Shojo Beat

My love STORY!!

Story **KAZUNE KAWAHARA**

Art **ARUKO**

12

MY love STORY!!

12

CONTENTS

STORY Thus Far...

Takeo Goda, a first-year high school student, is a hot-blooded guy who is 6'6" tall and weighs 265 pounds. Boys look up to him, but the girls he falls in love with all end up liking his handsome best friend, Makoto Sunakawa! But that all changes when Takeo saves Rinko Yamato from a groper on the train, and she becomes his girlfriend.

As they date, Takeo's heart starts to race at the thought of Yamato, and he desperately fights his urges. Not knowing the reason for Takeo's strange behavior, Yamato grows concerned. But upon learning of Takeo's desire for her, she is overjoyed! During a school trip, they are able to talk about their feelings, and they deepen their bond in the process.

Later, Yamato wants to be stronger so that Takeo doesn't have to protect her all the time. Takeo decides to teach her how to tumble so that she can fall without hurting herself. Meanwhile, a transfer student named Tanaka starts to hang around Sunakawa, but this guy is not what he seems!

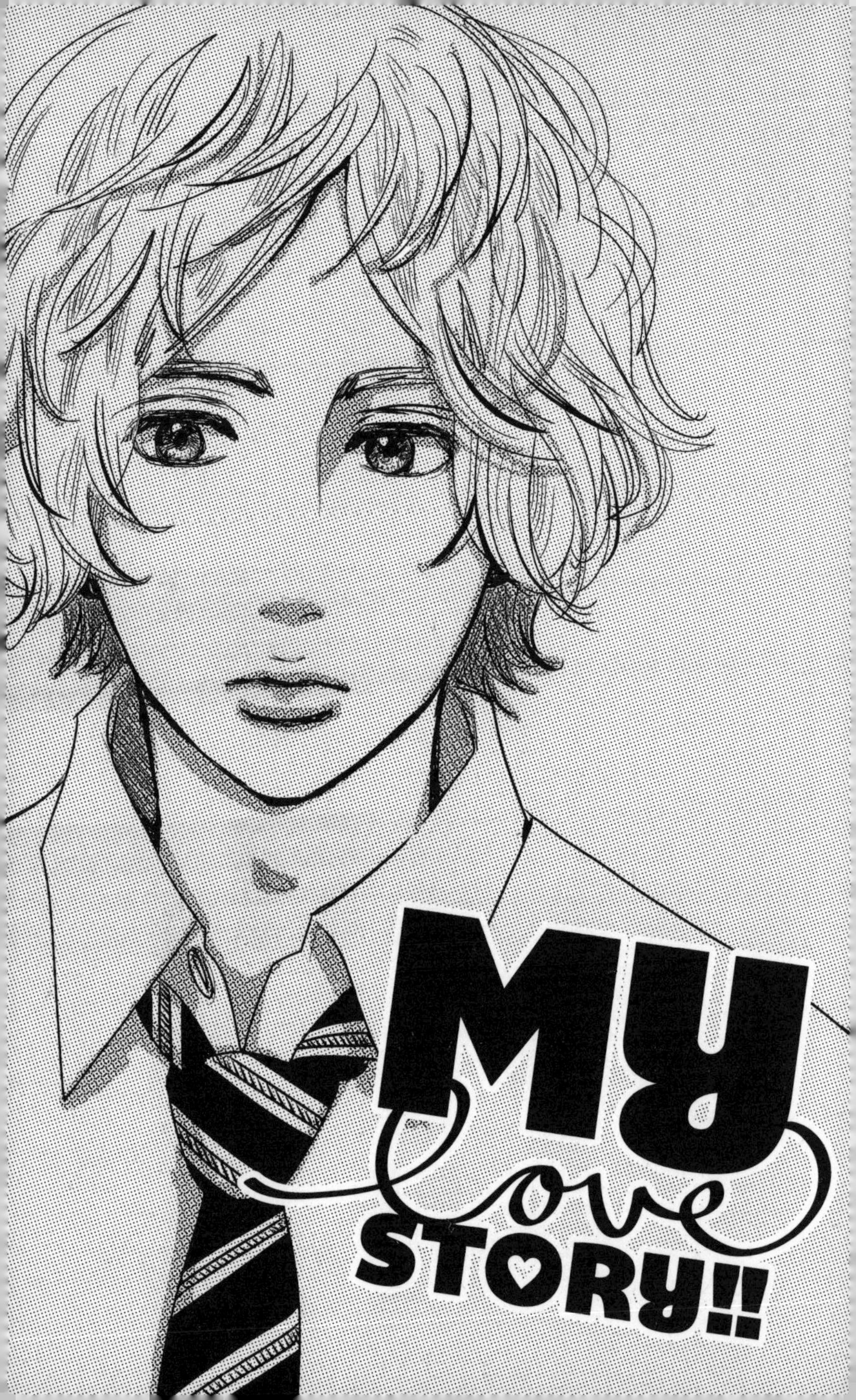
MY love STORY!!

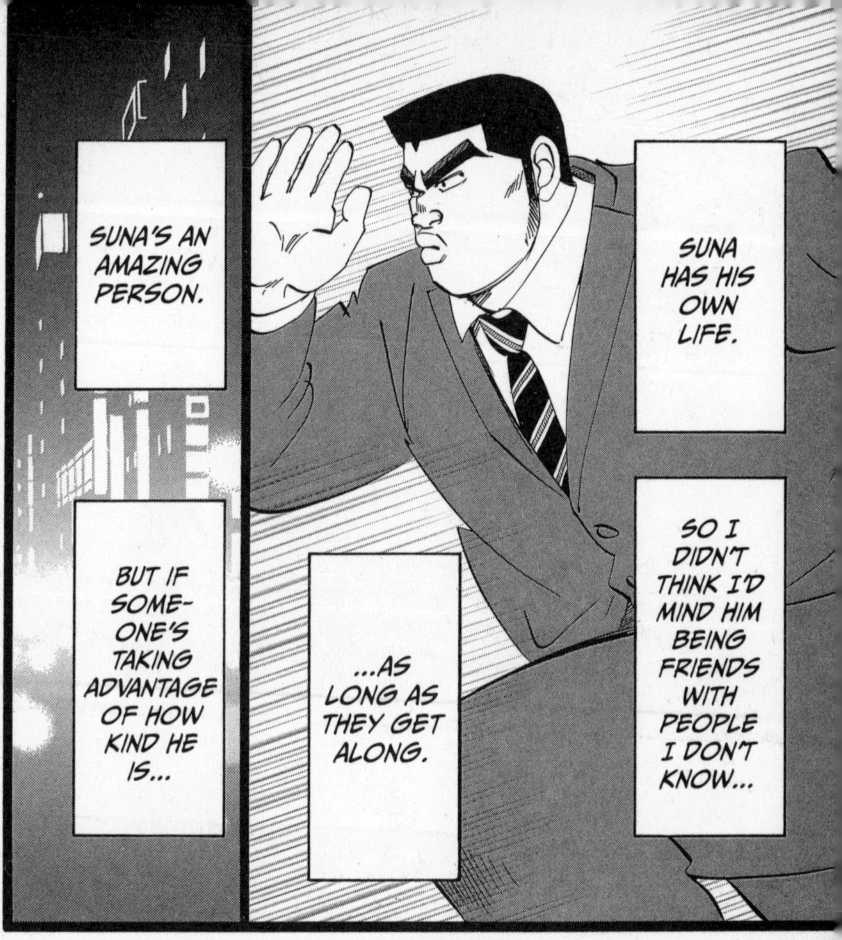
SUNA HAS HIS OWN LIFE.
SO I DIDN'T THINK I'D MIND HIM BEING FRIENDS WITH PEOPLE I DON'T KNOW...
...AS LONG AS THEY GET ALONG.
SUNA'S AN AMAZING PERSON.
BUT IF SOME-ONE'S TAKING ADVANTAGE OF HOW KIND HE IS...

MY love STORY!!

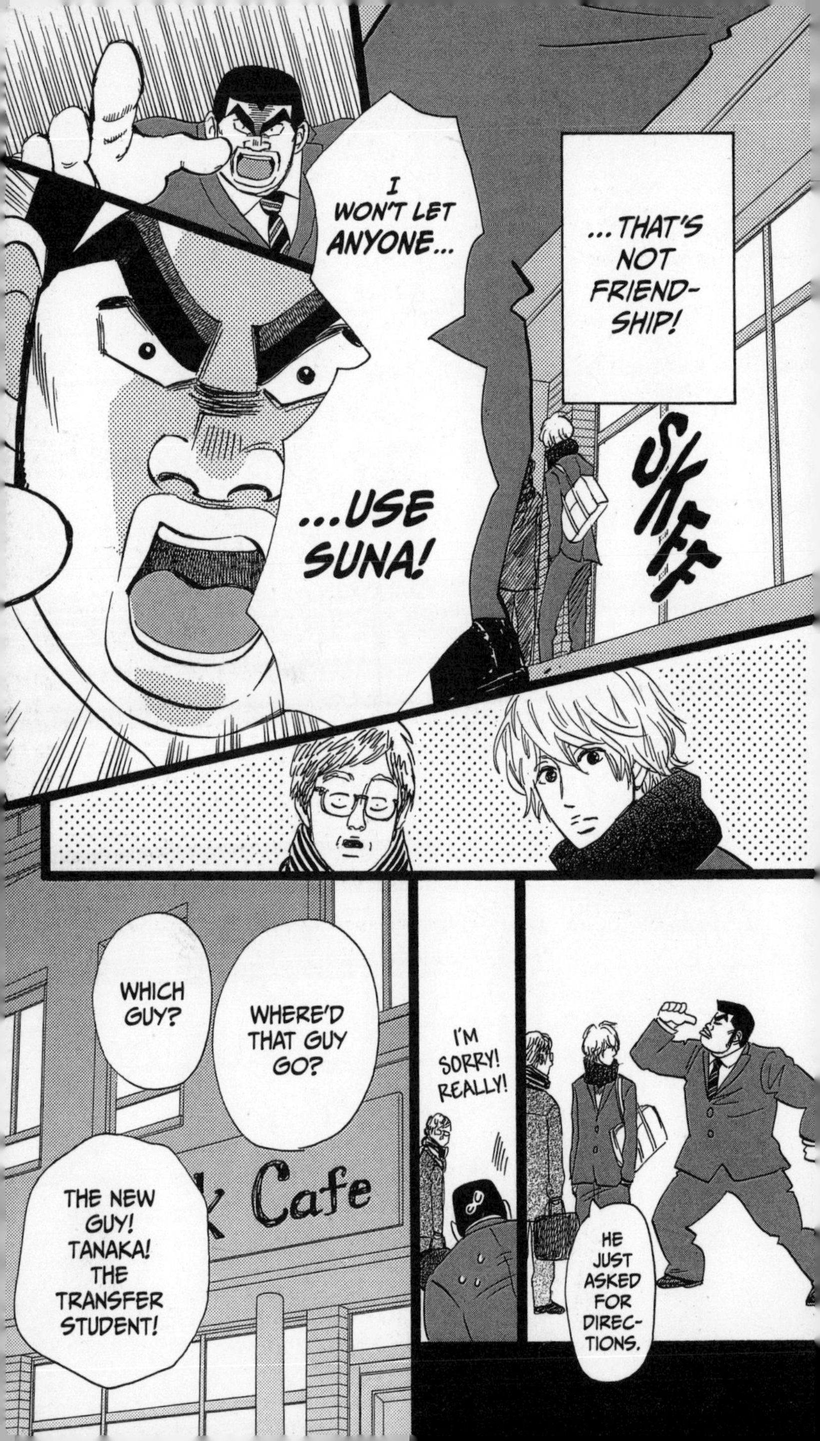
...THAT'S NOT FRIEND-SHIP!
SKFF
I WON'T LET ANYONE...
...USE SUNA!
HE JUST ASKED FOR DIREC-TIONS.
I'M SORRY! REALLY!
WHERE'D THAT GUY GO?
WHICH GUY?
Cafe
THE NEW GUY! TANAKA! THE TRANSFER STUDENT!

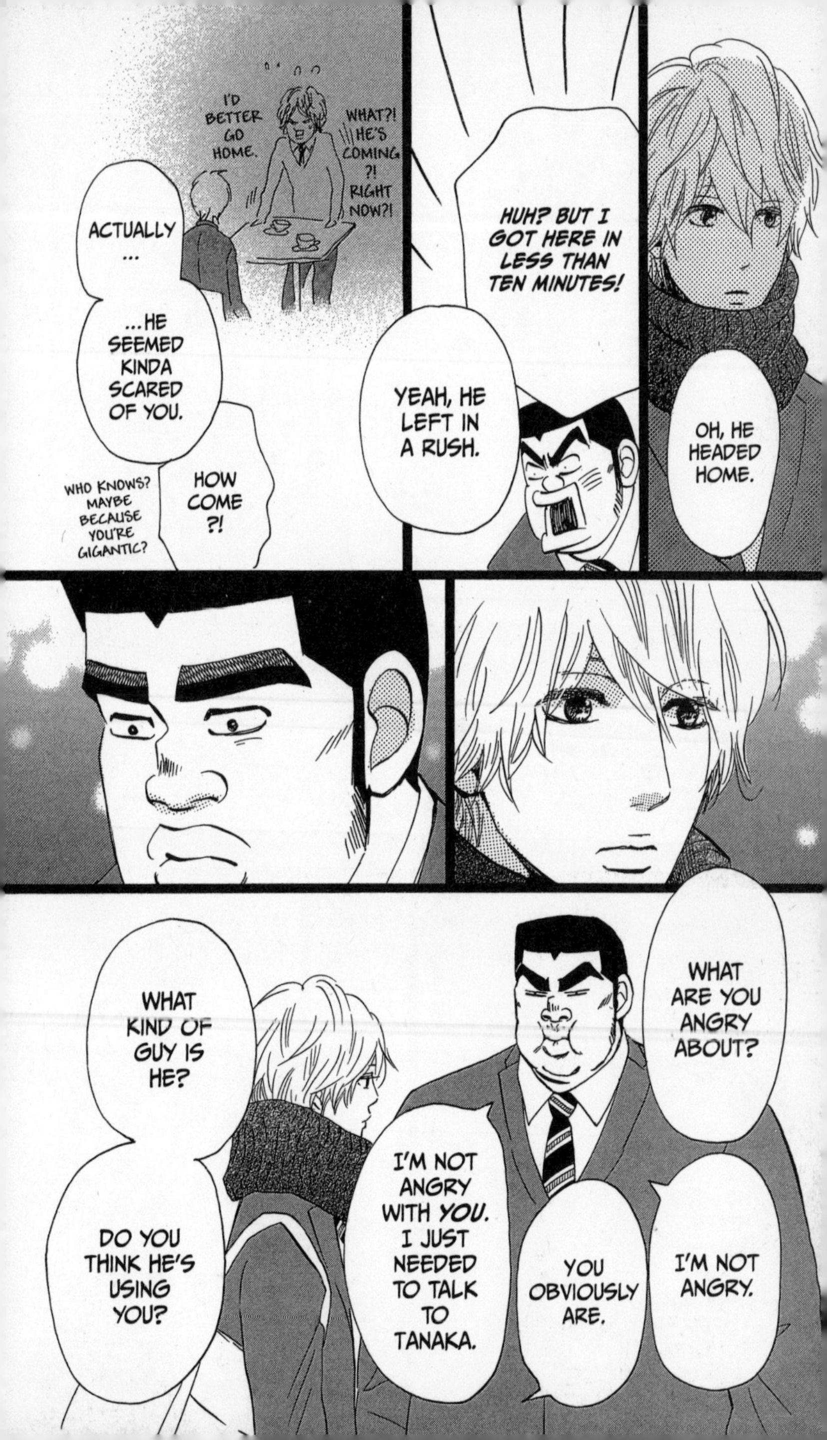
OH, HE HEADED HOME.
HUH? BUT I GOT HERE IN LESS THAN TEN MINUTES!
YEAH, HE LEFT IN A RUSH.
ACTUALLY ...
...HE SEEMED KINDA SCARED OF YOU.
I'D BETTER GO HOME.
WHAT?! HE'S COMING ?! RIGHT NOW?!
HOW COME ?!
WHO KNOWS? MAYBE BECAUSE YOU'RE GIGANTIC?
WHAT ARE YOU ANGRY ABOUT?
I'M NOT ANGRY.
YOU OBVIOUSLY ARE.
I'M NOT ANGRY WITH YOU. I JUST NEEDED TO TALK TO TANAKA.
WHAT KIND OF GUY IS HE?
DO YOU THINK HE'S USING YOU?

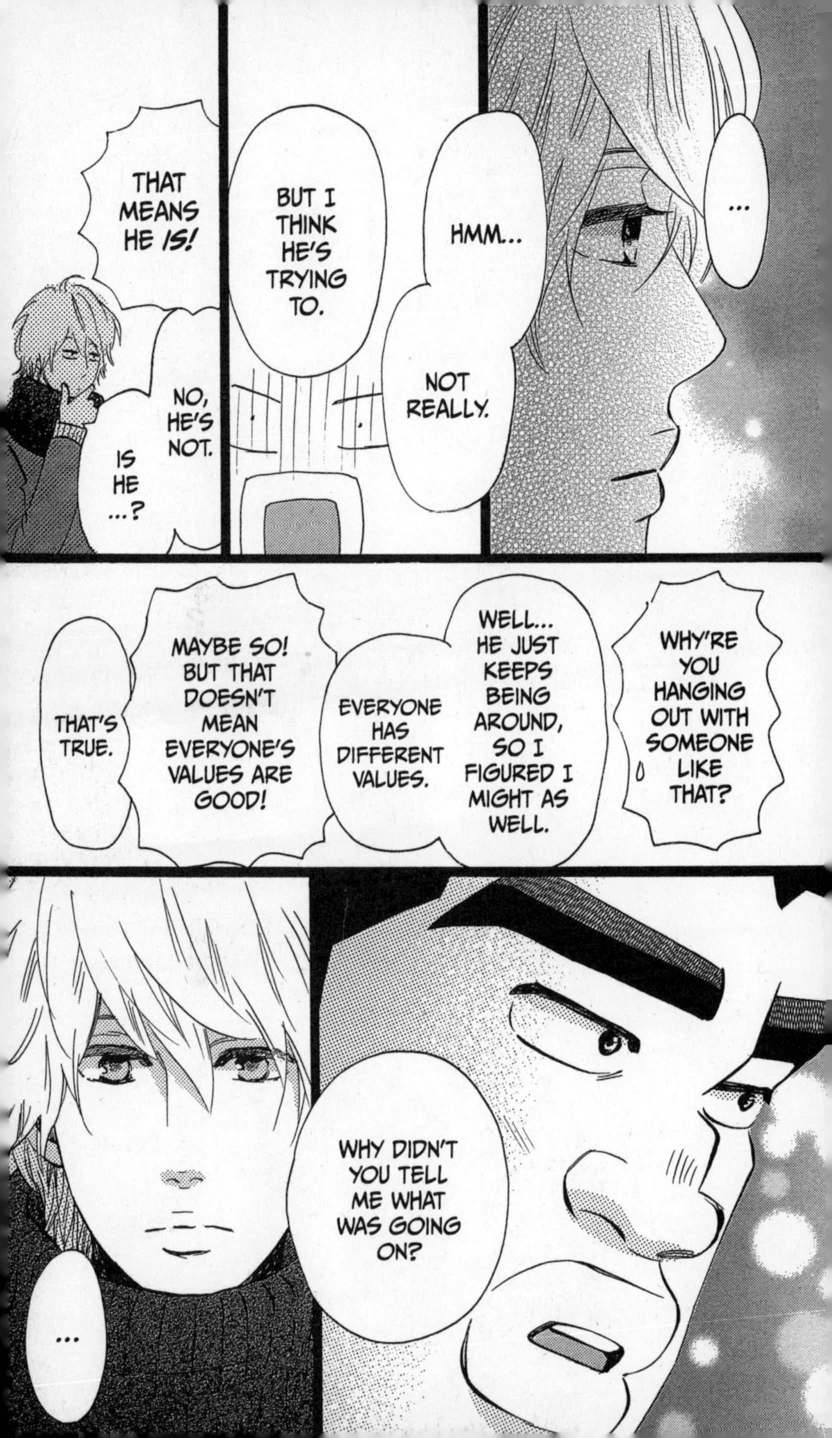
...
HMM...
NOT REALLY.
BUT I THINK HE'S TRYING TO.
IS HE ...?
NO, HE'S NOT.
THAT MEANS HE *IS*!
WHY'RE YOU HANGING OUT WITH SOMEONE LIKE THAT?
WELL... HE JUST KEEPS BEING AROUND, SO I FIGURED I MIGHT AS WELL.
EVERYONE HAS DIFFERENT VALUES.
MAYBE SO! BUT THAT DOESN'T MEAN EVERYONE'S VALUES ARE GOOD!
THAT'S TRUE.
WHY DIDN'T YOU TELL ME WHAT WAS GOING ON?
...

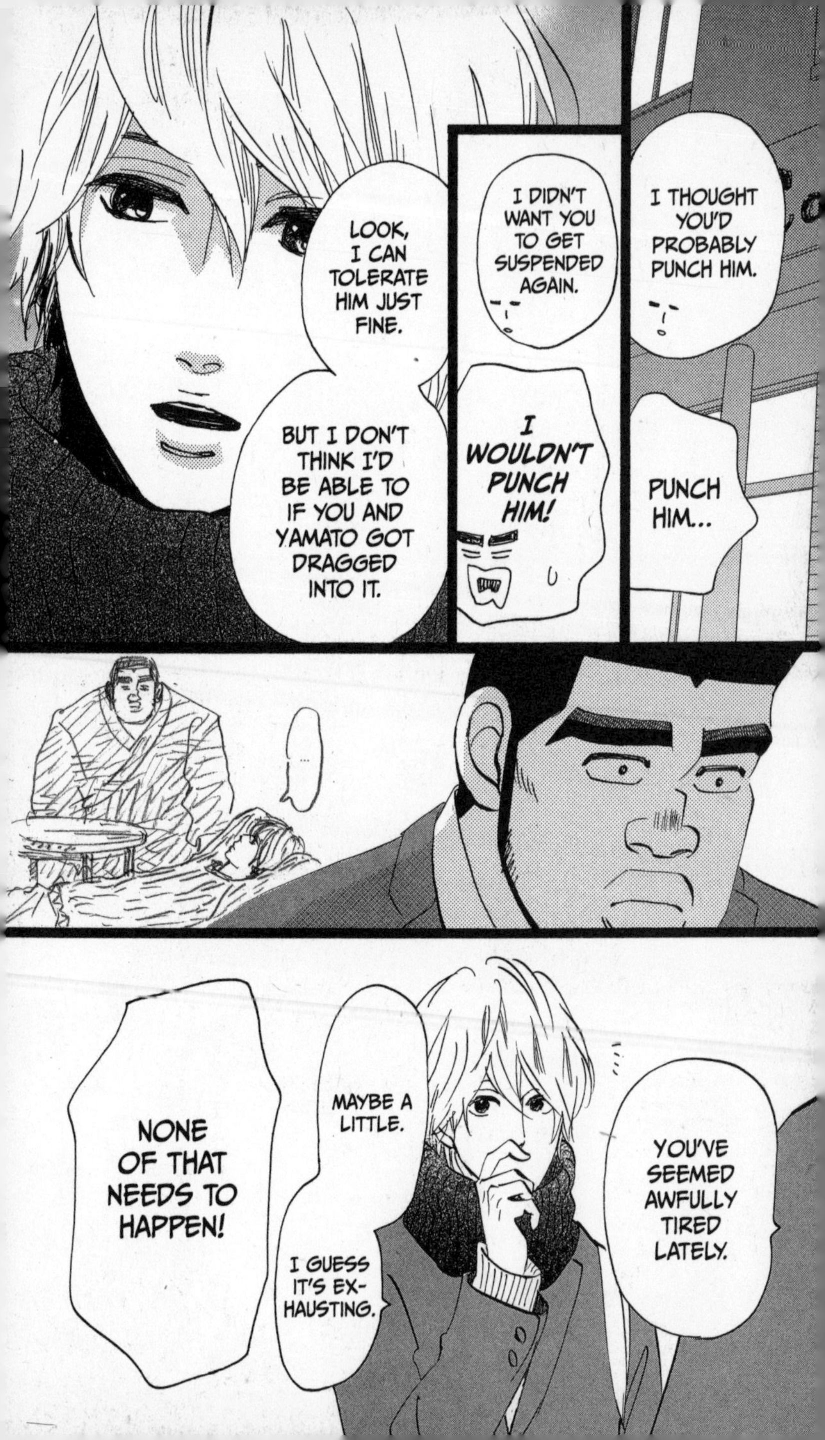
I THOUGHT YOU'D PROBABLY PUNCH HIM.
PUNCH HIM...
I DIDN'T WANT YOU TO GET SUSPENDED AGAIN.
I WOULDN'T PUNCH HIM!
LOOK, I CAN TOLERATE HIM JUST FINE.
BUT I DON'T THINK I'D BE ABLE TO IF YOU AND YAMATO GOT DRAGGED INTO IT.
...
YOU'VE SEEMED AWFULLY TIRED LATELY.
MAYBE A LITTLE.
I GUESS IT'S EX-HAUSTING.
NONE OF THAT NEEDS TO HAPPEN!

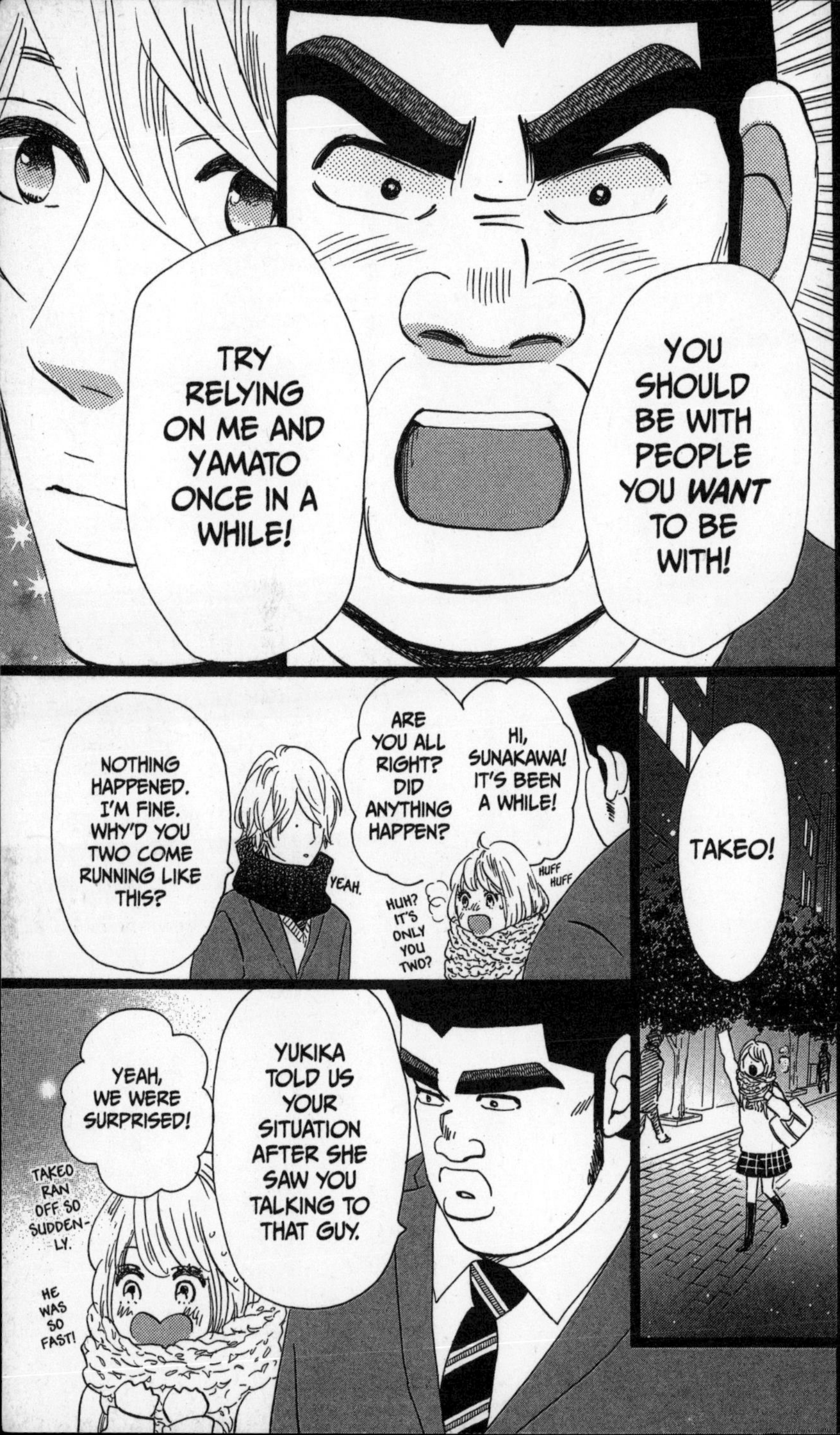
YOU SHOULD BE WITH PEOPLE YOU *WANT* TO BE WITH!
TRY RELYING ON ME AND YAMATO ONCE IN A WHILE!
TAKEO!
HI, SUNAKAWA! IT'S BEEN A WHILE!
ARE YOU ALL RIGHT? DID ANYTHING HAPPEN?
HUFF HUFF
HUH? IT'S ONLY YOU TWO?
YEAH.
NOTHING HAPPENED. I'M FINE. WHY'D YOU TWO COME RUNNING LIKE THIS?
YUKIKA TOLD US YOUR SITUATION AFTER SHE SAW YOU TALKING TO THAT GUY.
YEAH, WE WERE SURPRISED!
TAKEO RAN OFF SO SUDDEN-LY.
HE WAS SO FAST!

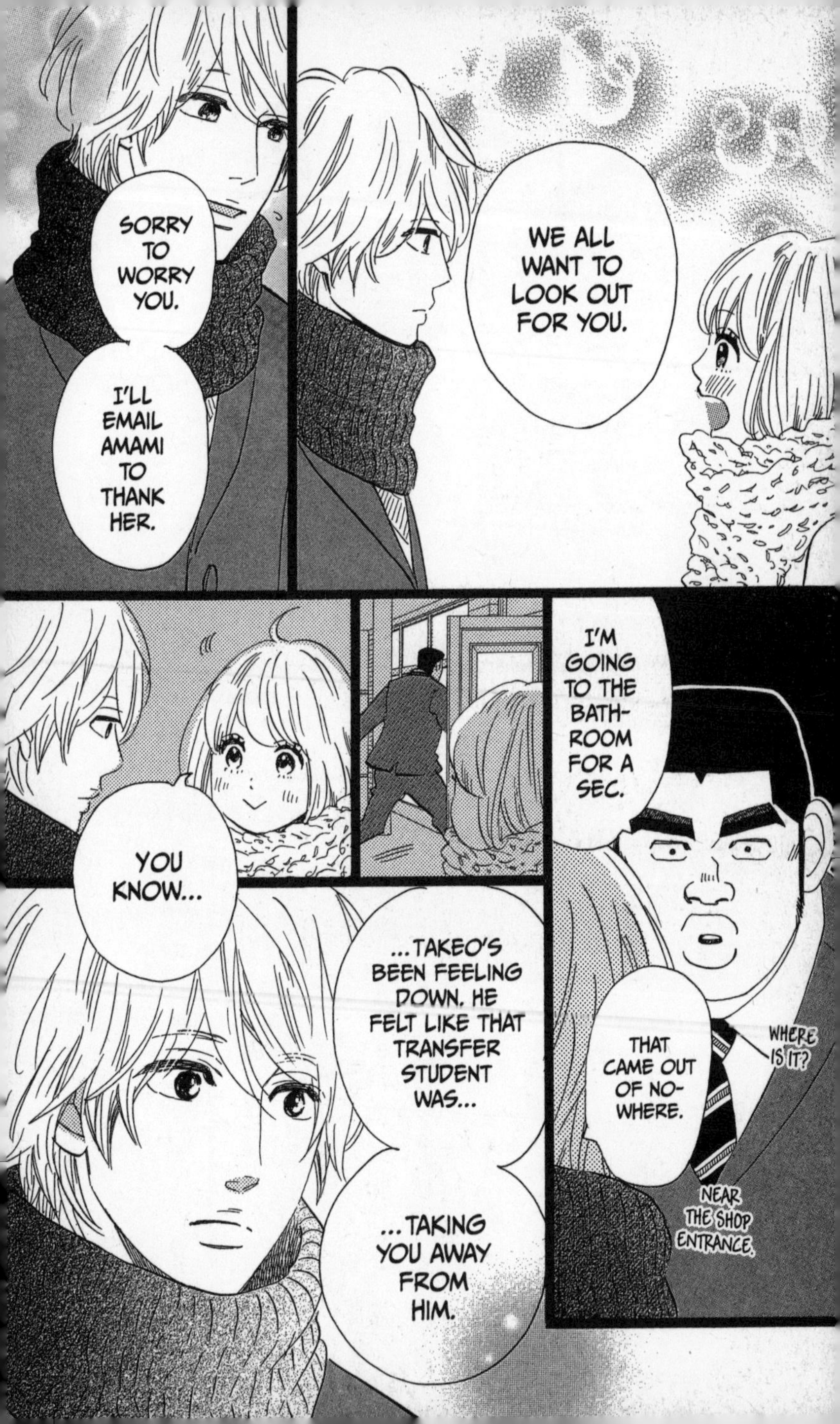
WE ALL WANT TO LOOK OUT FOR YOU.
SORRY TO WORRY YOU.
I'LL EMAIL AMAMI TO THANK HER.
I'M GOING TO THE BATH-ROOM FOR A SEC.
THAT CAME OUT OF NO-WHERE.
WHERE IS IT?
NEAR THE SHOP ENTRANCE.
YOU KNOW...
...TAKEO'S BEEN FEELING DOWN. HE FELT LIKE THAT TRANSFER STUDENT WAS...
...TAKING YOU AWAY FROM HIM.

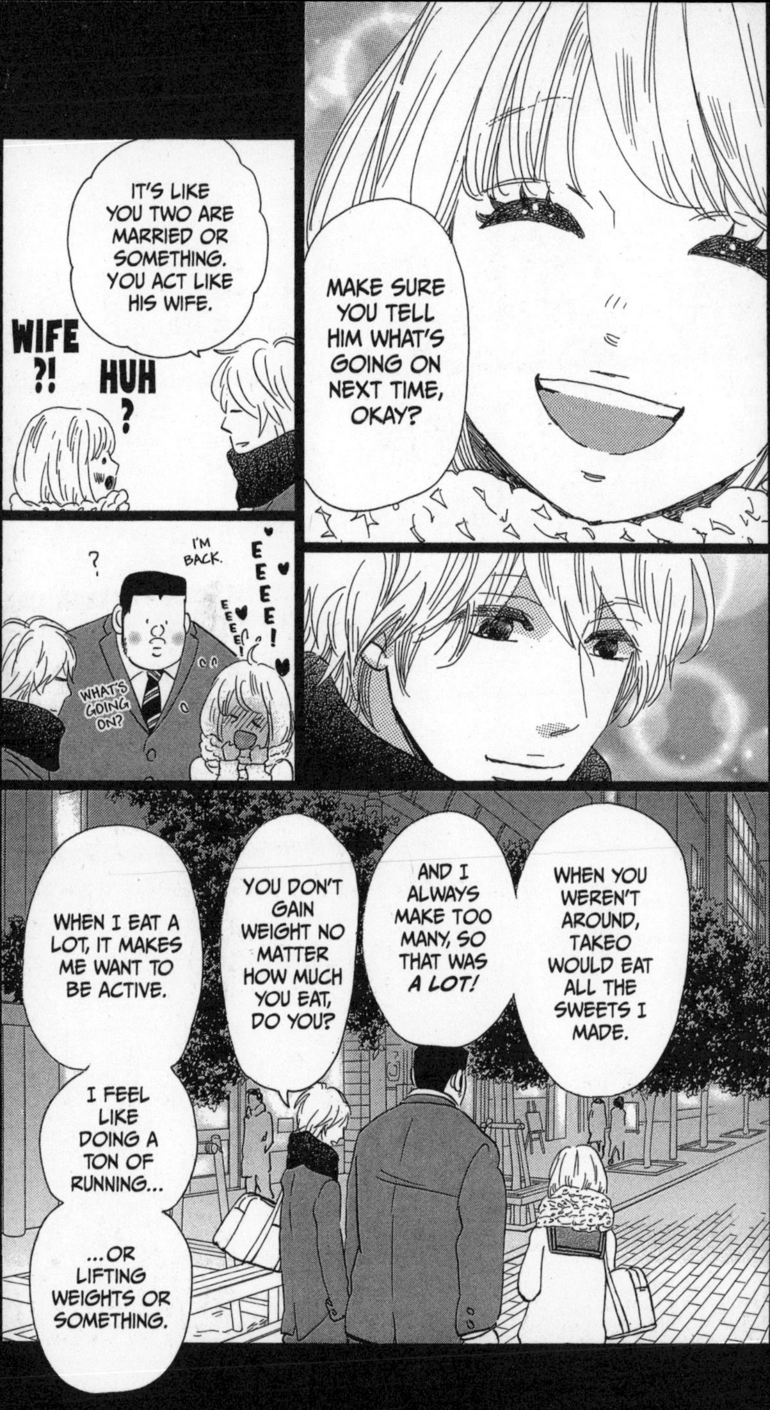
MAKE SURE YOU TELL HIM WHAT'S GOING ON NEXT TIME, OKAY?
IT'S LIKE YOU TWO ARE MARRIED OR SOMETHING. YOU ACT LIKE HIS WIFE.
HUH?
WIFE?!
EEEE!
EEEE!
I'M BACK.
?
WHAT'S GOING ON?
WHEN YOU WEREN'T AROUND, TAKEO WOULD EAT ALL THE SWEETS I MADE.
AND I ALWAYS MAKE TOO MANY, SO THAT WAS A LOT!
YOU DON'T GAIN WEIGHT NO MATTER HOW MUCH YOU EAT, DO YOU?
WHEN I EAT A LOT, IT MAKES ME WANT TO BE ACTIVE.
I FEEL LIKE DOING A TON OF RUNNING...
...OR LIFTING WEIGHTS OR SOMETHING.

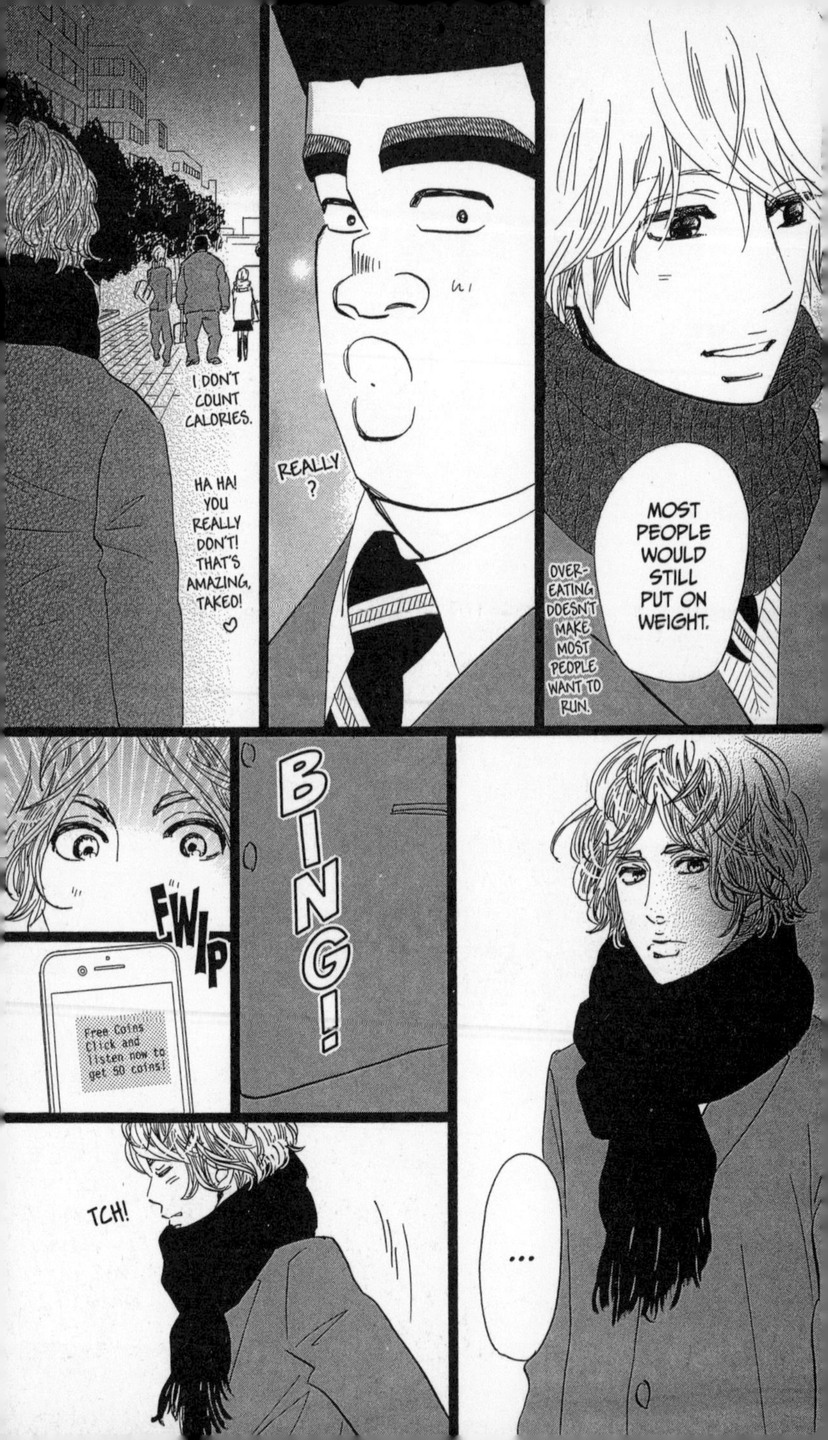
MOST PEOPLE WOULD STILL PUT ON WEIGHT.
OVER-EATING DOESN'T MAKE MOST PEOPLE WANT TO RUN.
REALLY?
I DON'T COUNT CALORIES.
HA HA! YOU REALLY DON'T! THAT'S AMAZING, TAKEO! ♡
...
BING!
FWIP
Free Coins
Click and listen now to get 50 coins!
TCH!

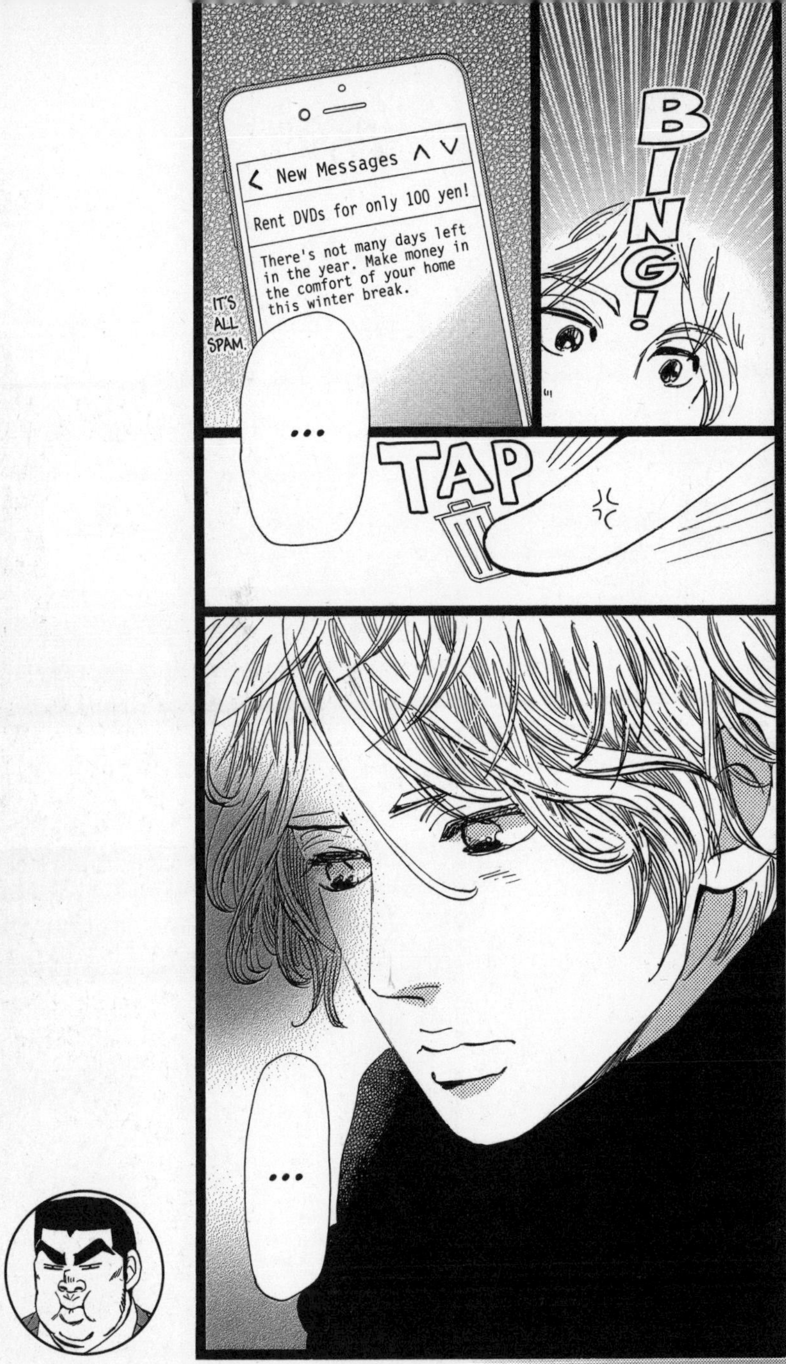
BING!
New Messages
Rent DVDs for only 100 yen!
There's not many days left in the year. Make money in the comfort of your home this winter break.
IT'S ALL SPAM.
...
TAP
...

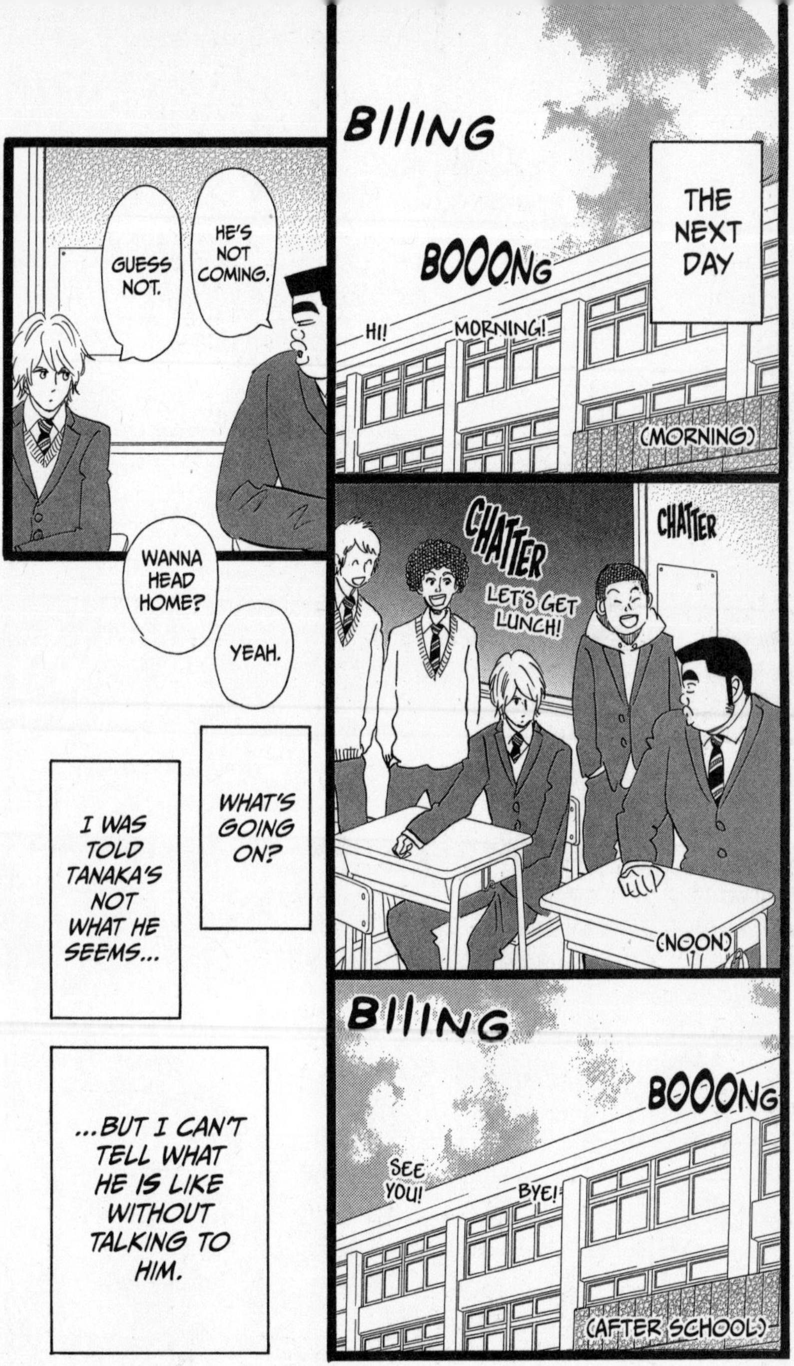
BIIING
THE NEXT DAY
BOOONG
MORNING!
HI!
(MORNING)
CHATTER
CHATTER
LET'S GET LUNCH!
(NOON)
BIIING
BOOONG
BYE!
SEE YOU!
(AFTER SCHOOL)
HE'S NOT COMING.
GUESS NOT.
WANNA HEAD HOME?
YEAH.
WHAT'S GOING ON?
I WAS TOLD TANAKA'S NOT WHAT HE SEEMS...
...BUT I CAN'T TELL WHAT HE IS LIKE WITHOUT TALKING TO HIM.

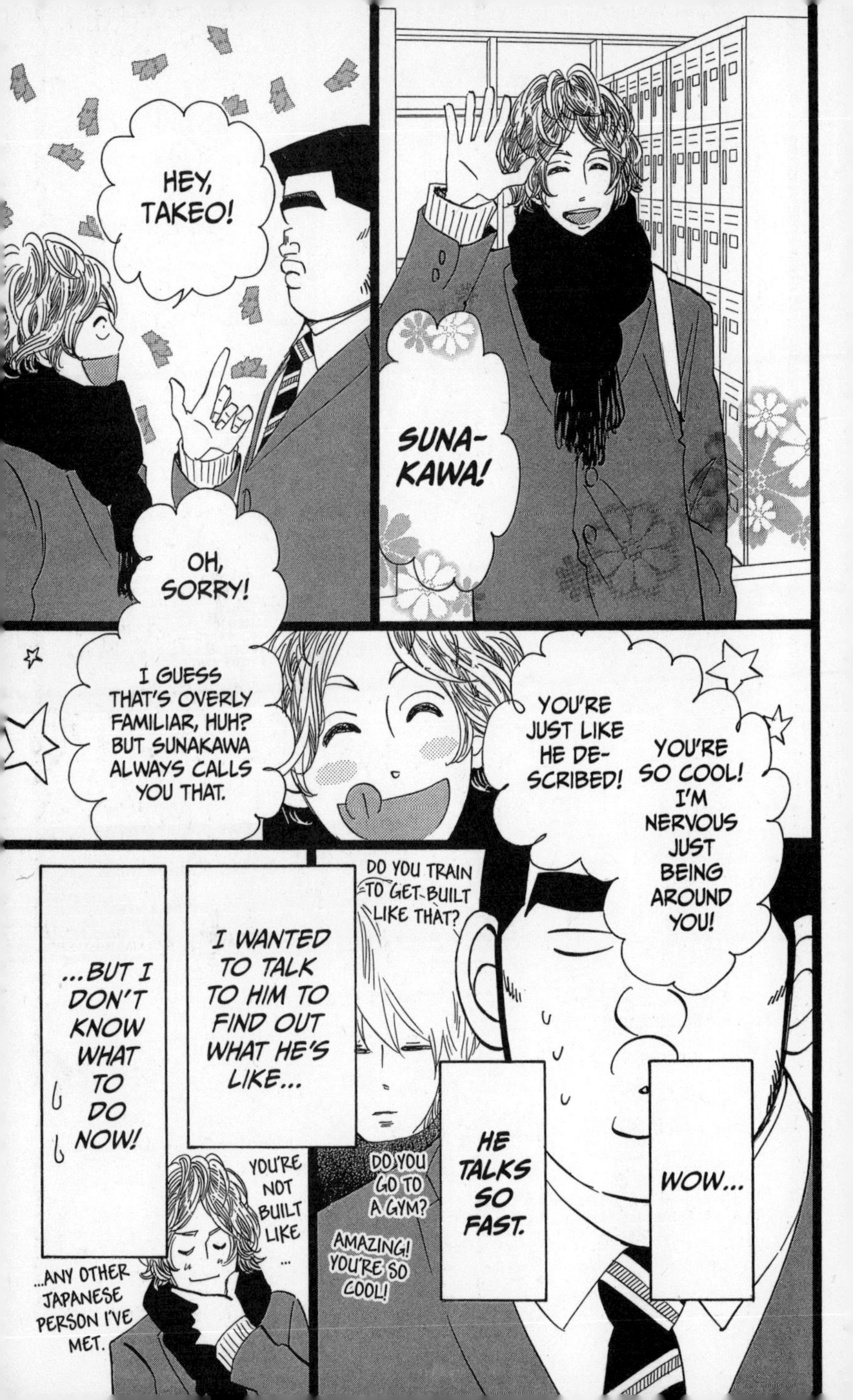
SUNA-KAWA!
HEY, TAKEO!
OH, SORRY!
I GUESS THAT'S OVERLY FAMILIAR, HUH? BUT SUNAKAWA ALWAYS CALLS YOU THAT.
YOU'RE JUST LIKE HE DE-SCRIBED!
YOU'RE SO COOL! I'M NERVOUS JUST BEING AROUND YOU!
WOW...
HE TALKS SO FAST.
DO YOU TRAIN TO GET BUILT LIKE THAT?
DO YOU GO TO A GYM?
AMAZING! YOU'RE SO COOL!
I WANTED TO TALK TO HIM TO FIND OUT WHAT HE'S LIKE...
YOU'RE NOT BUILT LIKE ...
...ANY OTHER JAPANESE PERSON I'VE MET.
...BUT I DON'T KNOW WHAT TO DO NOW!

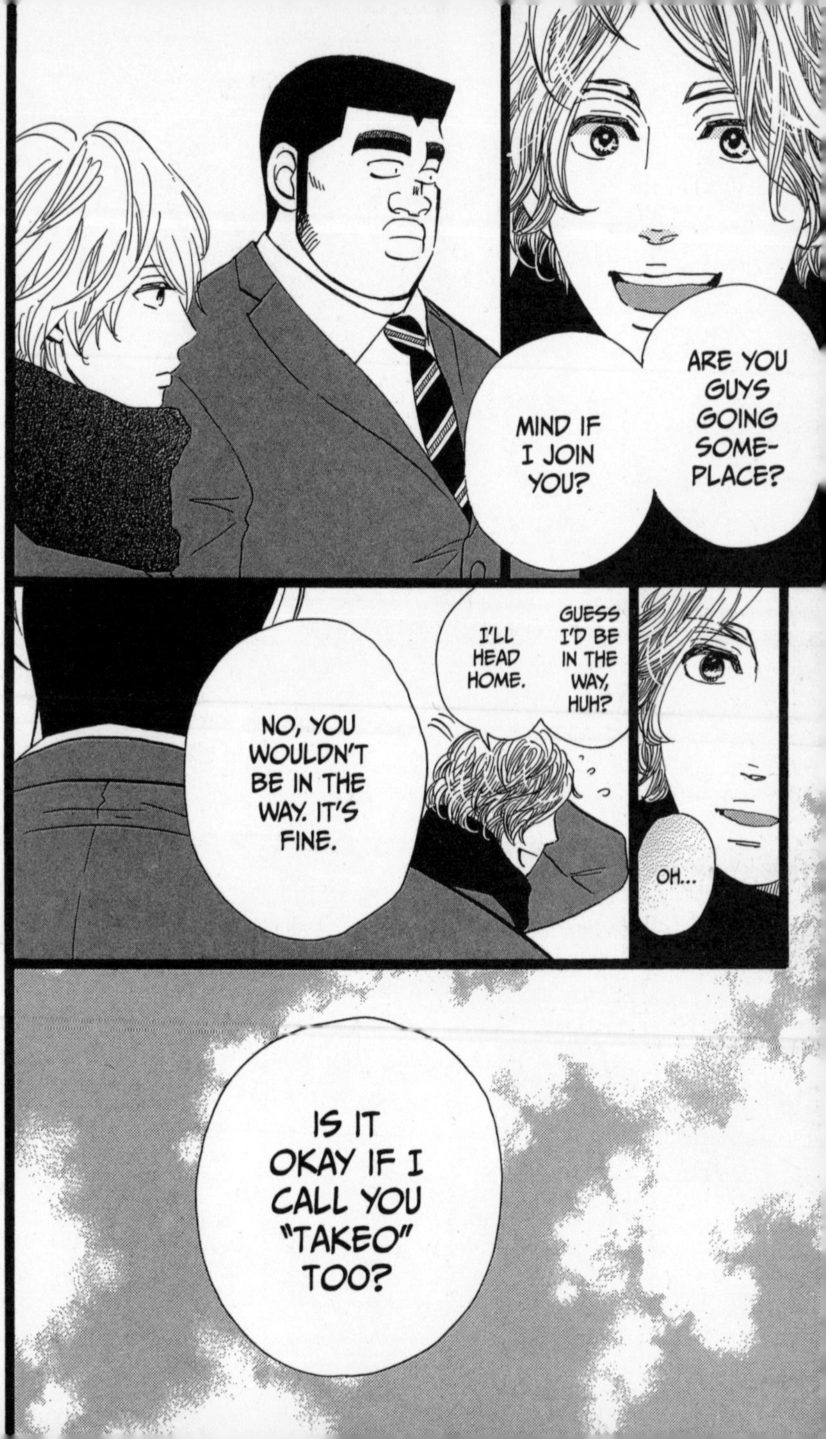
ARE YOU GUYS GOING SOME-PLACE?
MIND IF I JOIN YOU?
OH...
GUESS I'D BE IN THE WAY, HUH?
I'LL HEAD HOME.
NO, YOU WOULDN'T BE IN THE WAY. IT'S FINE.
IS IT OKAY IF I CALL YOU "TAKEO" TOO?

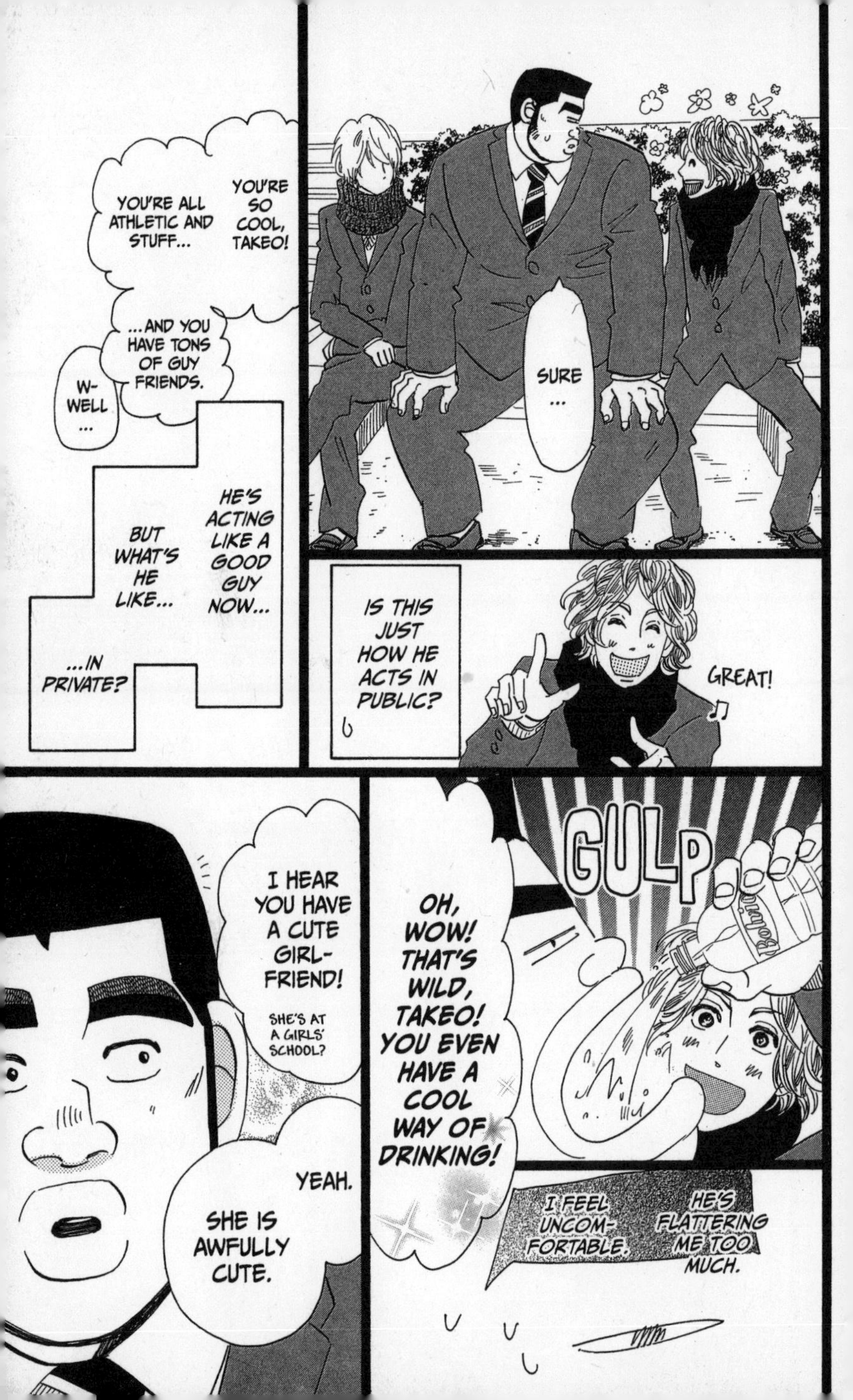
SURE ...
YOU'RE SO COOL, TAKEO!
YOU'RE ALL ATHLETIC AND STUFF...
...AND YOU HAVE TONS OF GUY FRIENDS.
W-WELL ...
HE'S ACTING LIKE A GOOD GUY NOW...
BUT WHAT'S HE LIKE...
...IN PRIVATE?
GREAT!
IS THIS JUST HOW HE ACTS IN PUBLIC?
GULP
OH, WOW! THAT'S WILD, TAKEO! YOU EVEN HAVE A COOL WAY OF DRINKING!
HE'S FLATTERING ME TOO MUCH.
I FEEL UNCOM-FORTABLE.
I HEAR YOU HAVE A CUTE GIRL-FRIEND!
SHE'S AT A GIRLS' SCHOOL?
YEAH.
SHE IS AWFULLY CUTE.

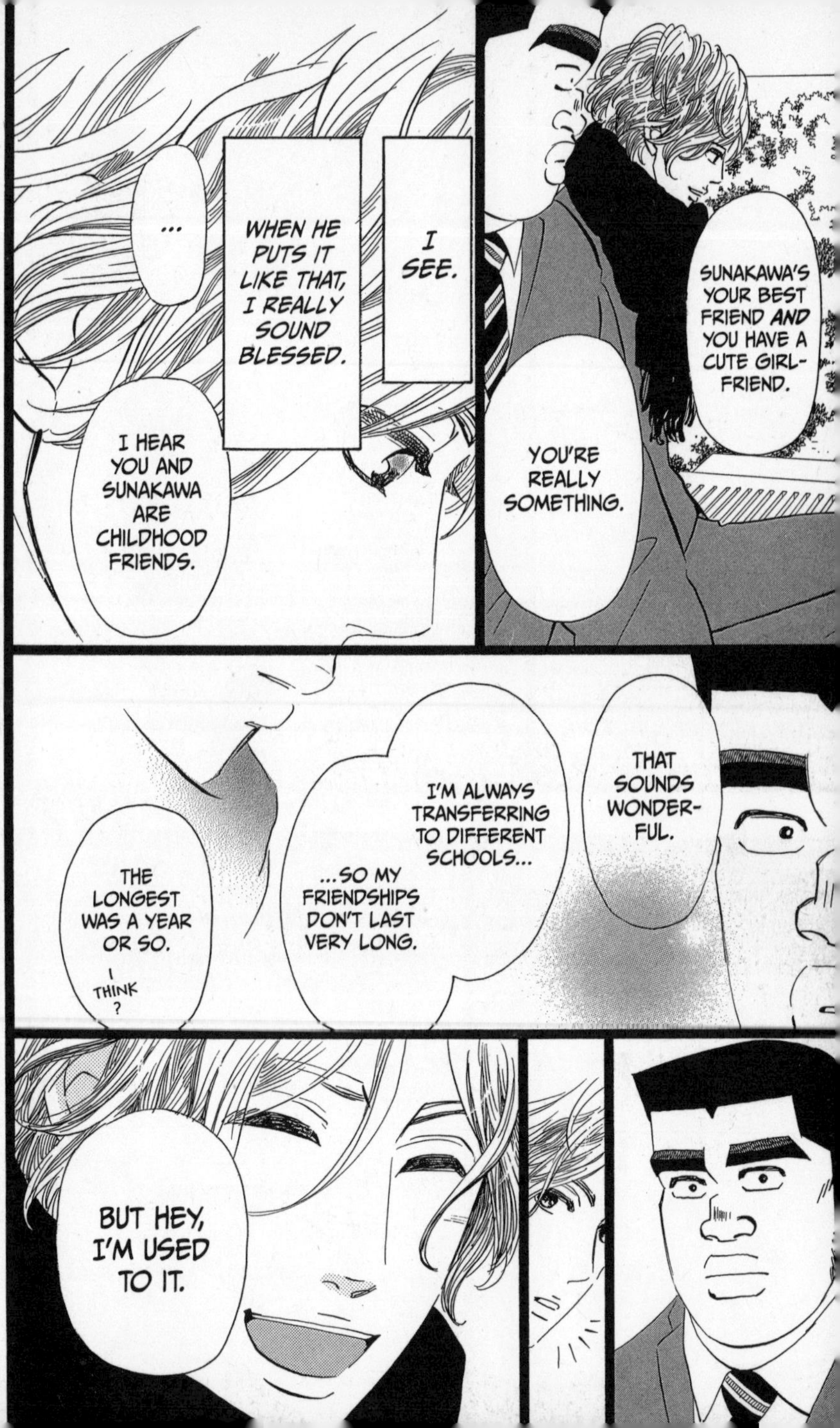
SUNAKAWA'S YOUR BEST FRIEND AND YOU HAVE A CUTE GIRL-FRIEND.
YOU'RE REALLY SOMETHING.
I SEE.
WHEN HE PUTS IT LIKE THAT, I REALLY SOUND BLESSED.
...
I HEAR YOU AND SUNAKAWA ARE CHILDHOOD FRIENDS.
THAT SOUNDS WONDER-FUL.
I'M ALWAYS TRANSFERRING TO DIFFERENT SCHOOLS...
...SO MY FRIENDSHIPS DON'T LAST VERY LONG.
THE LONGEST WAS A YEAR OR SO.
I THINK?
BUT HEY, I'M USED TO IT.

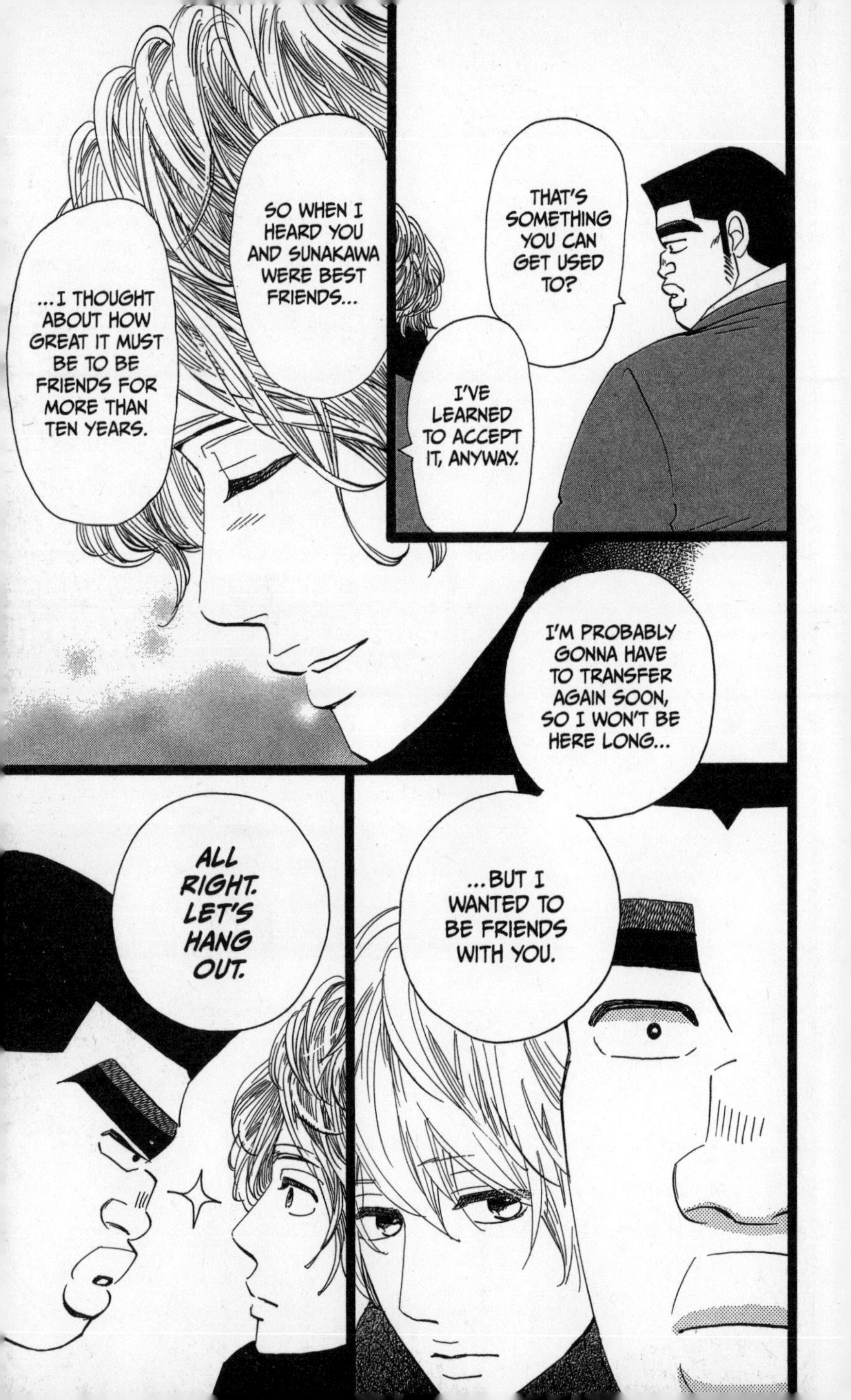
THAT'S SOMETHING YOU CAN GET USED TO?
I'VE LEARNED TO ACCEPT IT, ANYWAY.
SO WHEN I HEARD YOU AND SUNAKAWA WERE BEST FRIENDS...
...I THOUGHT ABOUT HOW GREAT IT MUST BE TO BE FRIENDS FOR MORE THAN TEN YEARS.
I'M PROBABLY GONNA HAVE TO TRANSFER AGAIN SOON, SO I WON'T BE HERE LONG...
...BUT I WANTED TO BE FRIENDS WITH YOU.
ALL RIGHT. LET'S HANG OUT.

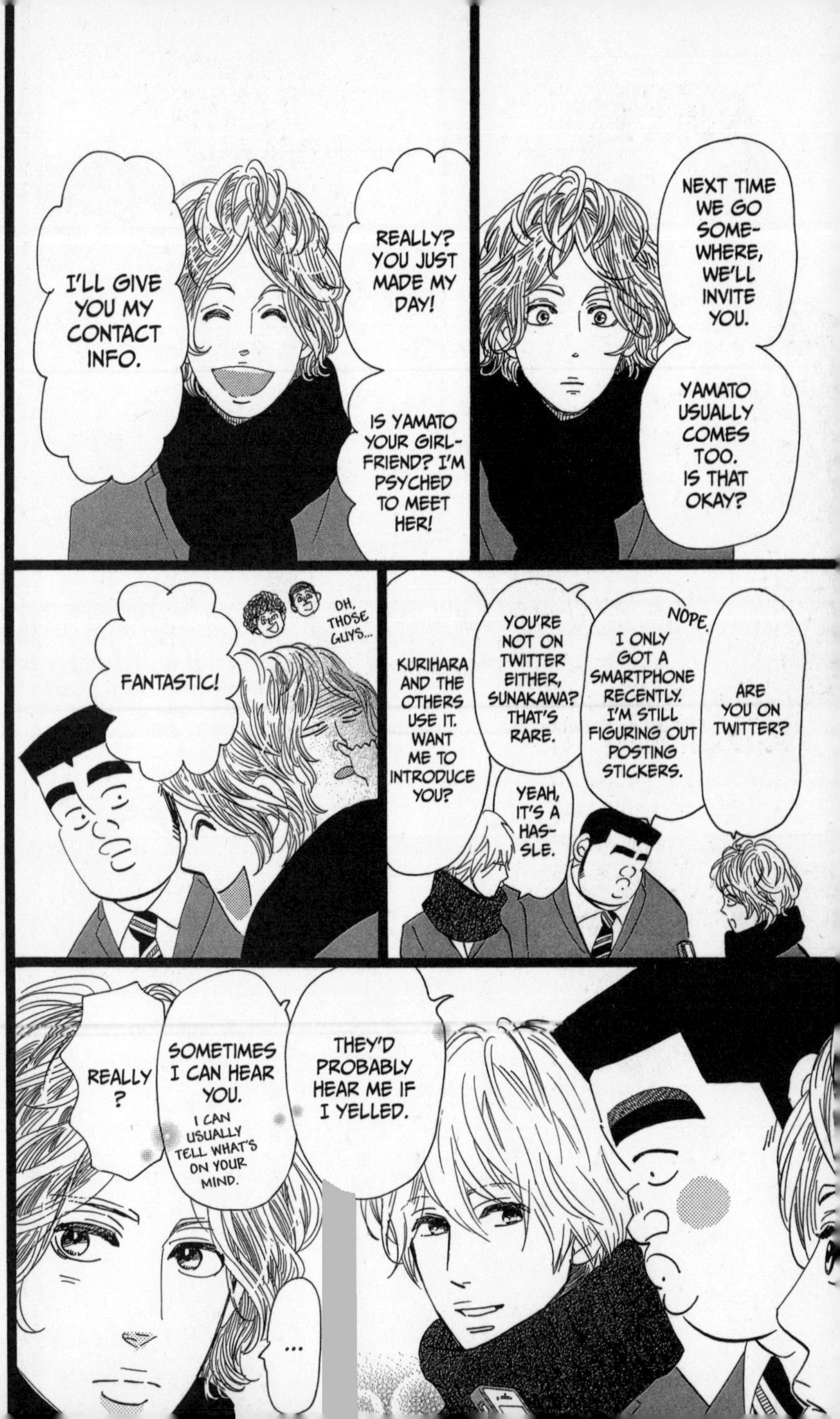
NEXT TIME WE GO SOME-WHERE, WE'LL INVITE YOU.
YAMATO USUALLY COMES TOO. IS THAT OKAY?
REALLY? YOU JUST MADE MY DAY!
IS YAMATO YOUR GIRL-FRIEND? I'M PSYCHED TO MEET HER!
I'LL GIVE YOU MY CONTACT INFO.
ARE YOU ON TWITTER?
NOPE.
I ONLY GOT A SMARTPHONE RECENTLY. I'M STILL FIGURING OUT POSTING STICKERS.
YOU'RE NOT ON TWITTER EITHER, SUNAKAWA? THAT'S RARE.
YEAH, IT'S A HAS-SLE.
KURIHARA AND THE OTHERS USE IT. WANT ME TO INTRODUCE YOU?
OH, THOSE GUYS...
FANTASTIC!
THEY'D PROBABLY HEAR ME IF I YELLED.
SOMETIMES I CAN HEAR YOU.
I CAN USUALLY TELL WHAT'S ON YOUR MIND.
REALLY?
...

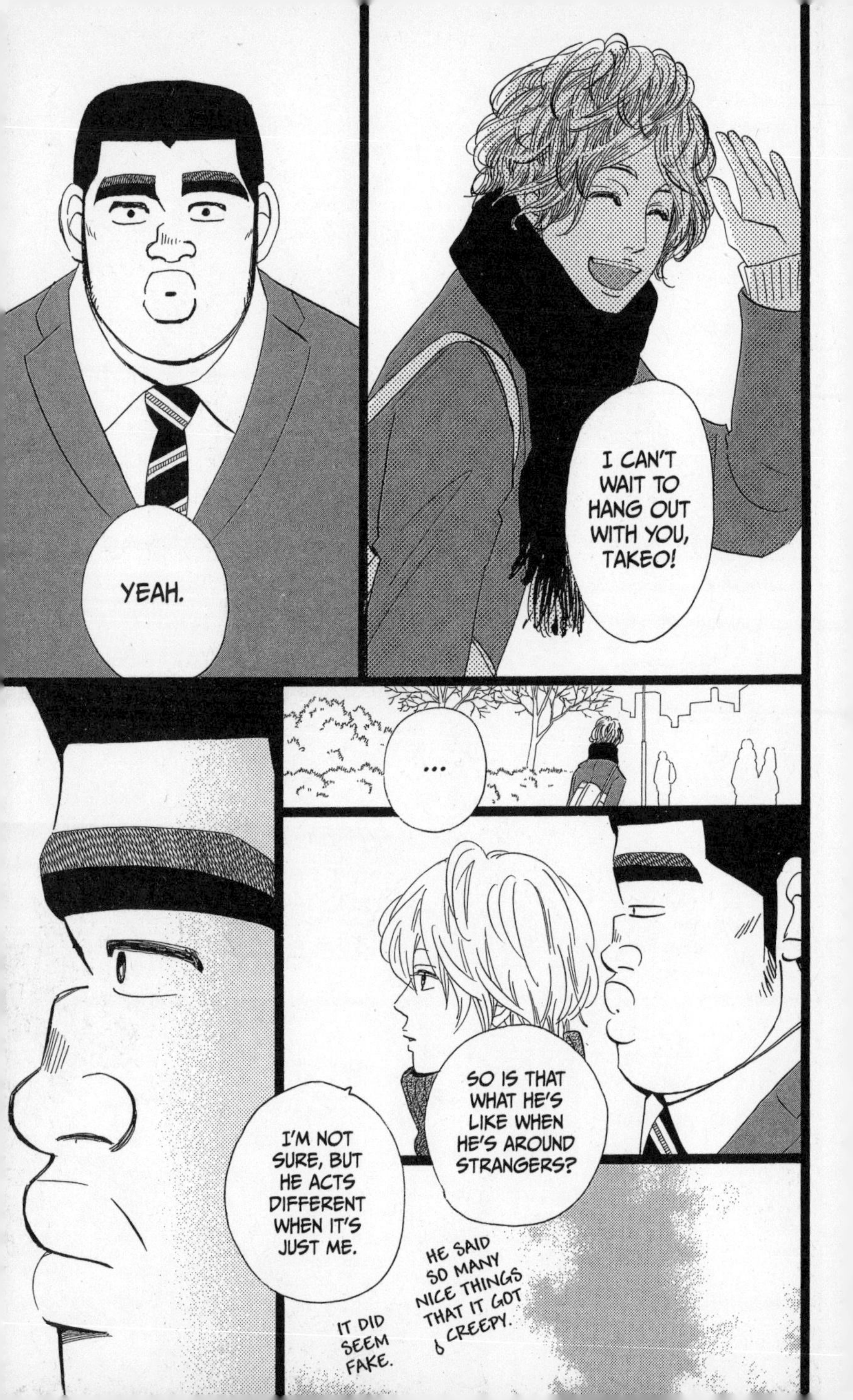
I CAN'T WAIT TO HANG OUT WITH YOU, TAKEO!
YEAH.
...
SO IS THAT WHAT HE'S LIKE WHEN HE'S AROUND STRANGERS?
I'M NOT SURE, BUT HE ACTS DIFFERENT WHEN IT'S JUST ME.
HE SAID SO MANY NICE THINGS THAT IT GOT CREEPY.
IT DID SEEM FAKE.

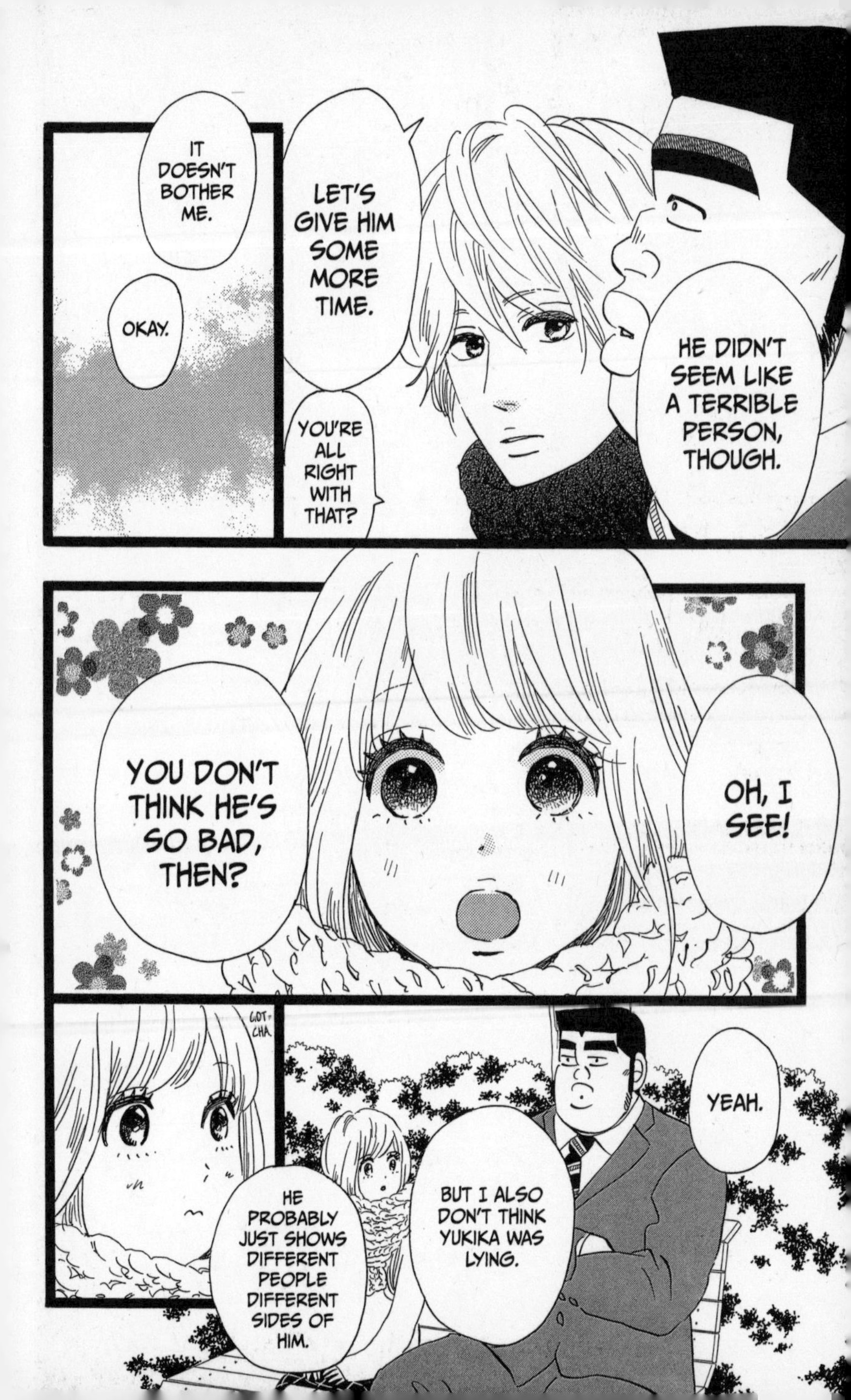
HE DIDN'T SEEM LIKE A TERRIBLE PERSON, THOUGH.
LET'S GIVE HIM SOME MORE TIME.
YOU'RE ALL RIGHT WITH THAT?
IT DOESN'T BOTHER ME.
OKAY.
OH, I SEE!
YOU DON'T THINK HE'S SO BAD, THEN?
YEAH.
BUT I ALSO DON'T THINK YUKIKA WAS LYING.
HE PROBABLY JUST SHOWS DIFFERENT PEOPLE DIFFERENT SIDES OF HIM.
GOT-CHA.

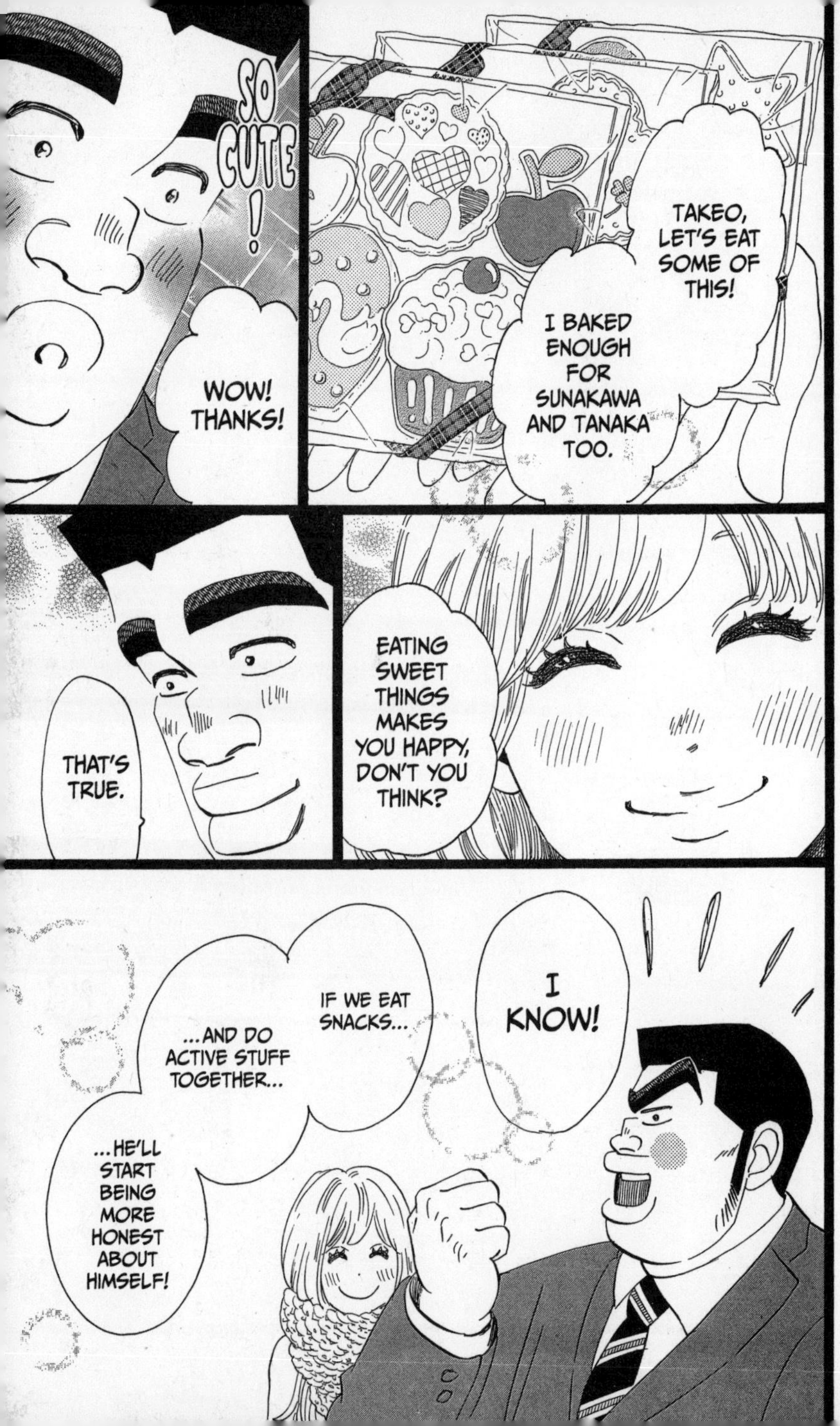
TAKEO, LET'S EAT SOME OF THIS!
I BAKED ENOUGH FOR SUNAKAWA AND TANAKA TOO.
SO CUTE!
WOW! THANKS!
EATING SWEET THINGS MAKES YOU HAPPY, DON'T YOU THINK?
THAT'S TRUE.
I KNOW!
IF WE EAT SNACKS...
...AND DO ACTIVE STUFF TOGETHER...
...HE'LL START BEING MORE HONEST ABOUT HIMSELF!

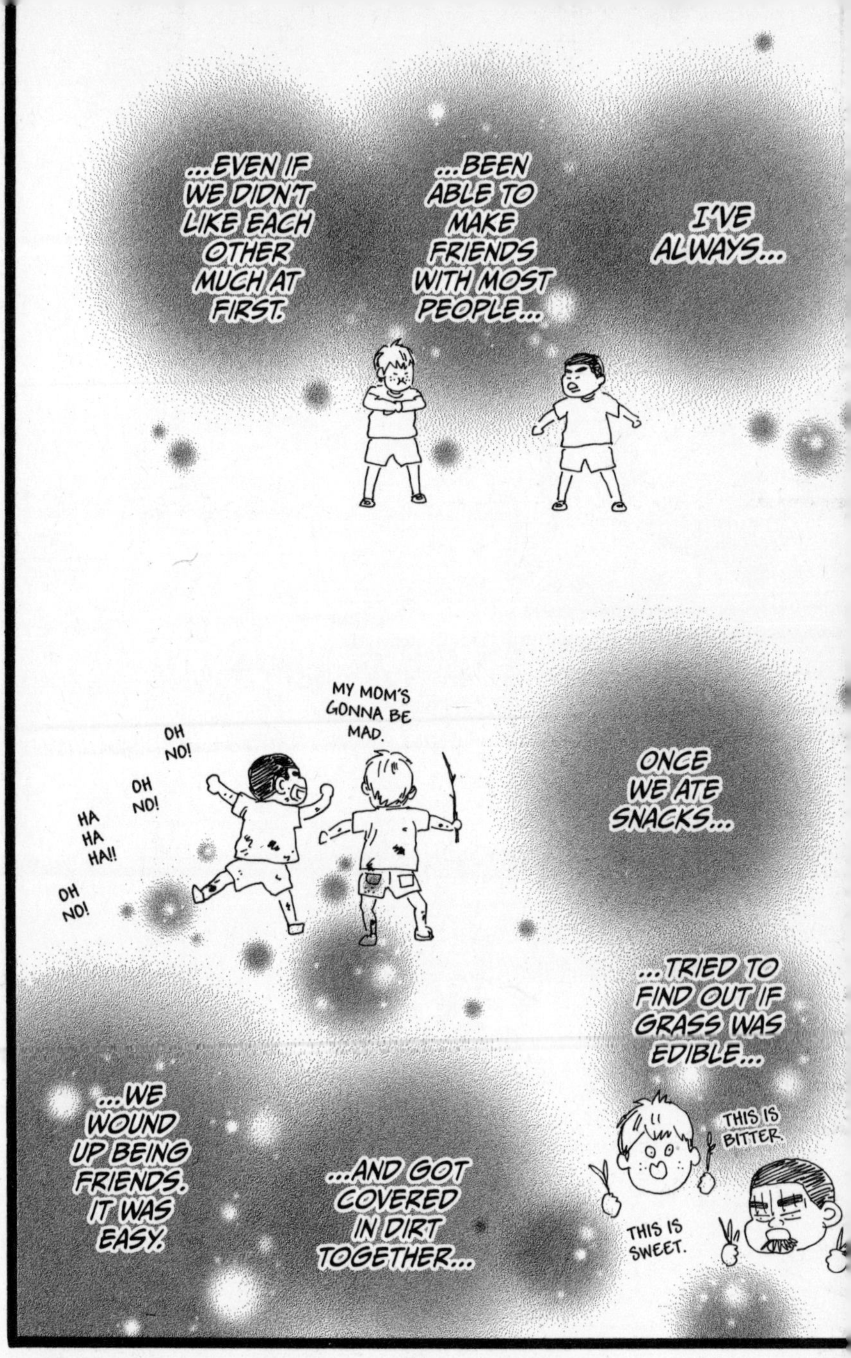
I'VE ALWAYS...
...BEEN ABLE TO MAKE FRIENDS WITH MOST PEOPLE...
...EVEN IF WE DIDN'T LIKE EACH OTHER MUCH AT FIRST.
ONCE WE ATE SNACKS...
MY MOM'S GONNA BE MAD.
OH NO!
OH NO!
HA HA HA!!
OH NO!
...TRIED TO FIND OUT IF GRASS WAS EDIBLE...
THIS IS BITTER.
THIS IS SWEET.
...AND GOT COVERED IN DIRT TOGETHER...
...WE WOUND UP BEING FRIENDS. IT WAS EASY.

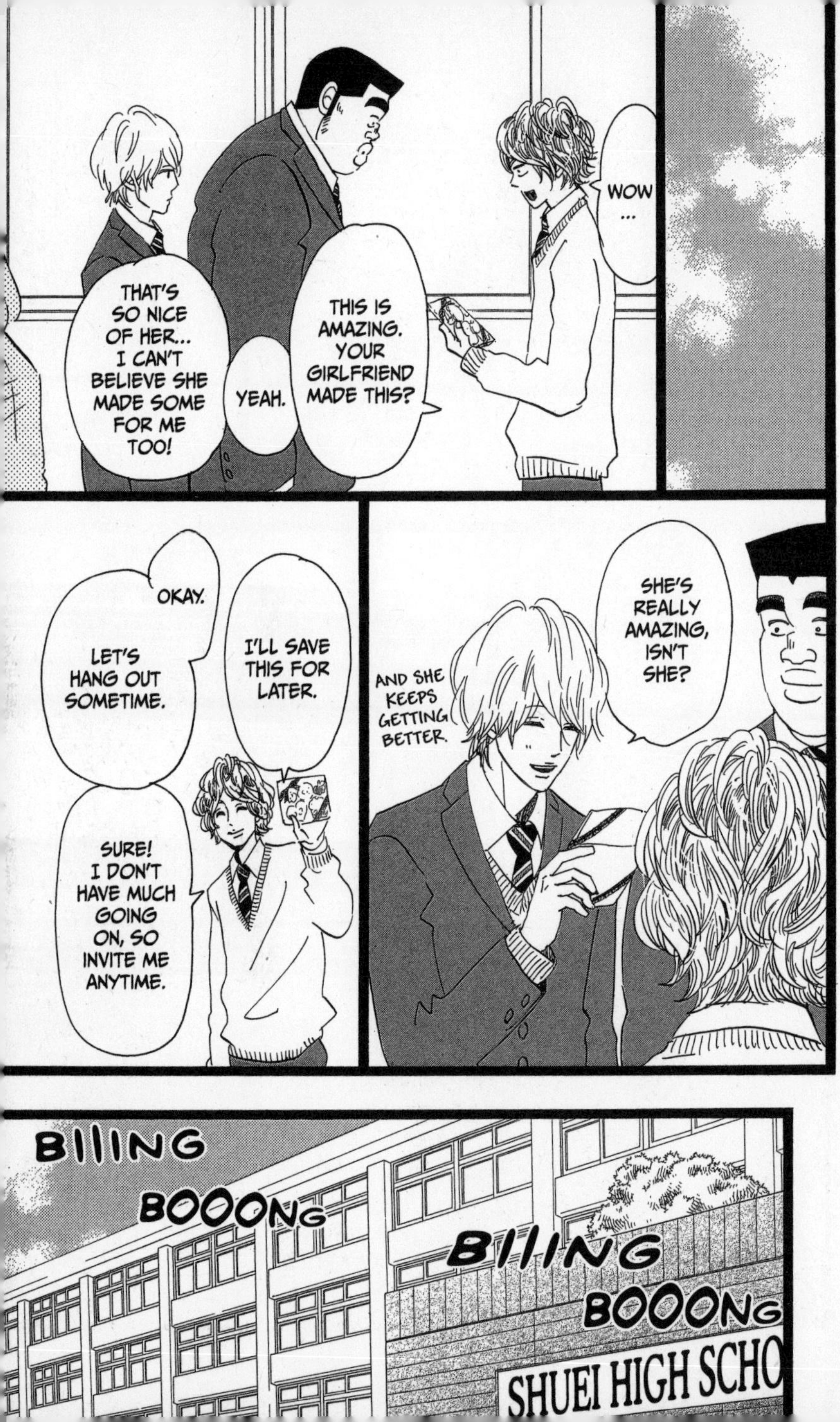
WOW ...
THIS IS AMAZING. YOUR GIRLFRIEND MADE THIS?
YEAH.
THAT'S SO NICE OF HER... I CAN'T BELIEVE SHE MADE SOME FOR ME TOO!
SHE'S REALLY AMAZING, ISN'T SHE?
AND SHE KEEPS GETTING BETTER.
I'LL SAVE THIS FOR LATER.
OKAY.
LET'S HANG OUT SOMETIME.
SURE! I DON'T HAVE MUCH GOING ON, SO INVITE ME ANYTIME.
BIIING
BOOONG
BIIING
BOOONG
SHUEI HIGH SCHO

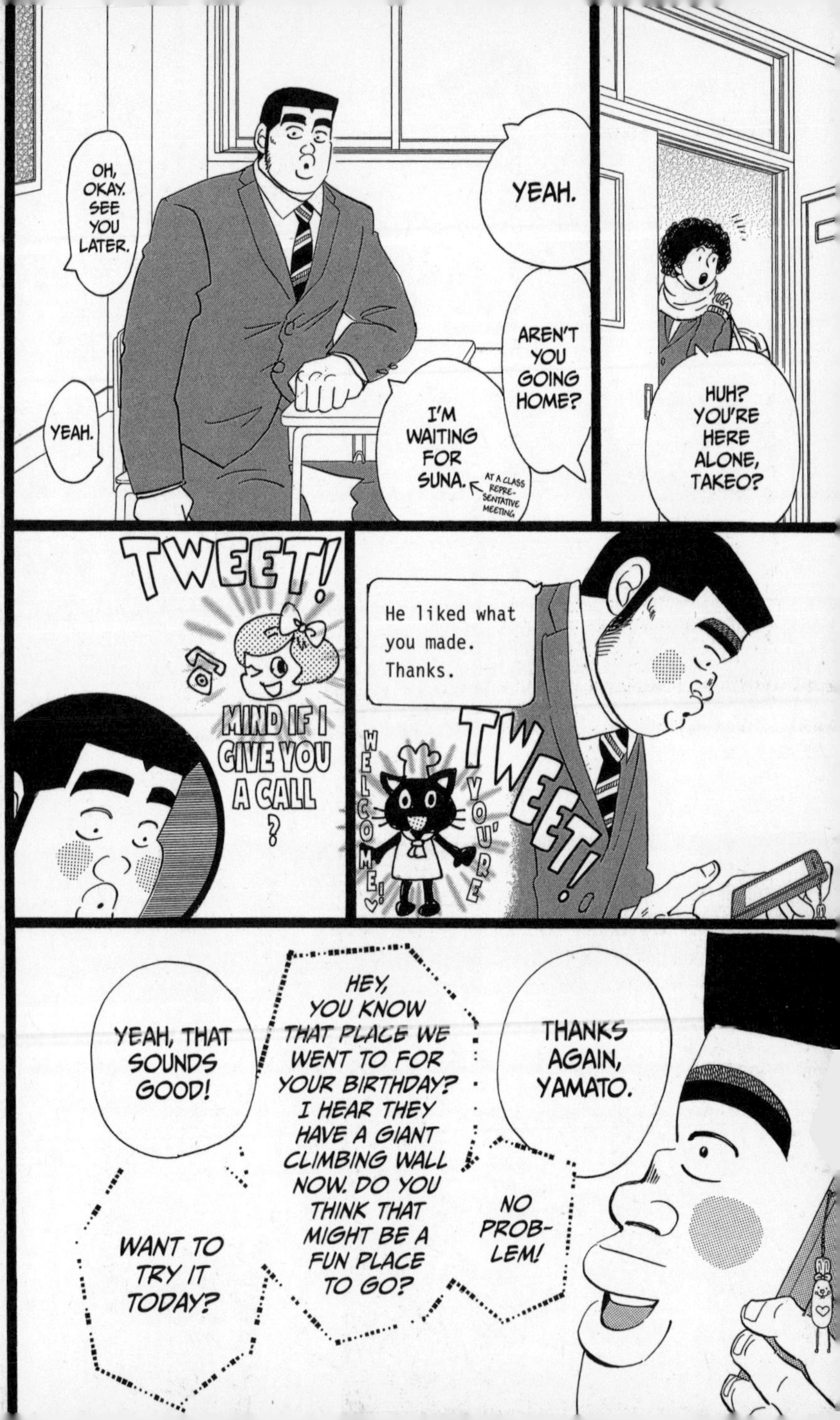
HUH? YOU'RE HERE ALONE, TAKEO?
YEAH.
AREN'T YOU GOING HOME?
I'M WAITING FOR SUNA.
AT A CLASS REPRESENTATIVE MEETING.
YEAH.
OH, OKAY. SEE YOU LATER.
He liked what you made. Thanks.
TWEET!
YOU'RE WELCOME!
TWEET!
MIND IF I GIVE YOU A CALL?
THANKS AGAIN, YAMATO.
NO PROB-LEM!
HEY, YOU KNOW THAT PLACE WE WENT TO FOR YOUR BIRTHDAY? I HEAR THEY HAVE A GIANT CLIMBING WALL NOW. DO YOU THINK THAT MIGHT BE A FUN PLACE TO GO?
WANT TO TRY IT TODAY?
YEAH, THAT SOUNDS GOOD!

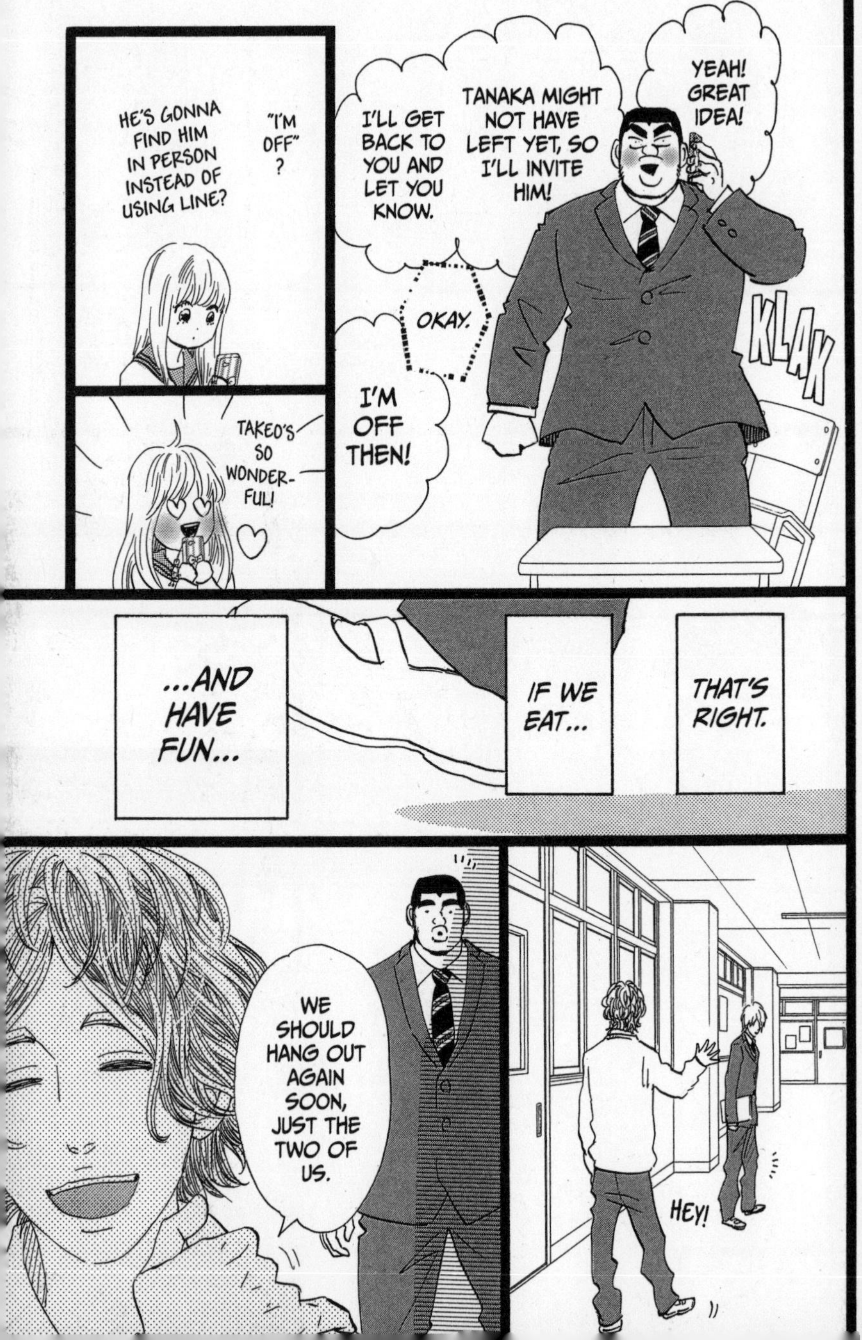
YEAH! GREAT IDEA!
TANAKA MIGHT NOT HAVE LEFT YET, SO I'LL INVITE HIM!
I'LL GET BACK TO YOU AND LET YOU KNOW.
OKAY.
I'M OFF THEN!
KLAK
"I'M OFF" ?
HE'S GONNA FIND HIM IN PERSON INSTEAD OF USING LINE?
TAKEO'S SO WONDER-FUL!
THAT'S RIGHT.
IF WE EAT...
...AND HAVE FUN...
HEY!
WE SHOULD HANG OUT AGAIN SOON, JUST THE TWO OF US.

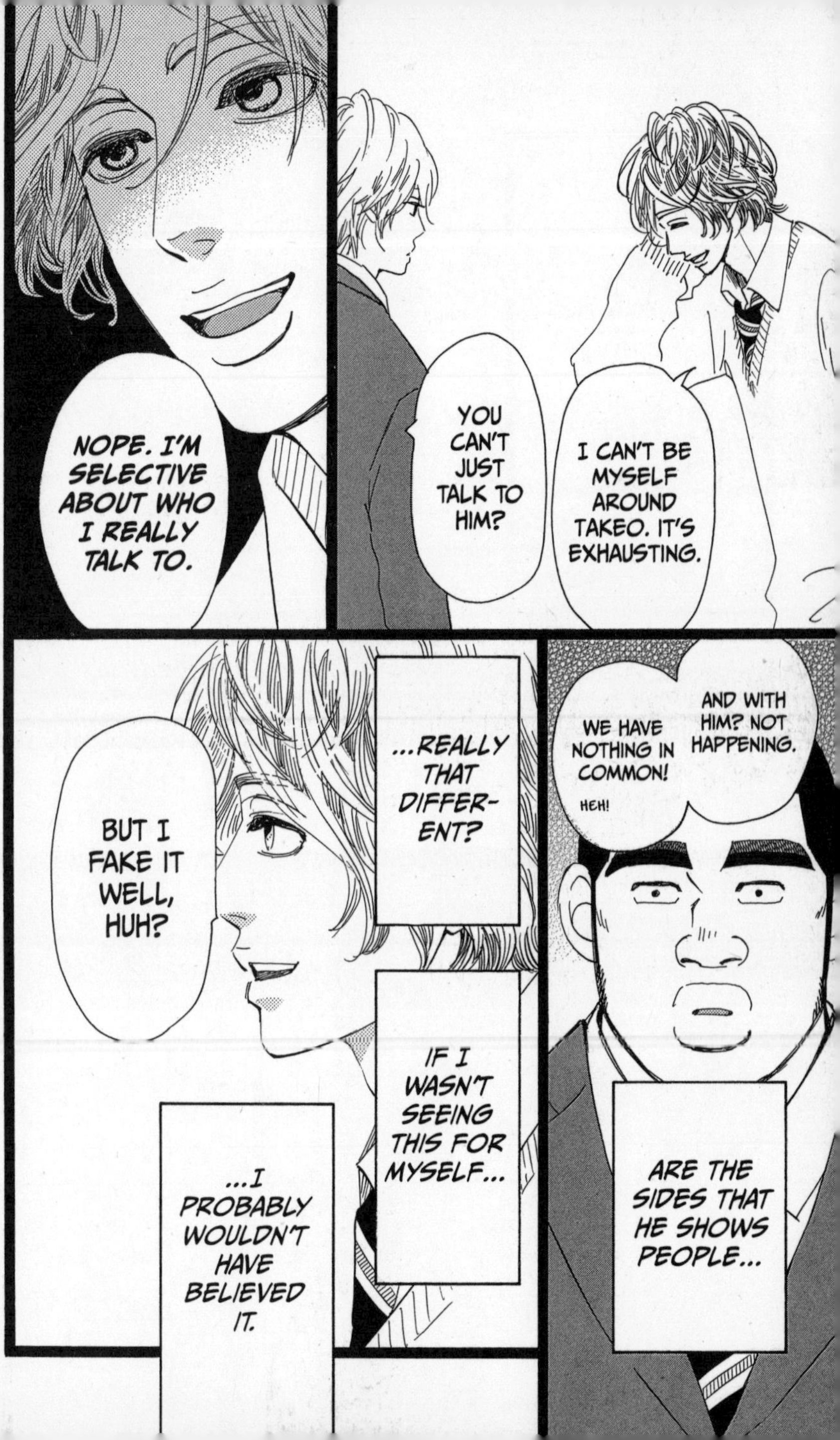
I CAN'T BE MYSELF AROUND TAKEO. IT'S EXHAUSTING.
YOU CAN'T JUST TALK TO HIM?
NOPE. I'M SELECTIVE ABOUT WHO I REALLY TALK TO.
AND WITH HIM? NOT HAPPENING.
WE HAVE NOTHING IN COMMON!
HEH!
ARE THE SIDES THAT HE SHOWS PEOPLE...
...REALLY THAT DIFFER-ENT?
BUT I FAKE IT WELL, HUH?
IF I WASN'T SEEING THIS FOR MYSELF...
...I PROBABLY WOULDN'T HAVE BELIEVED IT.

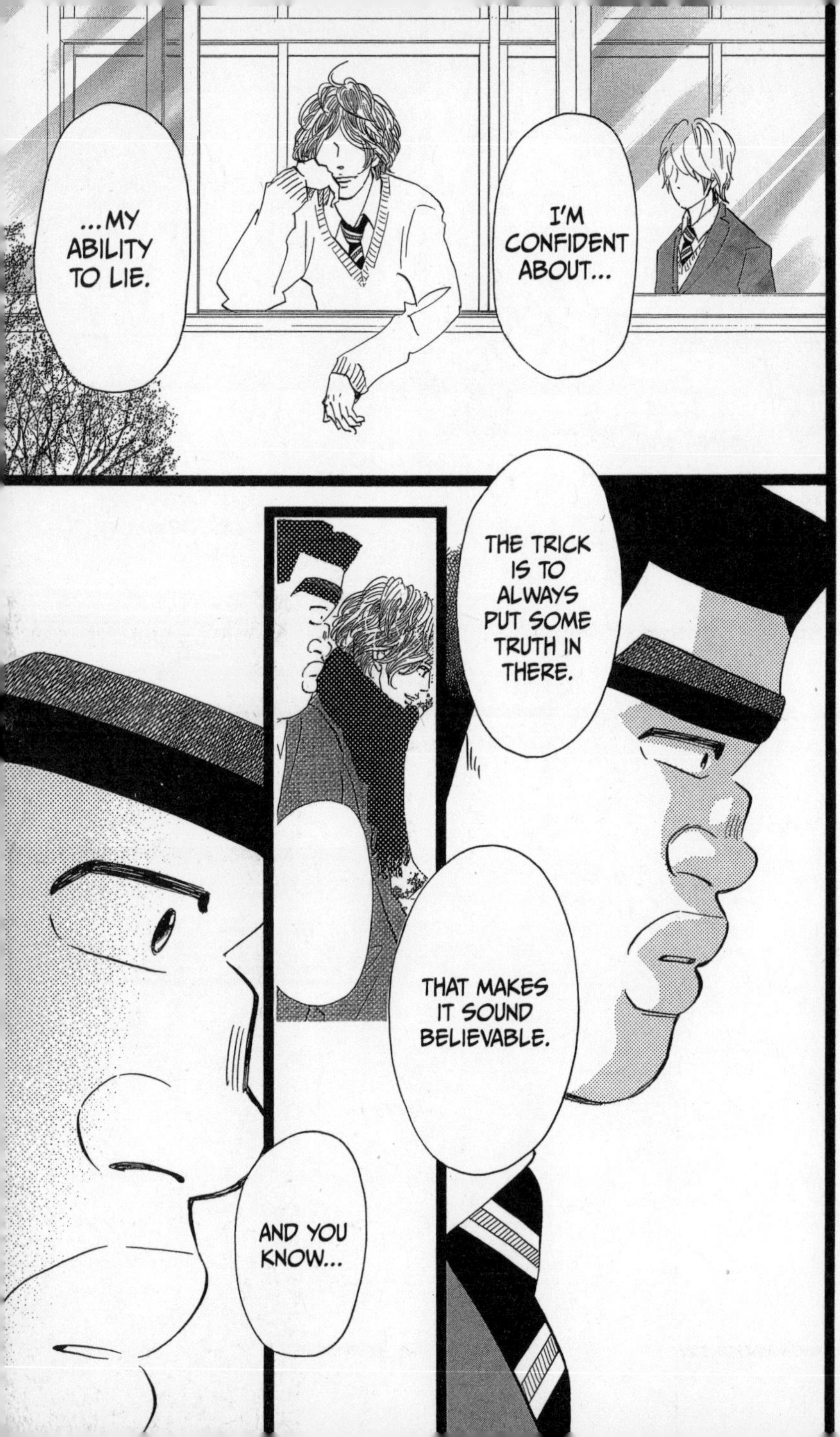
I'M CONFIDENT ABOUT...
...MY ABILITY TO LIE.
THE TRICK IS TO ALWAYS PUT SOME TRUTH IN THERE.
THAT MAKES IT SOUND BELIEVABLE.
AND YOU KNOW...

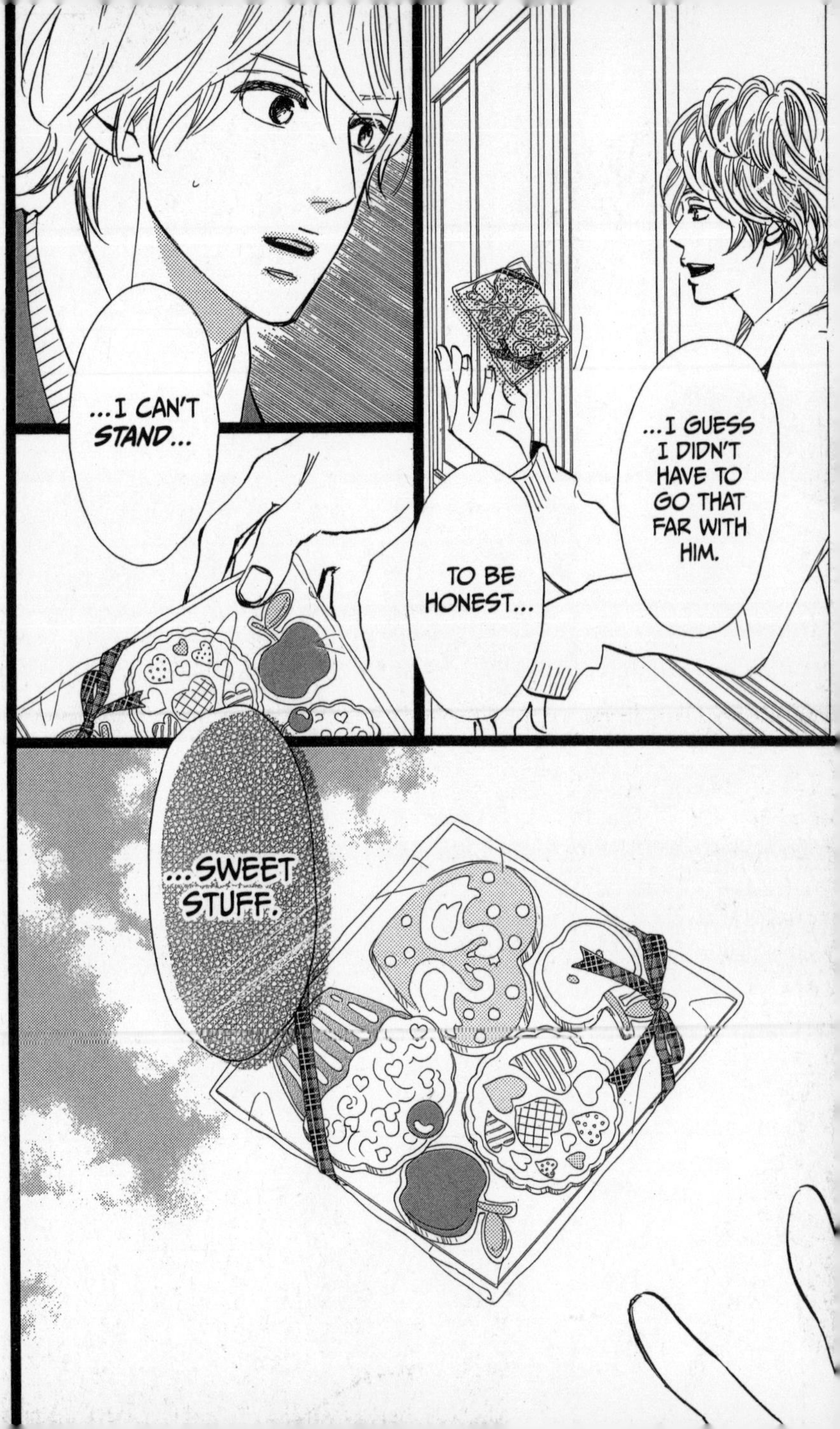
...I GUESS I DIDN'T HAVE TO GO THAT FAR WITH HIM.
TO BE HONEST...
...I CAN'T STAND...
...SWEET STUFF.

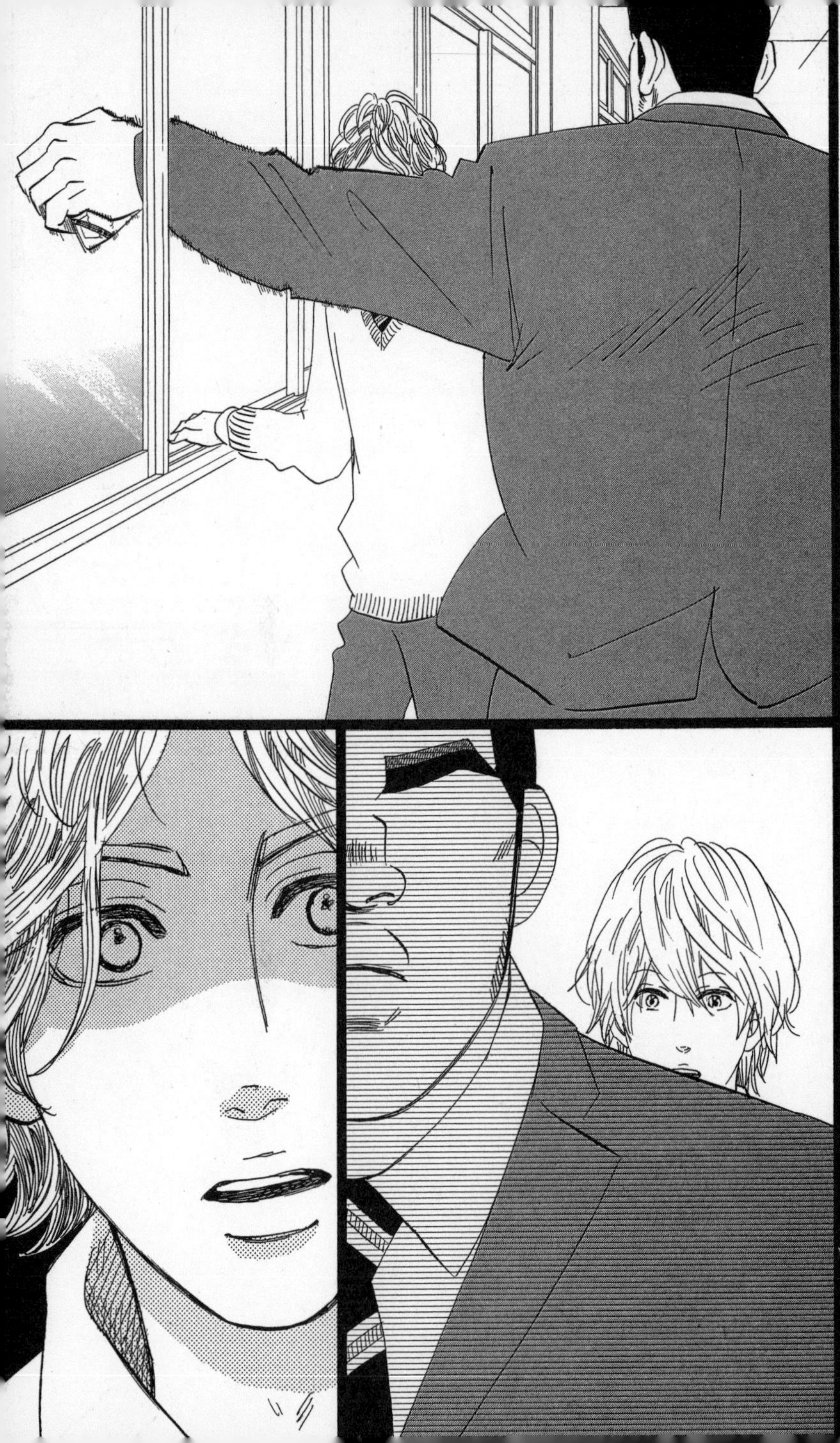

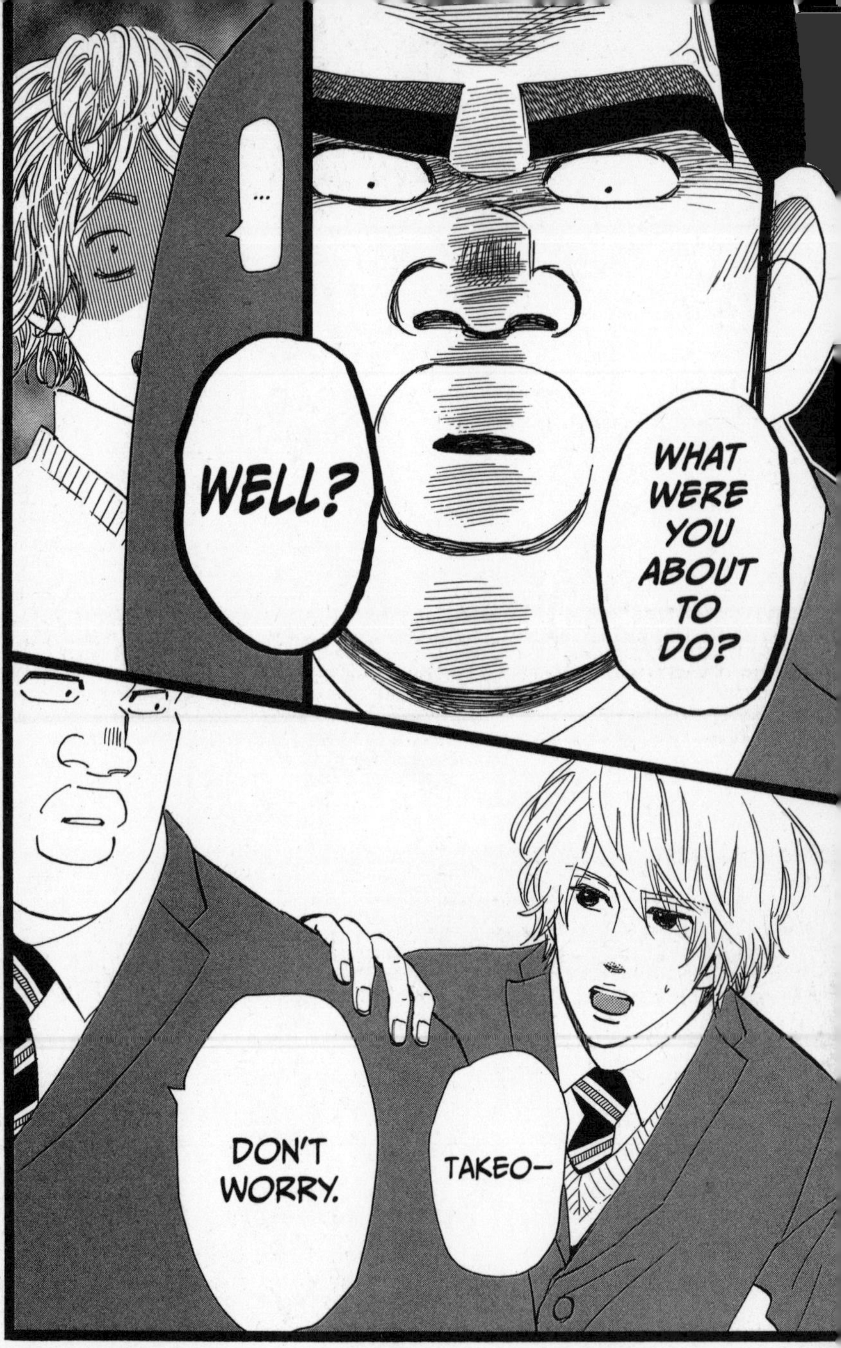
WHAT WERE YOU ABOUT TO DO?
WELL?
...
TAKEO—
DON'T WORRY.

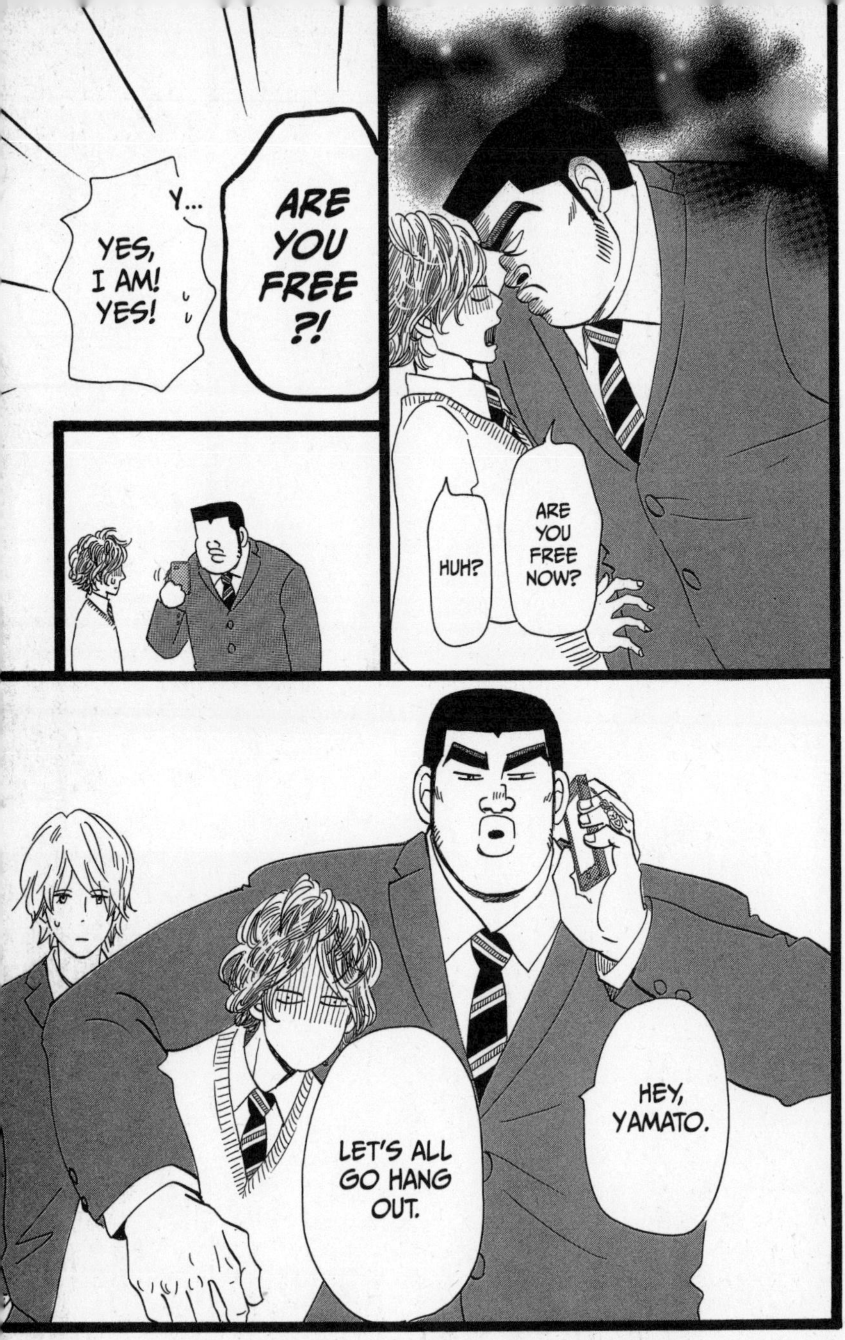
ARE YOU FREE NOW?
HUH?
ARE YOU FREE ?!
Y...
YES, I AM! YES!
HEY, YAMATO.
LET'S ALL GO HANG OUT.

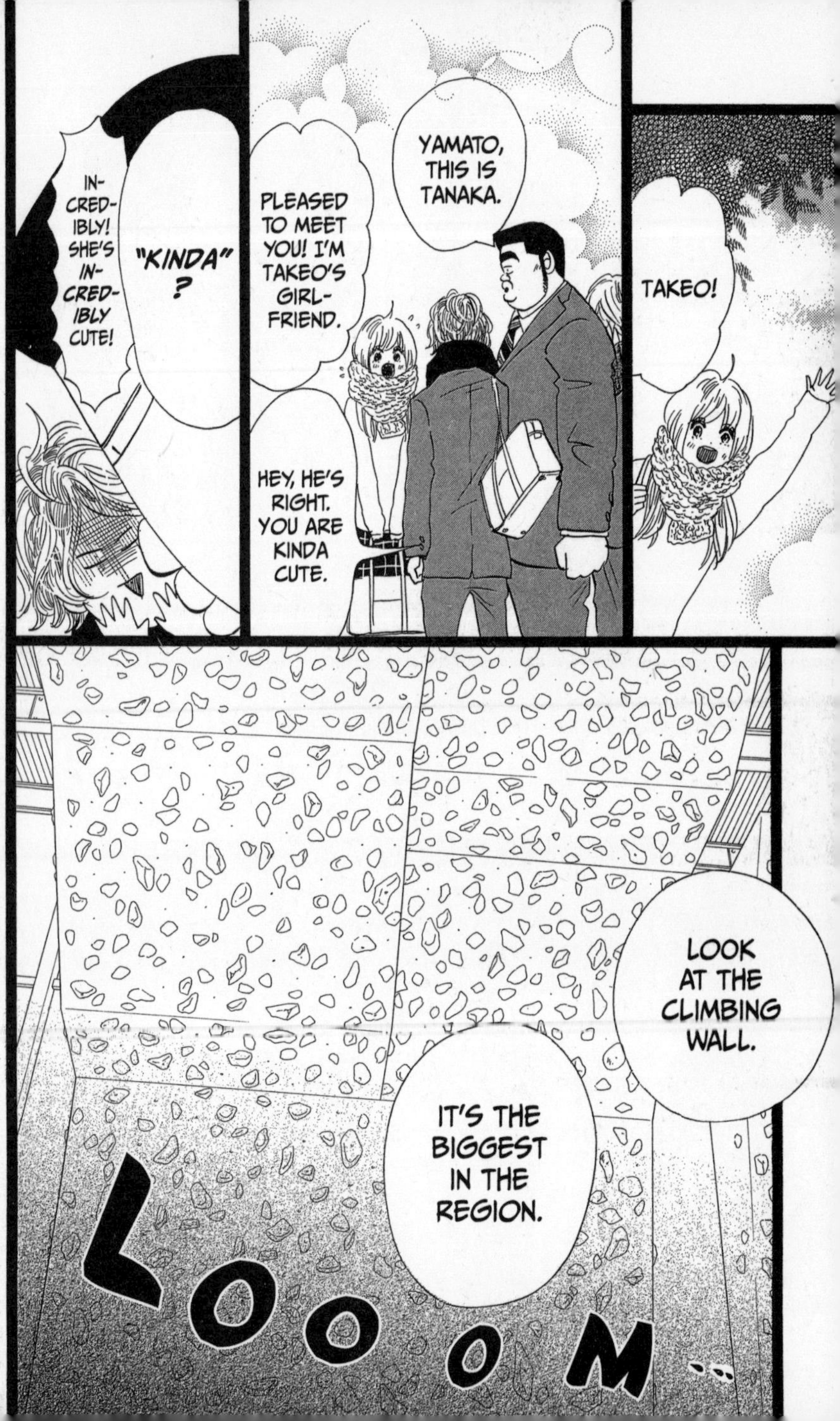
TAKEO!
YAMATO, THIS IS TANAKA.
PLEASED TO MEET YOU! I'M TAKEO'S GIRL-FRIEND.
HEY, HE'S RIGHT. YOU ARE KINDA CUTE.
"KINDA"?
IN-CRED-IBLY! SHE'S IN-CRED-IBLY CUTE!
LOOK AT THE CLIMBING WALL.
IT'S THE BIGGEST IN THE REGION.
LOOOOM...

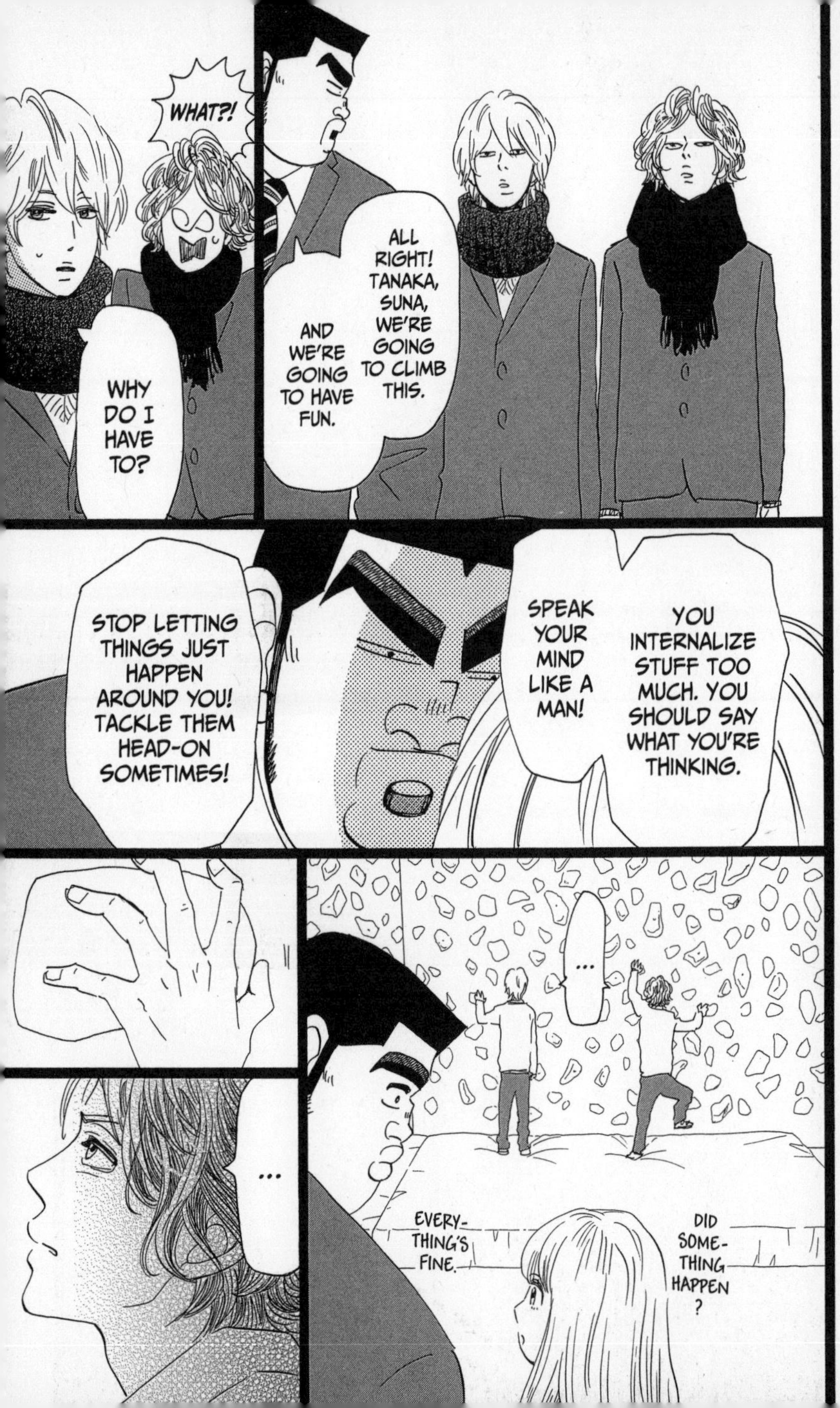
ALL RIGHT! TANAKA, SUNA, WE'RE GOING TO CLIMB THIS.
AND WE'RE GOING TO HAVE FUN.
WHAT?!
WHY DO I HAVE TO?
YOU INTERNALIZE STUFF TOO MUCH. YOU SHOULD SAY WHAT YOU'RE THINKING.
SPEAK YOUR MIND LIKE A MAN!
STOP LETTING THINGS JUST HAPPEN AROUND YOU! TACKLE THEM HEAD-ON SOMETIMES!
...
DID SOME-THING HAPPEN?
EVERY-THING'S FINE.
...

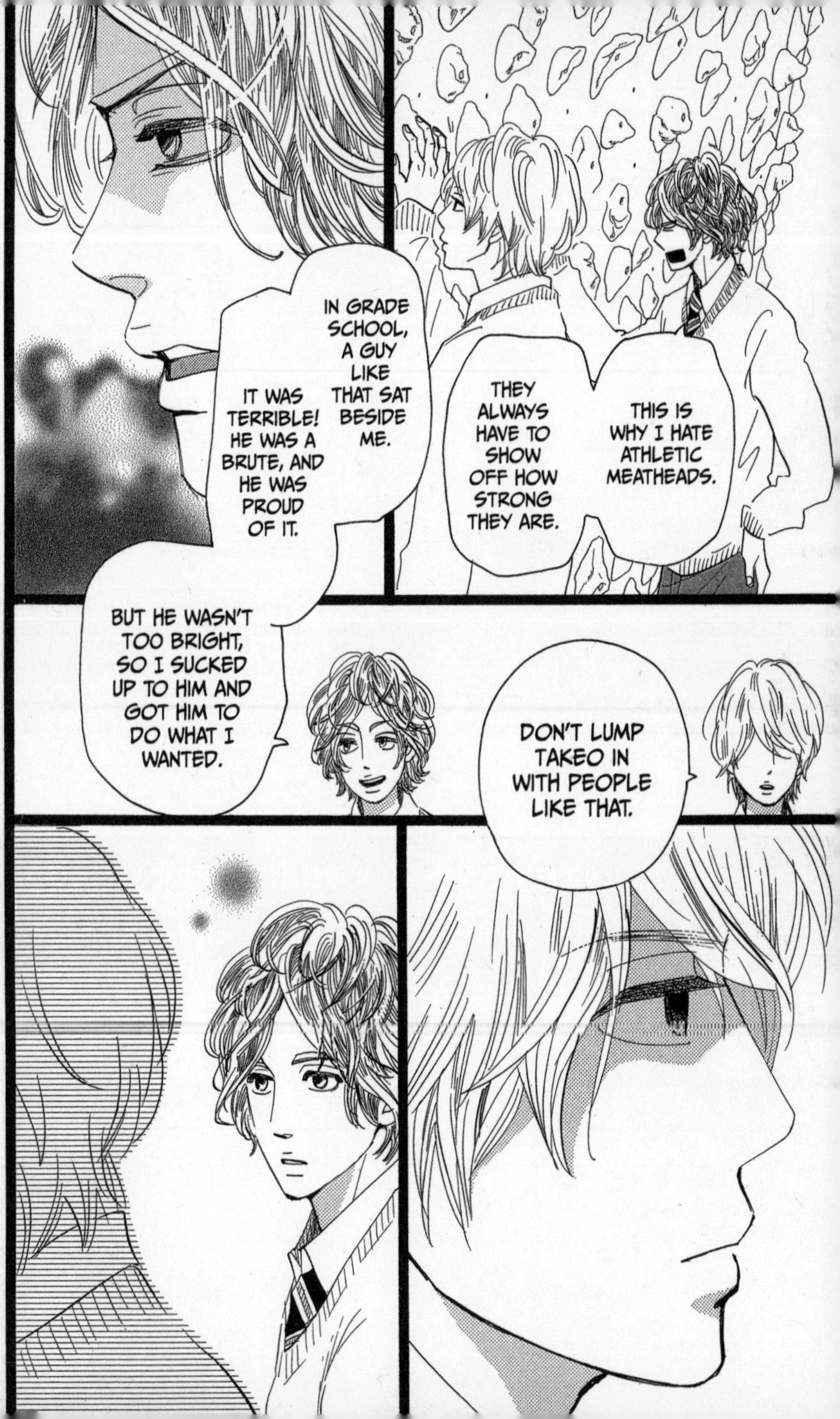
THIS IS WHY I HATE ATHLETIC MEATHEADS.
THEY ALWAYS HAVE TO SHOW OFF HOW STRONG THEY ARE.
IN GRADE SCHOOL, A GUY LIKE THAT SAT BESIDE ME.
IT WAS TERRIBLE! HE WAS A BRUTE, AND HE WAS PROUD OF IT.
BUT HE WASN'T TOO BRIGHT, SO I SUCKED UP TO HIM AND GOT HIM TO DO WHAT I WANTED.
DON'T LUMP TAKEO IN WITH PEOPLE LIKE THAT.

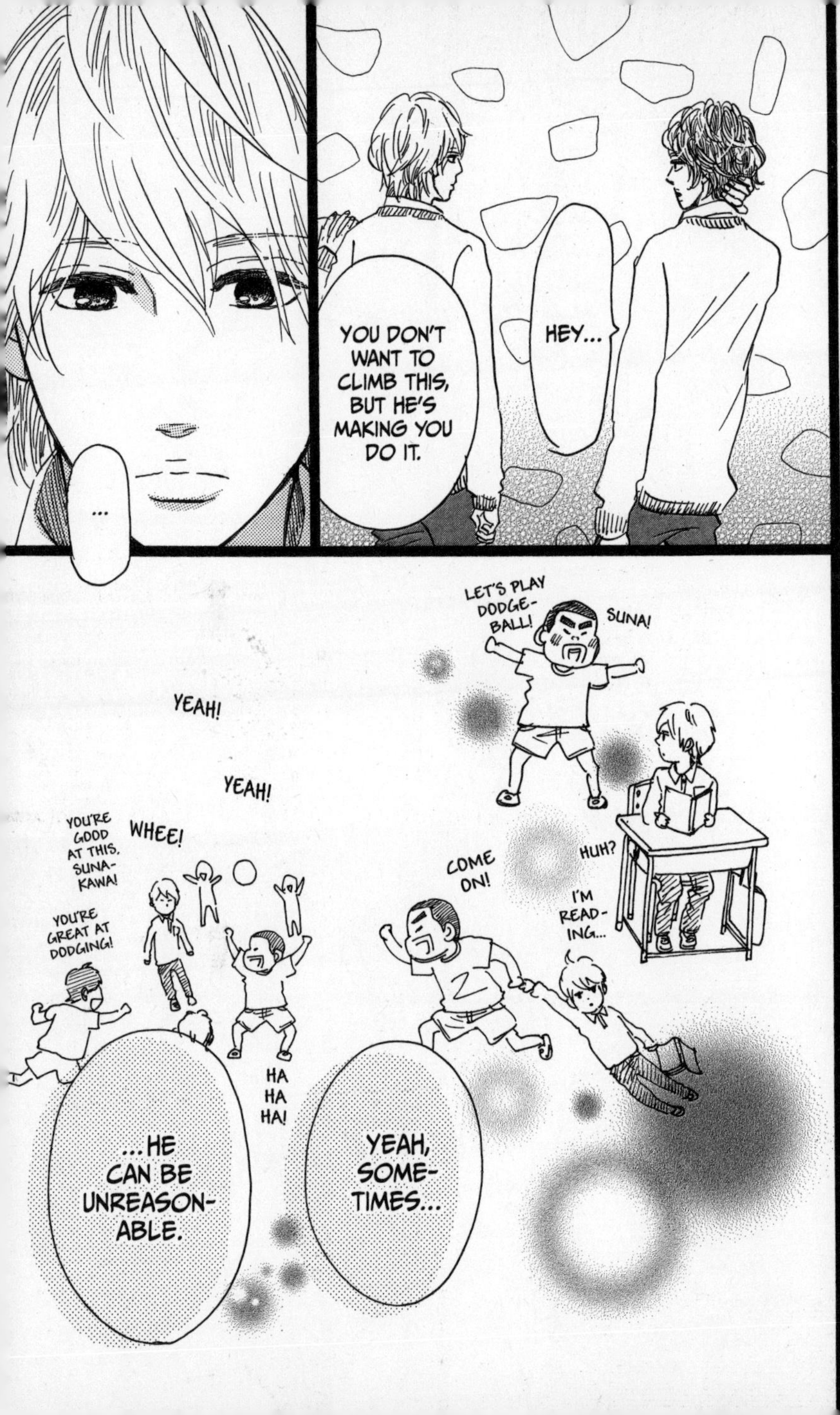
HEY...
YOU DON'T WANT TO CLIMB THIS, BUT HE'S MAKING YOU DO IT.
...
LET'S PLAY DODGE-BALL!
SUNA!
HUH?
I'M READ-ING...
COME ON!
YEAH!
YEAH!
WHEE!
YOU'RE GOOD AT THIS, SUNA-KAWA!
YOU'RE GREAT AT DODGING!
HA HA HA!
YEAH, SOME-TIMES...
...HE CAN BE UNREASON-ABLE.

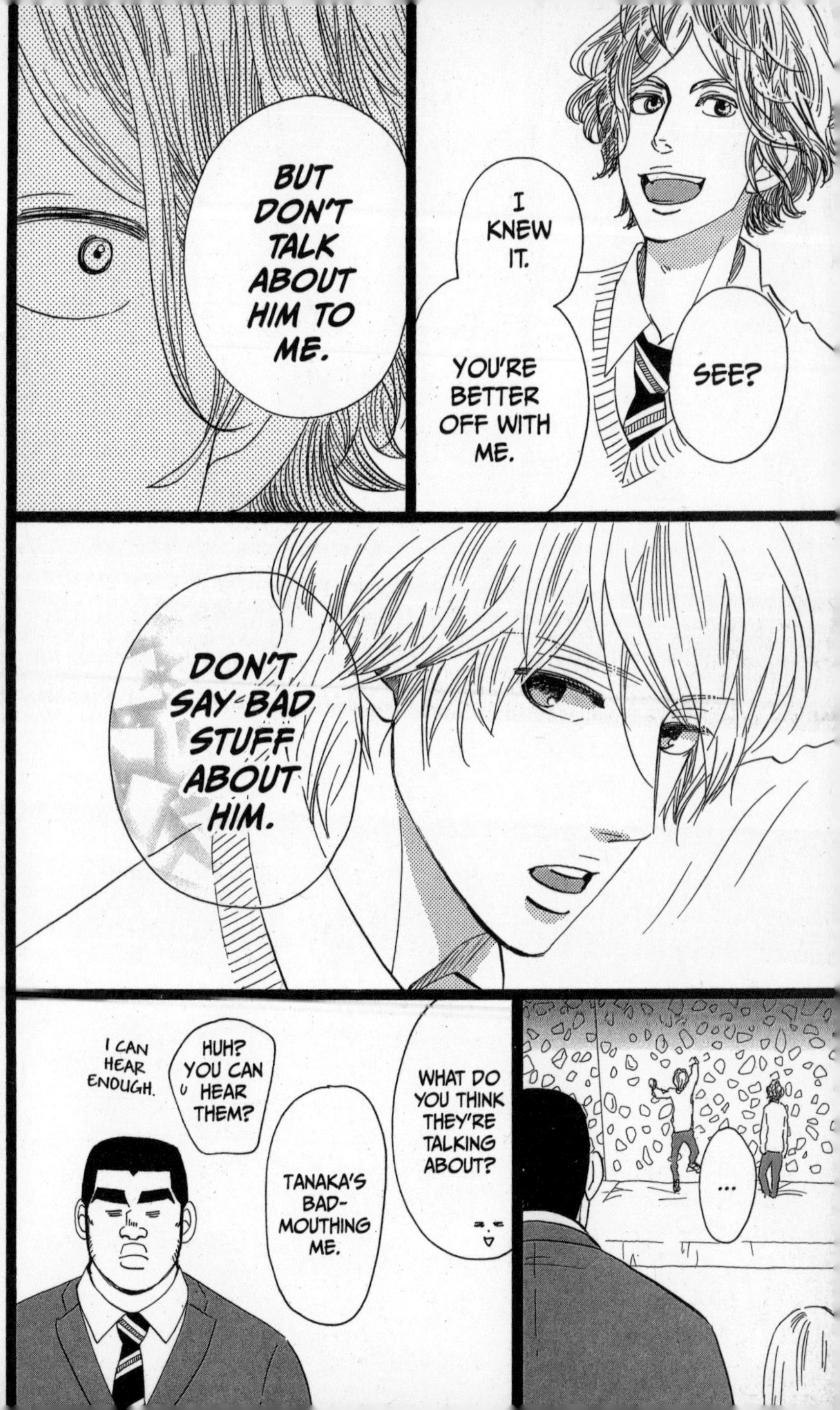
SEE?
I KNEW IT.
YOU'RE BETTER OFF WITH ME.
BUT DON'T TALK ABOUT HIM TO ME.
DON'T SAY BAD STUFF ABOUT HIM.
...
WHAT DO YOU THINK THEY'RE TALKING ABOUT?
TANAKA'S BAD-MOUTHING ME.
HUH? YOU CAN HEAR THEM?
I CAN HEAR ENOUGH.

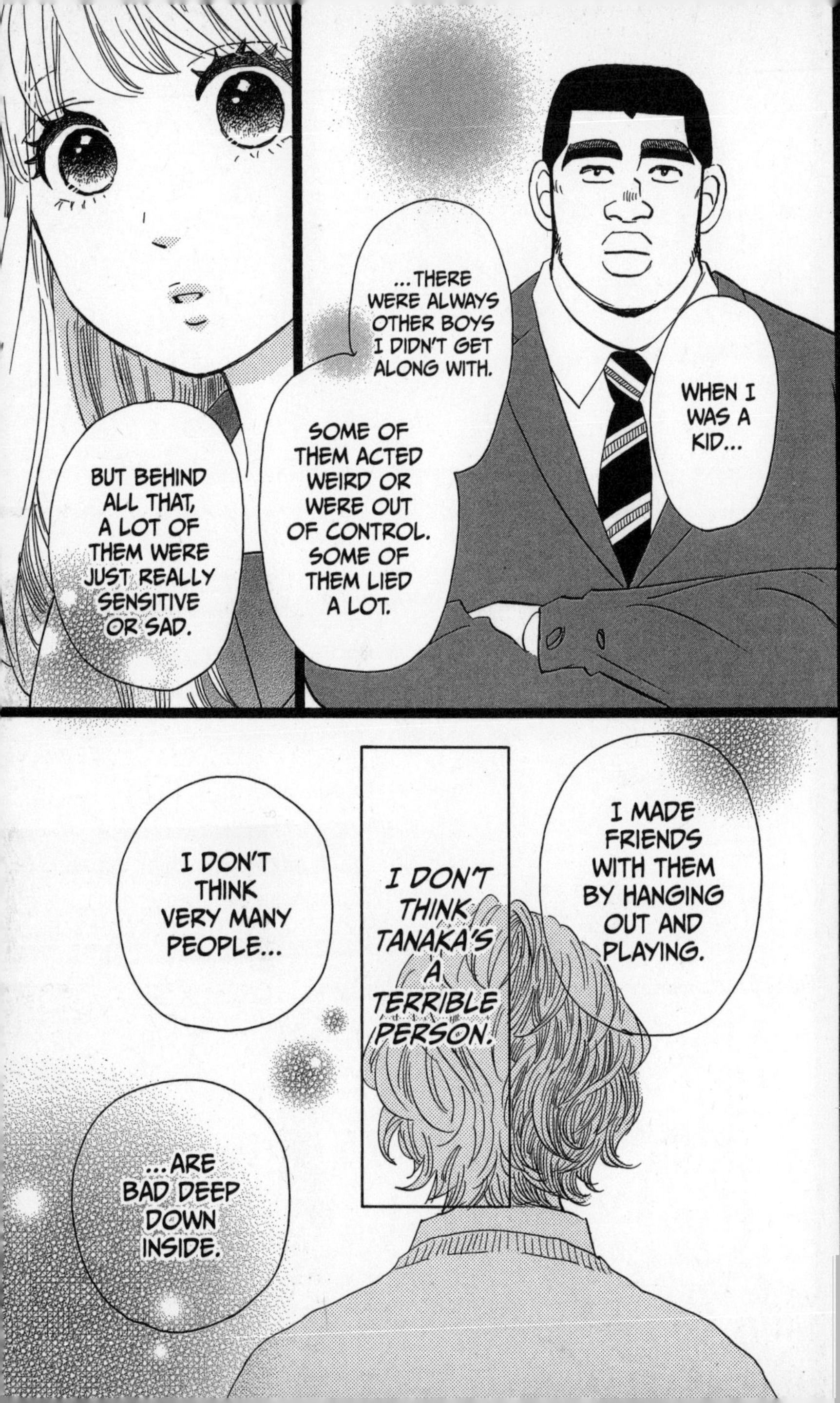
WHEN I WAS A KID...
...THERE WERE ALWAYS OTHER BOYS I DIDN'T GET ALONG WITH.
SOME OF THEM ACTED WEIRD OR WERE OUT OF CONTROL. SOME OF THEM LIED A LOT.
BUT BEHIND ALL THAT, A LOT OF THEM WERE JUST REALLY SENSITIVE OR SAD.
I MADE FRIENDS WITH THEM BY HANGING OUT AND PLAYING.
I DON'T THINK TANAKA'S A TERRIBLE PERSON.
I DON'T THINK VERY MANY PEOPLE...
...ARE BAD DEEP DOWN INSIDE.

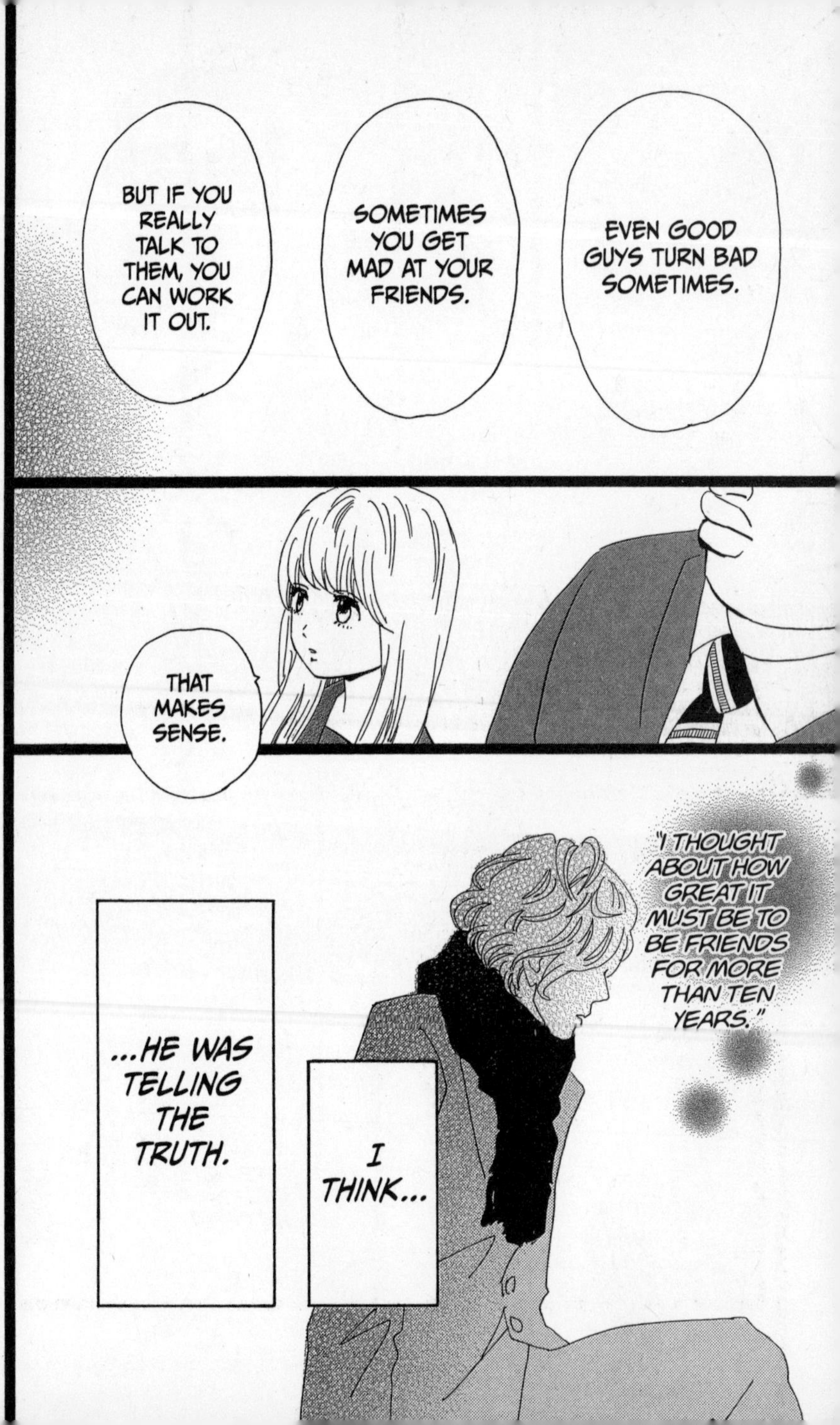
EVEN GOOD GUYS TURN BAD SOMETIMES.
SOMETIMES YOU GET MAD AT YOUR FRIENDS.
BUT IF YOU REALLY TALK TO THEM, YOU CAN WORK IT OUT.
THAT MAKES SENSE.
"I THOUGHT ABOUT HOW GREAT IT MUST BE TO BE FRIENDS FOR MORE THAN TEN YEARS."
I THINK...
...HE WAS TELLING THE TRUTH.

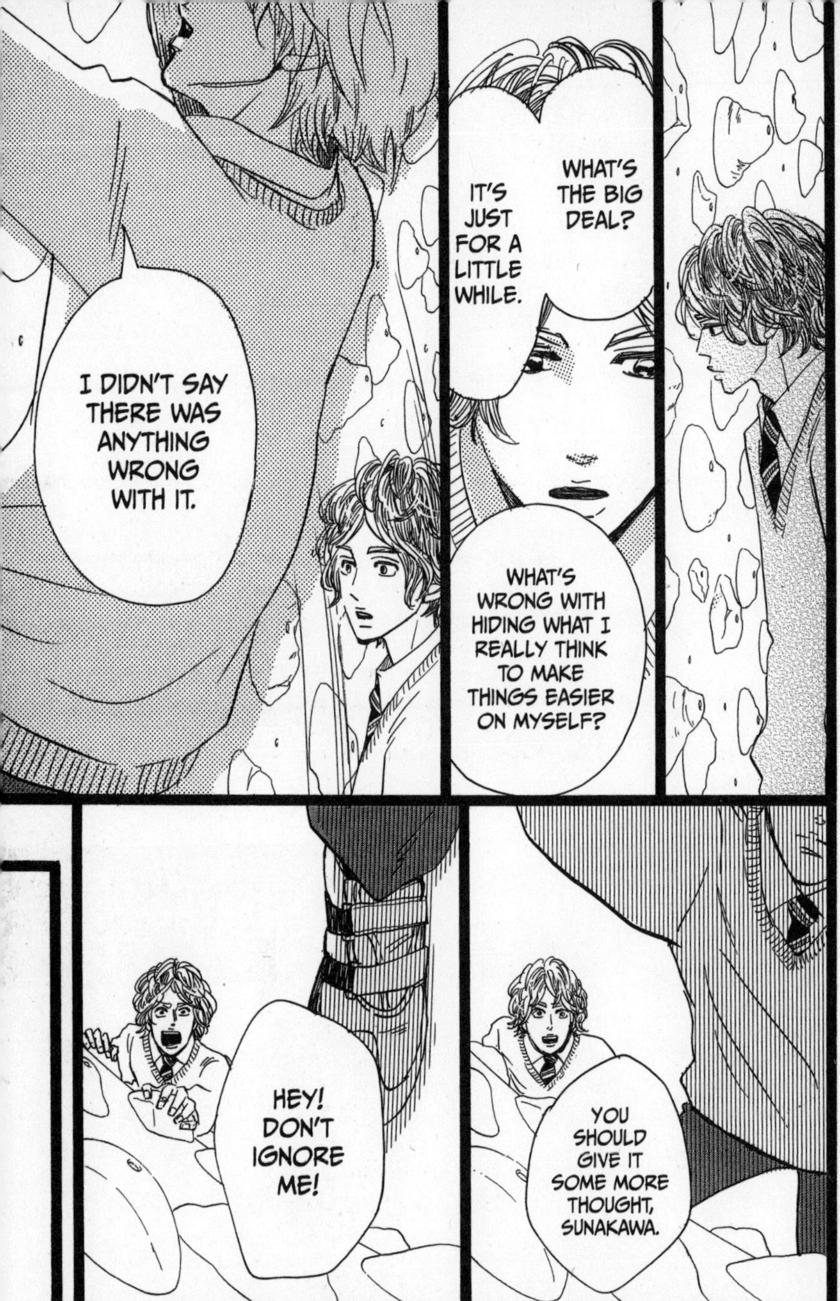
WHAT'S THE BIG DEAL?
IT'S JUST FOR A LITTLE WHILE.
WHAT'S WRONG WITH HIDING WHAT I REALLY THINK TO MAKE THINGS EASIER ON MYSELF?
I DIDN'T SAY THERE WAS ANYTHING WRONG WITH IT.
YOU SHOULD GIVE IT SOME MORE THOUGHT, SUNAKAWA.
HEY! DON'T IGNORE ME!

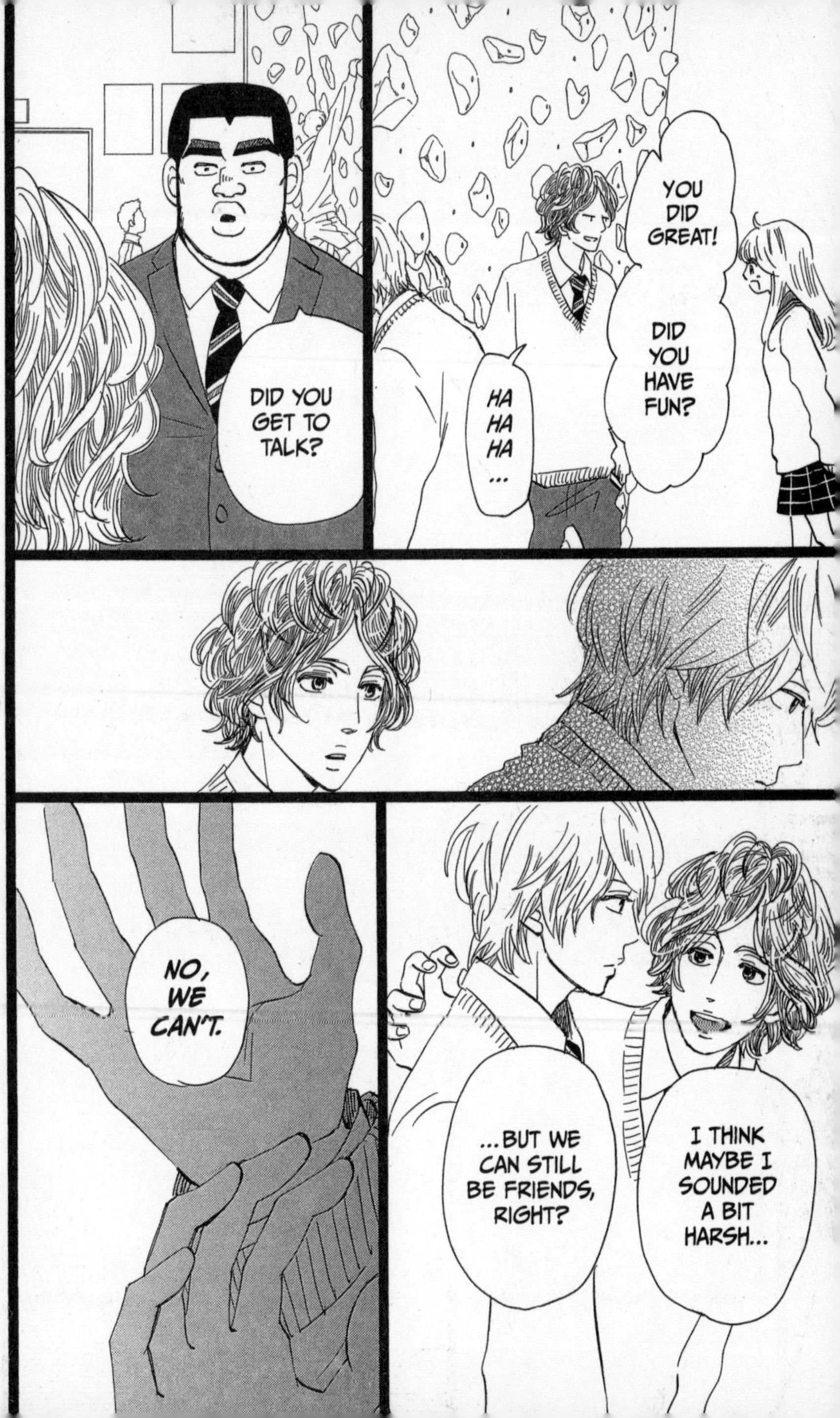
YOU DID GREAT!
DID YOU HAVE FUN?
HA HA HA ...
DID YOU GET TO TALK?
I THINK MAYBE I SOUNDED A BIT HARSH...
...BUT WE CAN STILL BE FRIENDS, RIGHT?
NO, WE CAN'T.

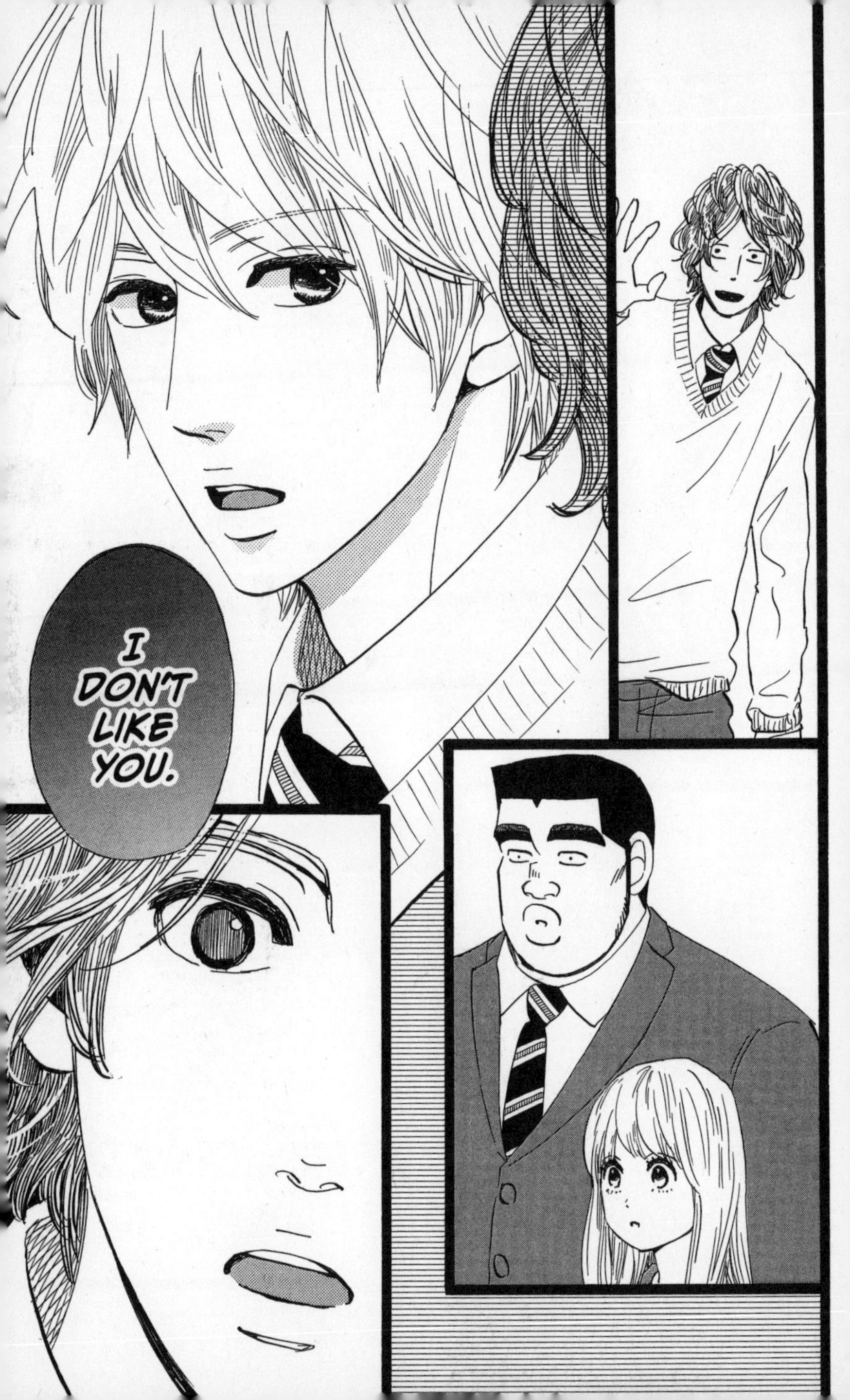
I DON'T LIKE YOU.

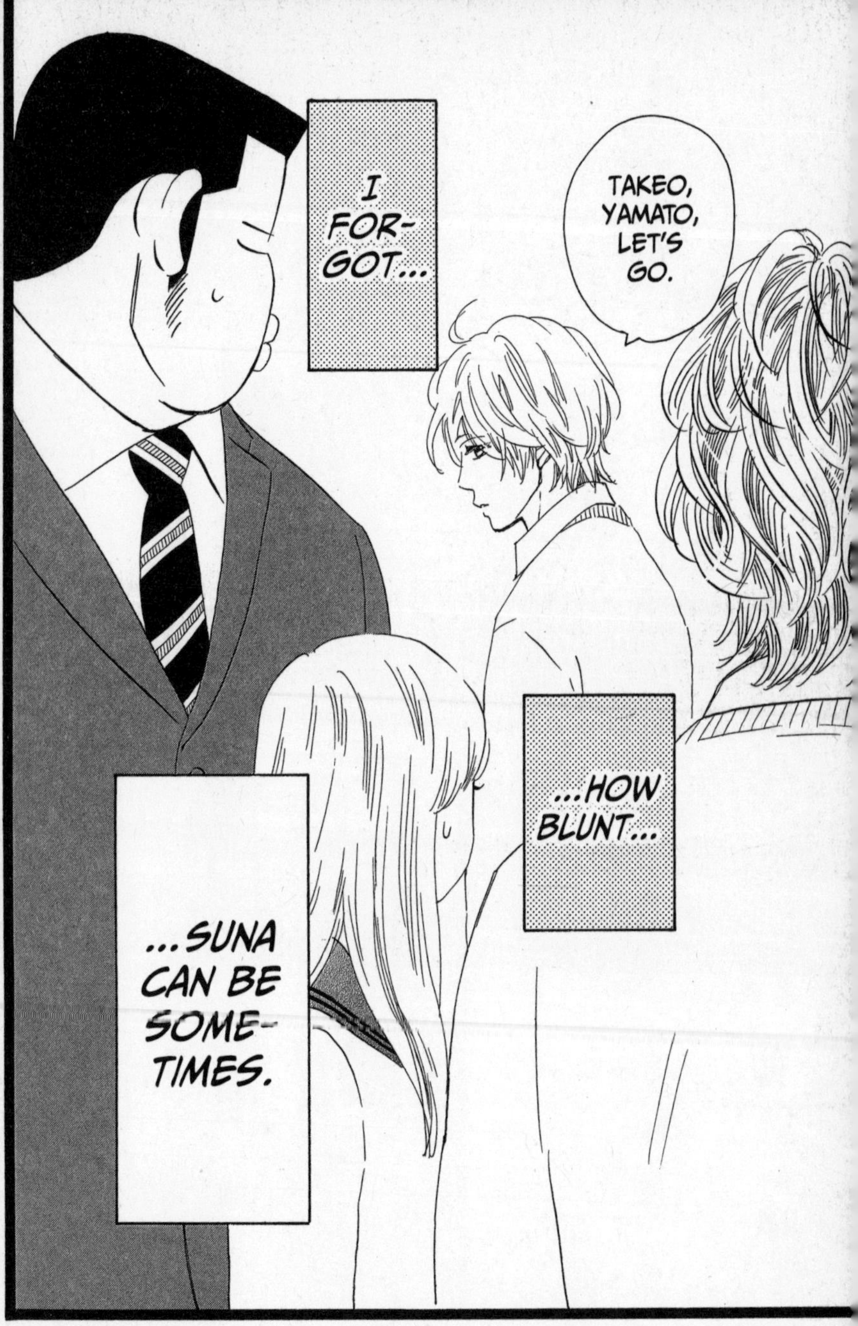
TAKEO, YAMATO, LET'S GO.
I FOR-GOT...
...HOW BLUNT...
...SUNA CAN BE SOME-TIMES.

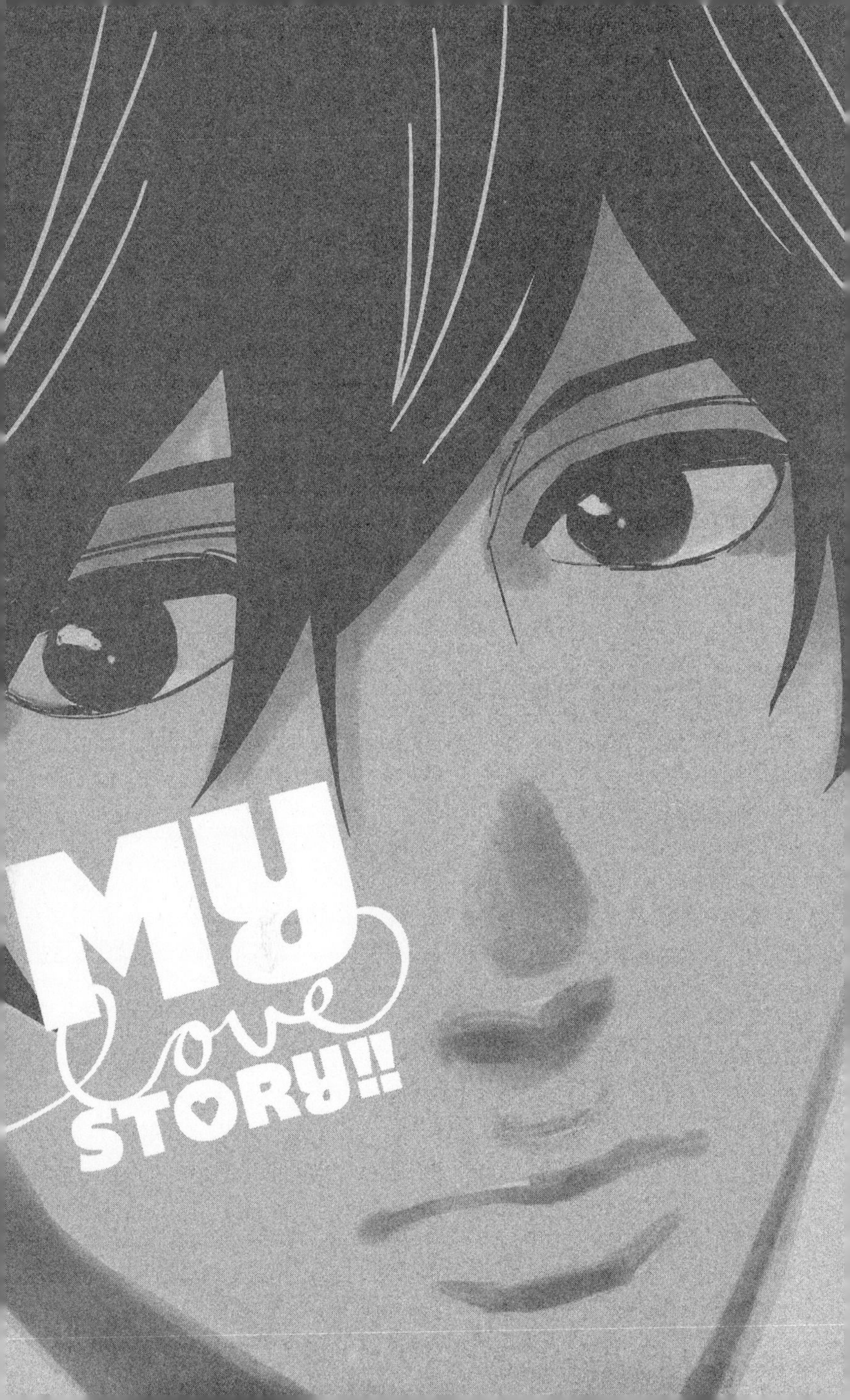
MY Love STORY!!

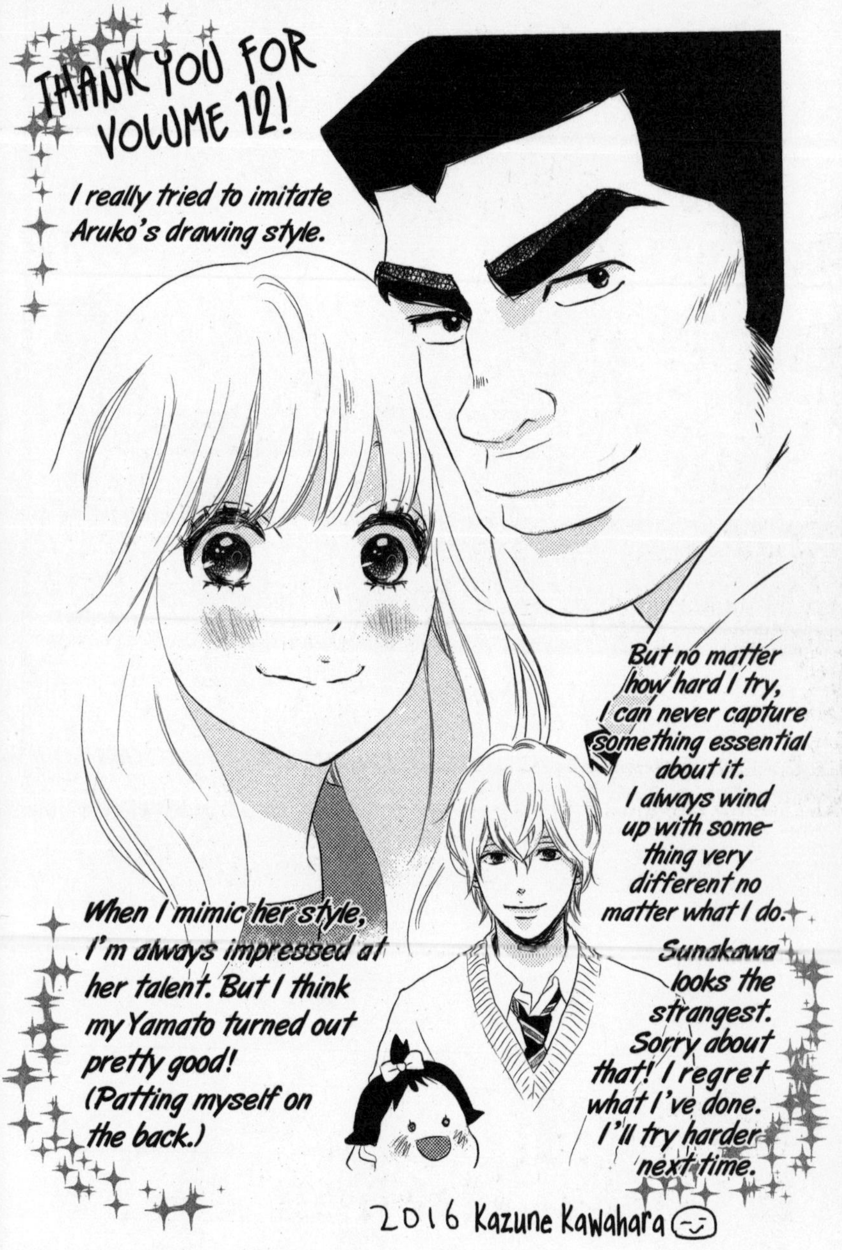
THANK YOU FOR VOLUME 12!
I really tried to imitate Aruko's drawing style.
When I mimic her style, I'm always impressed at her talent. But I think my Yamato turned out pretty good! (Patting myself on the back.)
But no matter how hard I try, I can never capture something essential about it. I always wind up with something very different no matter what I do.
Sunakawa looks the strangest. Sorry about that! I regret what I've done. I'll try harder next time.
2016 Kazune Kawahara

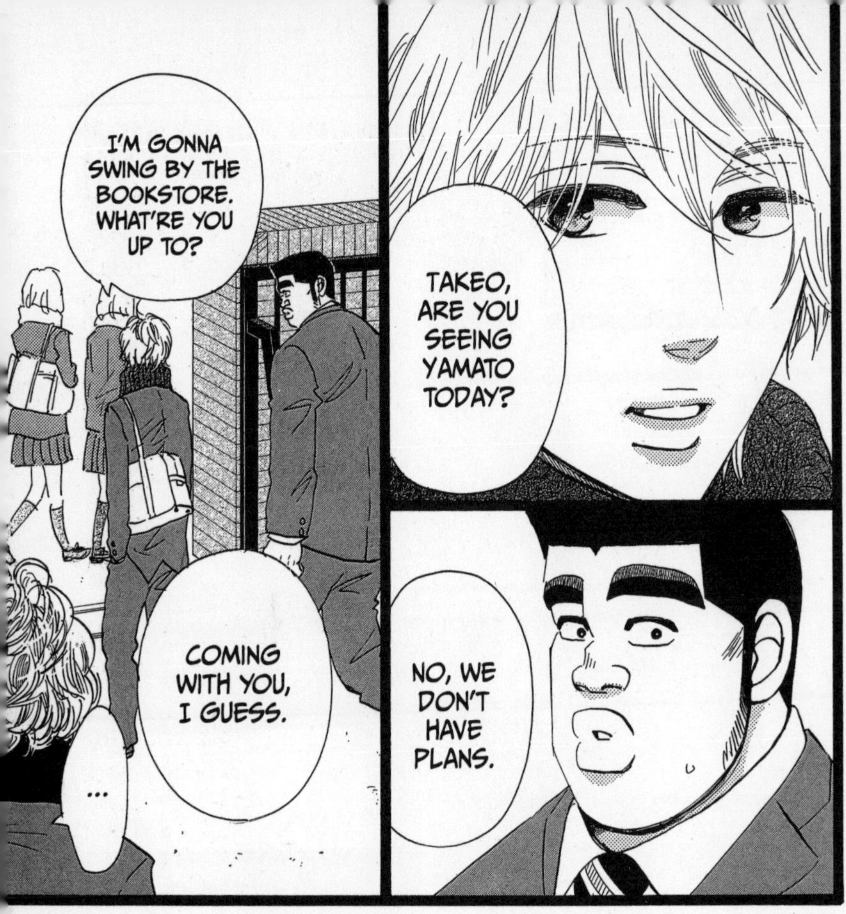
TAKEO, ARE YOU SEEING YAMATO TODAY?
NO, WE DON'T HAVE PLANS.
I'M GONNA SWING BY THE BOOKSTORE. WHAT'RE YOU UP TO?
COMING WITH YOU, I GUESS.
...

MY love STORY!!

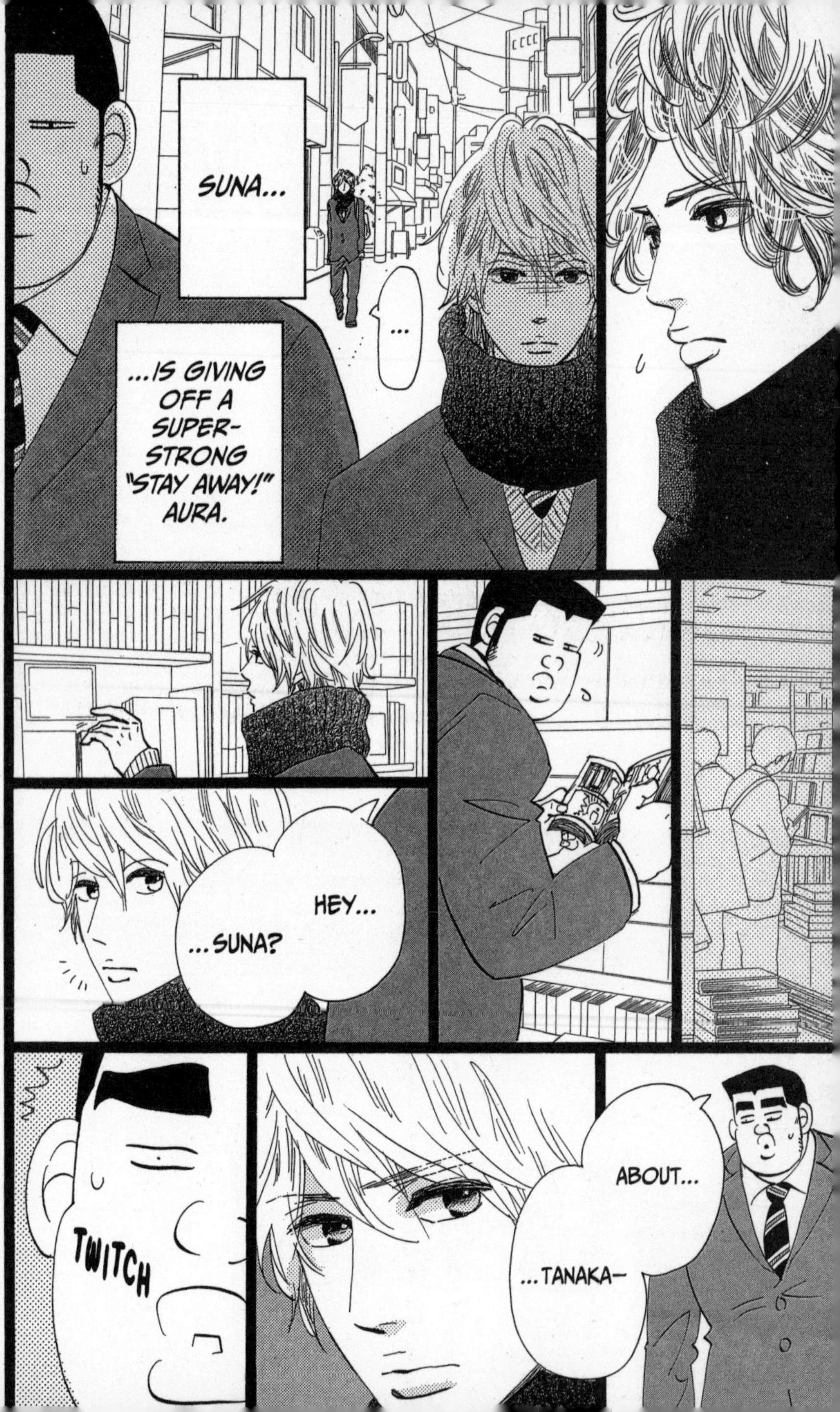
SUNA...
...
...IS GIVING OFF A SUPER-STRONG "STAY AWAY!" AURA.
HEY... ...SUNA?
ABOUT... ...TANAKA—
TWITCH

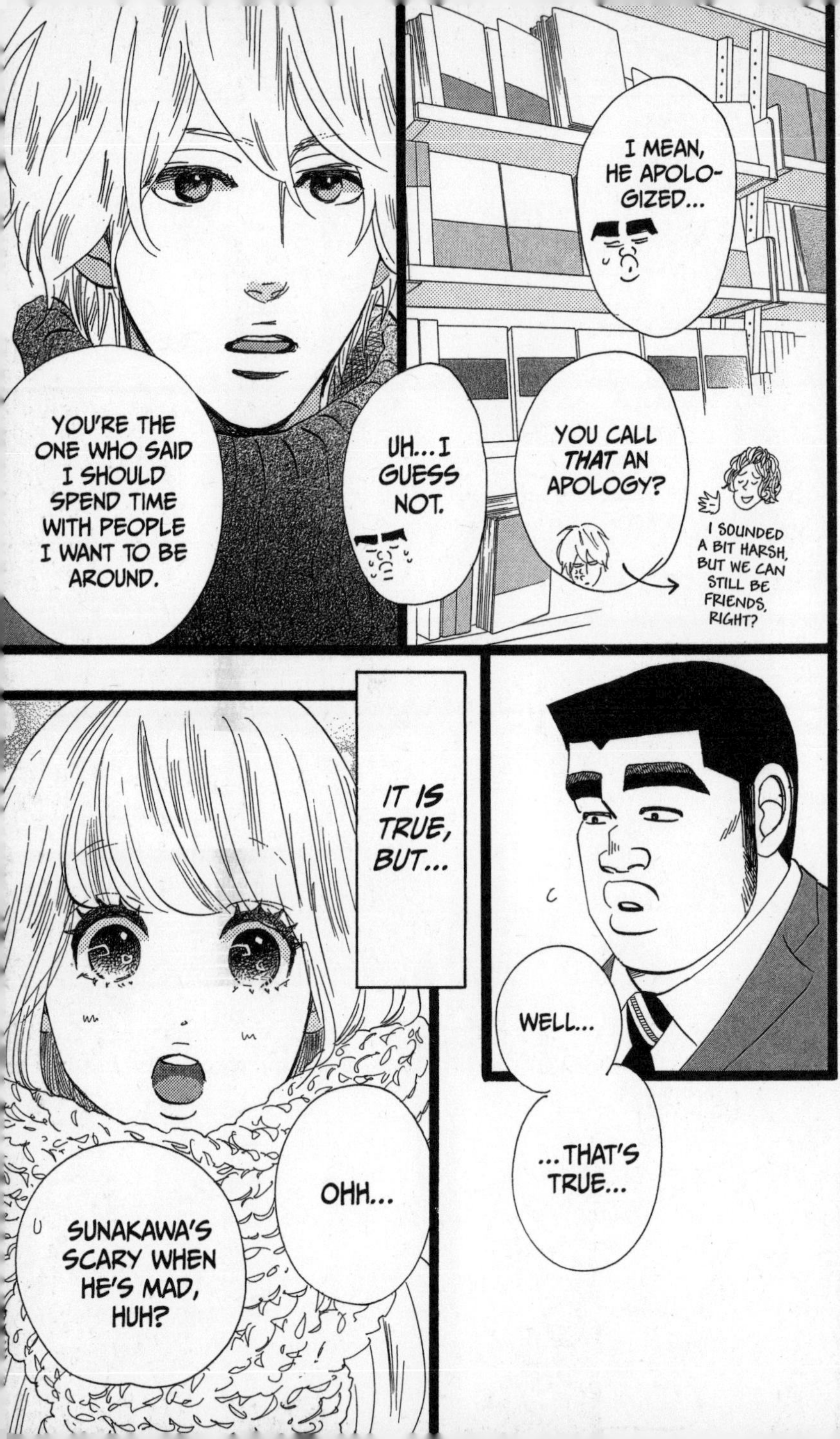
I MEAN, HE APOLOGIZED...
YOU CALL THAT AN APOLOGY?
I SOUNDED A BIT HARSH, BUT WE CAN STILL BE FRIENDS, RIGHT?
UH...I GUESS NOT.
YOU'RE THE ONE WHO SAID I SHOULD SPEND TIME WITH PEOPLE I WANT TO BE AROUND.
WELL...
...THAT'S TRUE...
IT IS TRUE, BUT...
OHH...
SUNAKAWA'S SCARY WHEN HE'S MAD, HUH?

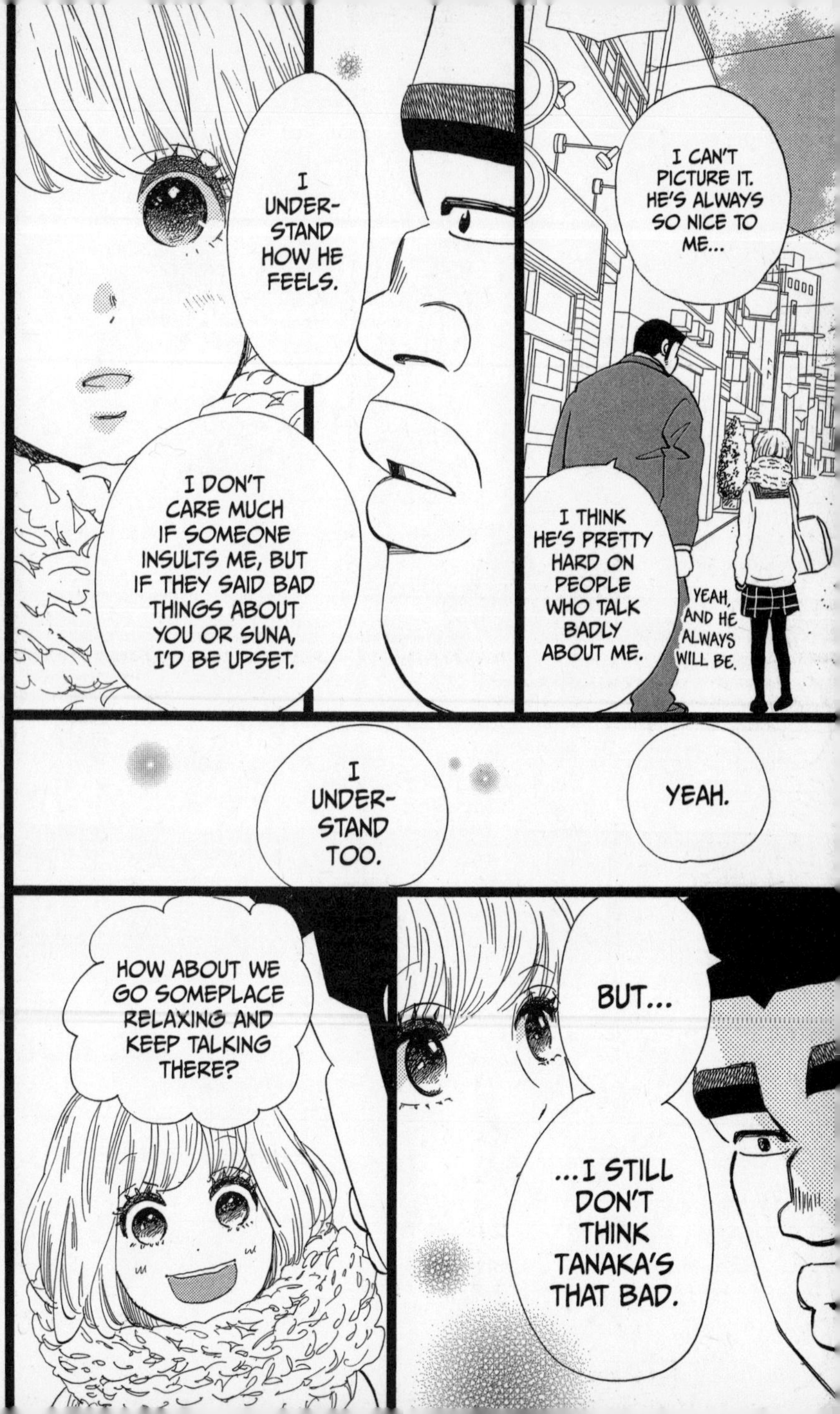
I CAN'T PICTURE IT. HE'S ALWAYS SO NICE TO ME...
I THINK HE'S PRETTY HARD ON PEOPLE WHO TALK BADLY ABOUT ME.
YEAH, AND HE ALWAYS WILL BE.
I UNDERSTAND HOW HE FEELS.
I DON'T CARE MUCH IF SOMEONE INSULTS ME, BUT IF THEY SAID BAD THINGS ABOUT YOU OR SUNA, I'D BE UPSET.
YEAH.
I UNDERSTAND TOO.
BUT...
...I STILL DON'T THINK TANAKA'S THAT BAD.
HOW ABOUT WE GO SOMEPLACE RELAXING AND KEEP TALKING THERE?

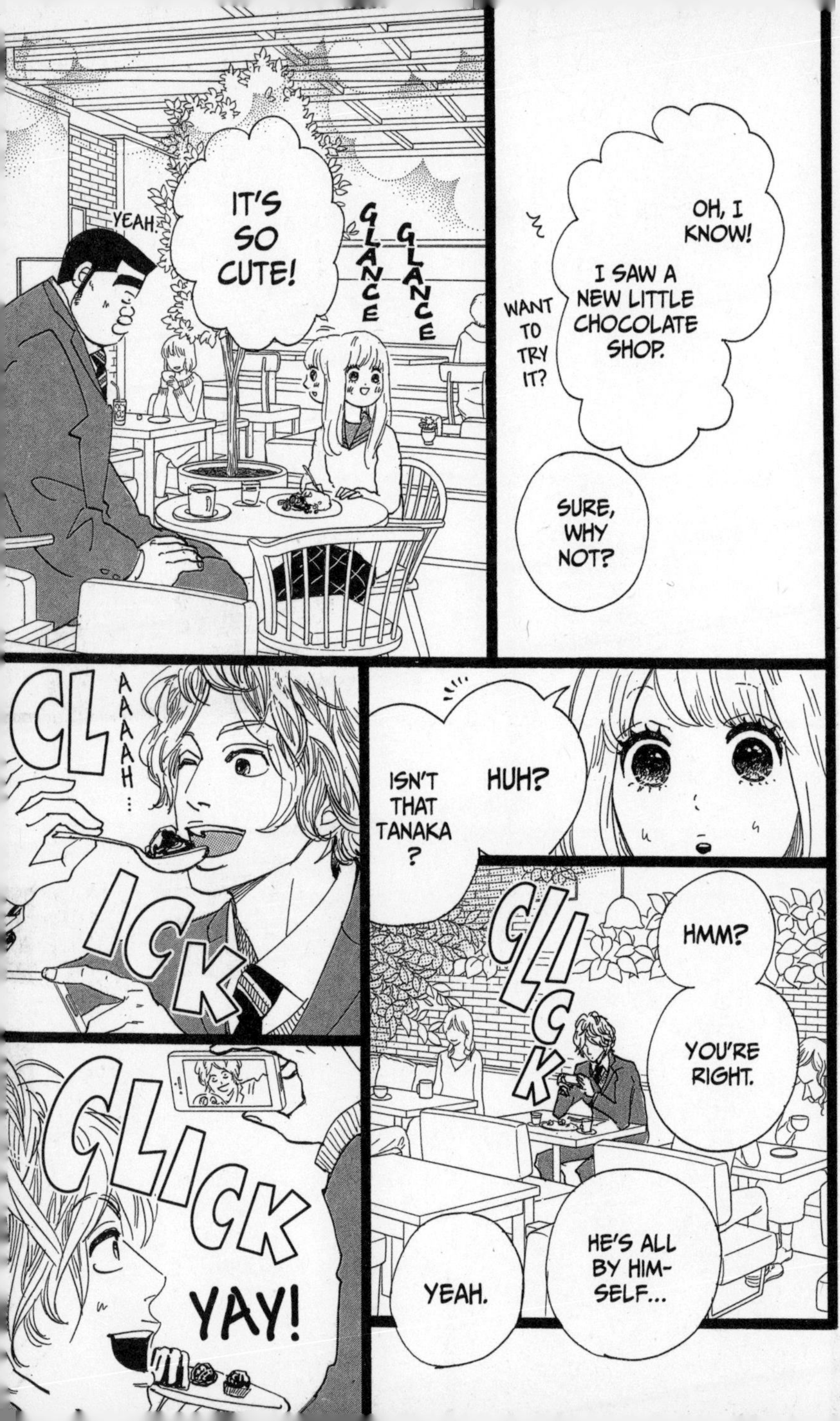
OH, I KNOW!
I SAW A NEW LITTLE CHOCOLATE SHOP.
WANT TO TRY IT?
SURE, WHY NOT?
IT'S SO CUTE!
GLANCE
GLANCE
YEAH.
HUH?
ISN'T THAT TANAKA?
HMM?
YOU'RE RIGHT.
HE'S ALL BY HIM-SELF...
YEAH.
CL
AAAAH...
ICK
CLICK
CLICK
YAY!

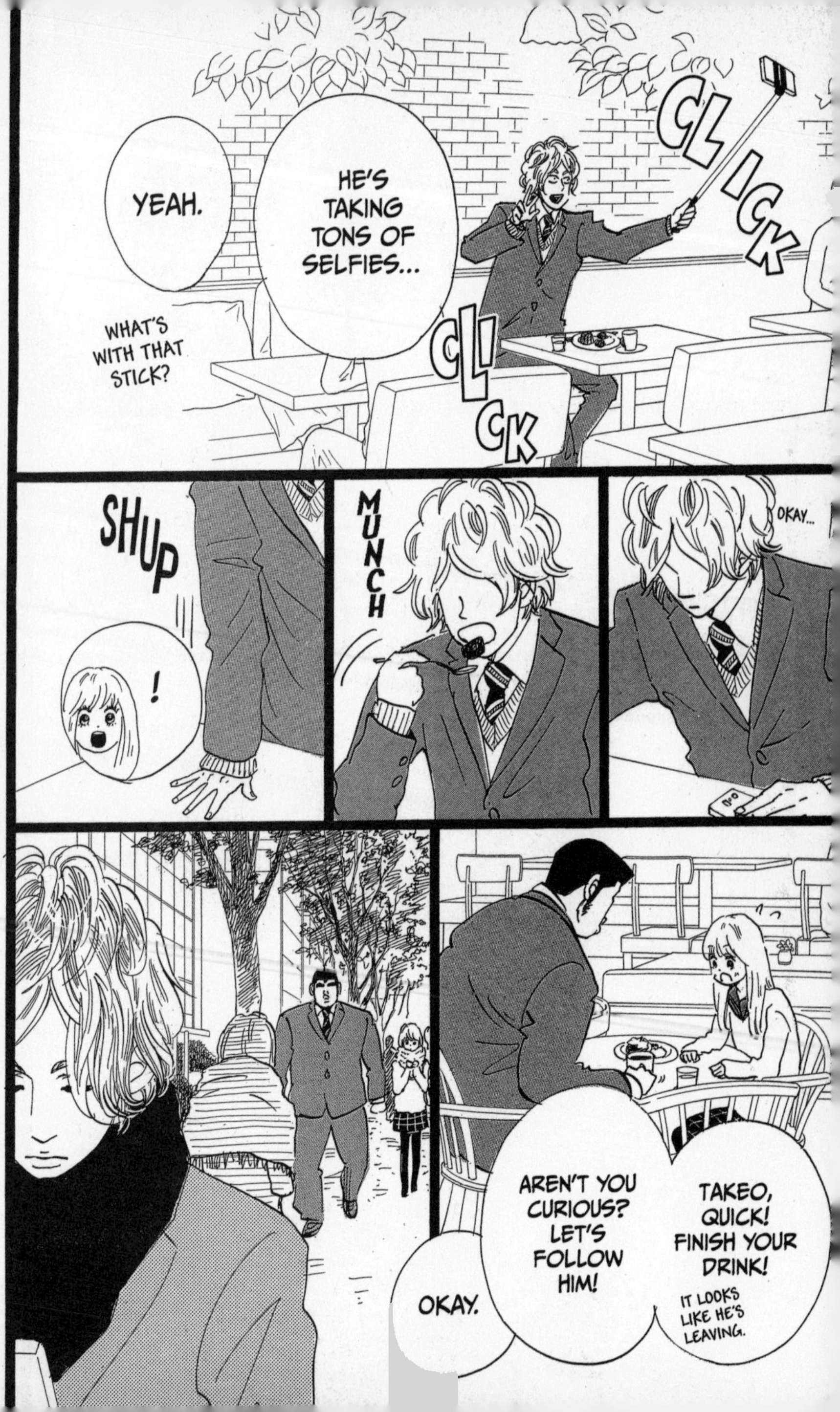
CLICK
CLICK
HE'S TAKING TONS OF SELFIES...
YEAH.
WHAT'S WITH THAT STICK?
OKAY...
MUNCH
SHUP
!
TAKEO, QUICK! FINISH YOUR DRINK!
IT LOOKS LIKE HE'S LEAVING.
AREN'T YOU CURIOUS? LET'S FOLLOW HIM!
OKAY.

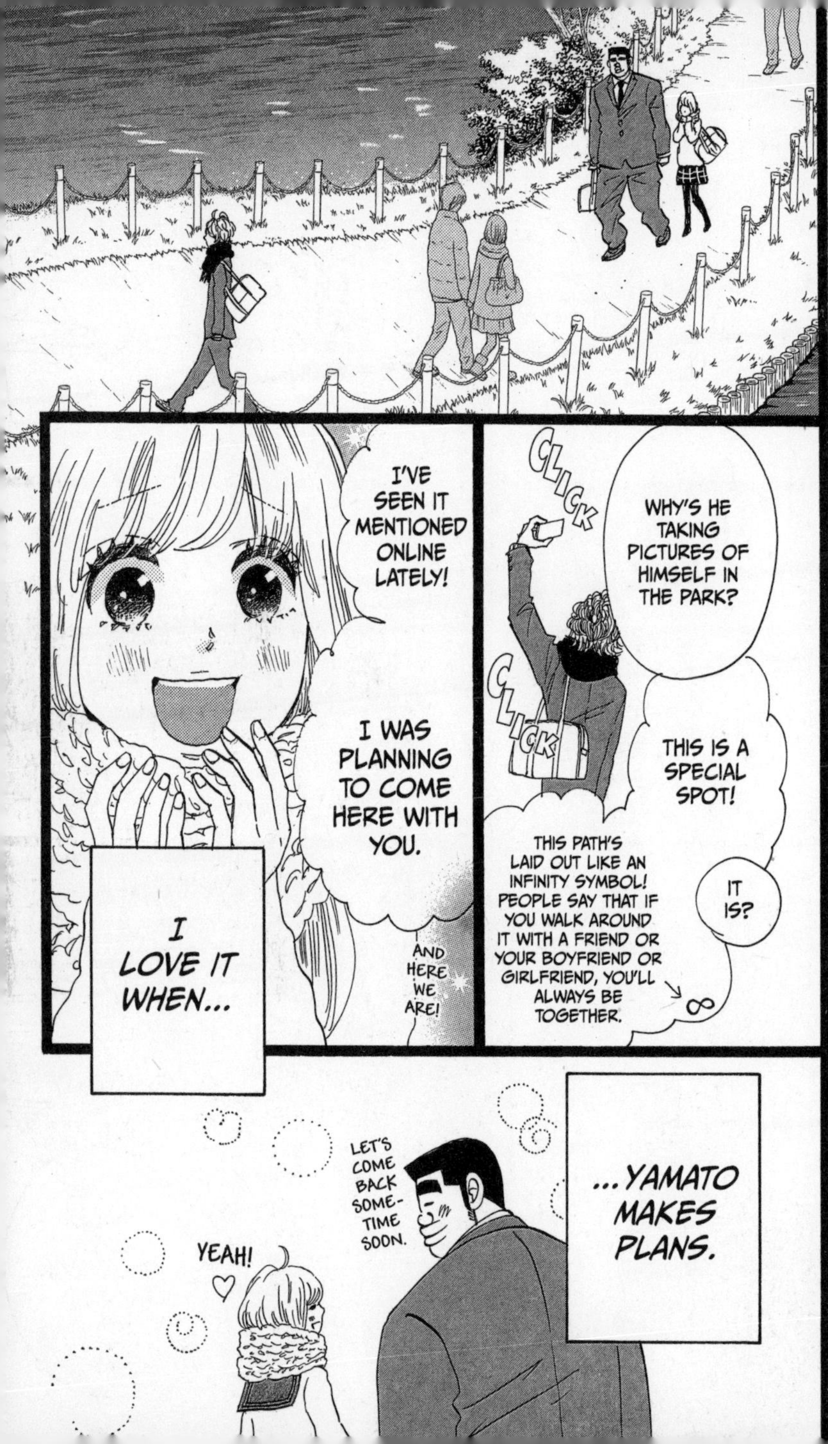
WHY'S HE TAKING PICTURES OF HIMSELF IN THE PARK?
CLICK
CLICK
THIS IS A SPECIAL SPOT!
IT IS?
THIS PATH'S LAID OUT LIKE AN INFINITY SYMBOL! PEOPLE SAY THAT IF YOU WALK AROUND IT WITH A FRIEND OR YOUR BOYFRIEND OR GIRLFRIEND, YOU'LL ALWAYS BE TOGETHER.
∞
I'VE SEEN IT MENTIONED ONLINE LATELY!
I WAS PLANNING TO COME HERE WITH YOU.
AND HERE WE ARE!
I LOVE IT WHEN...
...YAMATO MAKES PLANS.
LET'S COME BACK SOME-TIME SOON.
YEAH!

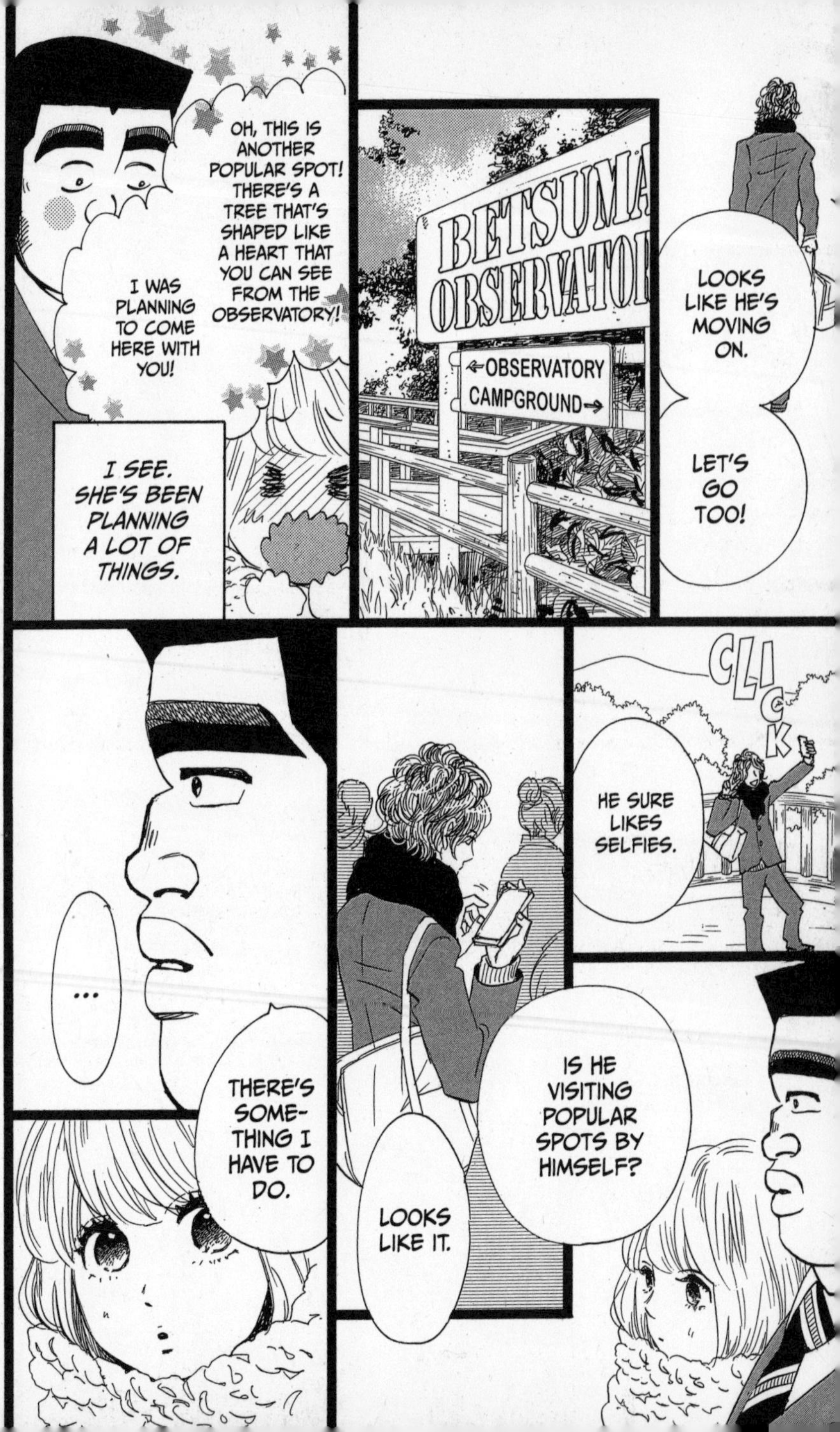
LOOKS LIKE HE'S MOVING ON.
LET'S GO TOO!
BETSUMA OBSERVATO
←OBSERVATORY
CAMPGROUND→
OH, THIS IS ANOTHER POPULAR SPOT! THERE'S A TREE THAT'S SHAPED LIKE A HEART THAT YOU CAN SEE FROM THE OBSERVATORY!
I WAS PLANNING TO COME HERE WITH YOU!
I SEE. SHE'S BEEN PLANNING A LOT OF THINGS.
CLICK
HE SURE LIKES SELFIES.
IS HE VISITING POPULAR SPOTS BY HIMSELF?
LOOKS LIKE IT.
...
THERE'S SOME-THING I HAVE TO DO.

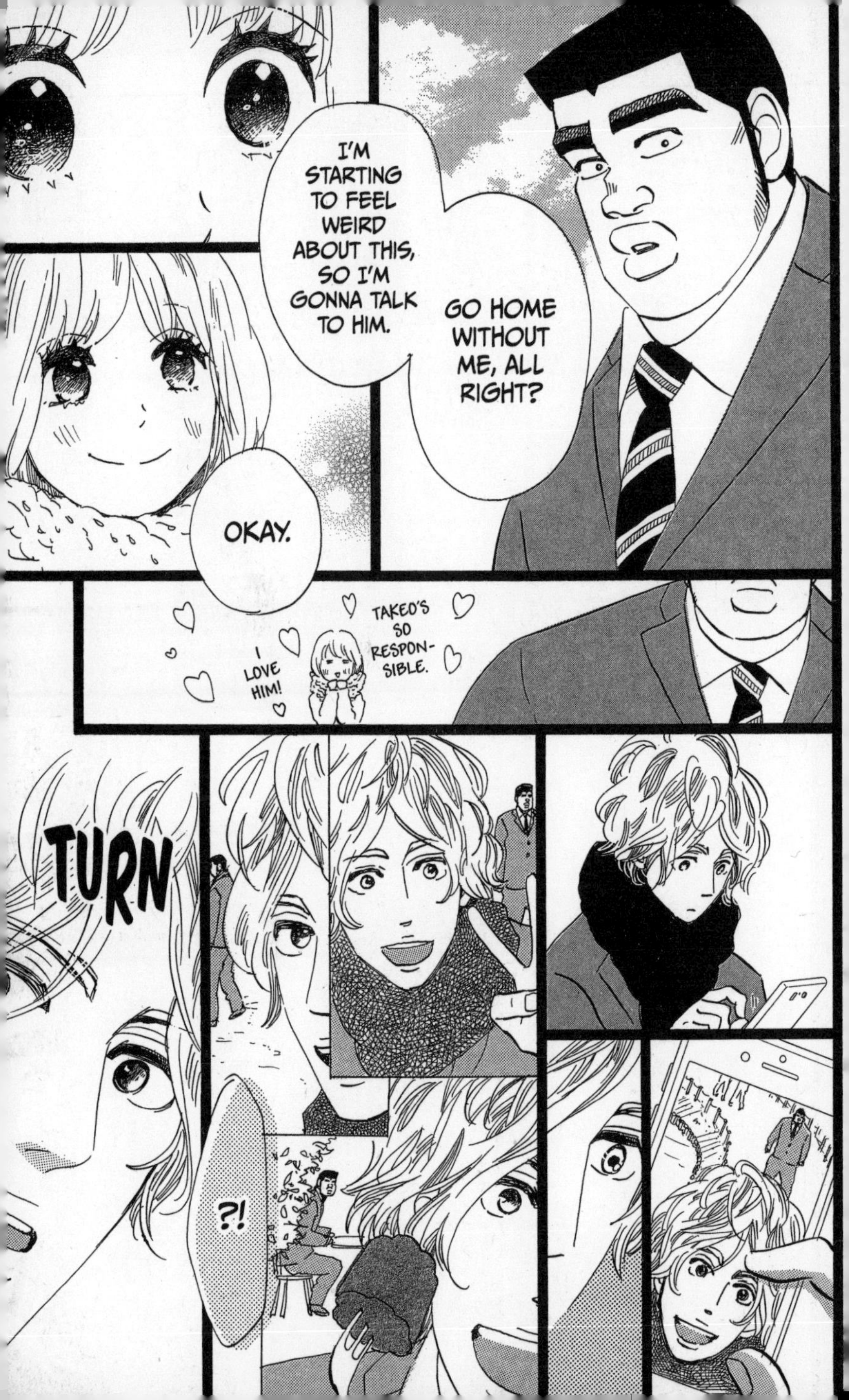
I'M STARTING TO FEEL WEIRD ABOUT THIS, SO I'M GONNA TALK TO HIM.
GO HOME WITHOUT ME, ALL RIGHT?
OKAY.
TAKEO'S SO RESPON-SIBLE.
I LOVE HIM!
TURN
?!

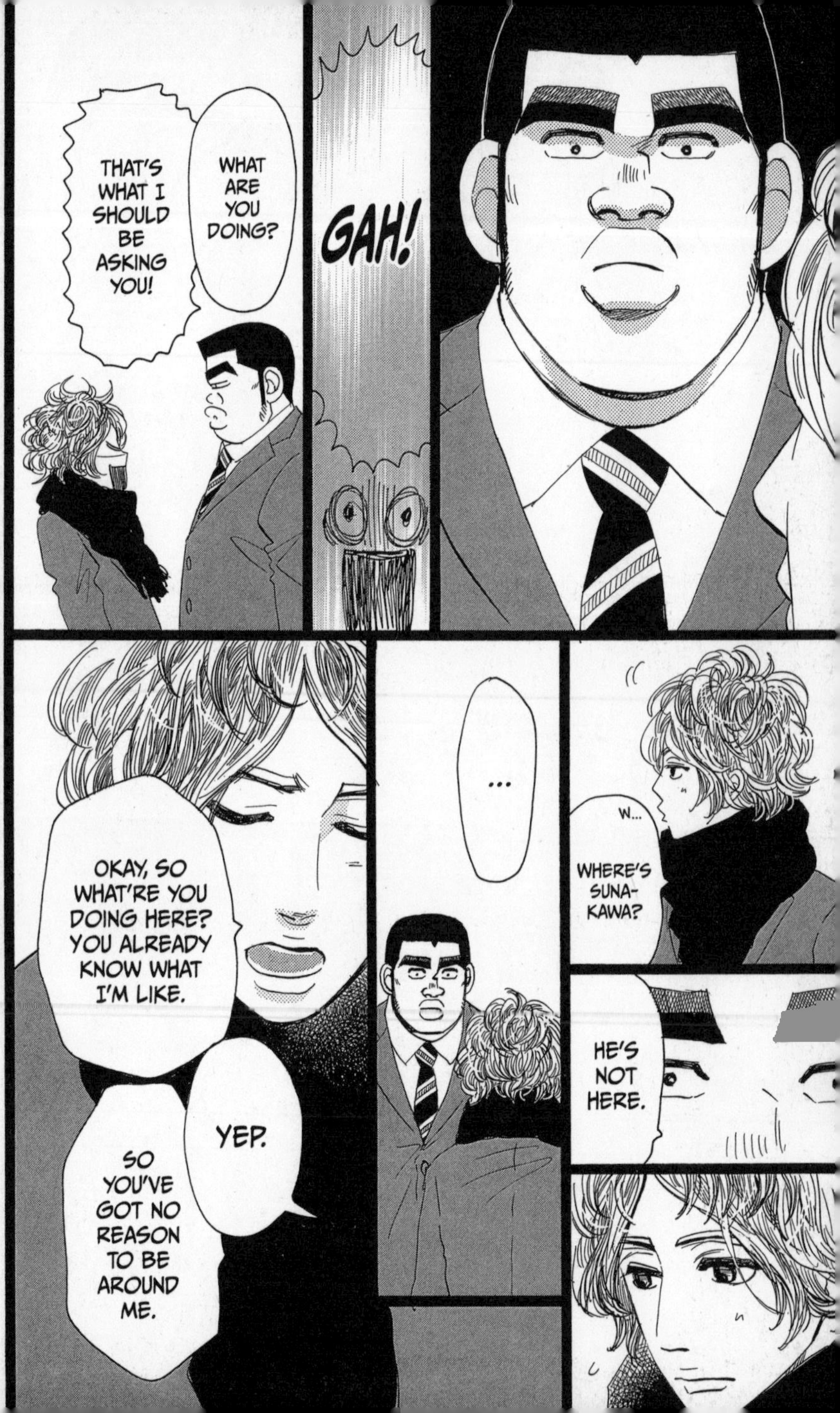
GAH!
WHAT ARE YOU DOING?
THAT'S WHAT I SHOULD BE ASKING YOU!
W...
WHERE'S SUNA-KAWA?
HE'S NOT HERE.
...
OKAY, SO WHAT'RE YOU DOING HERE? YOU ALREADY KNOW WHAT I'M LIKE.
YEP.
SO YOU'VE GOT NO REASON TO BE AROUND ME.

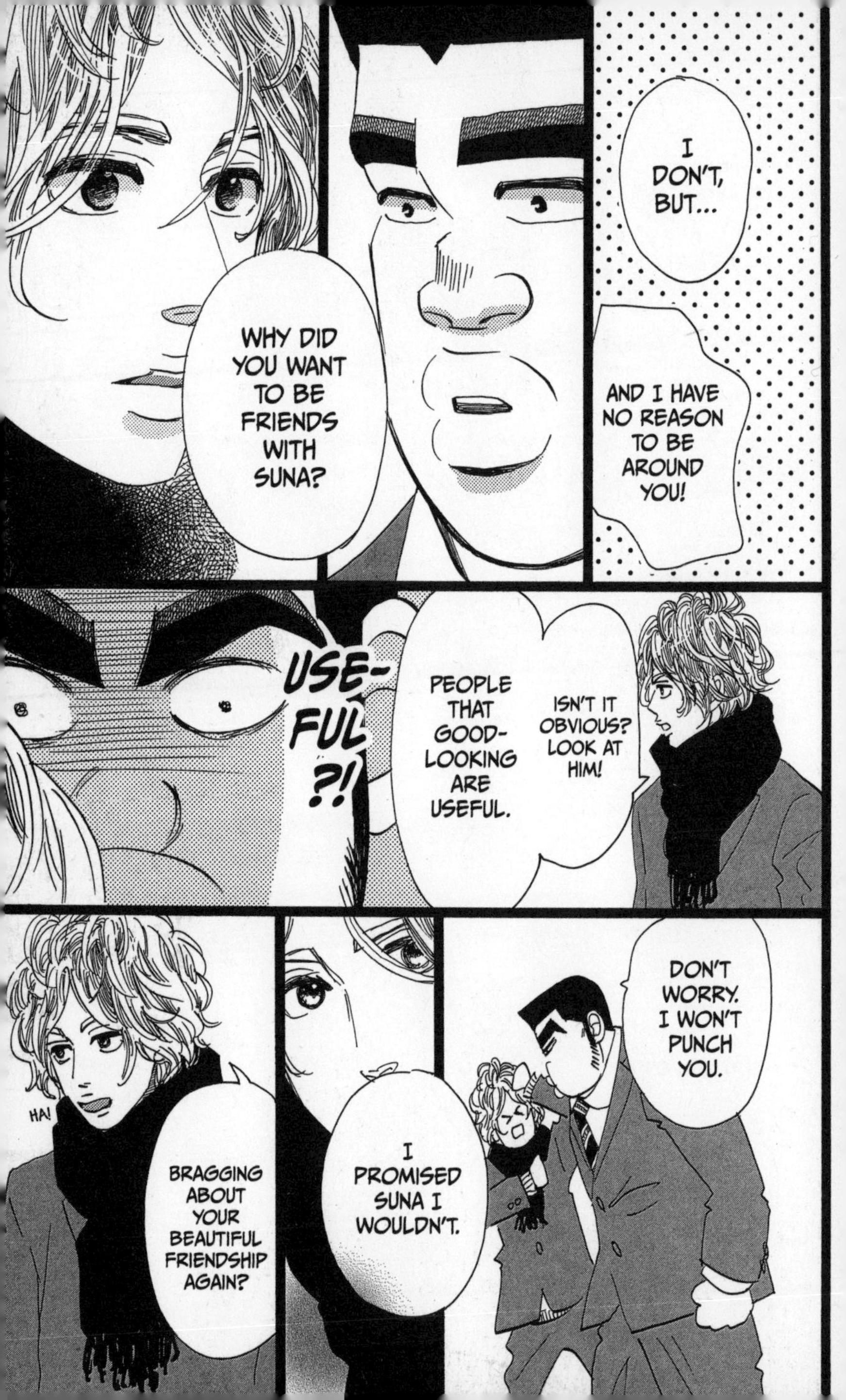
I DON'T, BUT...
AND I HAVE NO REASON TO BE AROUND YOU!
WHY DID YOU WANT TO BE FRIENDS WITH SUNA?
PEOPLE THAT GOOD-LOOKING ARE USEFUL.
ISN'T IT OBVIOUS? LOOK AT HIM!
USE-FUL ?!
DON'T WORRY. I WON'T PUNCH YOU.
I PROMISED SUNA I WOULDN'T.
BRAGGING ABOUT YOUR BEAUTIFUL FRIENDSHIP AGAIN?
HA!

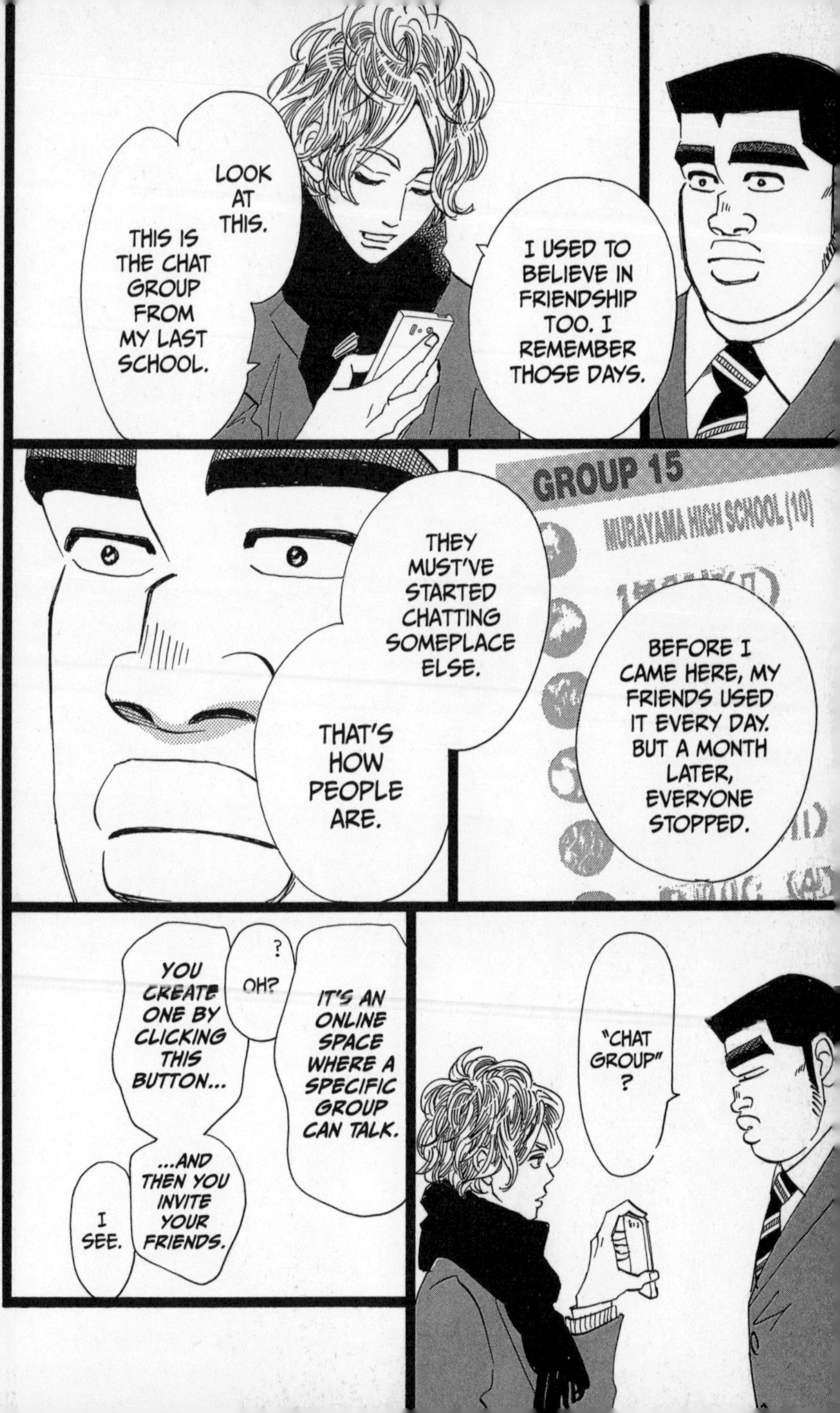
LOOK AT THIS.
THIS IS THE CHAT GROUP FROM MY LAST SCHOOL.
I USED TO BELIEVE IN FRIENDSHIP TOO. I REMEMBER THOSE DAYS.
GROUP 15
MURAYAMA HIGH SCHOOL [10]
BEFORE I CAME HERE, MY FRIENDS USED IT EVERY DAY. BUT A MONTH LATER, EVERYONE STOPPED.
THEY MUST'VE STARTED CHATTING SOMEPLACE ELSE.
THAT'S HOW PEOPLE ARE.
"CHAT GROUP"?
?
IT'S AN ONLINE SPACE WHERE A SPECIFIC GROUP CAN TALK.
OH?
YOU CREATE ONE BY CLICKING THIS BUTTON...
...AND THEN YOU INVITE YOUR FRIENDS.
I SEE.

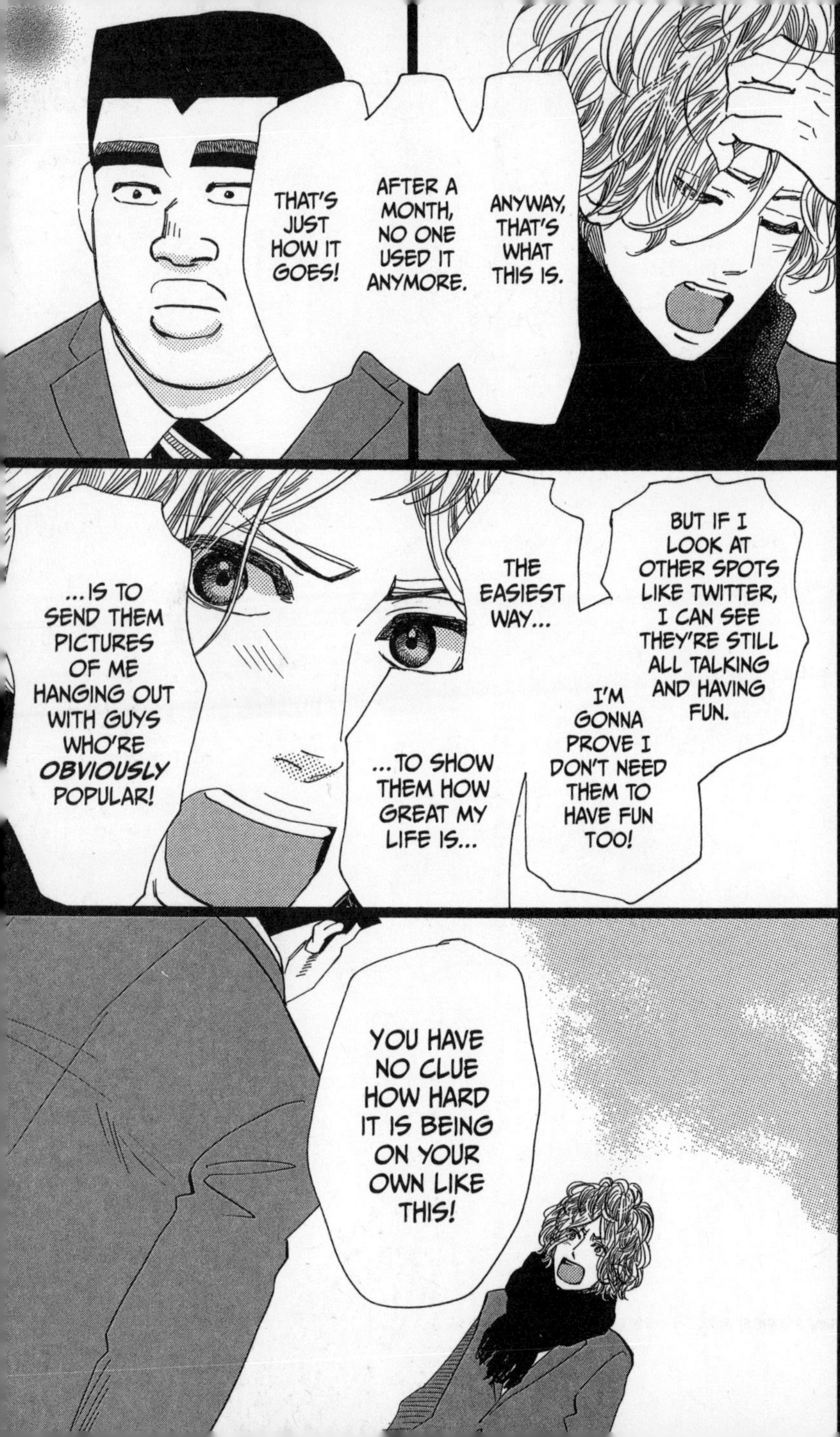
ANYWAY, THAT'S WHAT THIS IS.
AFTER A MONTH, NO ONE USED IT ANYMORE.
THAT'S JUST HOW IT GOES!
BUT IF I LOOK AT OTHER SPOTS LIKE TWITTER, I CAN SEE THEY'RE STILL ALL TALKING AND HAVING FUN.
I'M GONNA PROVE I DON'T NEED THEM TO HAVE FUN TOO!
THE EASIEST WAY...
...TO SHOW THEM HOW GREAT MY LIFE IS...
...IS TO SEND THEM PICTURES OF ME HANGING OUT WITH GUYS WHO'RE *OBVIOUSLY* POPULAR!
YOU HAVE NO CLUE HOW HARD IT IS BEING ON YOUR OWN LIKE THIS!

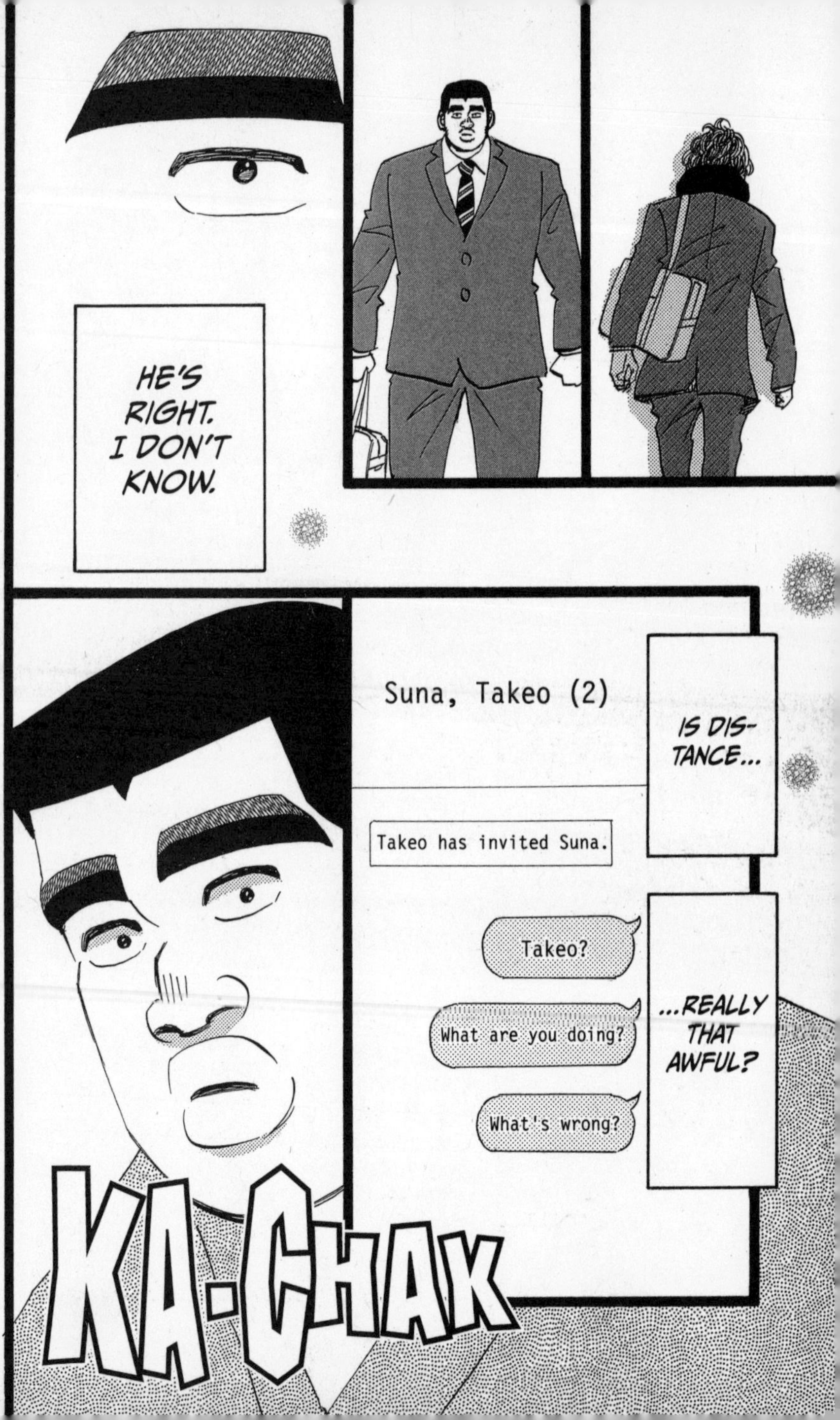
HE'S RIGHT. I DON'T KNOW.
IS DISTANCE...
...REALLY THAT AWFUL?
Suna, Takeo (2)
Takeo has invited Suna.
Takeo?
What are you doing?
What's wrong?
KA-CHAK

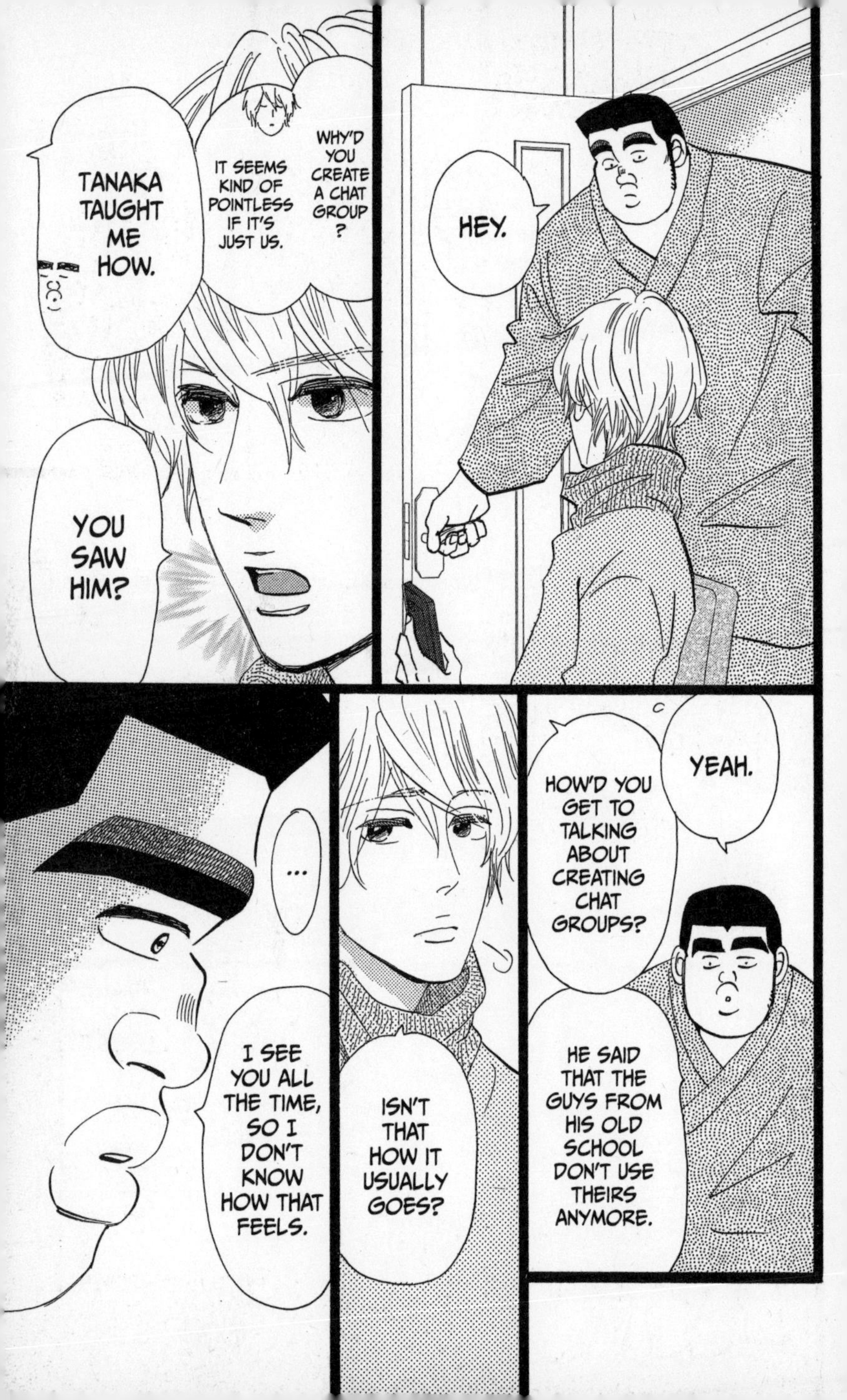
HEY.
WHY'D YOU CREATE A CHAT GROUP?
IT SEEMS KIND OF POINTLESS IF IT'S JUST US.
TANAKA TAUGHT ME HOW.
YOU SAW HIM?
YEAH.
HOW'D YOU GET TO TALKING ABOUT CREATING CHAT GROUPS?
HE SAID THAT THE GUYS FROM HIS OLD SCHOOL DON'T USE THEIRS ANYMORE.
ISN'T THAT HOW IT USUALLY GOES?
...
I SEE YOU ALL THE TIME, SO I DON'T KNOW HOW THAT FEELS.

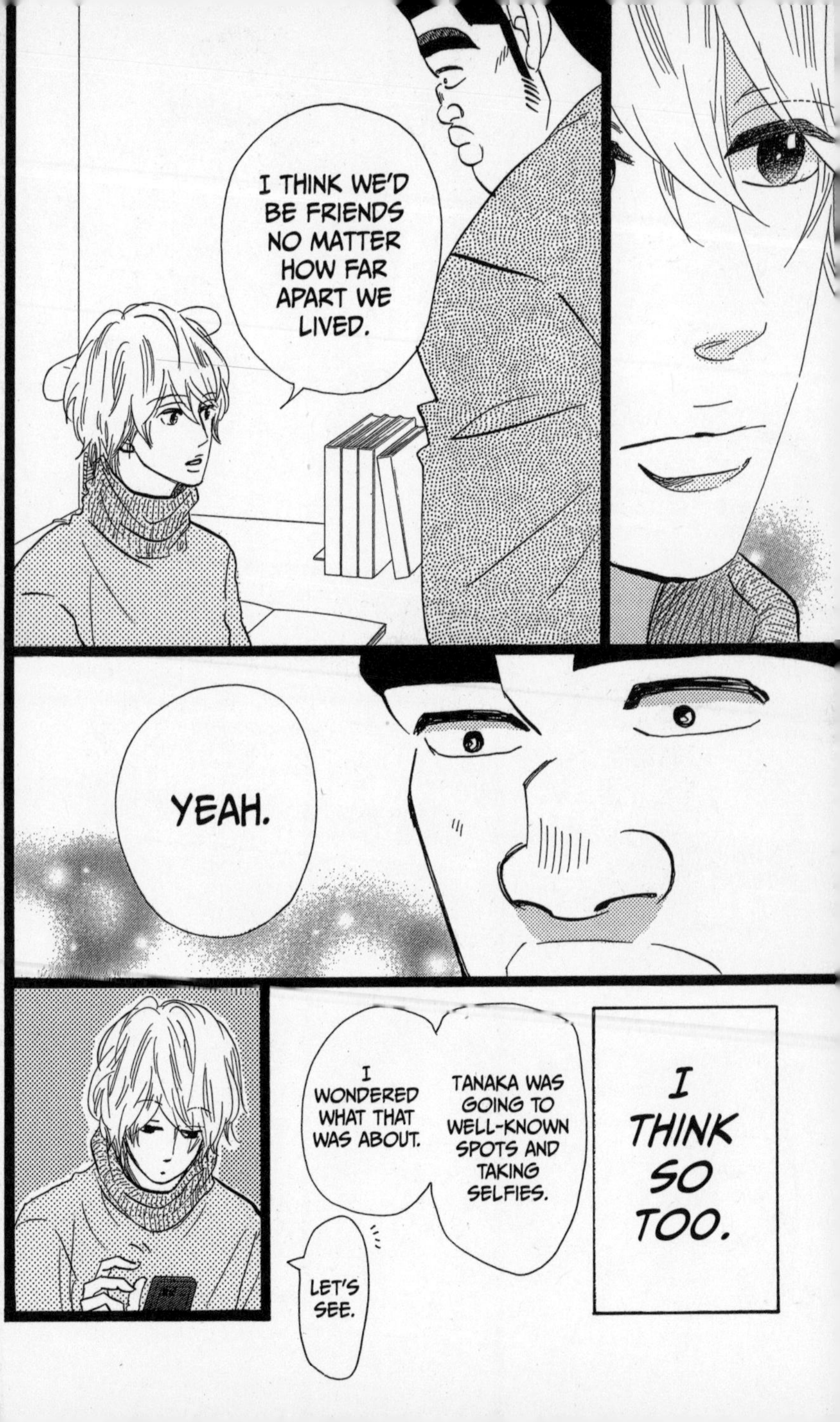
I THINK WE'D BE FRIENDS NO MATTER HOW FAR APART WE LIVED.
YEAH.
I THINK SO TOO.
I WONDERED WHAT THAT WAS ABOUT.
TANAKA WAS GOING TO WELL-KNOWN SPOTS AND TAKING SELFIES.
LET'S SEE.

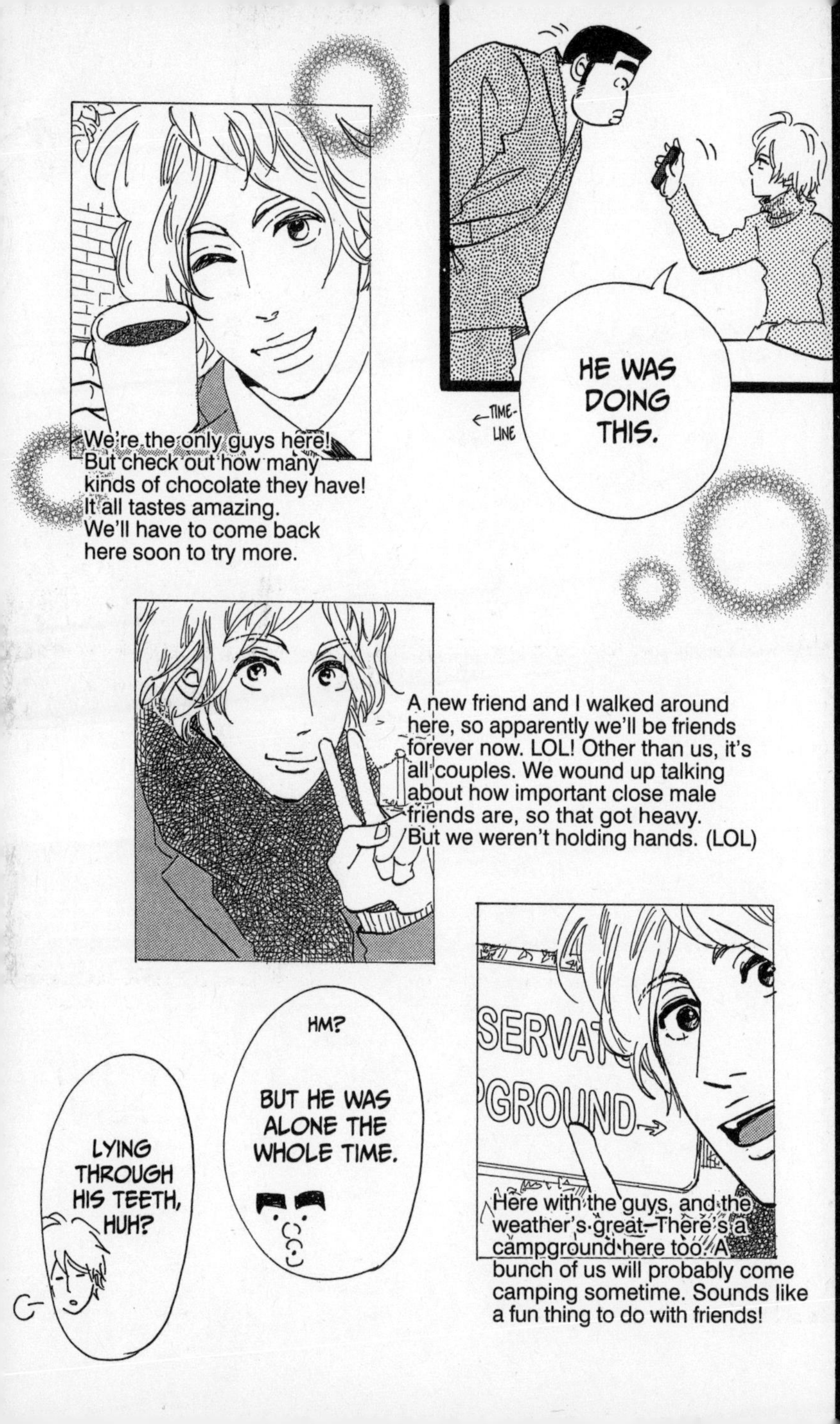
HE WAS DOING THIS.
←TIME-LINE
We're the only guys here! But check out how many kinds of chocolate they have! It all tastes amazing. We'll have to come back here soon to try more.
A new friend and I walked around here, so apparently we'll be friends forever now. LOL! Other than us, it's all couples. We wound up talking about how important close male friends are, so that got heavy. But we weren't holding hands. (LOL)
SERVAT
GROUND
Here with the guys, and the weather's great. There's a campground here too. A bunch of us will probably come camping sometime. Sounds like a fun thing to do with friends!
HM?
BUT HE WAS ALONE THE WHOLE TIME.
LYING THROUGH HIS TEETH, HUH?

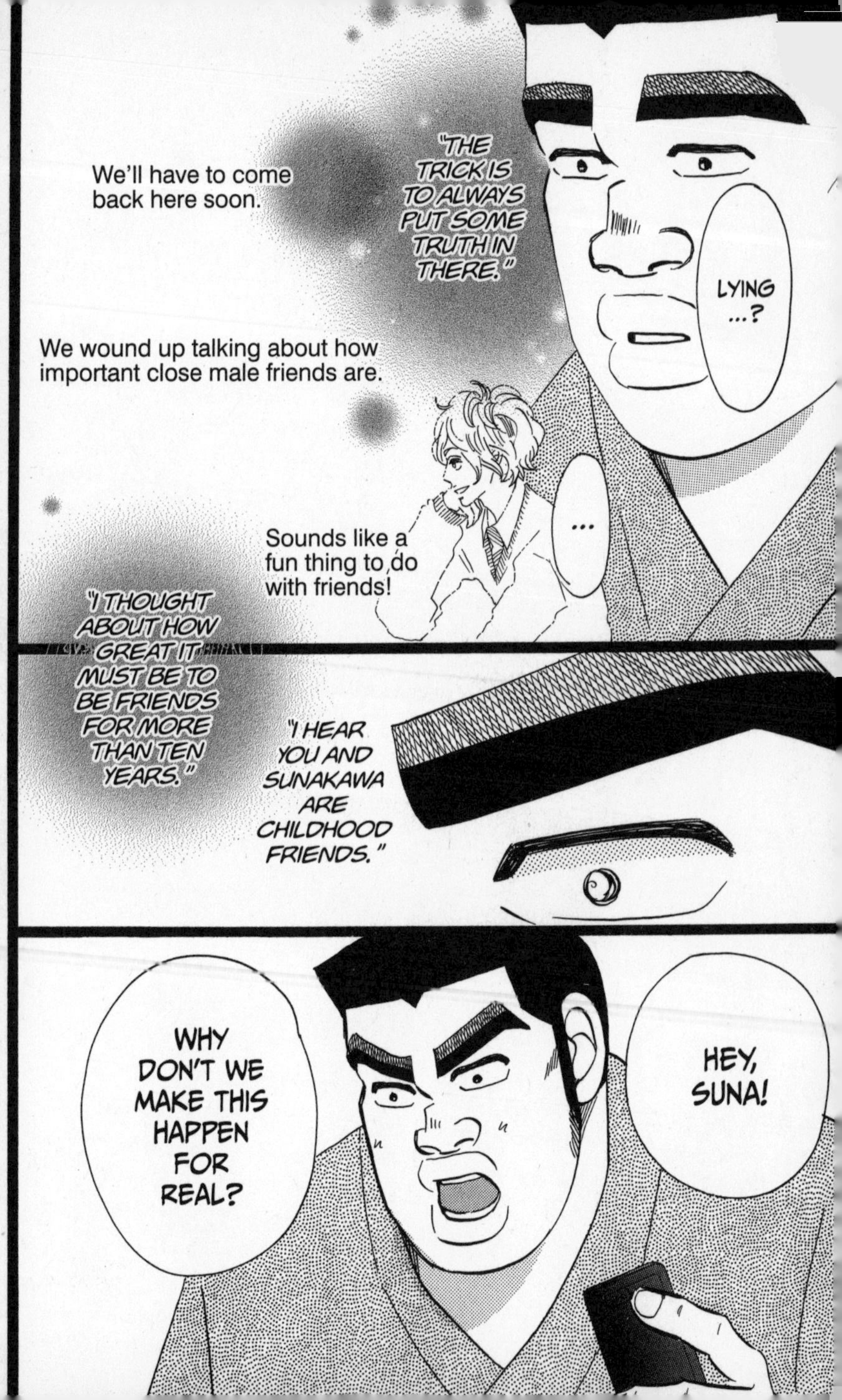
LYING ...?
"THE TRICK IS TO ALWAYS PUT SOME TRUTH IN THERE."
We'll have to come back here soon.
We wound up talking about how important close male friends are.
...
Sounds like a fun thing to do with friends!
"I THOUGHT ABOUT HOW GREAT IT MUST BE TO BE FRIENDS FOR MORE THAN TEN YEARS."
"I HEAR YOU AND SUNAKAWA ARE CHILDHOOD FRIENDS."
HEY, SUNA!
WHY DON'T WE MAKE THIS HAPPEN FOR REAL?

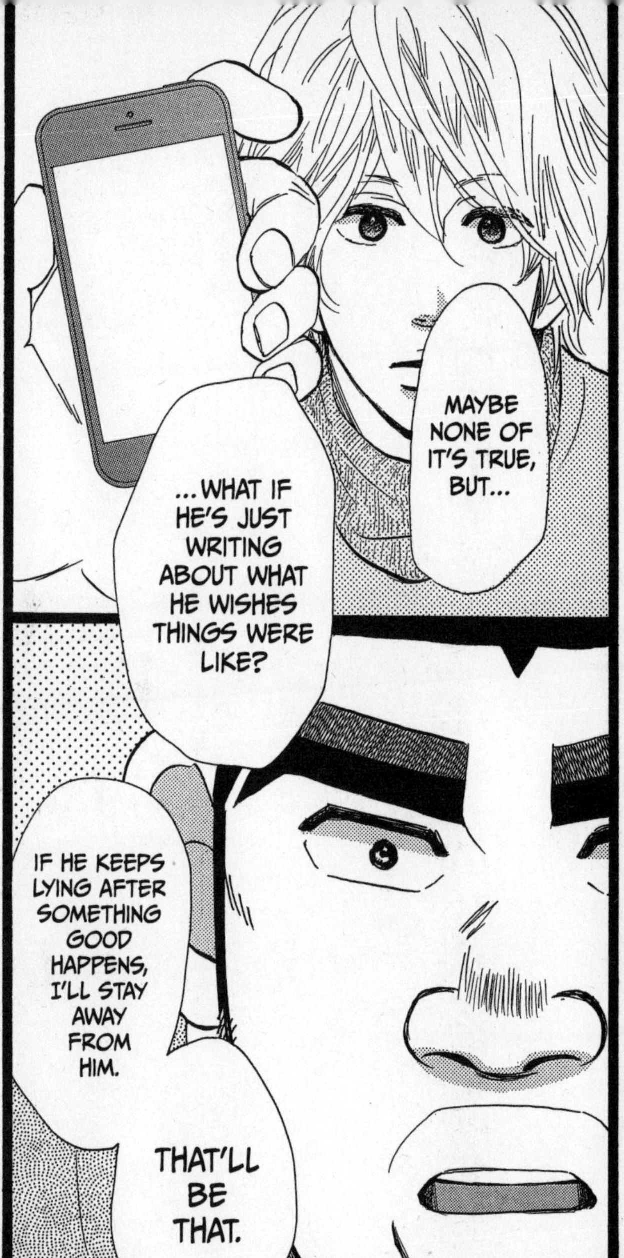
MAYBE NONE OF IT'S TRUE, BUT...
...WHAT IF HE'S JUST WRITING ABOUT WHAT HE WISHES THINGS WERE LIKE?
IF HE KEEPS LYING AFTER SOMETHING GOOD HAPPENS, I'LL STAY AWAY FROM HIM.
THAT'LL BE THAT.
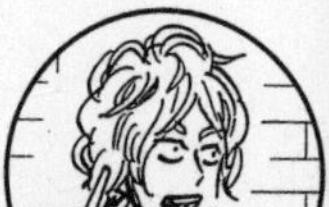

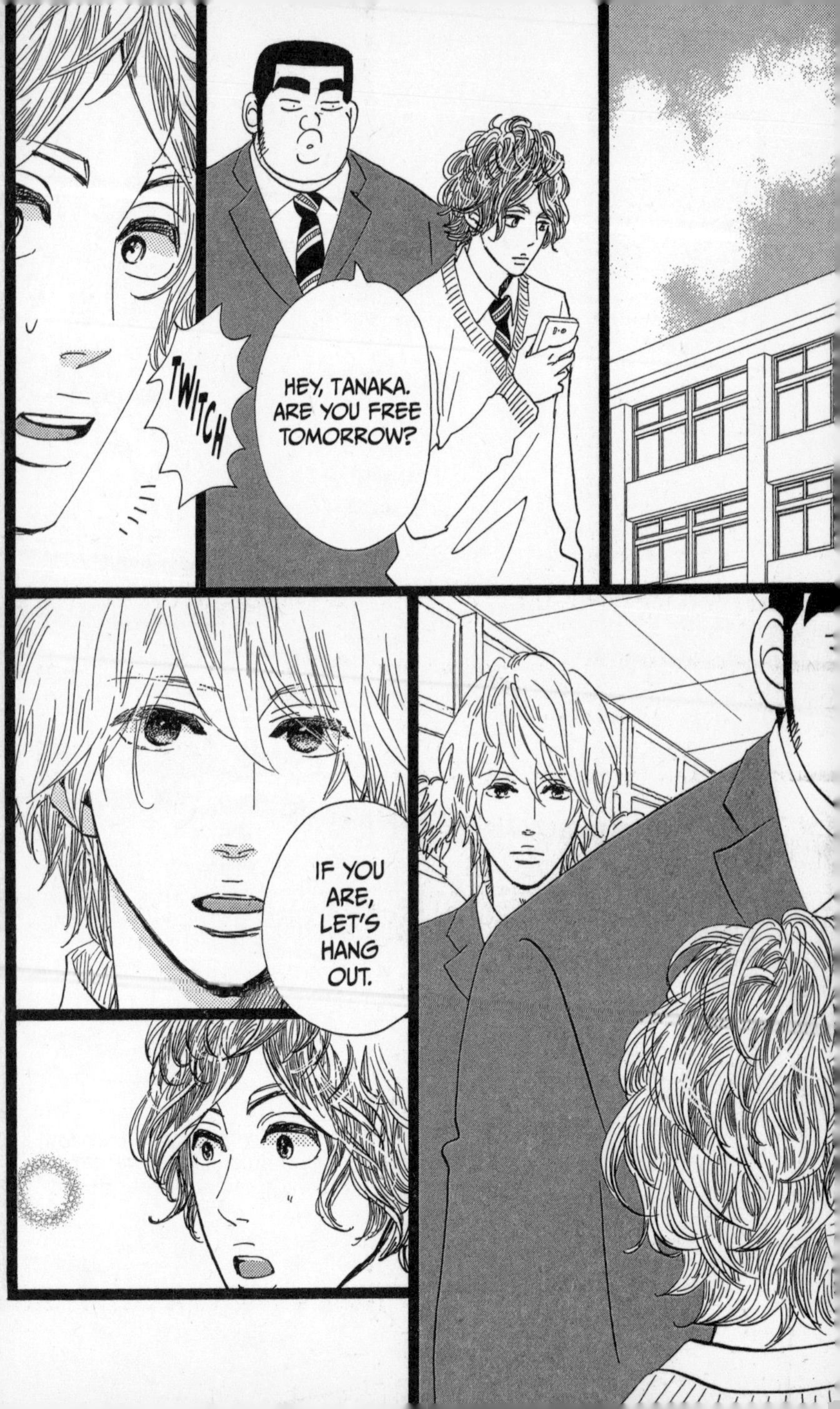
HEY, TANAKA. ARE YOU FREE TOMORROW?
TWITCH
IF YOU ARE, LET'S HANG OUT.

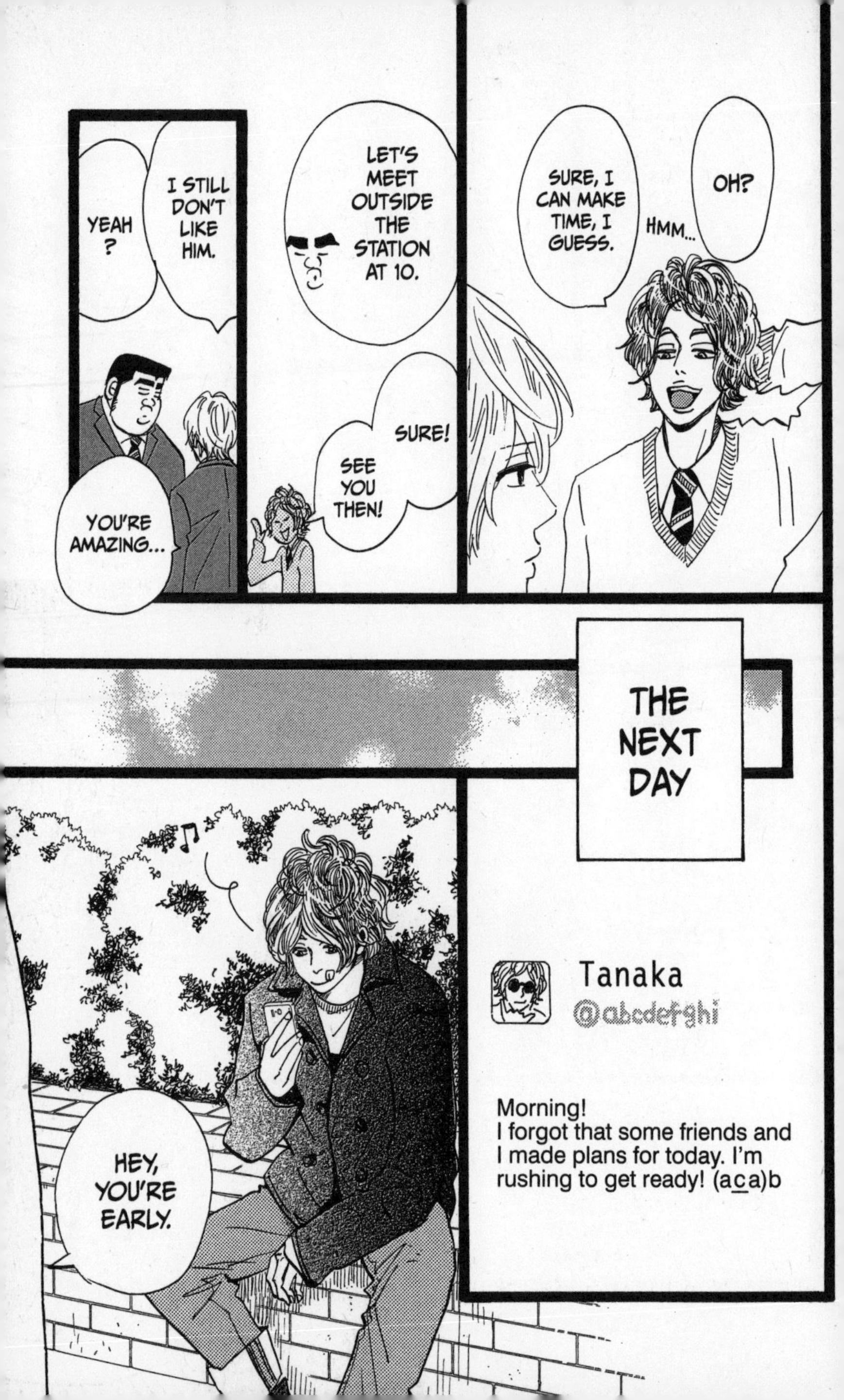
OH?
HMM...
SURE, I CAN MAKE TIME, I GUESS.
LET'S MEET OUTSIDE THE STATION AT 10.
SURE!
SEE YOU THEN!
I STILL DON'T LIKE HIM.
YEAH?
YOU'RE AMAZING...
THE NEXT DAY
Tanaka
@abcdefghi
Morning!
I forgot that some friends and I made plans for today. I'm rushing to get ready! (a_a)b
HEY, YOU'RE EARLY.

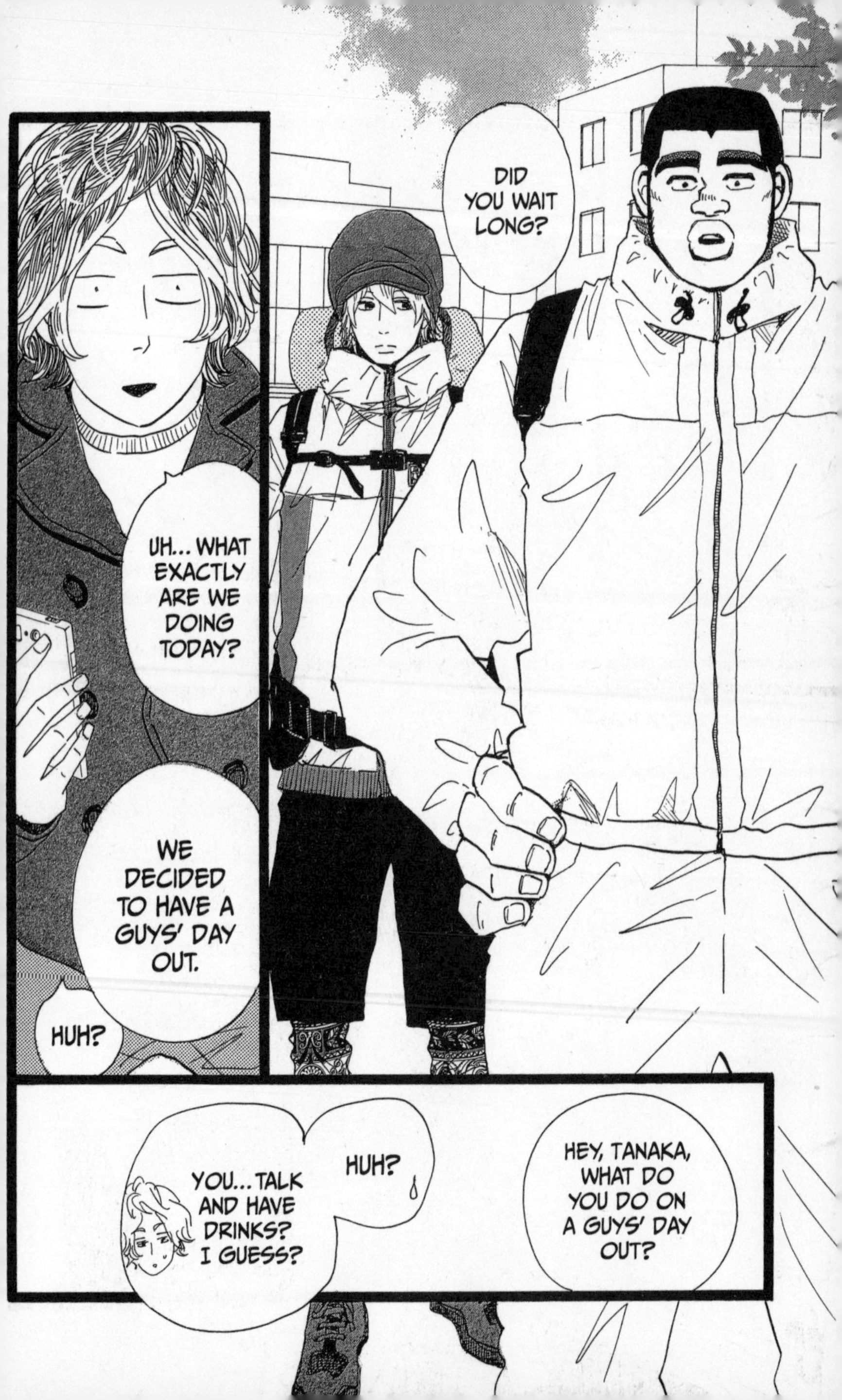
DID YOU WAIT LONG?
UH... WHAT EXACTLY ARE WE DOING TODAY?
WE DECIDED TO HAVE A GUYS' DAY OUT.
HUH?
HEY, TANAKA, WHAT DO YOU DO ON A GUYS' DAY OUT?
HUH?
YOU... TALK AND HAVE DRINKS? I GUESS?

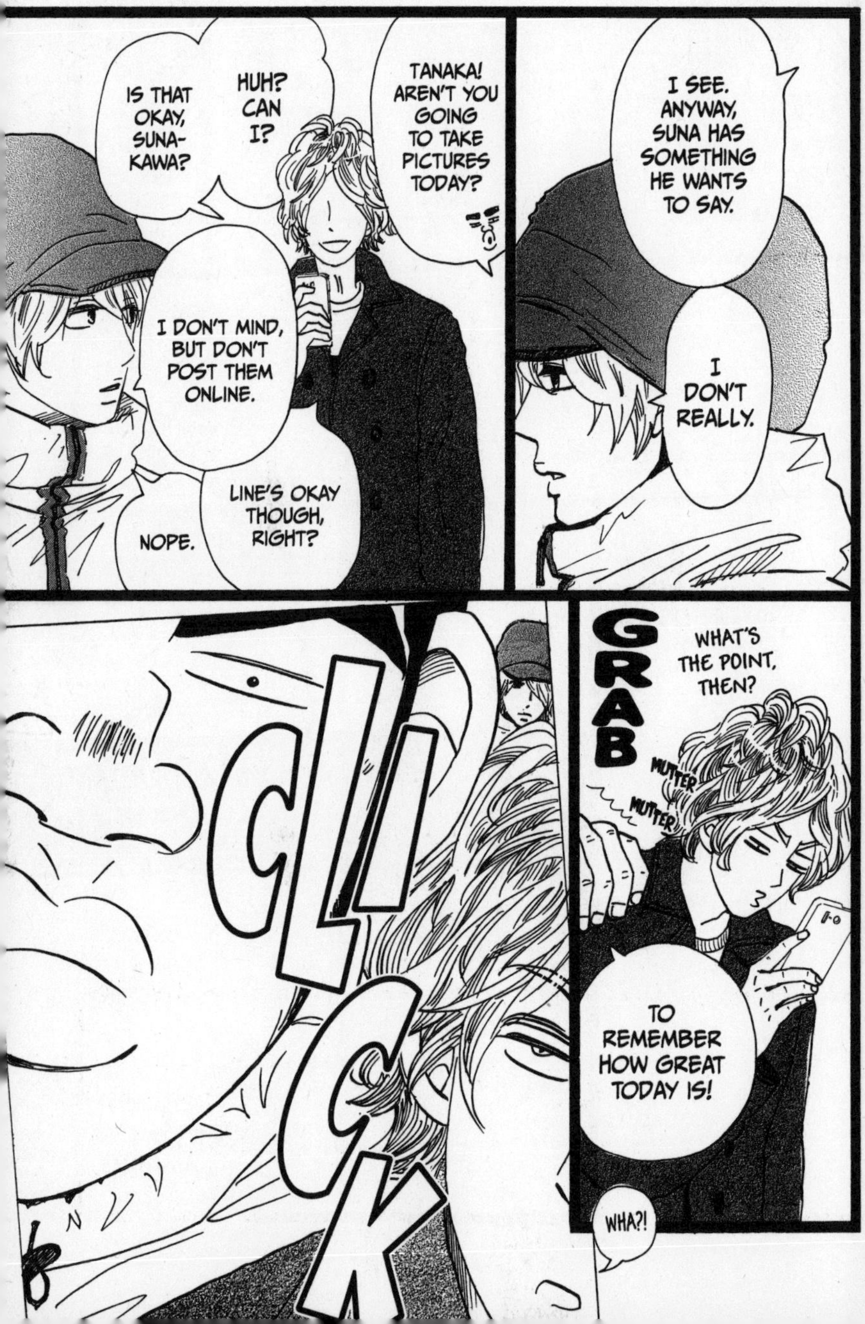
I SEE. ANYWAY, SUNA HAS SOMETHING HE WANTS TO SAY.
I DON'T REALLY.
TANAKA! AREN'T YOU GOING TO TAKE PICTURES TODAY?
HUH? CAN I?
IS THAT OKAY, SUNA-KAWA?
I DON'T MIND, BUT DON'T POST THEM ONLINE.
LINE'S OKAY THOUGH, RIGHT?
NOPE.
WHAT'S THE POINT, THEN?
GRAB
MUTTER MUTTER
TO REMEMBER HOW GREAT TODAY IS!
WHA?!
CLICK

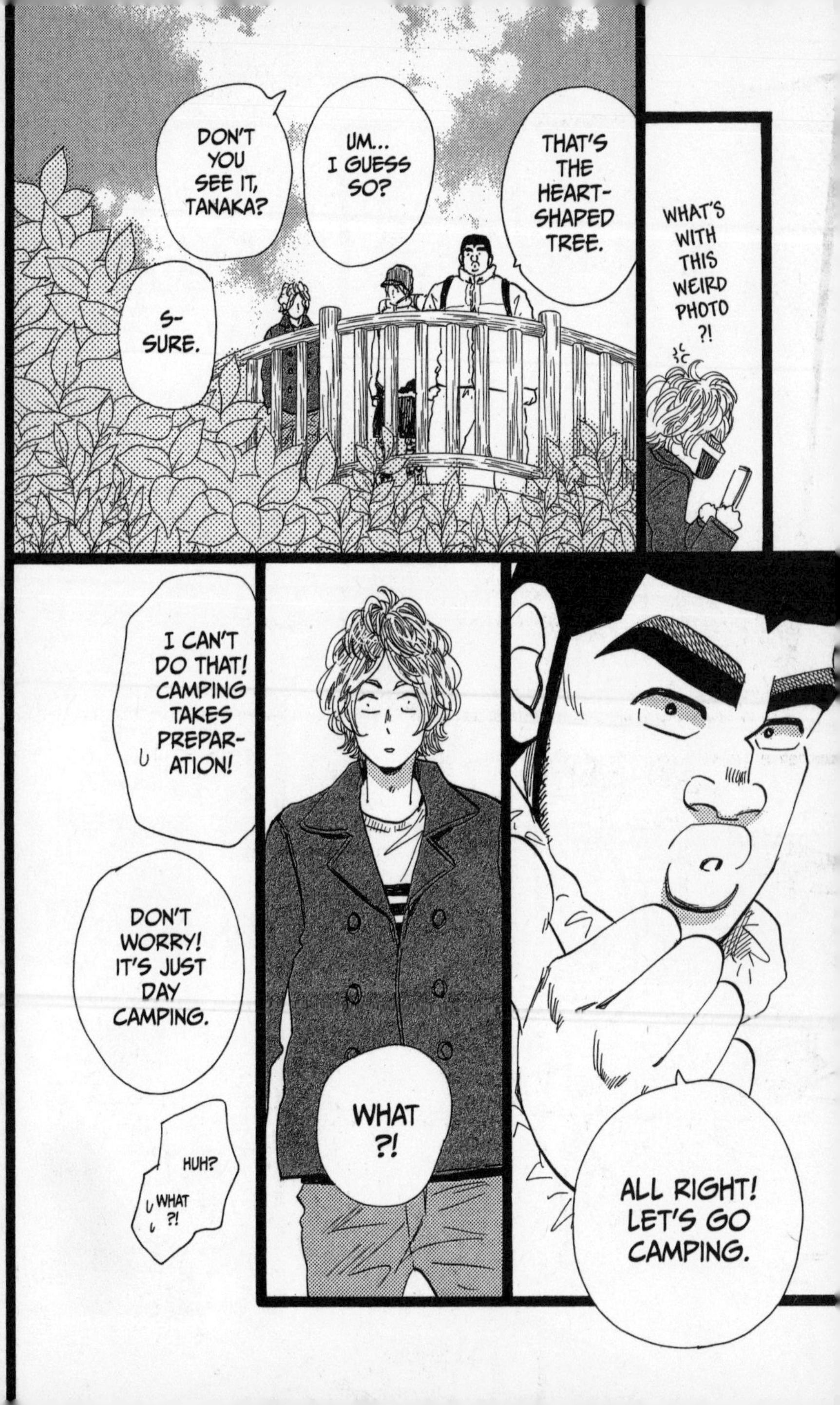
WHAT'S WITH THIS WEIRD PHOTO ?!
THAT'S THE HEART-SHAPED TREE.
UM... I GUESS SO?
DON'T YOU SEE IT, TANAKA?
S-SURE.
ALL RIGHT! LET'S GO CAMPING.
WHAT ?!
I CAN'T DO THAT! CAMPING TAKES PREPAR-ATION!
DON'T WORRY! IT'S JUST DAY CAMPING.
HUH?
WHAT ?!

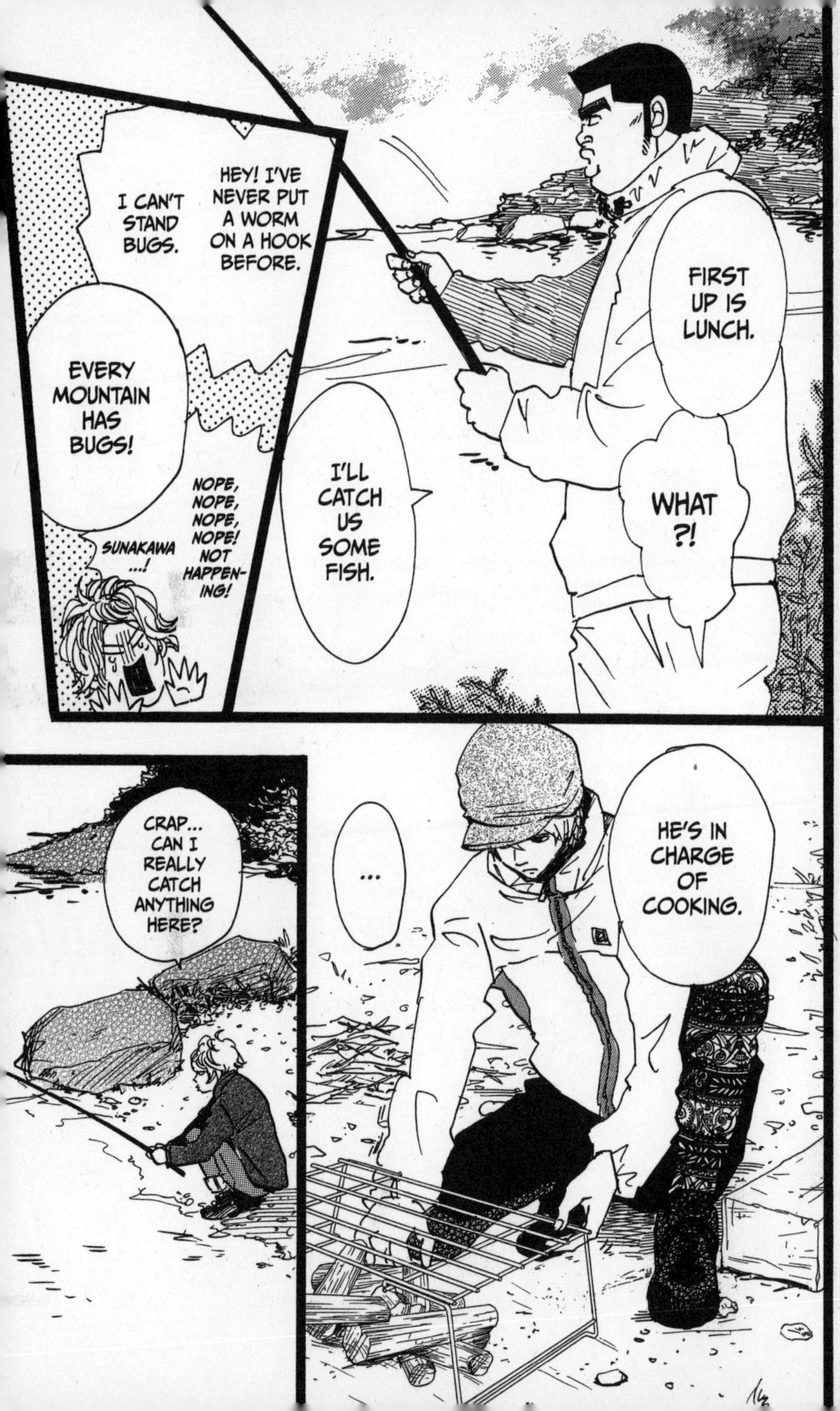
FIRST UP IS LUNCH.
WHAT ?!
I'LL CATCH US SOME FISH.
HEY! I'VE NEVER PUT A WORM ON A HOOK BEFORE.
I CAN'T STAND BUGS.
EVERY MOUNTAIN HAS BUGS!
NOPE, NOPE, NOPE, NOPE! NOT HAPPENING!
SUNAKAWA ...!
HE'S IN CHARGE OF COOKING.
...
CRAP... CAN I REALLY CATCH ANYTHING HERE?

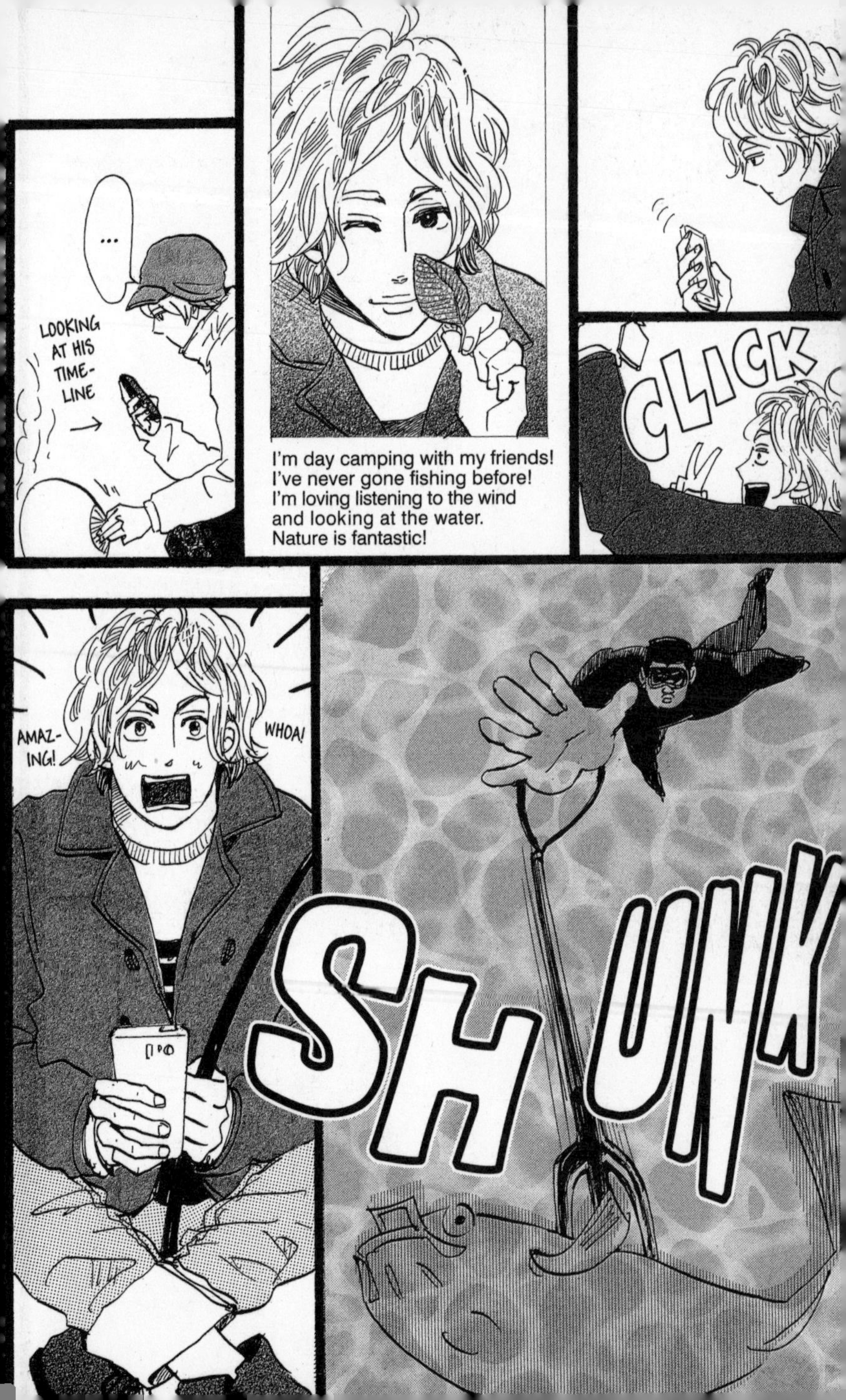
CLICK
I'm day camping with my friends!
I've never gone fishing before!
I'm loving listening to the wind
and looking at the water.
Nature is fantastic!
...
LOOKING AT HIS TIME-LINE
SHUNK
WHOA!
AMAZ-ING!

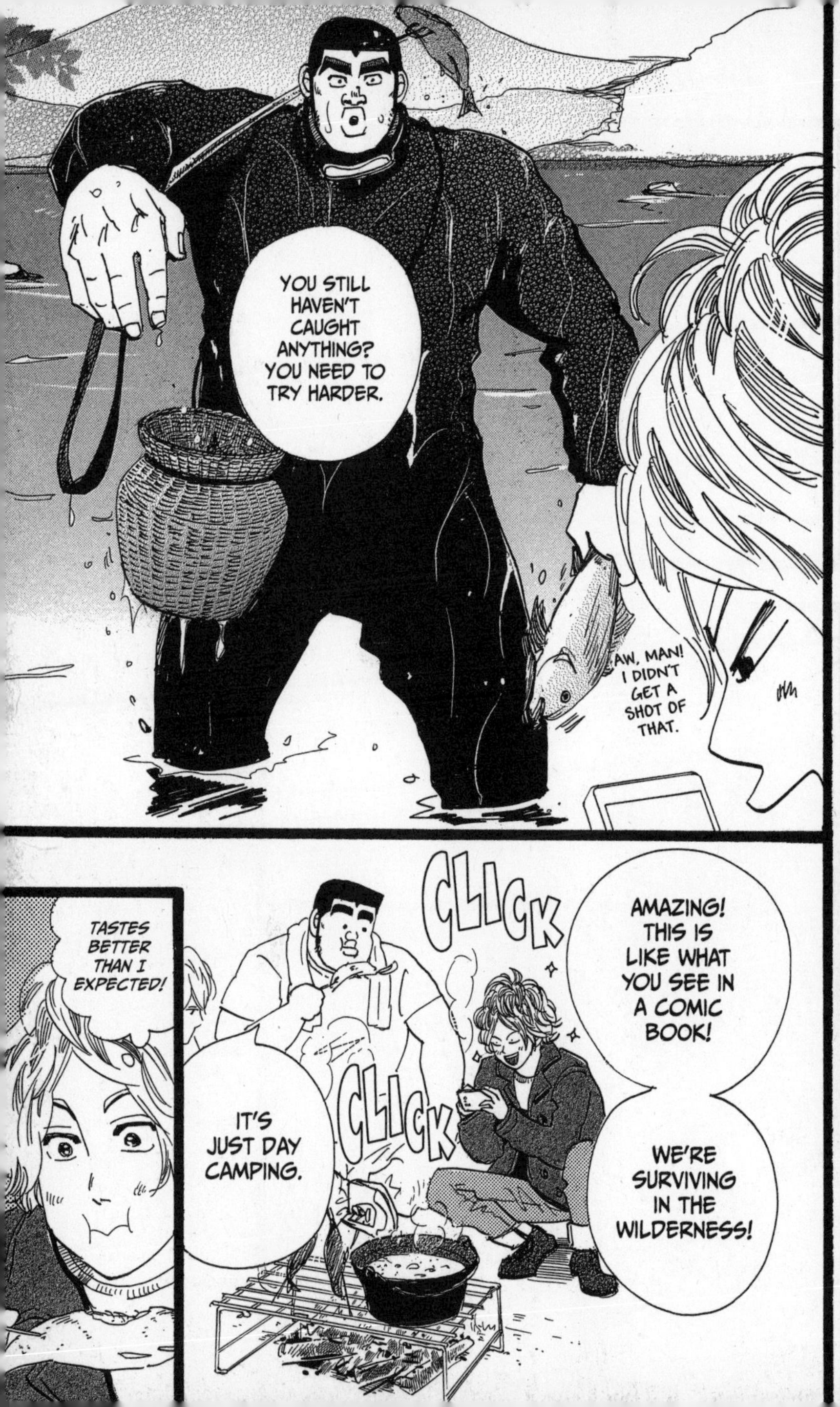
YOU STILL HAVEN'T CAUGHT ANYTHING? YOU NEED TO TRY HARDER.
AW, MAN! I DIDN'T GET A SHOT OF THAT.
CLICK
AMAZING! THIS IS LIKE WHAT YOU SEE IN A COMIC BOOK!
WE'RE SURVIVING IN THE WILDERNESS!
CLICK
IT'S JUST DAY CAMPING.
TASTES BETTER THAN I EXPECTED!

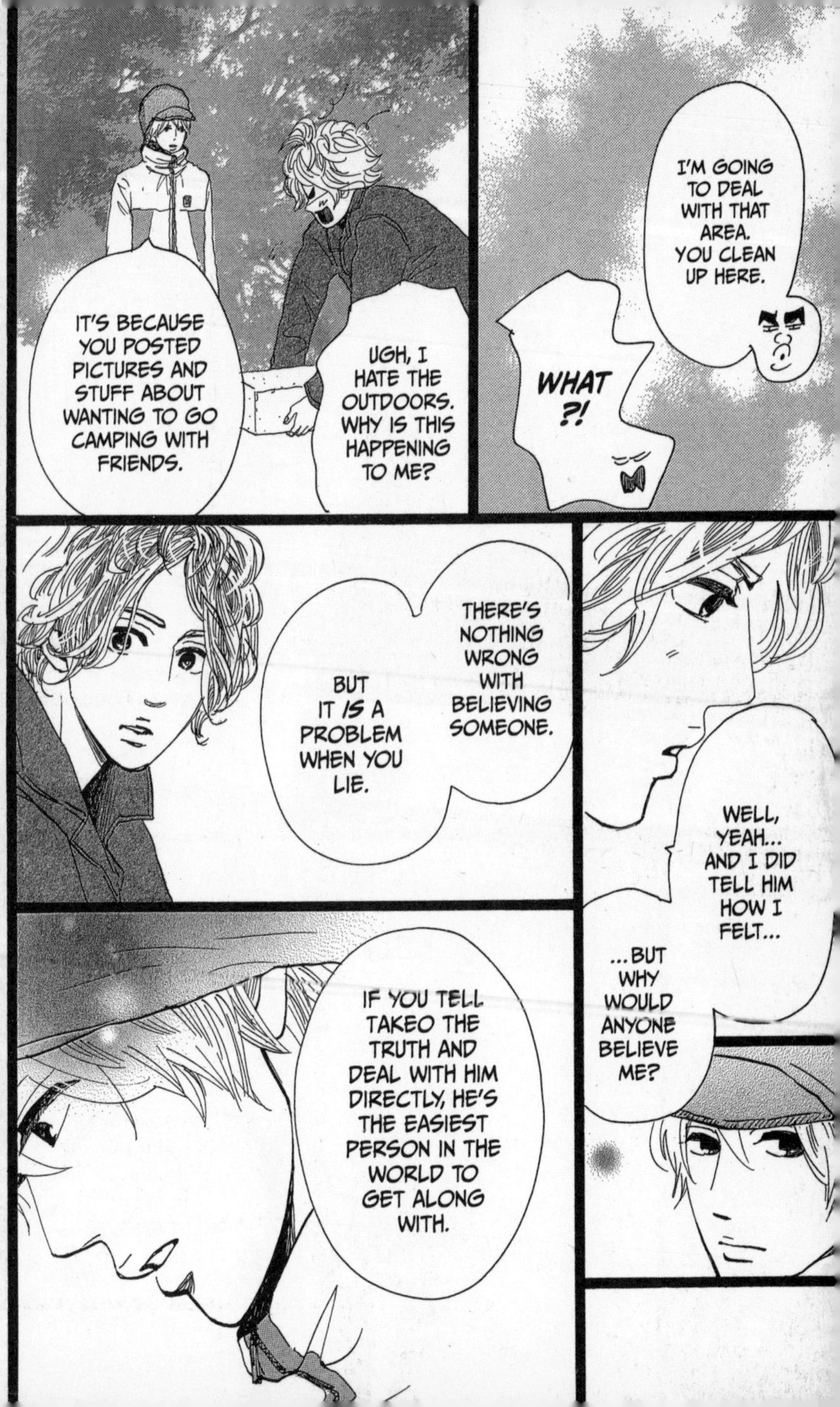
I'M GOING TO DEAL WITH THAT AREA. YOU CLEAN UP HERE.
WHAT ?!
UGH, I HATE THE OUTDOORS. WHY IS THIS HAPPENING TO ME?
IT'S BECAUSE YOU POSTED PICTURES AND STUFF ABOUT WANTING TO GO CAMPING WITH FRIENDS.
WELL, YEAH... AND I DID TELL HIM HOW I FELT...
THERE'S NOTHING WRONG WITH BELIEVING SOMEONE.
BUT IT IS A PROBLEM WHEN YOU LIE.
...BUT WHY WOULD ANYONE BELIEVE ME?
IF YOU TELL TAKEO THE TRUTH AND DEAL WITH HIM DIRECTLY, HE'S THE EASIEST PERSON IN THE WORLD TO GET ALONG WITH.

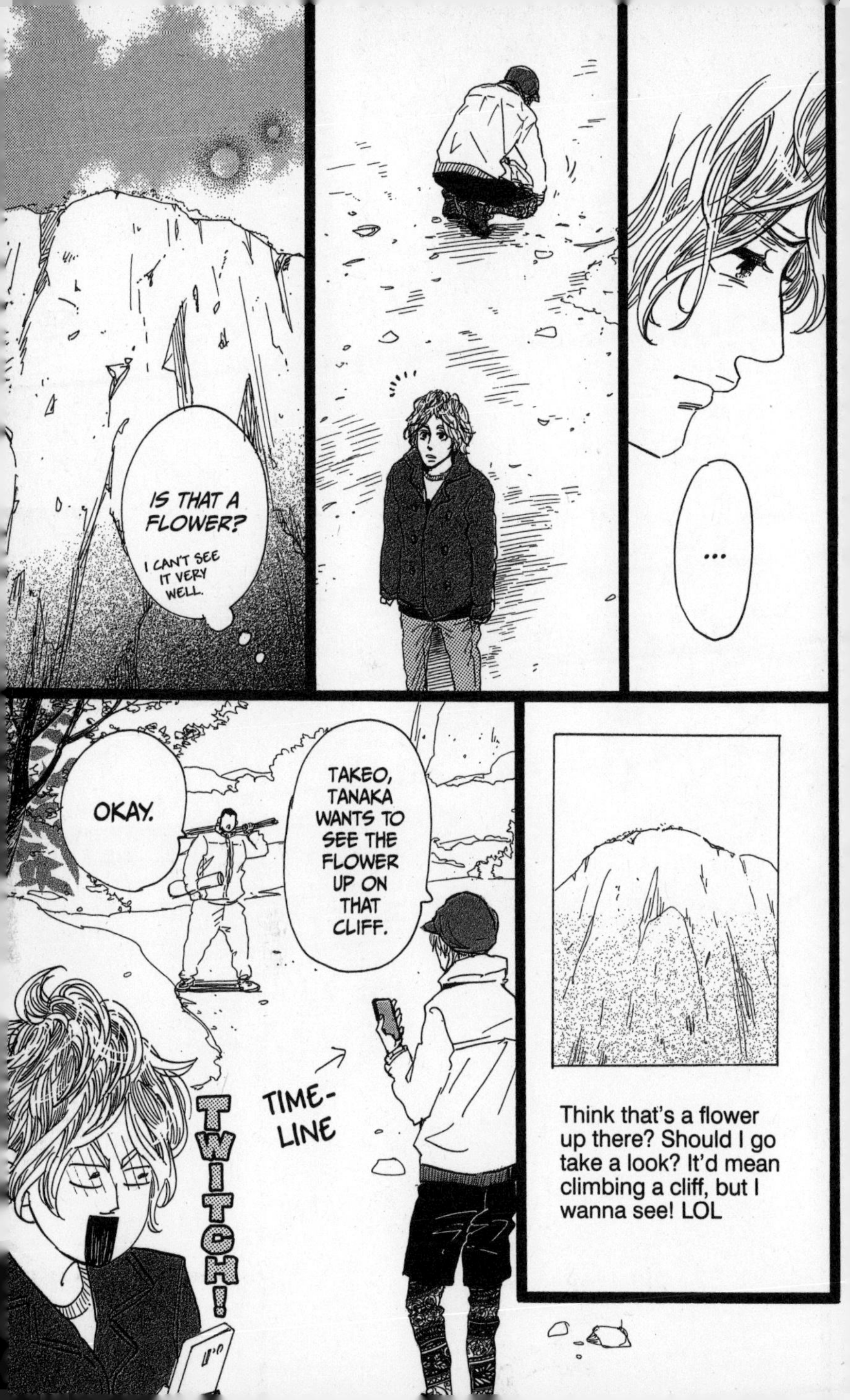
...
IS THAT A FLOWER?
I CAN'T SEE IT VERY WELL.
Think that's a flower up there? Should I go take a look? It'd mean climbing a cliff, but I wanna see! LOL
TAKEO, TANAKA WANTS TO SEE THE FLOWER UP ON THAT CLIFF.
OKAY.
TIME-LINE
TWITCH!

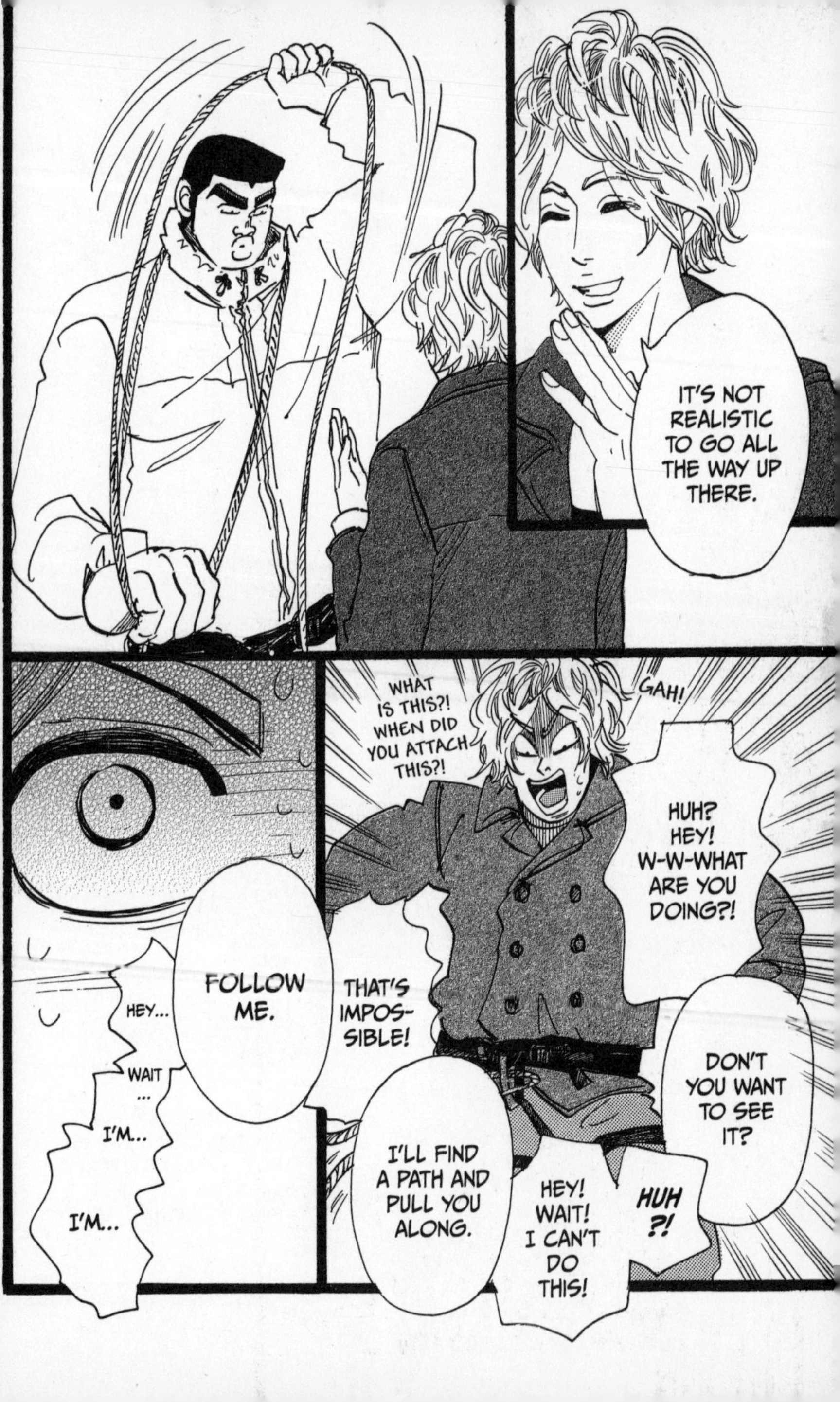
IT'S NOT REALISTIC TO GO ALL THE WAY UP THERE.
GAH!
HUH? HEY! W-W-WHAT ARE YOU DOING?!
WHAT IS THIS?! WHEN DID YOU ATTACH THIS?!
DON'T YOU WANT TO SEE IT?
HUH ?!
HEY! WAIT! I CAN'T DO THIS!
THAT'S IMPOS-SIBLE!
I'LL FIND A PATH AND PULL YOU ALONG.
FOLLOW ME.
HEY...
WAIT ...
I'M...
I'M...

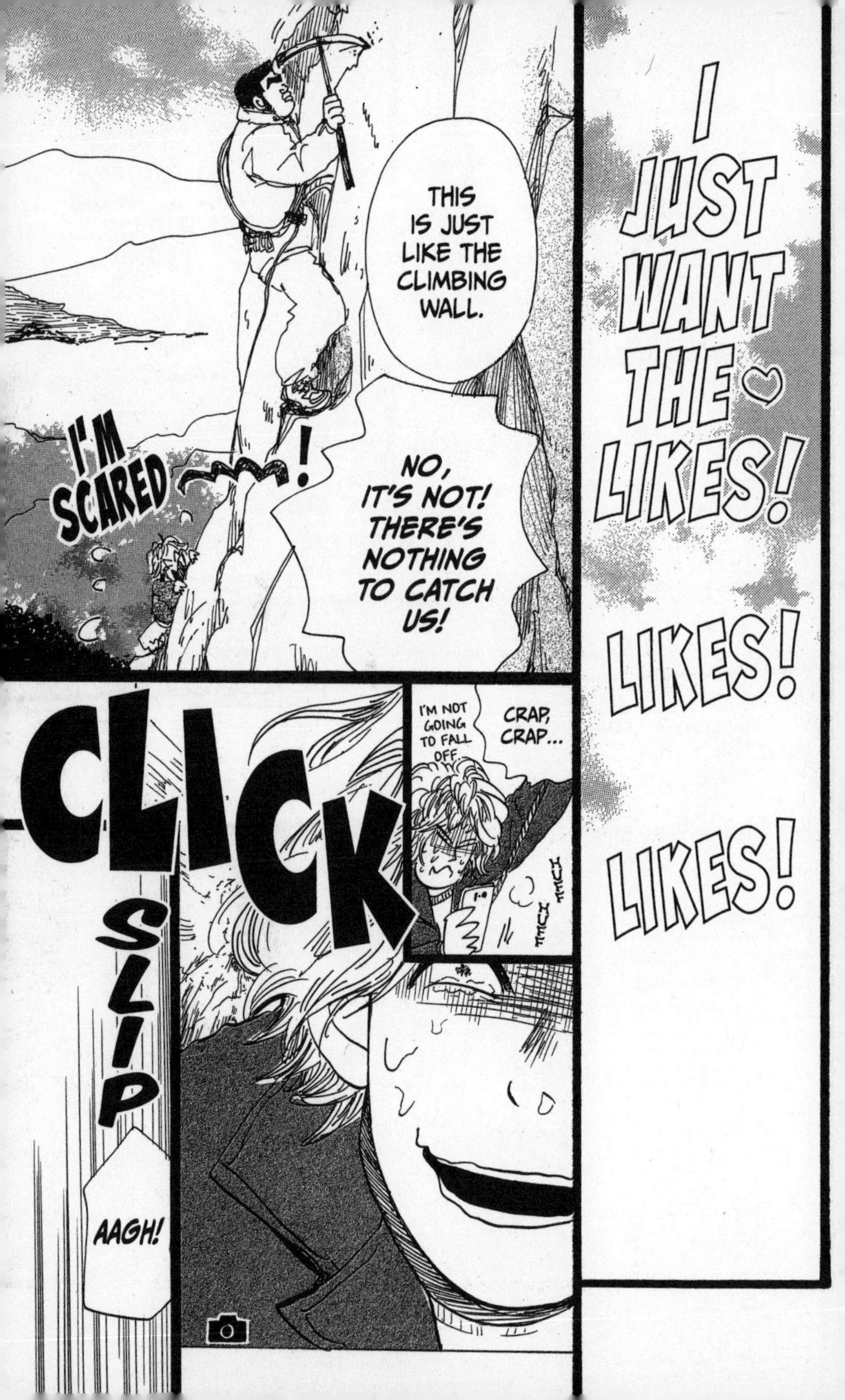
I JUST WANT THE ♡ LIKES!
LIKES!
LIKES!
THIS IS JUST LIKE THE CLIMBING WALL.
NO, IT'S NOT! THERE'S NOTHING TO CATCH US!
I'M SCARED!
CRAP, CRAP...
I'M NOT GOING TO FALL OFF.
HUFF HUFF
CLICK
SLIP
AAGH!

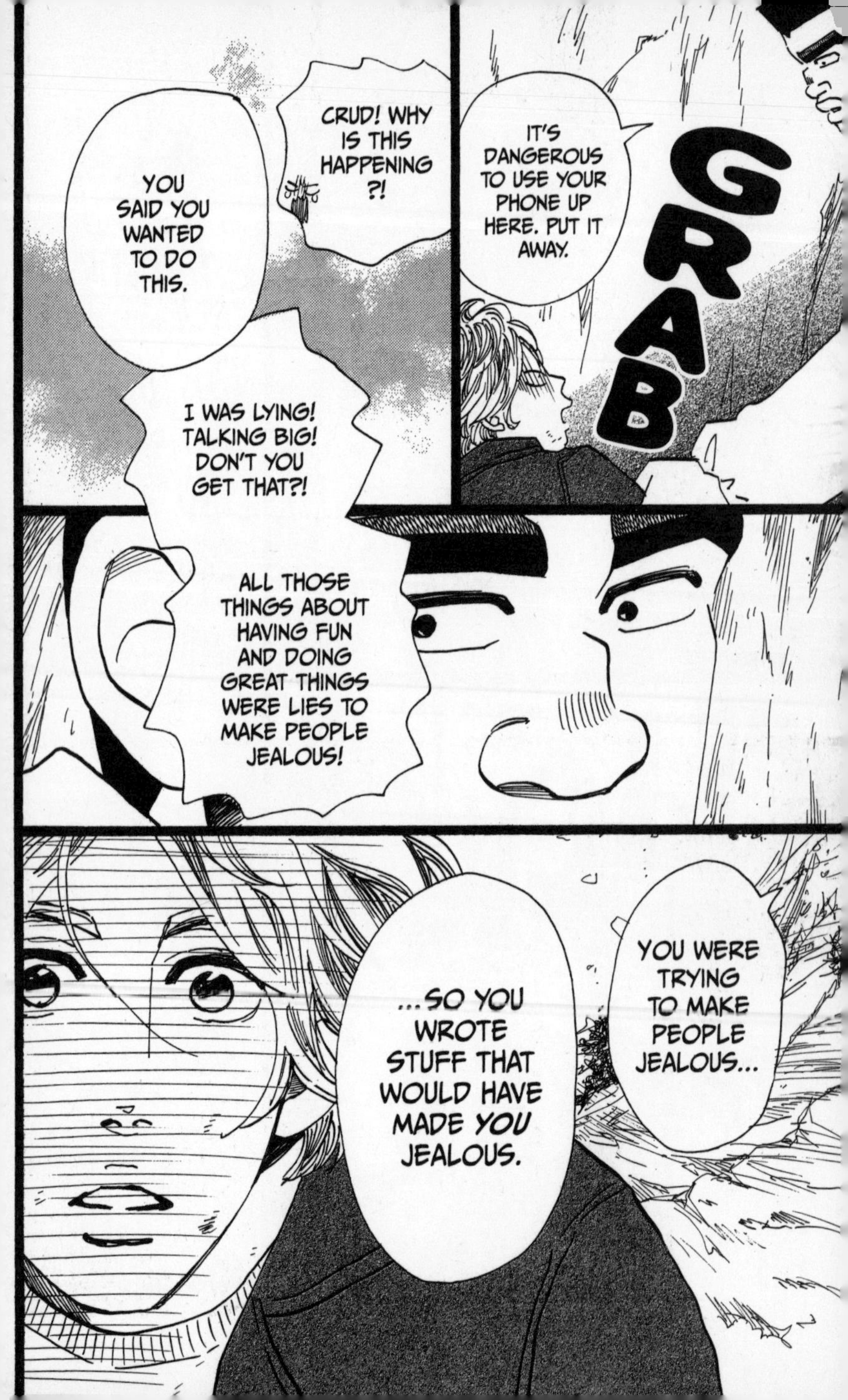
GRAB
IT'S DANGEROUS TO USE YOUR PHONE UP HERE. PUT IT AWAY.
CRUD! WHY IS THIS HAPPENING ?!
YOU SAID YOU WANTED TO DO THIS.
I WAS LYING! TALKING BIG! DON'T YOU GET THAT?!
ALL THOSE THINGS ABOUT HAVING FUN AND DOING GREAT THINGS WERE LIES TO MAKE PEOPLE JEALOUS!
YOU WERE TRYING TO MAKE PEOPLE JEALOUS...
...SO YOU WROTE STUFF THAT WOULD HAVE MADE *YOU* JEALOUS.

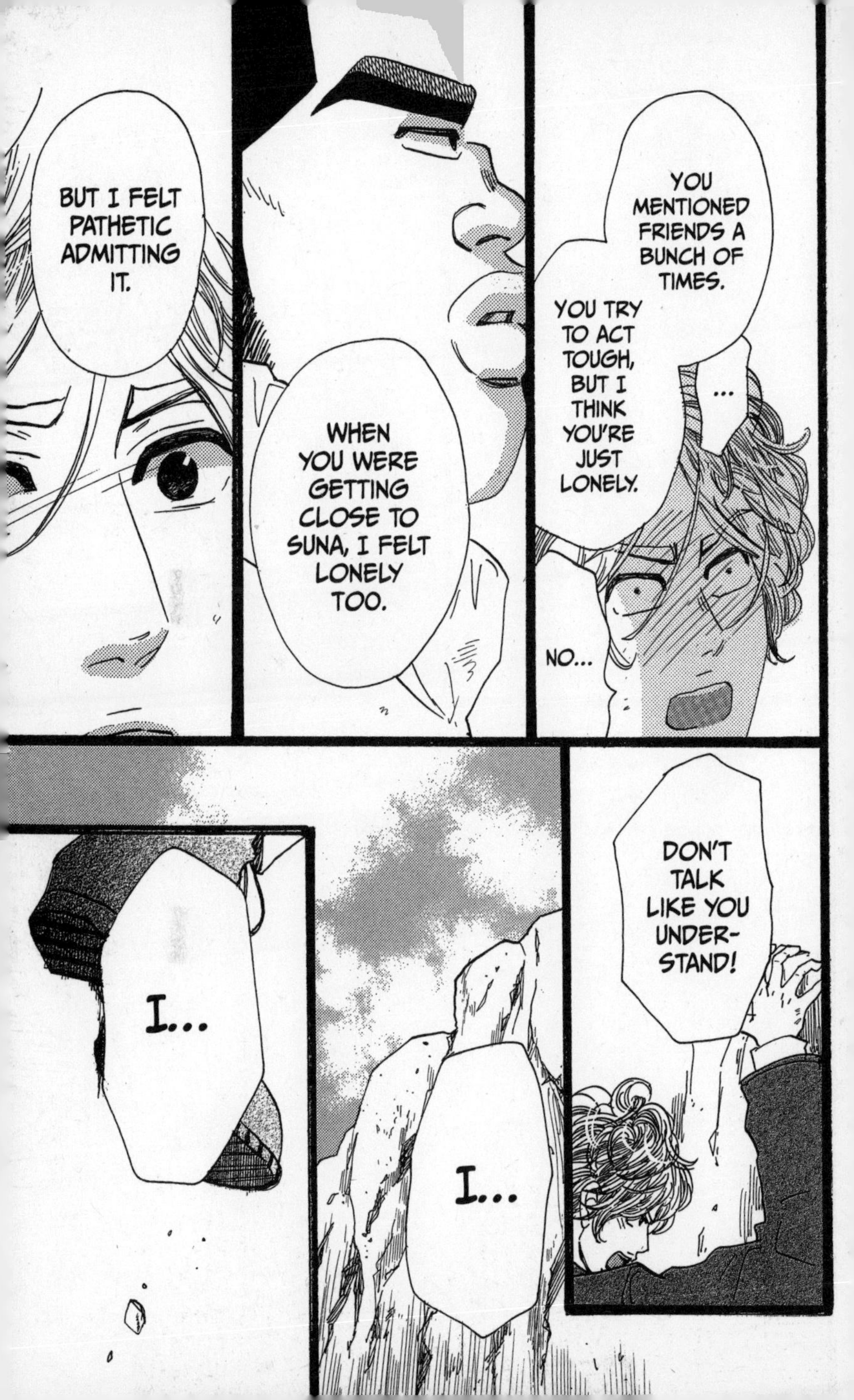
YOU MENTIONED FRIENDS A BUNCH OF TIMES.
YOU TRY TO ACT TOUGH, BUT I THINK YOU'RE JUST LONELY.
...
NO...
WHEN YOU WERE GETTING CLOSE TO SUNA, I FELT LONELY TOO.
BUT I FELT PATHETIC ADMITTING IT.
DON'T TALK LIKE YOU UNDER-STAND!
I...
I...

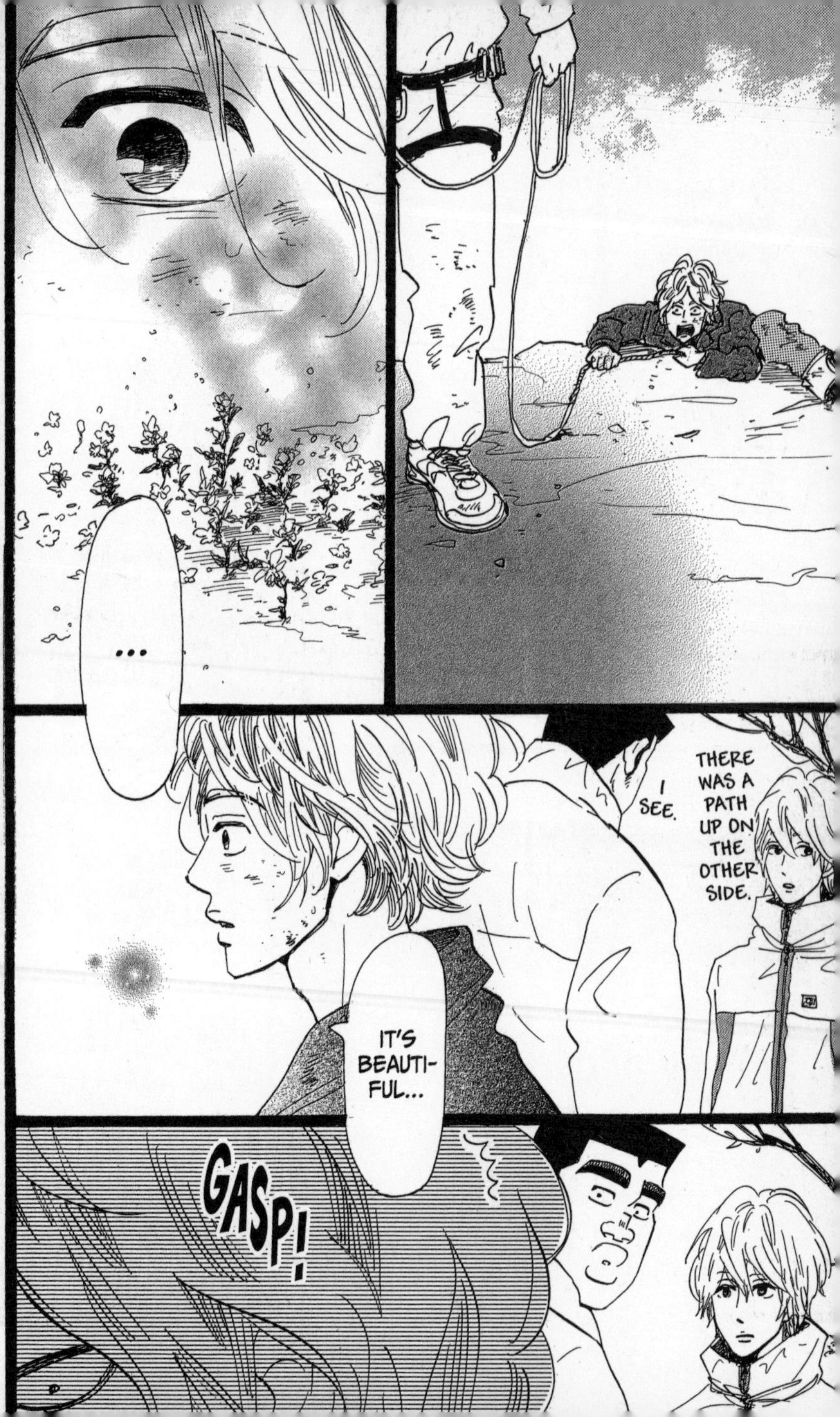
...
THERE WAS A PATH UP ON THE OTHER SIDE.
I SEE.
IT'S BEAUTI-FUL...
GASP!

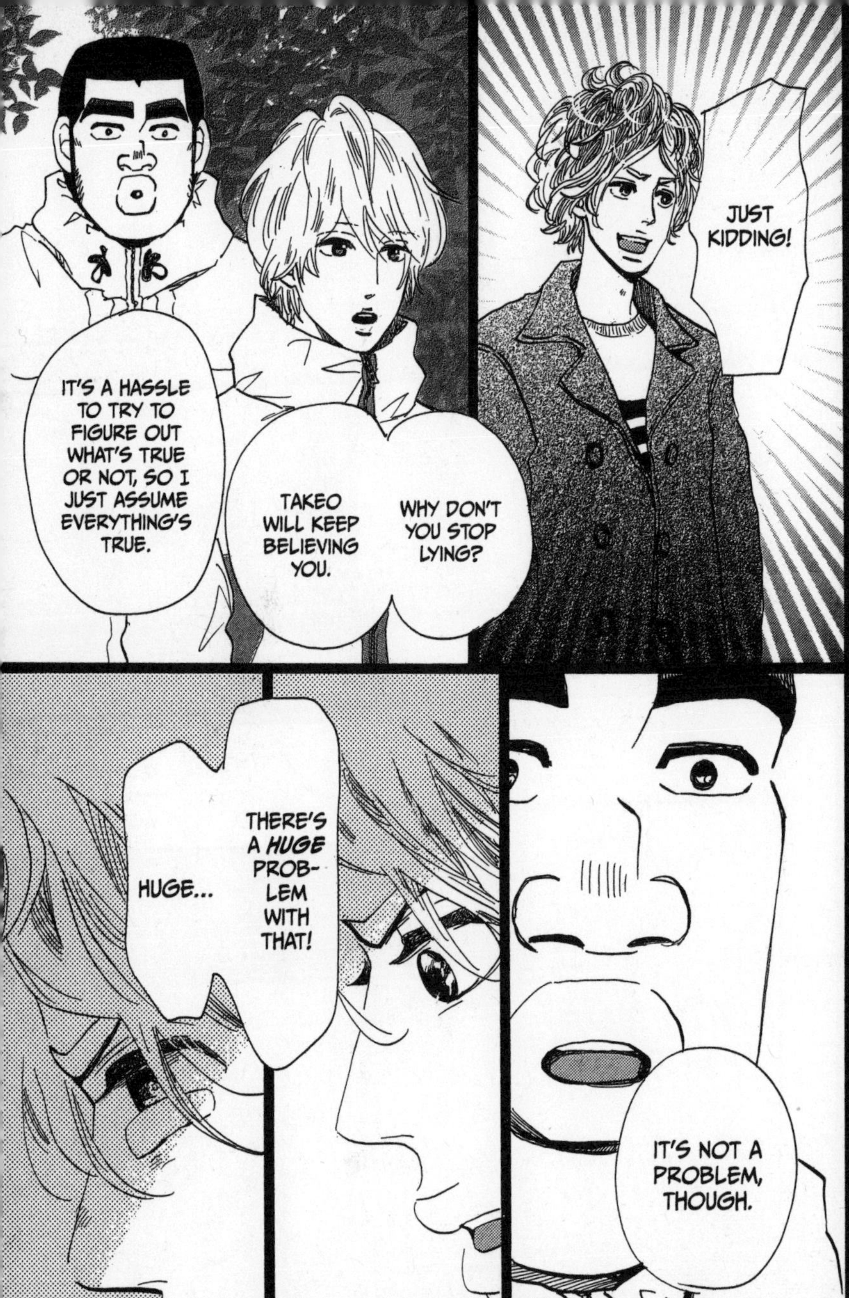
JUST KIDDING!
WHY DON'T YOU STOP LYING?
TAKEO WILL KEEP BELIEVING YOU.
IT'S A HASSLE TO TRY TO FIGURE OUT WHAT'S TRUE OR NOT, SO I JUST ASSUME EVERYTHING'S TRUE.
IT'S NOT A PROBLEM, THOUGH.
THERE'S A *HUGE* PROB-LEM WITH THAT!
HUGE...

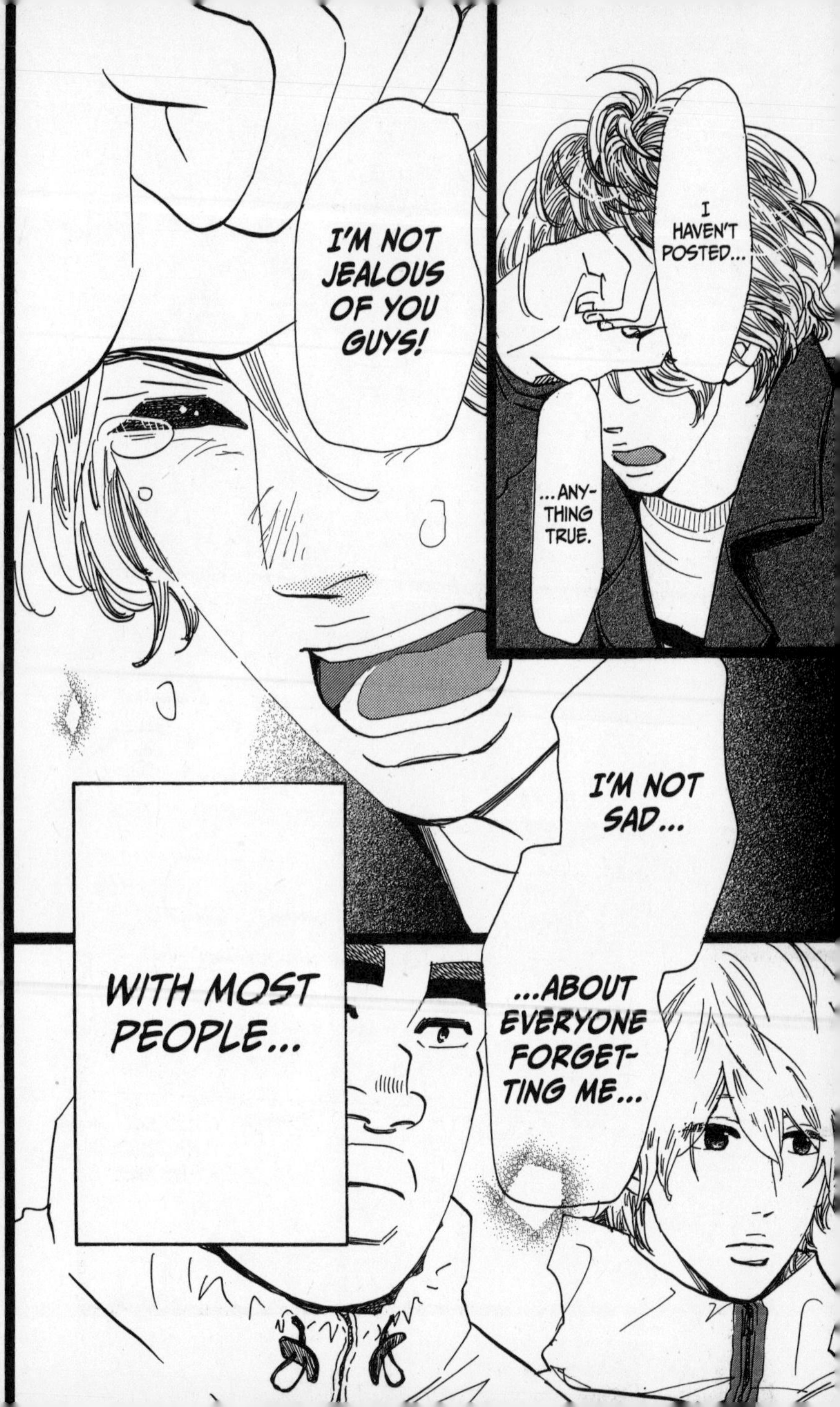
I HAVEN'T POSTED...
...ANYTHING TRUE.
I'M NOT JEALOUS OF YOU GUYS!
I'M NOT SAD...
...ABOUT EVERYONE FORGETTING ME...
WITH MOST PEOPLE...

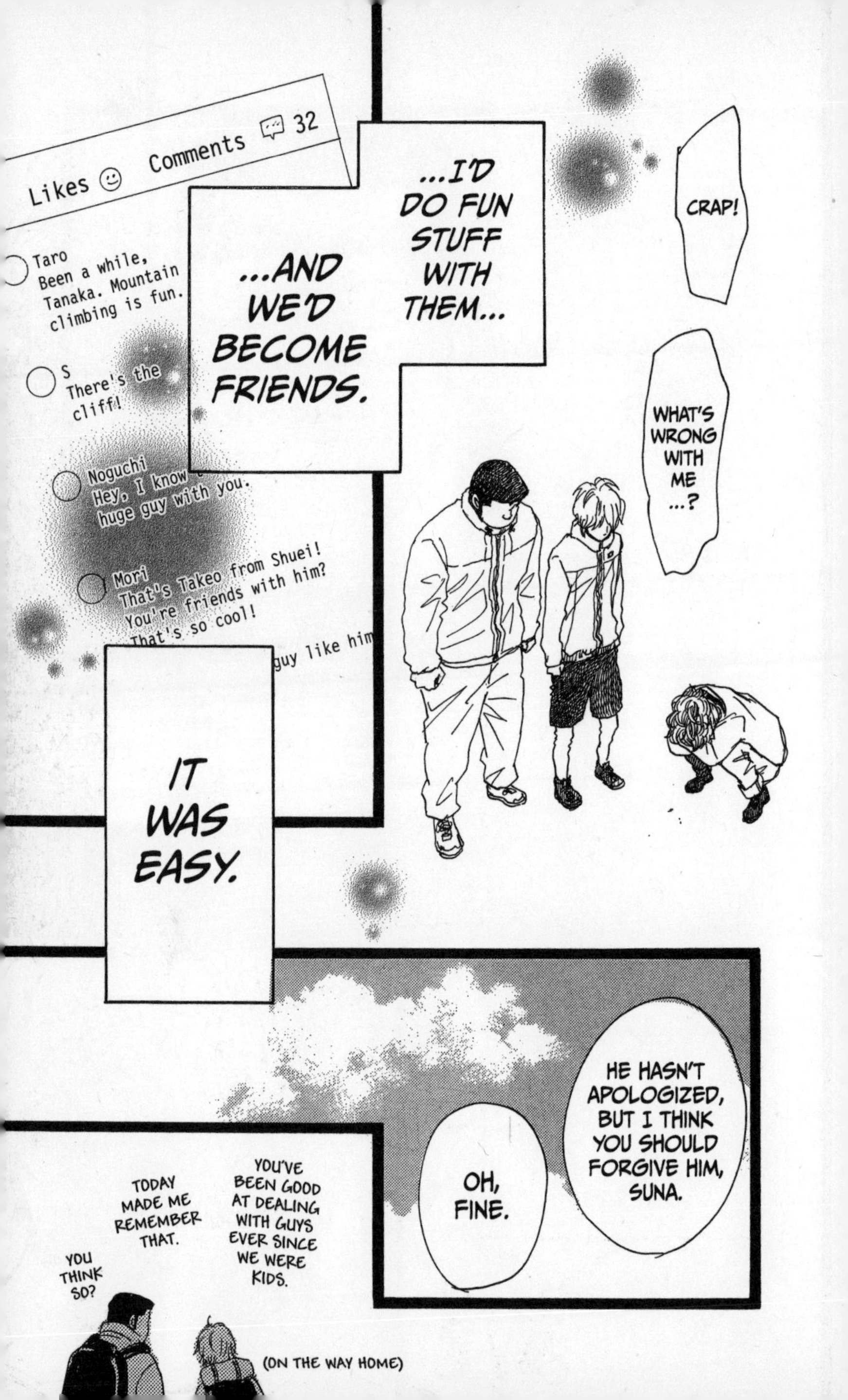
CRAP!
WHAT'S WRONG WITH ME ...?
...I'D DO FUN STUFF WITH THEM...
...AND WE'D BECOME FRIENDS.
Likes
Comments 32
Taro
Been a while, Tanaka. Mountain climbing is fun.
S
There's the cliff!
Noguchi
Hey, I know
huge guy with you.
Mori
That's Takeo from Shuei! You're friends with him? That's so cool!
guy like him
IT WAS EASY.
HE HASN'T APOLOGIZED, BUT I THINK YOU SHOULD FORGIVE HIM, SUNA.
OH, FINE.
YOU'VE BEEN GOOD AT DEALING WITH GUYS EVER SINCE WE WERE KIDS.
TODAY MADE ME REMEMBER THAT.
YOU THINK SO?
(ON THE WAY HOME)

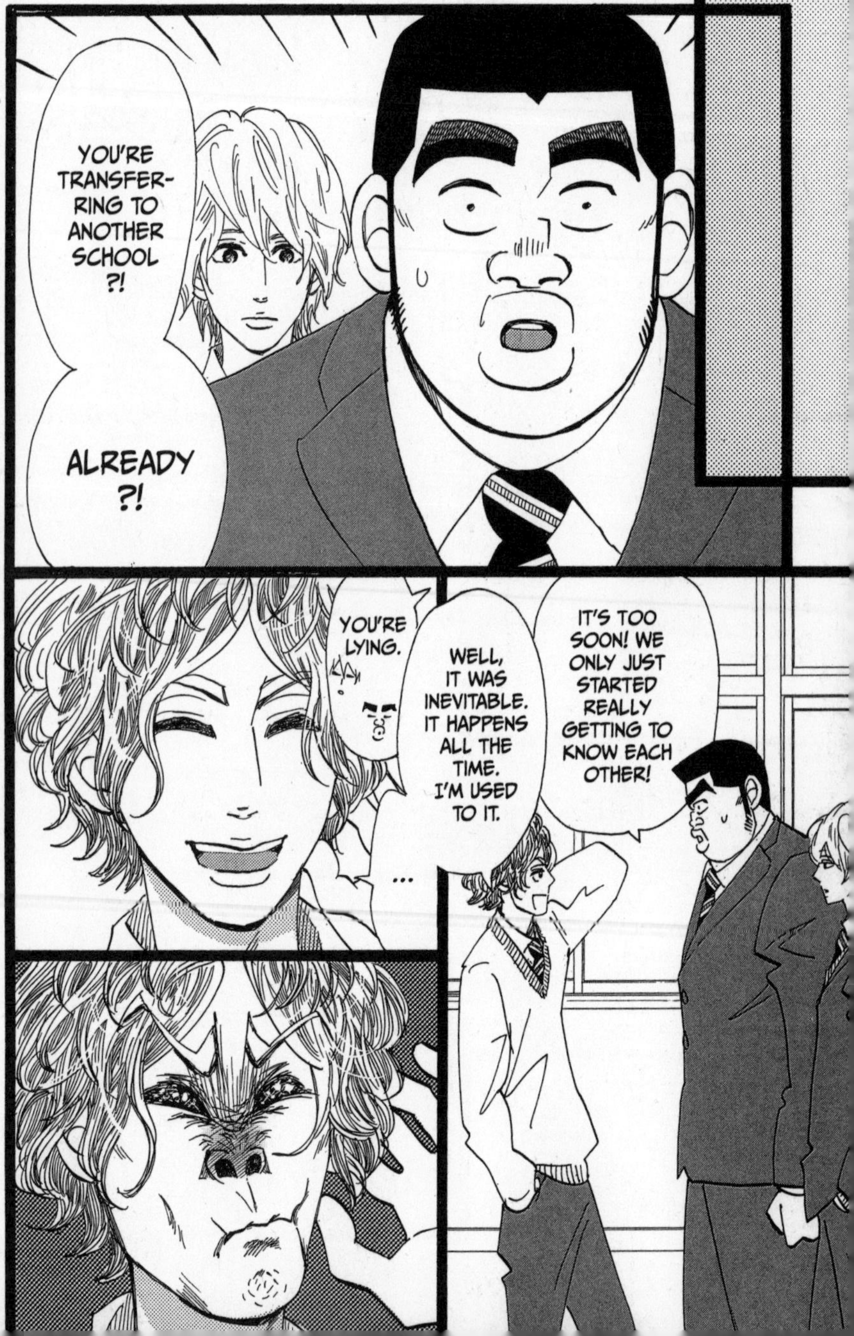
YOU'RE TRANSFER-RING TO ANOTHER SCHOOL ?!
ALREADY ?!
IT'S TOO SOON! WE ONLY JUST STARTED REALLY GETTING TO KNOW EACH OTHER!
WELL, IT WAS INEVITABLE. IT HAPPENS ALL THE TIME. I'M USED TO IT.
...
YOU'RE LYING.

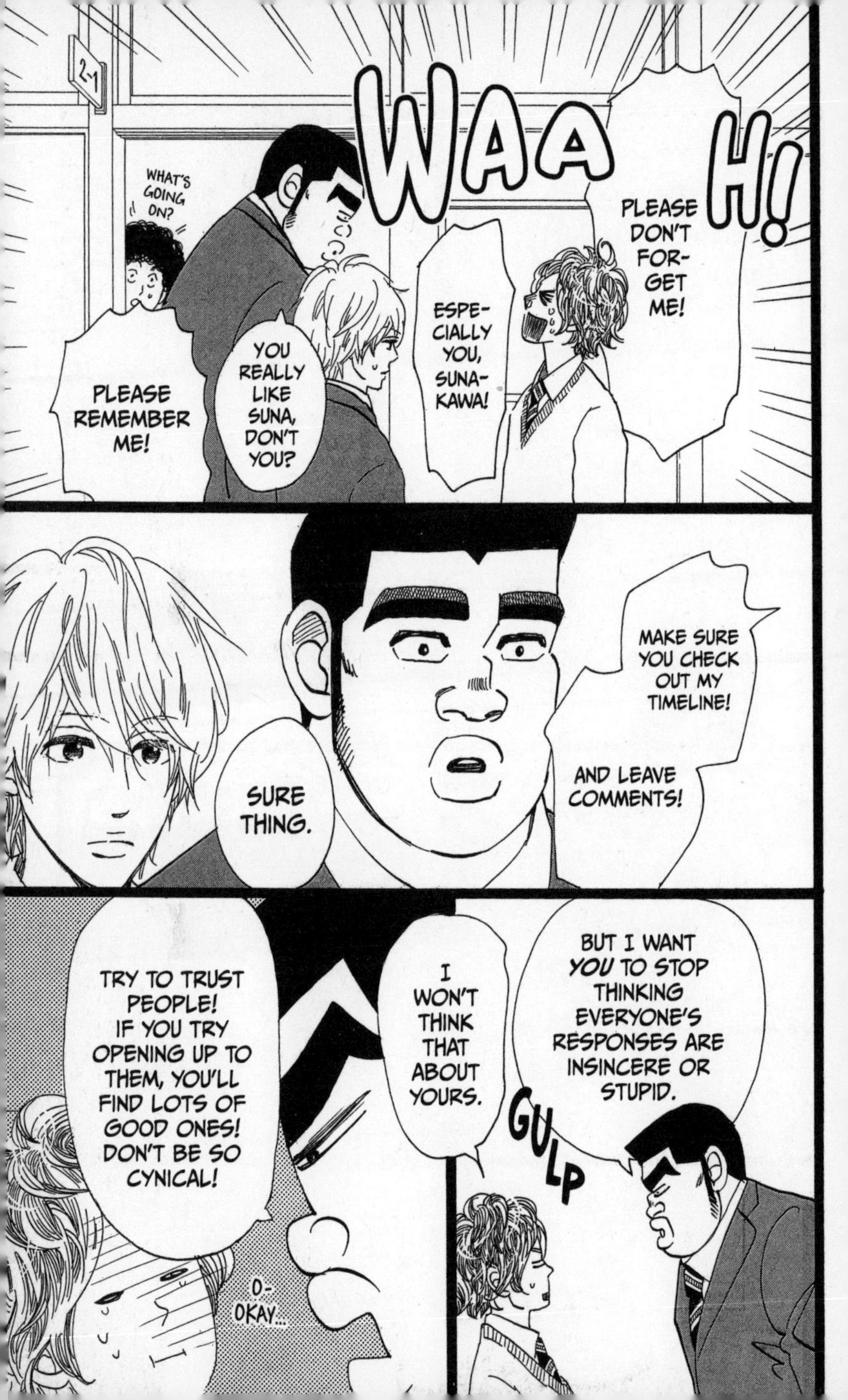
WAAH!
PLEASE DON'T FOR-GET ME!
ESPE-CIALLY YOU, SUNA-KAWA!
YOU REALLY LIKE SUNA, DON'T YOU?
PLEASE REMEMBER ME!
WHAT'S GOING ON?
2-1
MAKE SURE YOU CHECK OUT MY TIMELINE!
AND LEAVE COMMENTS!
SURE THING.
BUT I WANT YOU TO STOP THINKING EVERYONE'S RESPONSES ARE INSINCERE OR STUPID.
GULP
I WON'T THINK THAT ABOUT YOURS.
TRY TO TRUST PEOPLE! IF YOU TRY OPENING UP TO THEM, YOU'LL FIND LOTS OF GOOD ONES! DON'T BE SO CYNICAL!
O-OKAY...

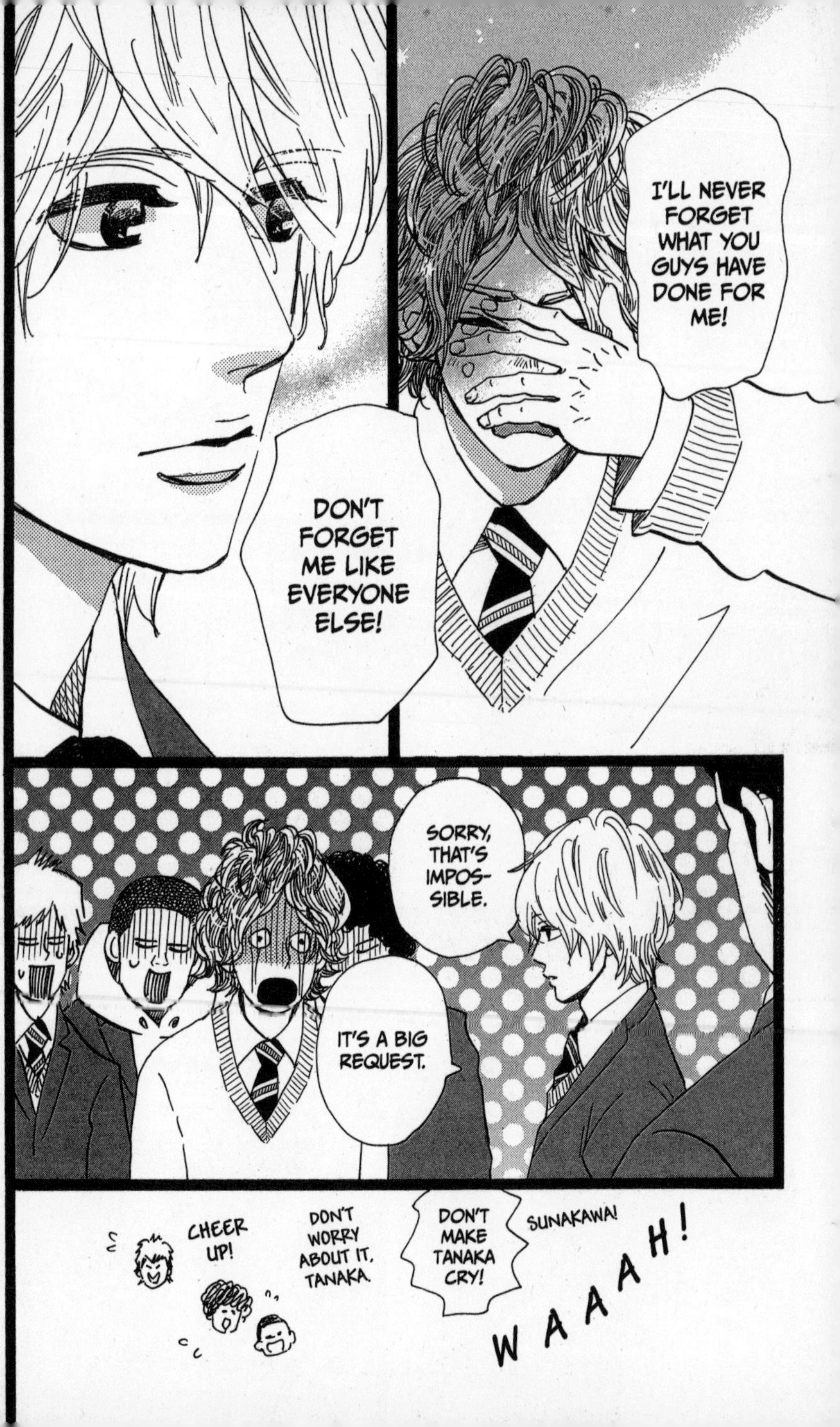
I'LL NEVER FORGET WHAT YOU GUYS HAVE DONE FOR ME!
DON'T FORGET ME LIKE EVERYONE ELSE!
SORRY, THAT'S IMPOS-SIBLE.
IT'S A BIG REQUEST.
WAAAH!
SUNAKAWA!
DON'T MAKE TANAKA CRY!
DON'T WORRY ABOUT IT, TANAKA.
CHEER UP!

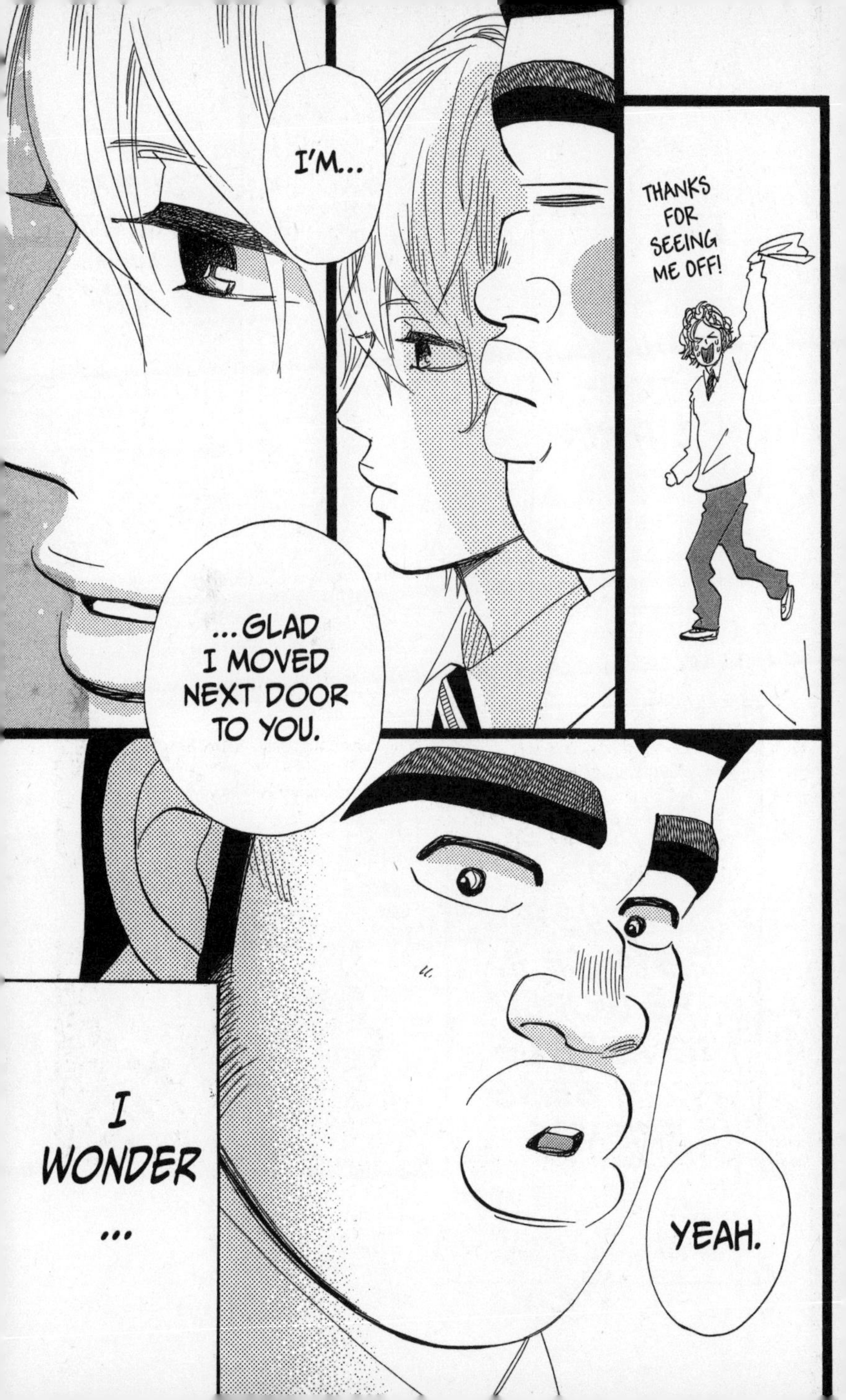
THANKS FOR SEEING ME OFF!
I'M...
...GLAD I MOVED NEXT DOOR TO YOU.
YEAH.
I WONDER ...

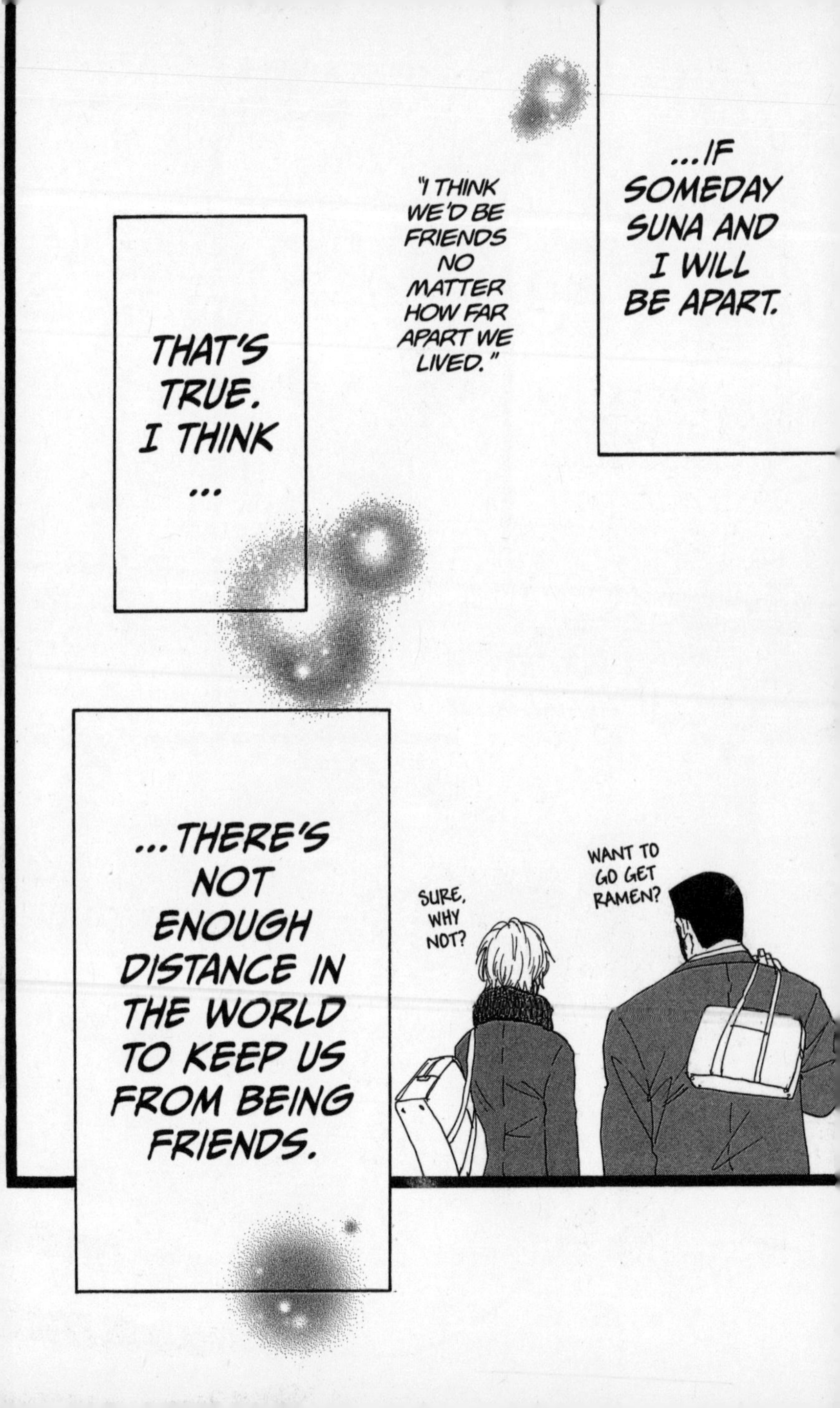
...IF SOMEDAY SUNA AND I WILL BE APART.
"I THINK WE'D BE FRIENDS NO MATTER HOW FAR APART WE LIVED."
THAT'S TRUE. I THINK ...
WANT TO GO GET RAMEN?
SURE, WHY NOT?
...THERE'S NOT ENOUGH DISTANCE IN THE WORLD TO KEEP US FROM BEING FRIENDS.

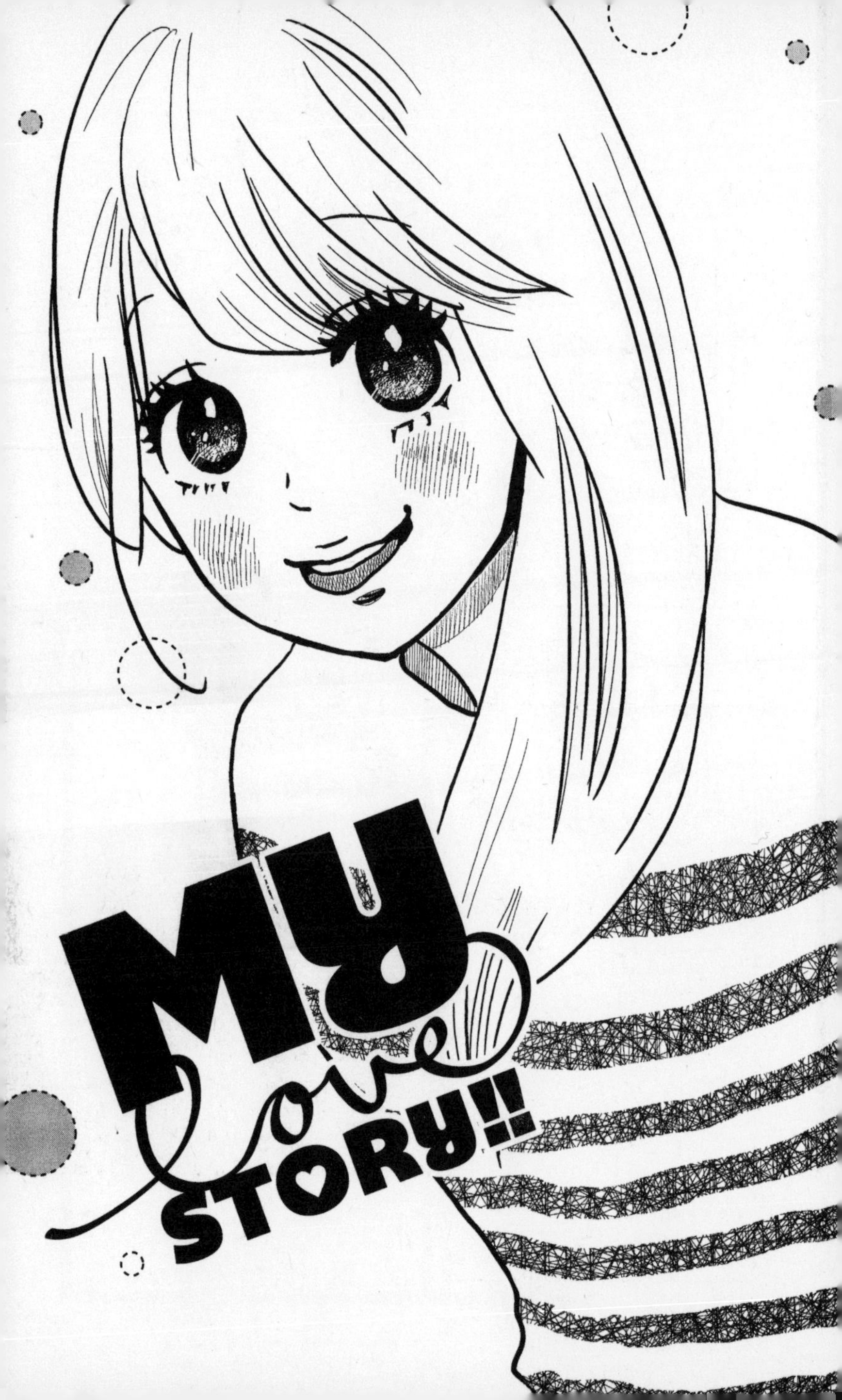
MY Love STORY!!

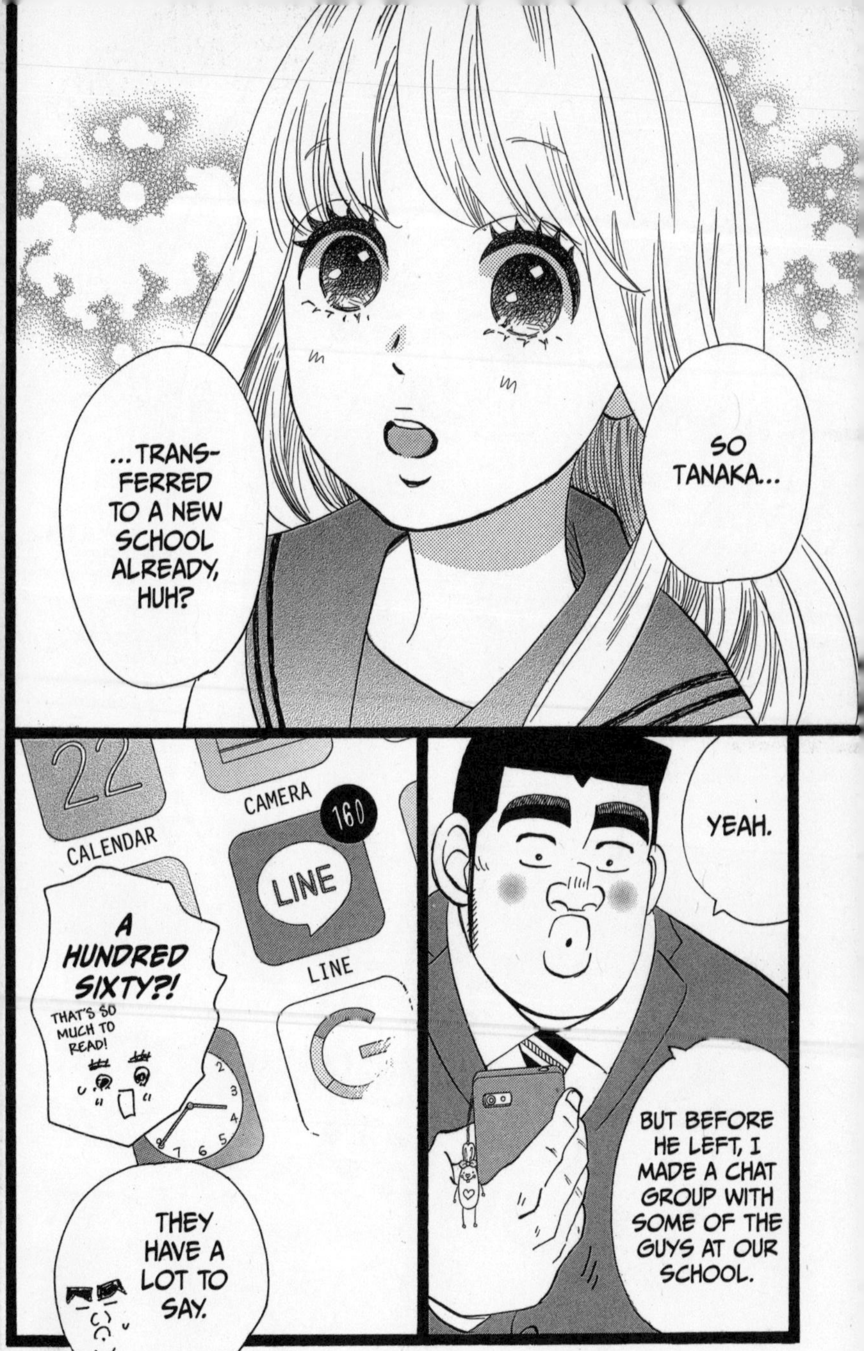
SO TANAKA...
...TRANSFERRED TO A NEW SCHOOL ALREADY, HUH?
YEAH.
BUT BEFORE HE LEFT, I MADE A CHAT GROUP WITH SOME OF THE GUYS AT OUR SCHOOL.
22
CALENDAR
CAMERA
160
LINE
LINE
A HUNDRED SIXTY?!
THAT'S SO MUCH TO READ!
THEY HAVE A LOT TO SAY.

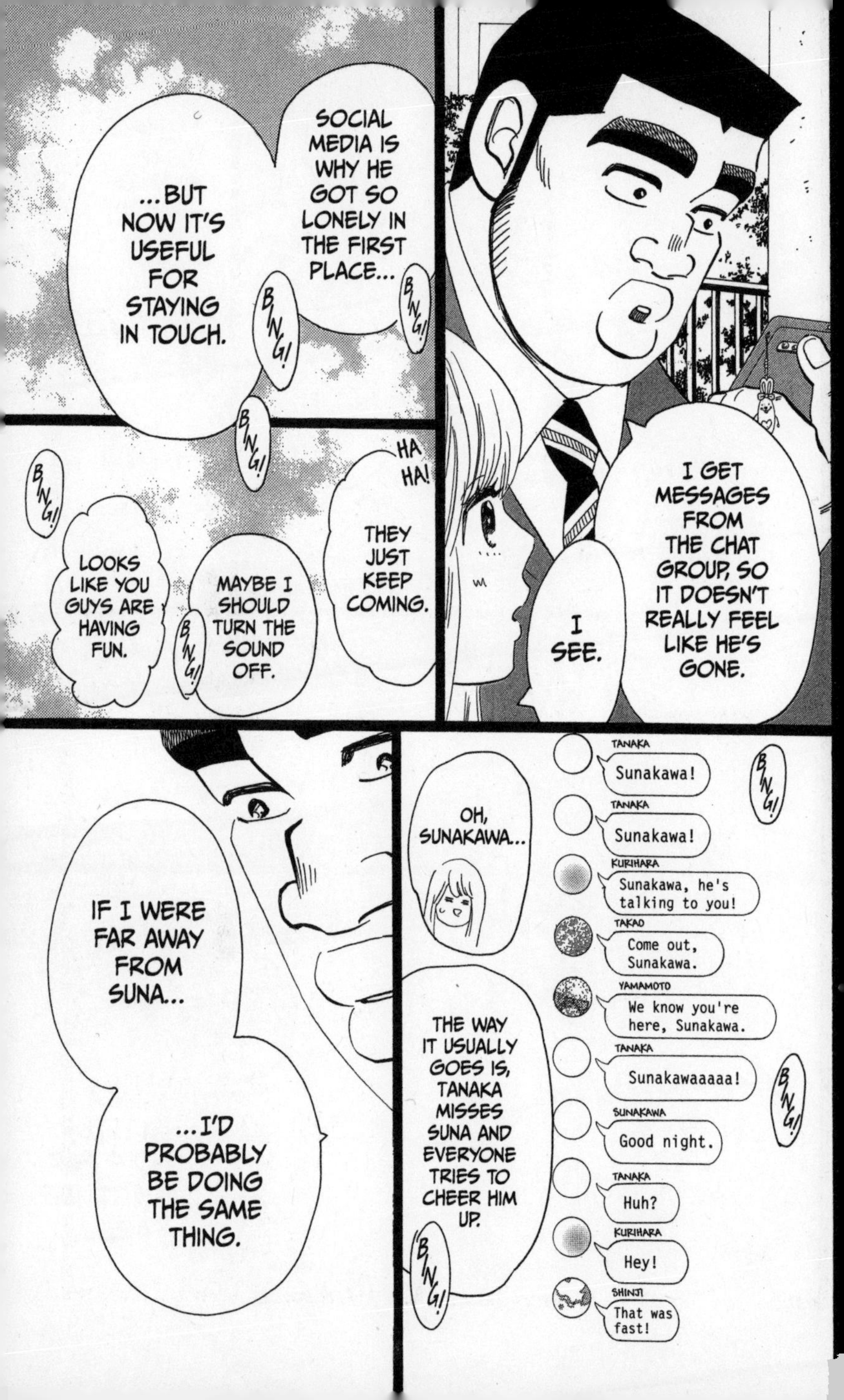
I GET MESSAGES FROM THE CHAT GROUP, SO IT DOESN'T REALLY FEEL LIKE HE'S GONE.
I SEE.
SOCIAL MEDIA IS WHY HE GOT SO LONELY IN THE FIRST PLACE...
BING!
...BUT NOW IT'S USEFUL FOR STAYING IN TOUCH.
BING!
BING!
HA HA!
THEY JUST KEEP COMING.
MAYBE I SHOULD TURN THE SOUND OFF.
BING!
LOOKS LIKE YOU GUYS ARE HAVING FUN.
BING!
BING!
TANAKA
Sunakawa!
TANAKA
Sunakawa!
KURIHARA
Sunakawa, he's talking to you!
TAKAO
Come out, Sunakawa.
YAMAMOTO
We know you're here, Sunakawa.
TANAKA
Sunakawaaaaa!
BING!
SUNAKAWA
Good night.
TANAKA
Huh?
KURIHARA
Hey!
SHINJI
That was fast!
OH, SUNAKAWA...
THE WAY IT USUALLY GOES IS, TANAKA MISSES SUNA AND EVERYONE TRIES TO CHEER HIM UP.
BING!
IF I WERE FAR AWAY FROM SUNA...
...I'D PROBABLY BE DOING THE SAME THING.

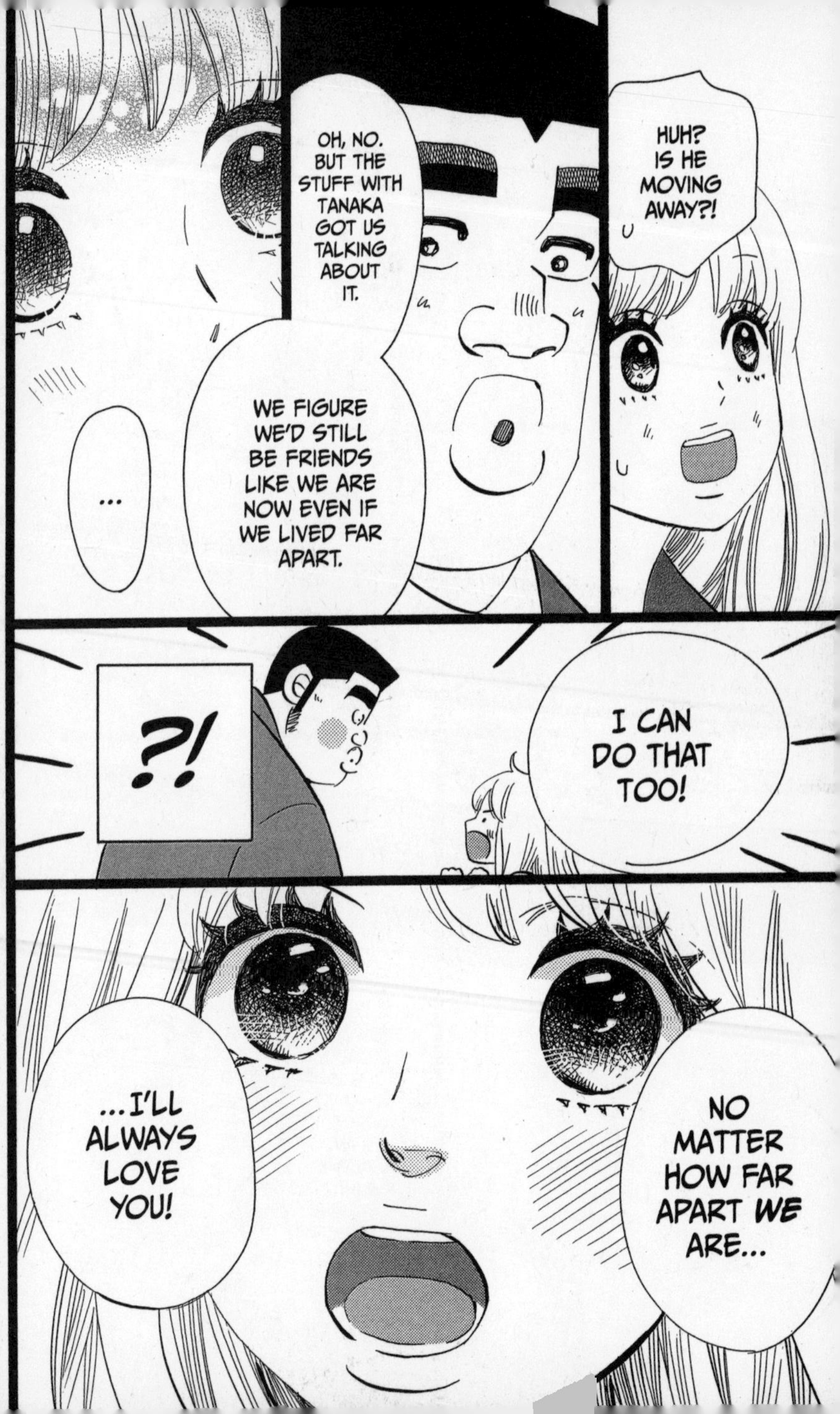
HUH? IS HE MOVING AWAY?!
OH, NO. BUT THE STUFF WITH TANAKA GOT US TALKING ABOUT IT.
WE FIGURE WE'D STILL BE FRIENDS LIKE WE ARE NOW EVEN IF WE LIVED FAR APART.
...
I CAN DO THAT TOO!
?!
NO MATTER HOW FAR APART WE ARE...
...I'LL ALWAYS LOVE YOU!

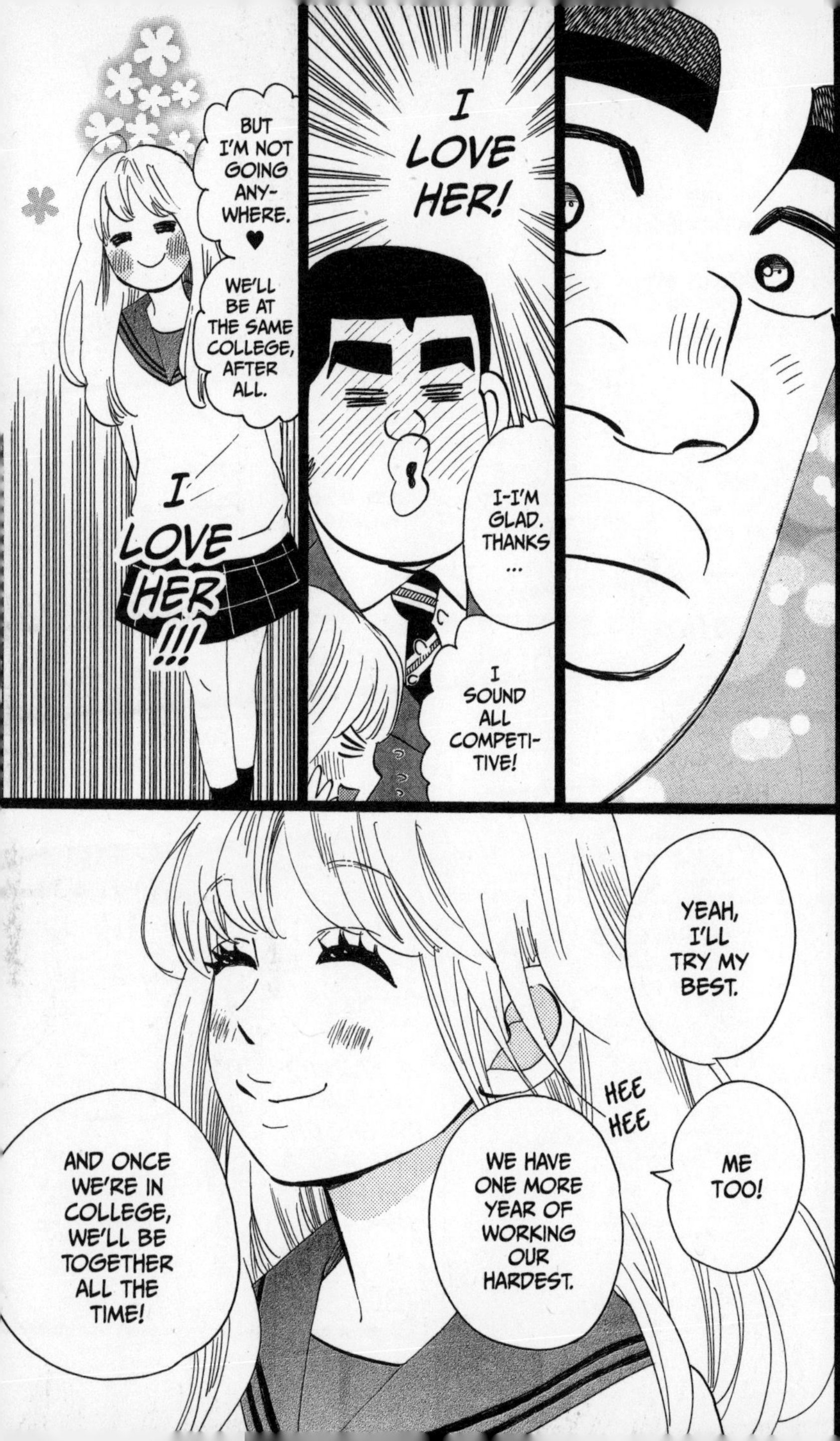
I LOVE HER!
I-I'M GLAD. THANKS...
I SOUND ALL COMPETI-TIVE!
BUT I'M NOT GOING ANY-WHERE. ♥
WE'LL BE AT THE SAME COLLEGE, AFTER ALL.
I LOVE HER!!!
YEAH, I'LL TRY MY BEST.
HEE HEE
ME TOO!
WE HAVE ONE MORE YEAR OF WORKING OUR HARDEST.
AND ONCE WE'RE IN COLLEGE, WE'LL BE TOGETHER ALL THE TIME!

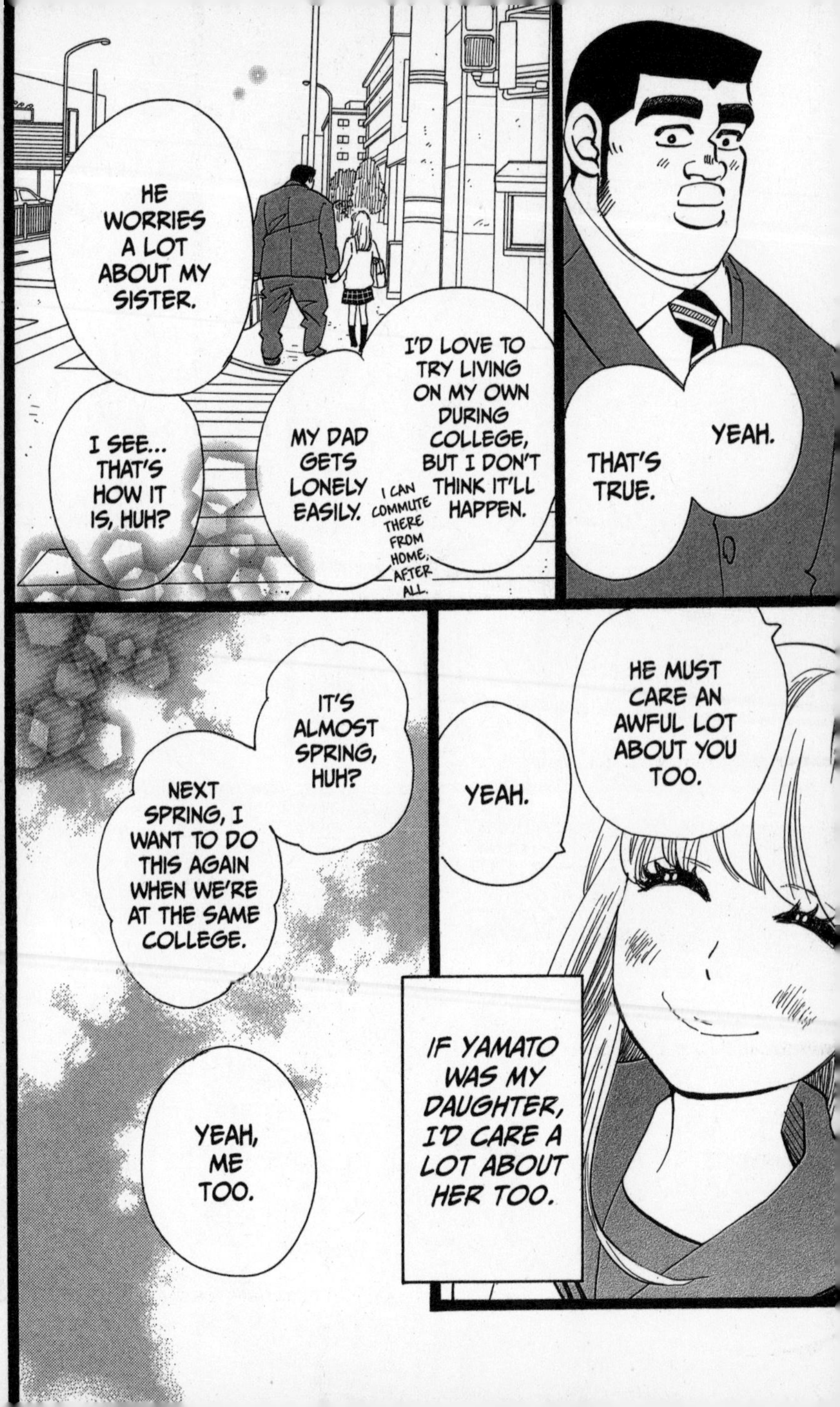
YEAH.
THAT'S TRUE.
HE WORRIES A LOT ABOUT MY SISTER.
I SEE... THAT'S HOW IT IS, HUH?
I'D LOVE TO TRY LIVING ON MY OWN DURING COLLEGE, BUT I DON'T THINK IT'LL HAPPEN.
MY DAD GETS LONELY EASILY.
I CAN COMMUTE THERE FROM HOME, AFTER ALL.
HE MUST CARE AN AWFUL LOT ABOUT YOU TOO.
YEAH.
IF YAMATO WAS MY DAUGHTER, I'D CARE A LOT ABOUT HER TOO.
IT'S ALMOST SPRING, HUH?
NEXT SPRING, I WANT TO DO THIS AGAIN WHEN WE'RE AT THE SAME COLLEGE.
YEAH, ME TOO.

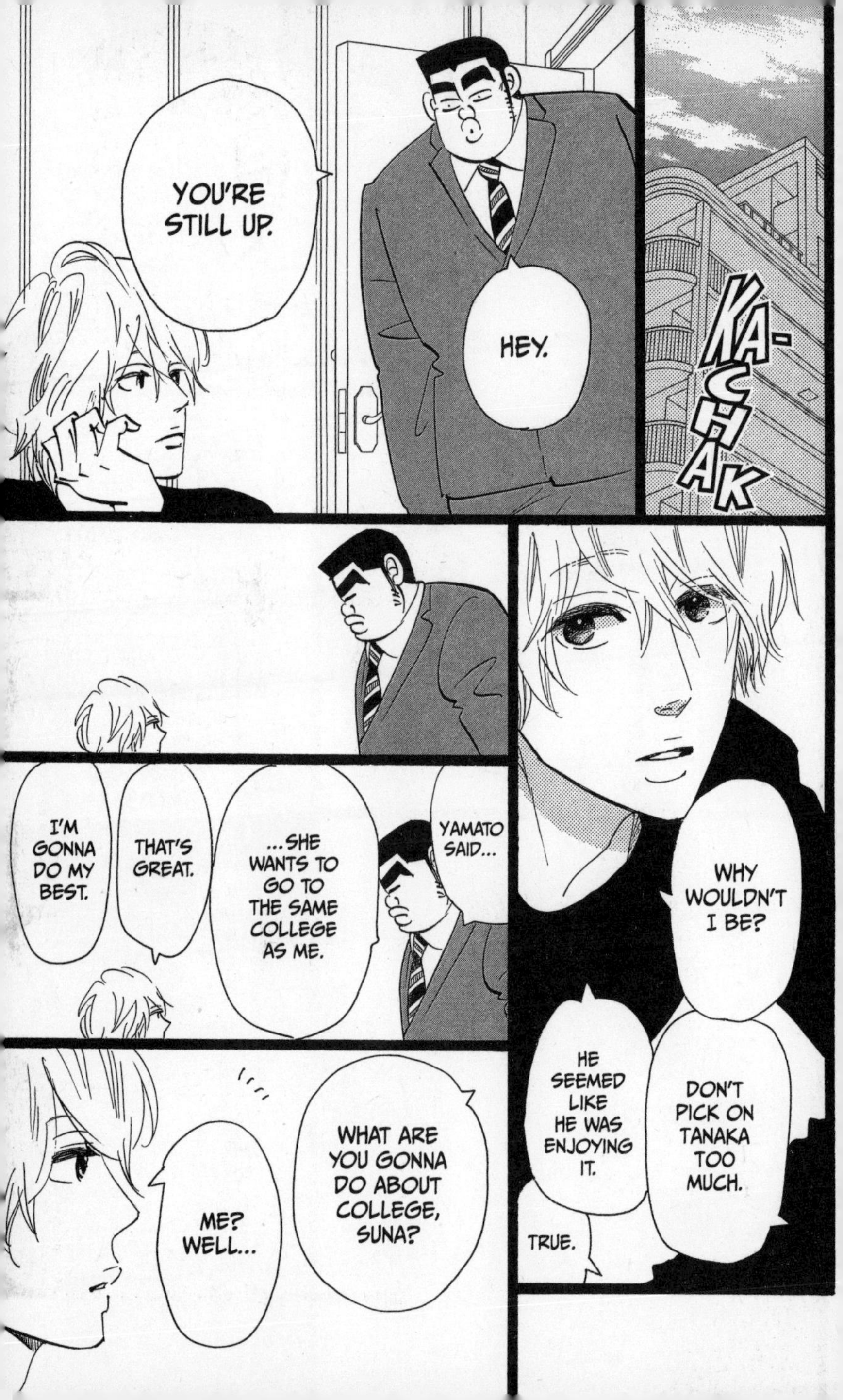
KA-CHAK
HEY.
YOU'RE STILL UP.
WHY WOULDN'T I BE?
DON'T PICK ON TANAKA TOO MUCH.
HE SEEMED LIKE HE WAS ENJOYING IT.
TRUE.
YAMATO SAID...
...SHE WANTS TO GO TO THE SAME COLLEGE AS ME.
THAT'S GREAT.
I'M GONNA DO MY BEST.
WHAT ARE YOU GONNA DO ABOUT COLLEGE, SUNA?
...
ME? WELL...

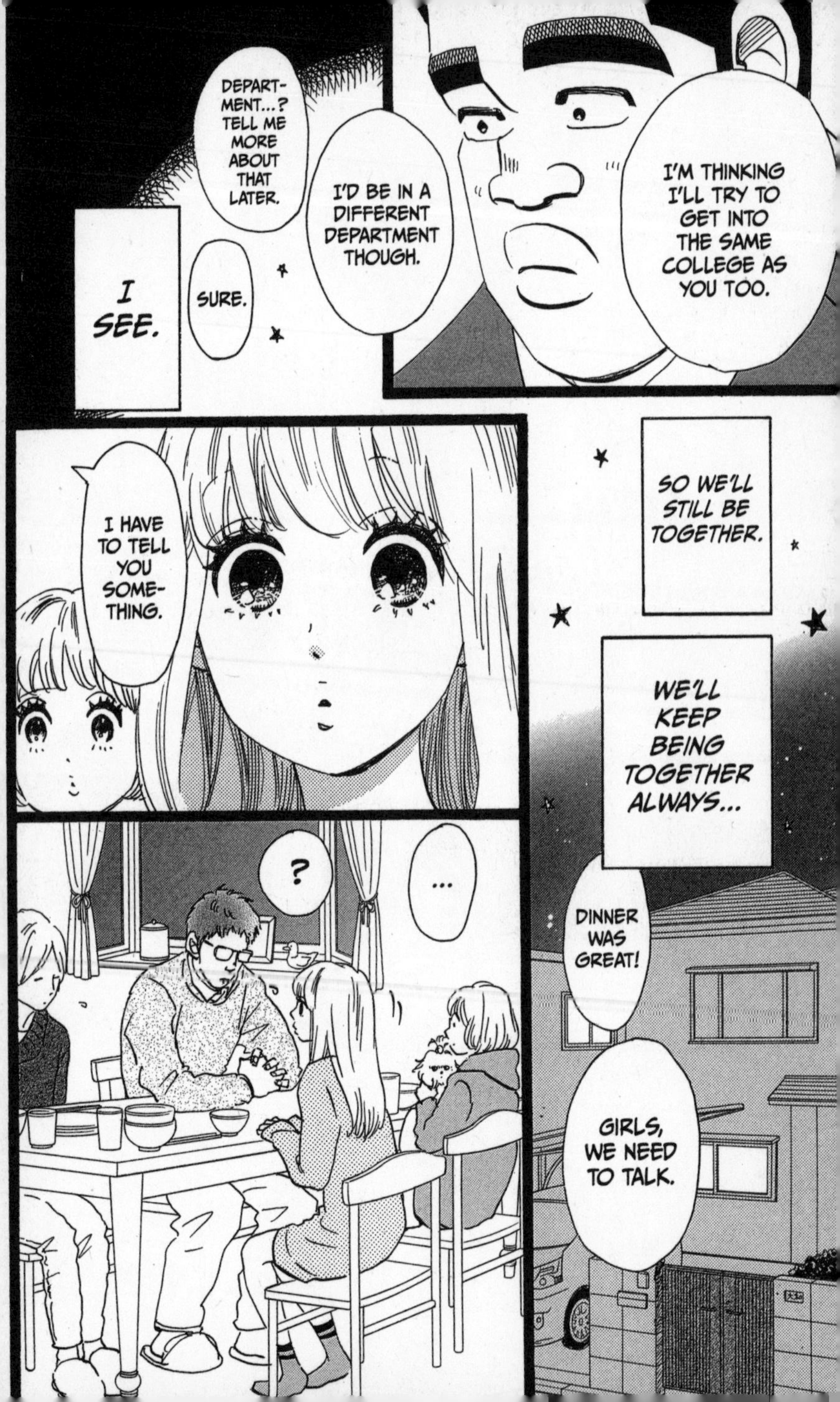
I'M THINKING I'LL TRY TO GET INTO THE SAME COLLEGE AS YOU TOO.
I'D BE IN A DIFFERENT DEPARTMENT THOUGH.
DEPARTMENT...? TELL ME MORE ABOUT THAT LATER.
SURE.
I SEE.
SO WE'LL STILL BE TOGETHER.
WE'LL KEEP BEING TOGETHER ALWAYS...
I HAVE TO TELL YOU SOMETHING.
DINNER WAS GREAT!
GIRLS, WE NEED TO TALK.
...
?

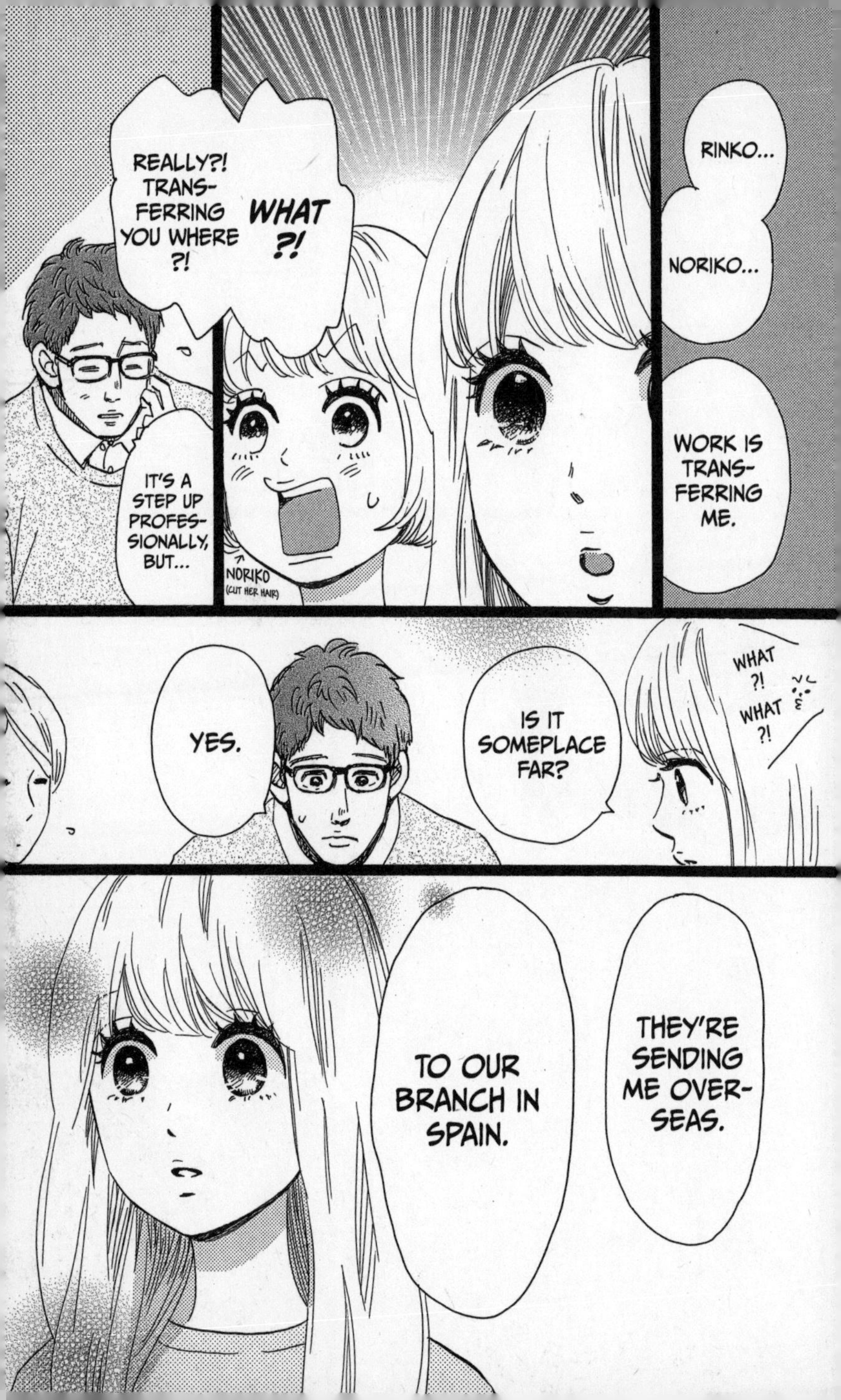
RINKO...
NORIKO...
WORK IS TRANSFERRING ME.
WHAT ?!
REALLY?! TRANSFERRING YOU WHERE ?!
IT'S A STEP UP PROFESSIONALLY, BUT...
NORIKO (CUT HER HAIR)
WHAT ?! WHAT ?!
IS IT SOMEPLACE FAR?
YES.
THEY'RE SENDING ME OVERSEAS.
TO OUR BRANCH IN SPAIN.

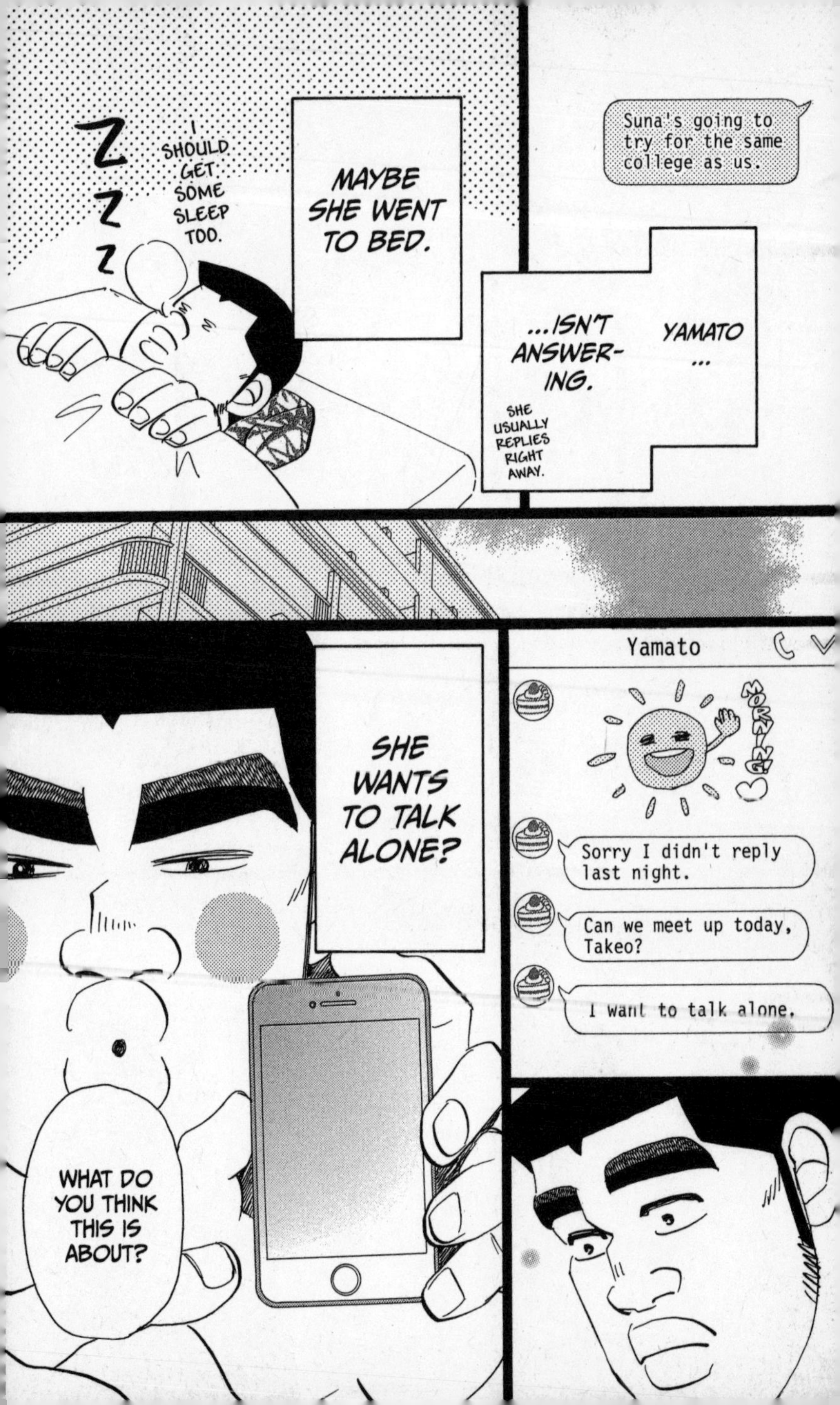
Suna's going to try for the same college as us.
YAMATO ...
...ISN'T ANSWERING.
SHE USUALLY REPLIES RIGHT AWAY.
MAYBE SHE WENT TO BED.
I SHOULD GET SOME SLEEP TOO.
Z Z Z
Yamato
MORNING!
Sorry I didn't reply last night.
Can we meet up today, Takeo?
I want to talk alone.
SHE WANTS TO TALK ALONE?
WHAT DO YOU THINK THIS IS ABOUT?

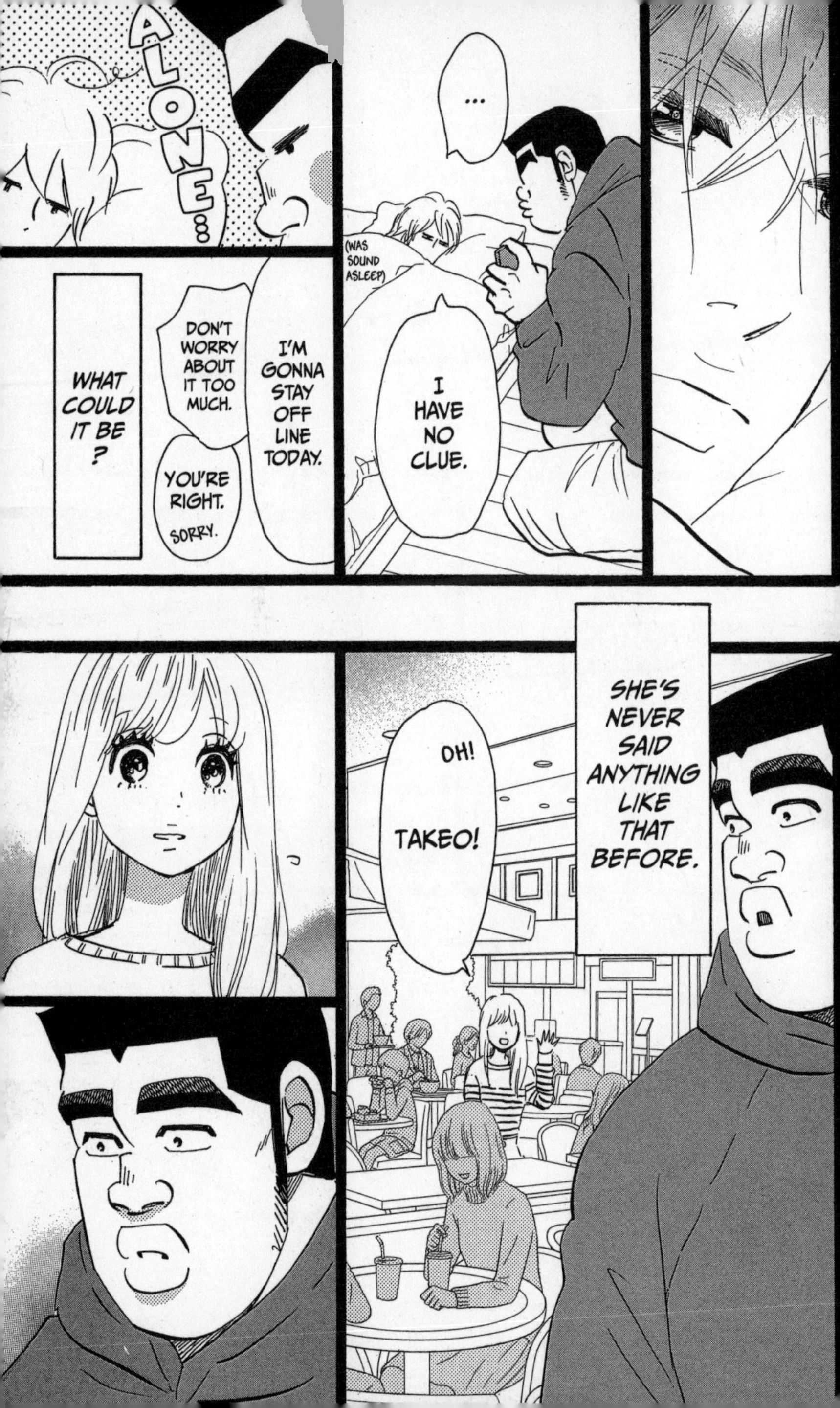
...
(WAS SOUND ASLEEP)
I HAVE NO CLUE.
ALONE...
I'M GONNA STAY OFF LINE TODAY.
DON'T WORRY ABOUT IT TOO MUCH.
YOU'RE RIGHT. SORRY.
WHAT COULD IT BE?
SHE'S NEVER SAID ANYTHING LIKE THAT BEFORE.
OH! TAKEO!

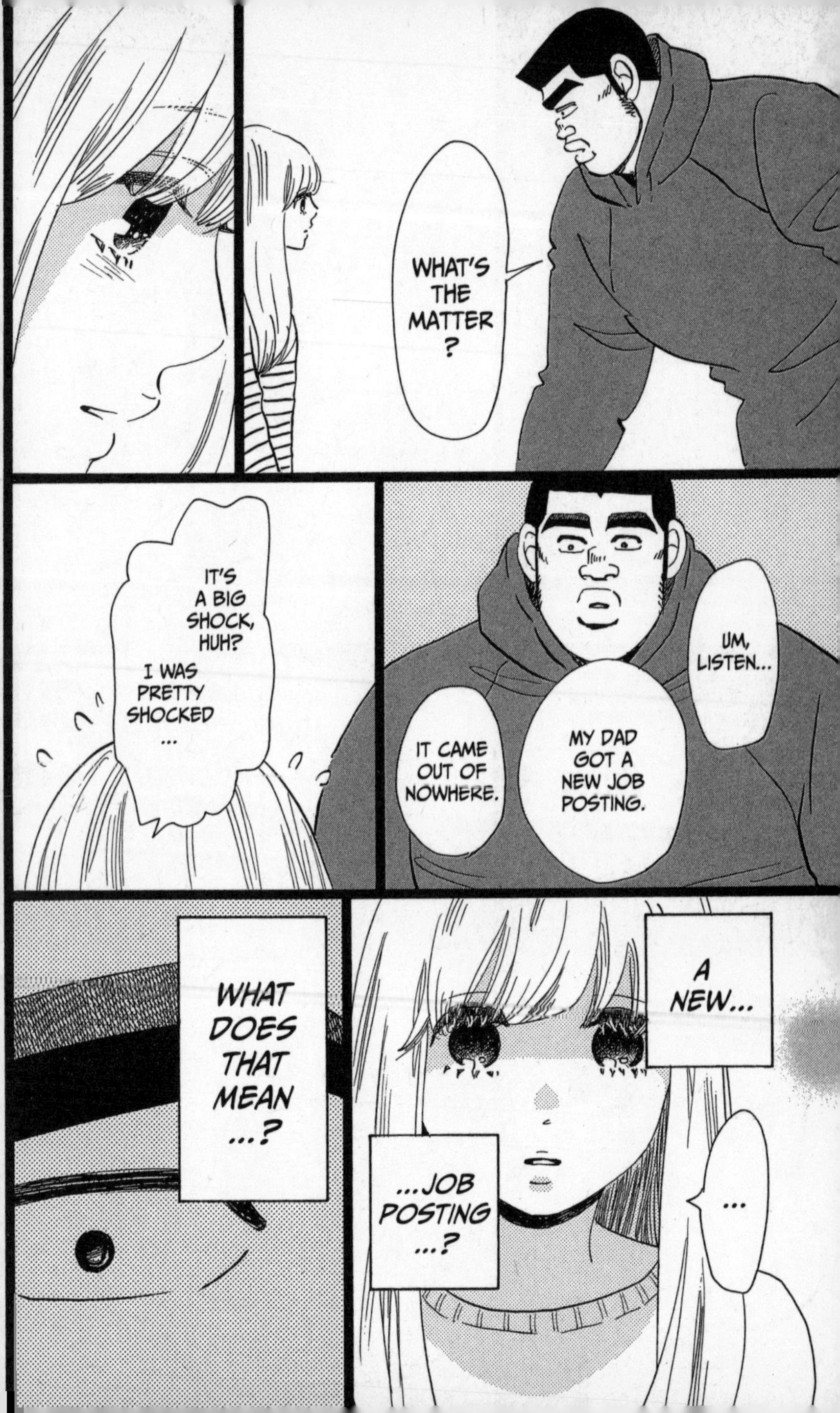
WHAT'S THE MATTER ?
UM, LISTEN...
MY DAD GOT A NEW JOB POSTING.
IT CAME OUT OF NOWHERE.
IT'S A BIG SHOCK, HUH?
I WAS PRETTY SHOCKED ...
A NEW...
...
...JOB POSTING ...?
WHAT DOES THAT MEAN ...?

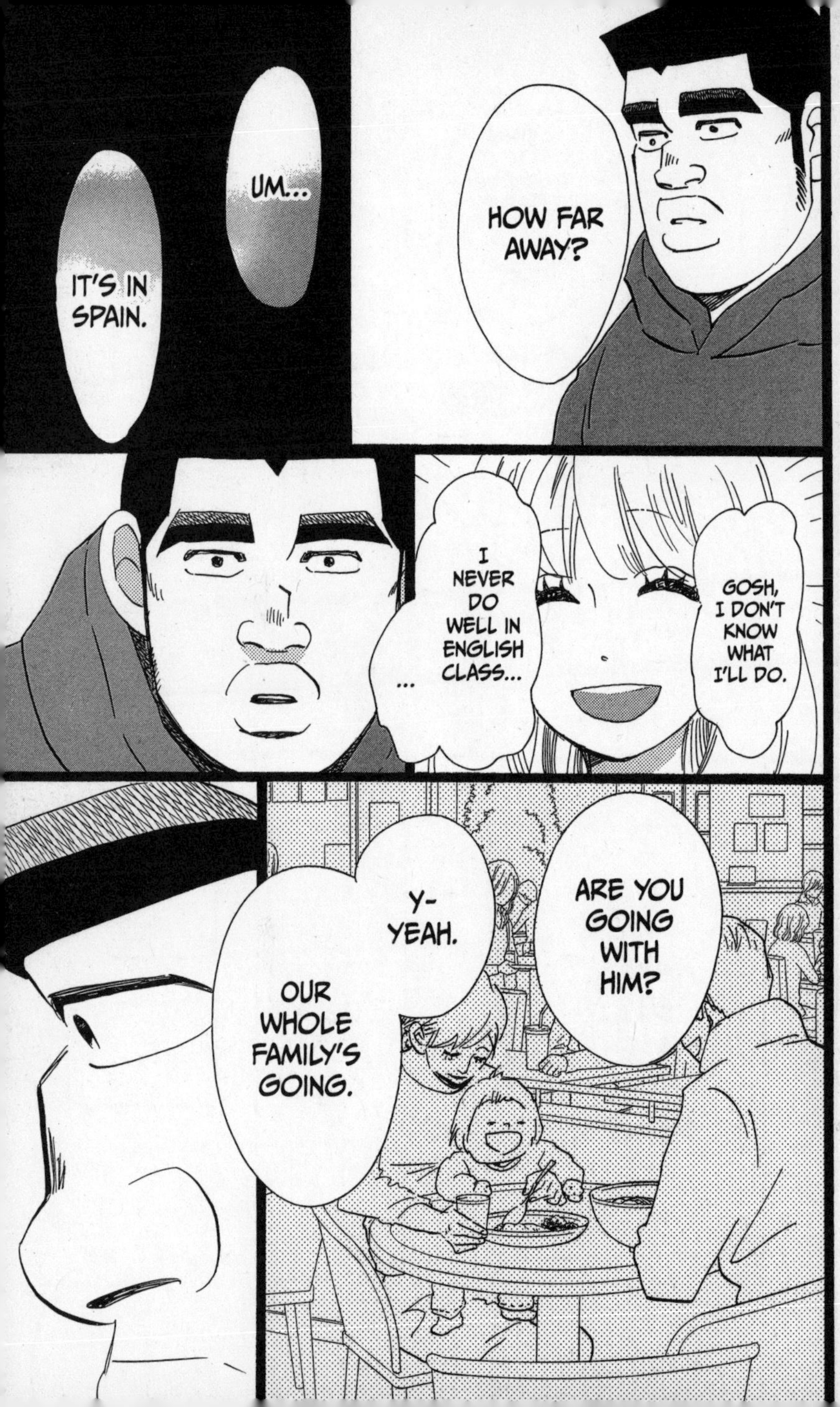
HOW FAR AWAY?
UM...
IT'S IN SPAIN.
GOSH, I DON'T KNOW WHAT I'LL DO.
I NEVER DO WELL IN ENGLISH CLASS...
...
ARE YOU GOING WITH HIM?
Y-YEAH.
OUR WHOLE FAMILY'S GOING.

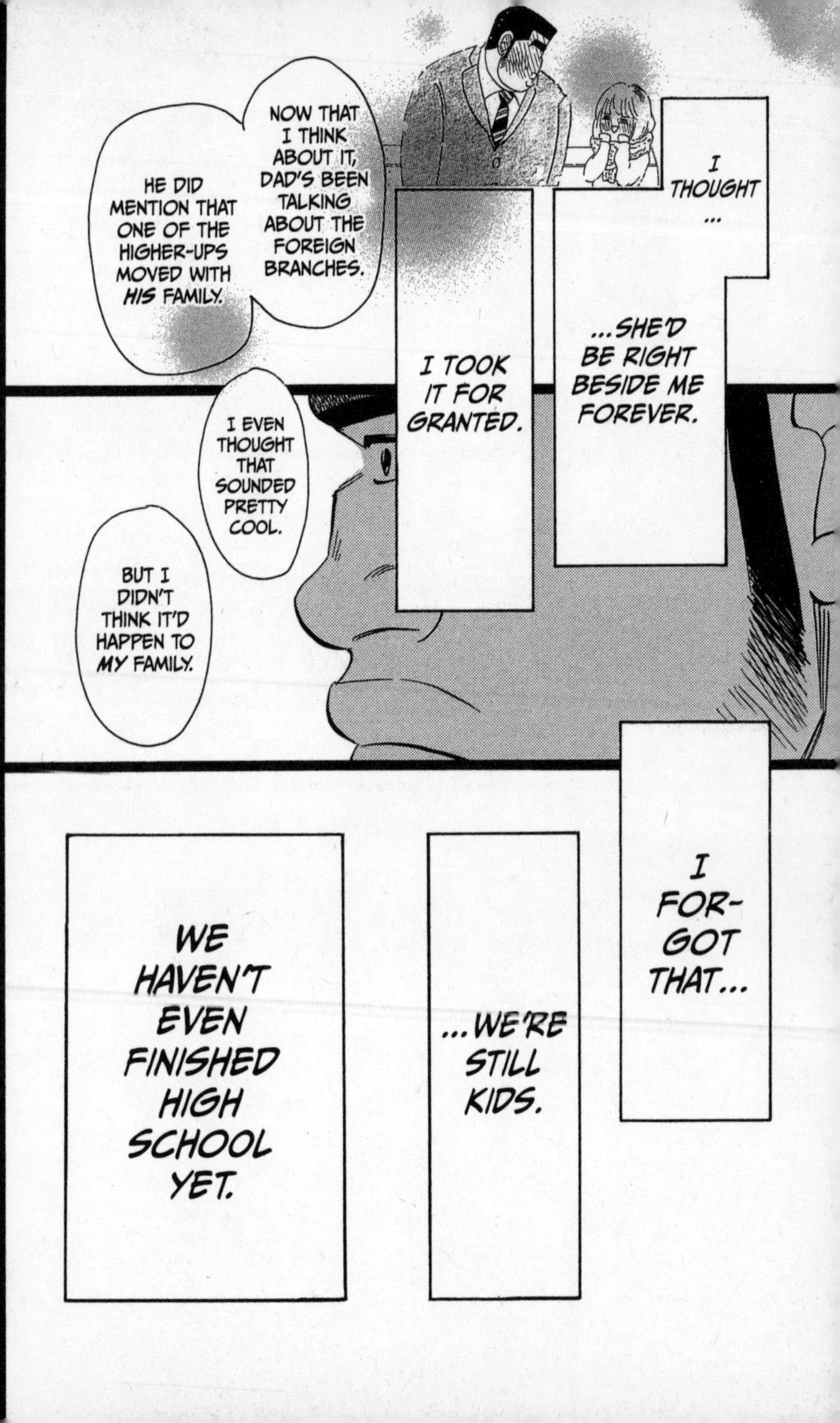
I THOUGHT ...
...SHE'D BE RIGHT BESIDE ME FOREVER.
I TOOK IT FOR GRANTED.
NOW THAT I THINK ABOUT IT, DAD'S BEEN TALKING ABOUT THE FOREIGN BRANCHES.
HE DID MENTION THAT ONE OF THE HIGHER-UPS MOVED WITH *HIS* FAMILY.
I EVEN THOUGHT THAT SOUNDED PRETTY COOL.
BUT I DIDN'T THINK IT'D HAPPEN TO *MY* FAMILY.
I FOR-GOT THAT...
...WE'RE STILL KIDS.
WE HAVEN'T EVEN FINISHED HIGH SCHOOL YET.

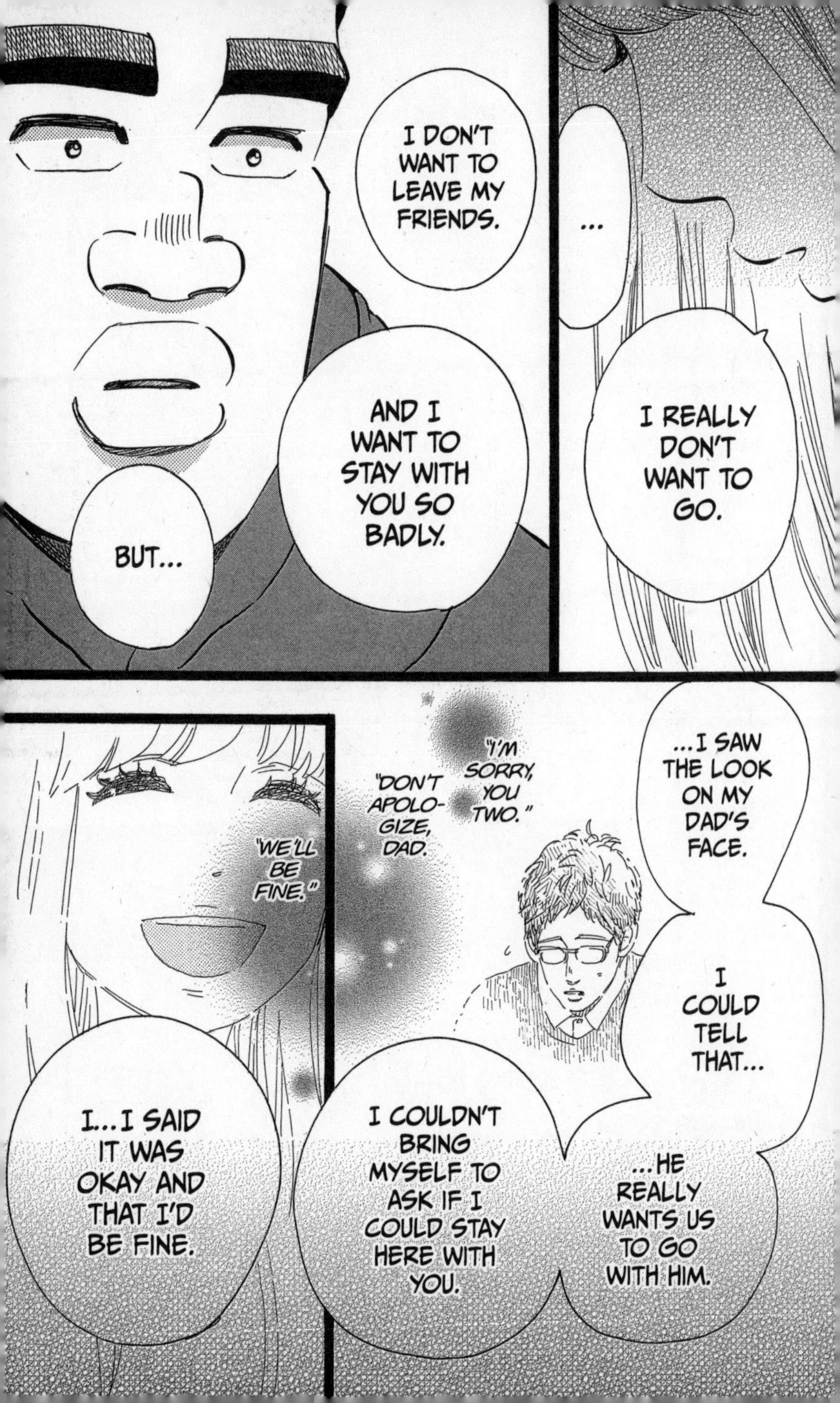
...
I REALLY DON'T WANT TO GO.
I DON'T WANT TO LEAVE MY FRIENDS.
AND I WANT TO STAY WITH YOU SO BADLY.
BUT...
...I SAW THE LOOK ON MY DAD'S FACE.
I COULD TELL THAT...
...HE REALLY WANTS US TO GO WITH HIM.
"I'M SORRY, YOU TWO."
"DON'T APOLOGIZE, DAD.
I COULDN'T BRING MYSELF TO ASK IF I COULD STAY HERE WITH YOU.
"WE'LL BE FINE."
I...I SAID IT WAS OKAY AND THAT I'D BE FINE.

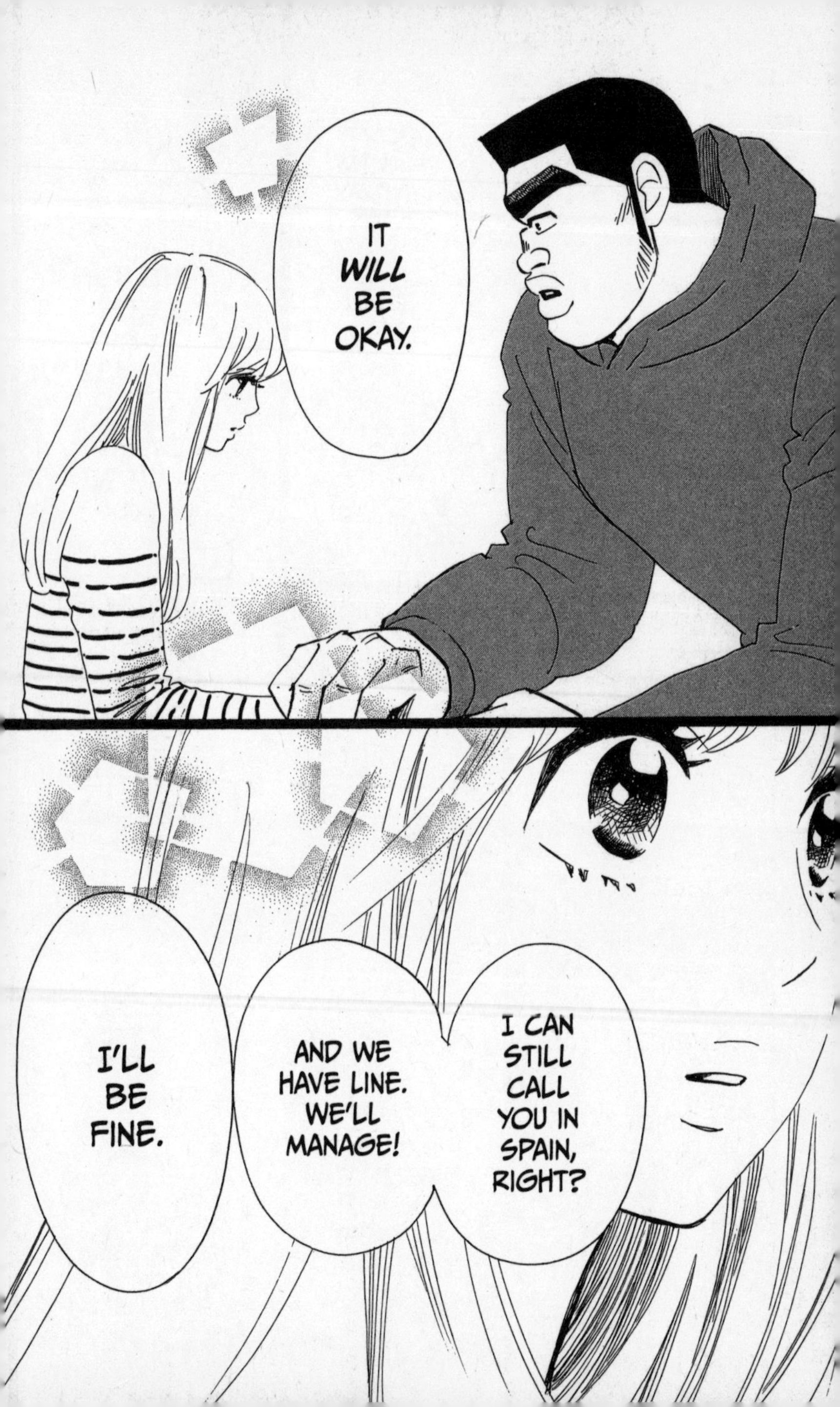
IT *WILL* BE OKAY.
I CAN STILL CALL YOU IN SPAIN, RIGHT?
AND WE HAVE LINE. WE'LL MANAGE!
I'LL BE FINE.

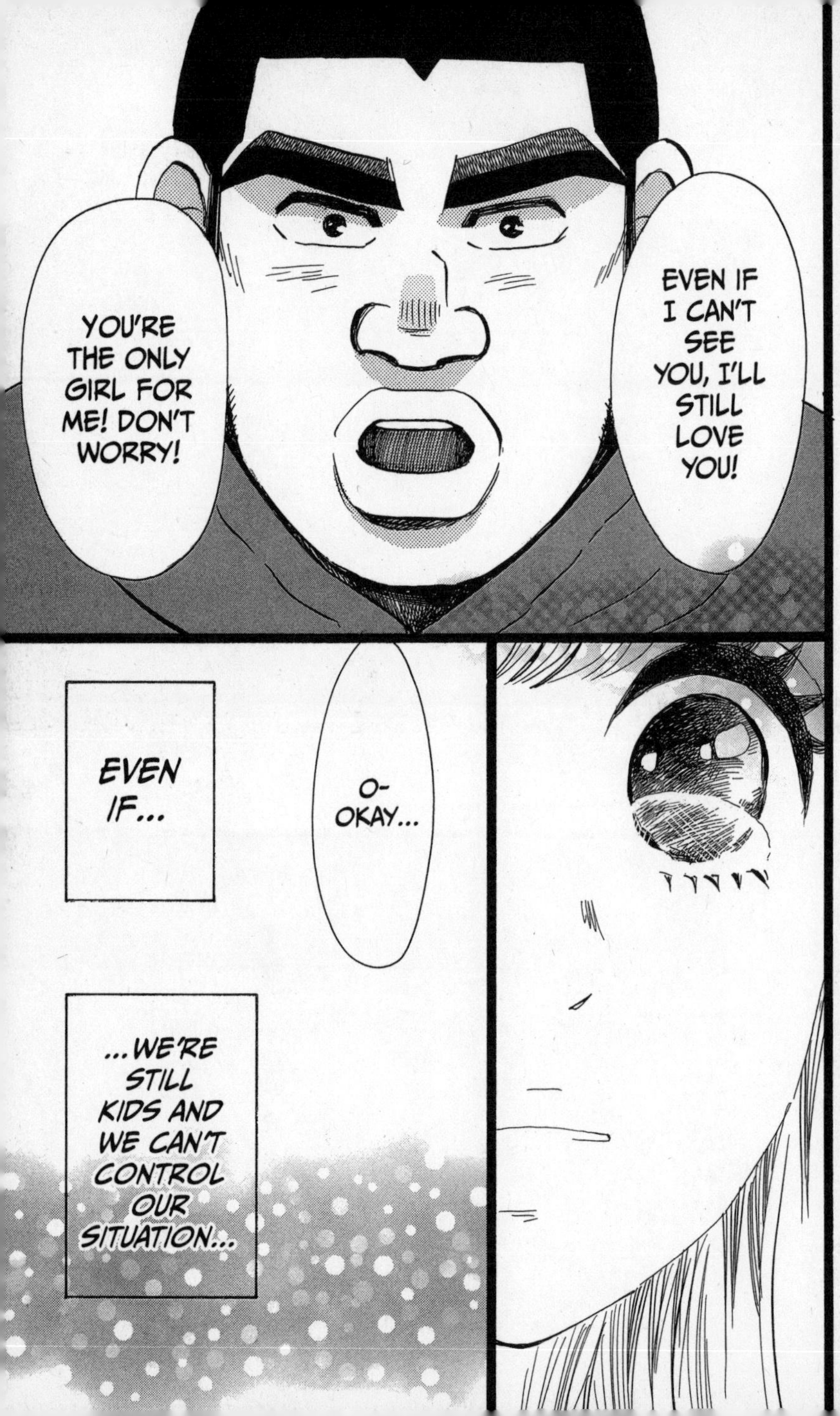
EVEN IF I CAN'T SEE YOU, I'LL STILL LOVE YOU!
YOU'RE THE ONLY GIRL FOR ME! DON'T WORRY!
O- OKAY...
EVEN IF...
...WE'RE STILL KIDS AND WE CAN'T CONTROL OUR SITUATION...

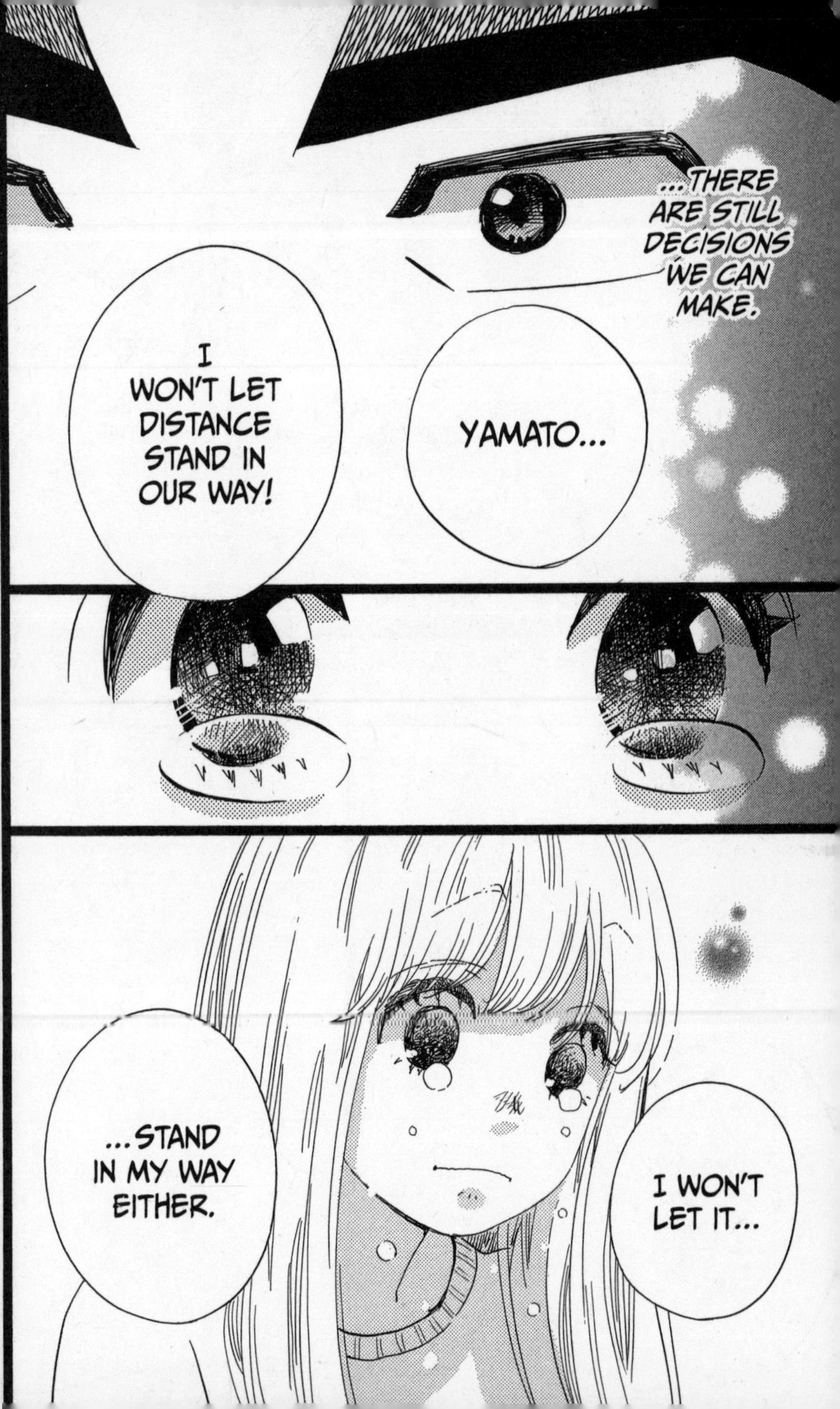
...THERE ARE STILL DECISIONS WE CAN MAKE.
YAMATO...
I WON'T LET DISTANCE STAND IN OUR WAY!
I WON'T LET IT...
...STAND IN MY WAY EITHER.

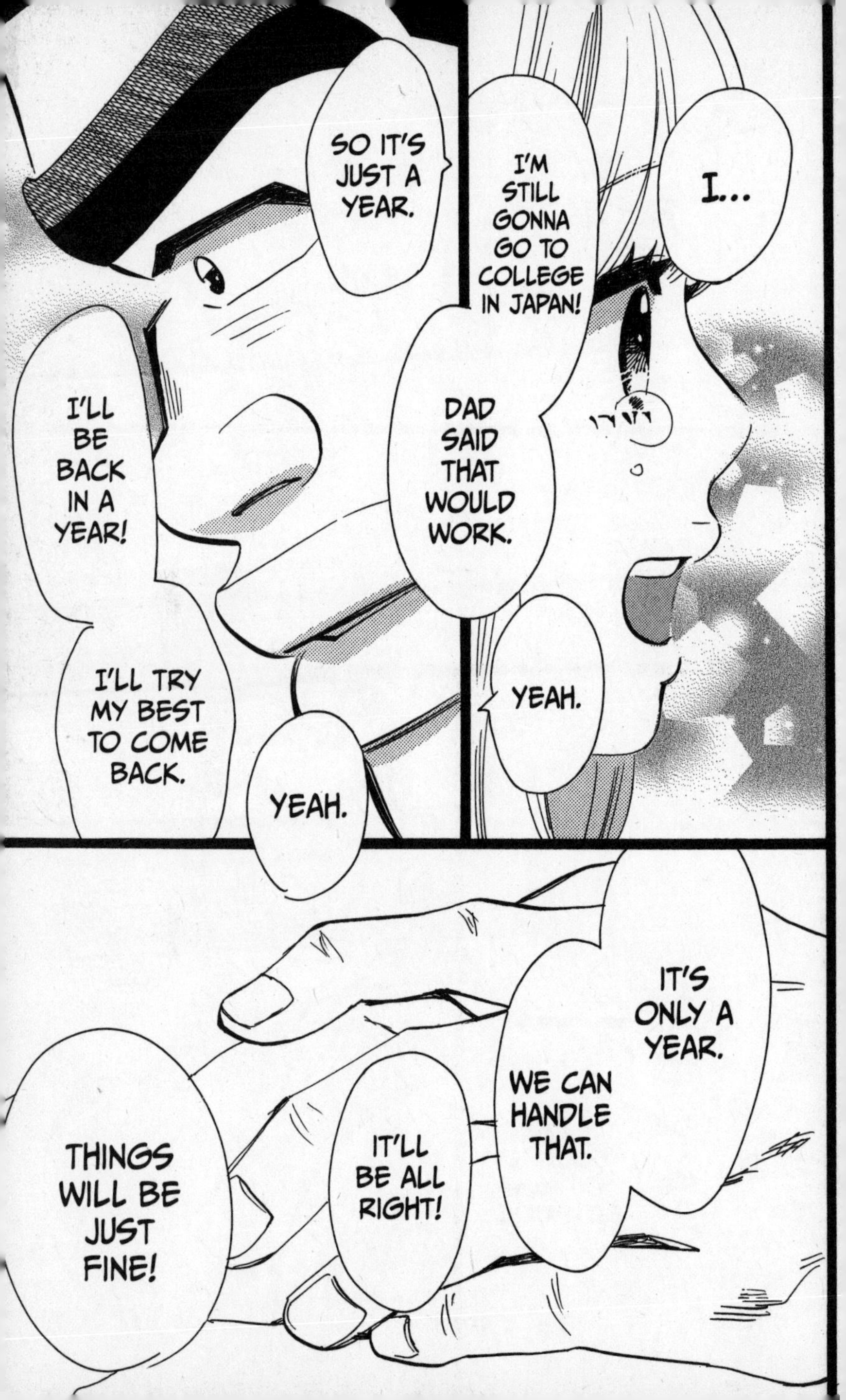
I...
I'M STILL GONNA GO TO COLLEGE IN JAPAN!
DAD SAID THAT WOULD WORK.
YEAH.
SO IT'S JUST A YEAR.
I'LL BE BACK IN A YEAR!
I'LL TRY MY BEST TO COME BACK.
YEAH.
IT'S ONLY A YEAR.
WE CAN HANDLE THAT.
IT'LL BE ALL RIGHT!
THINGS WILL BE JUST FINE!

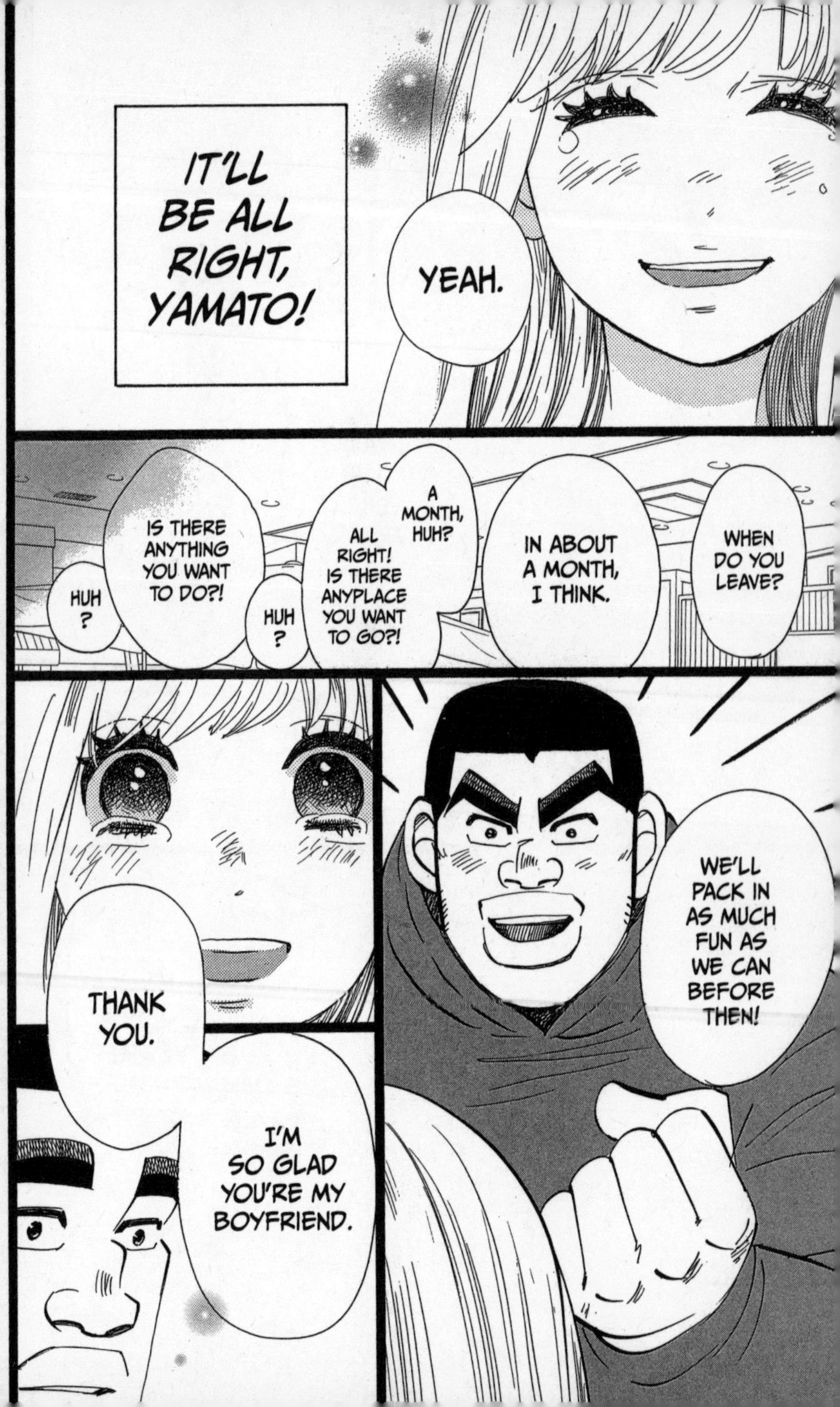
YEAH.
IT'LL BE ALL RIGHT, YAMATO!
WHEN DO YOU LEAVE?
IN ABOUT A MONTH, I THINK.
A MONTH, HUH?
ALL RIGHT! IS THERE ANYPLACE YOU WANT TO GO?!
HUH?
IS THERE ANYTHING YOU WANT TO DO?!
HUH?
WE'LL PACK IN AS MUCH FUN AS WE CAN BEFORE THEN!
THANK YOU.
I'M SO GLAD YOU'RE MY BOYFRIEND.

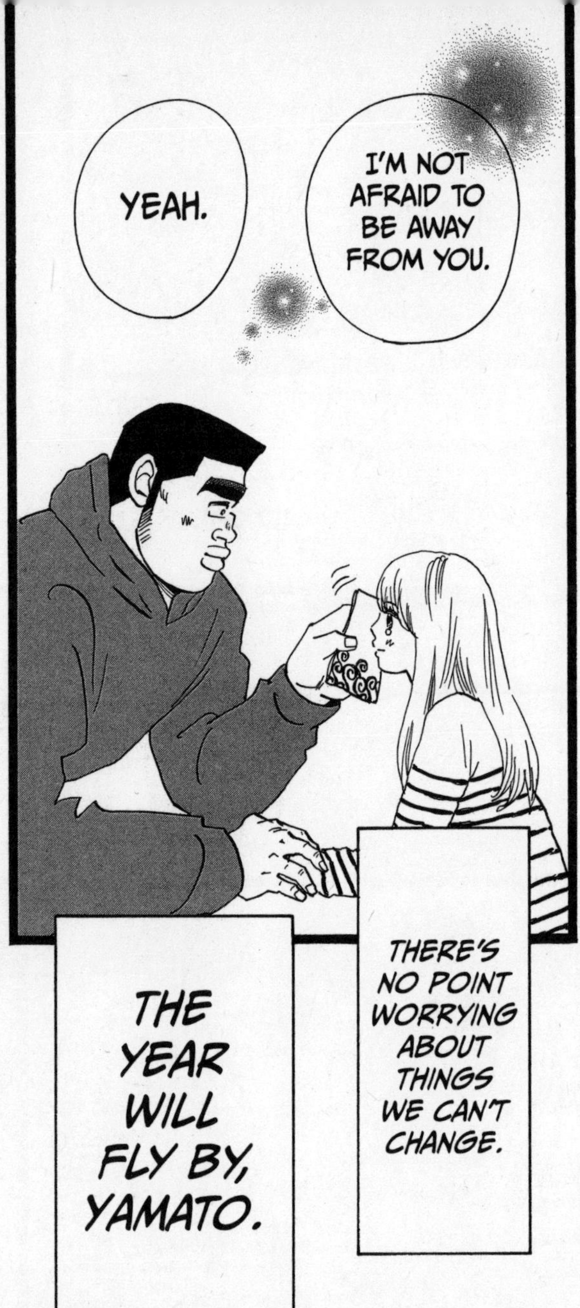
I'M NOT AFRAID TO BE AWAY FROM YOU.
YEAH.
THERE'S NO POINT WORRYING ABOUT THINGS WE CAN'T CHANGE.
THE YEAR WILL FLY BY, YAMATO.

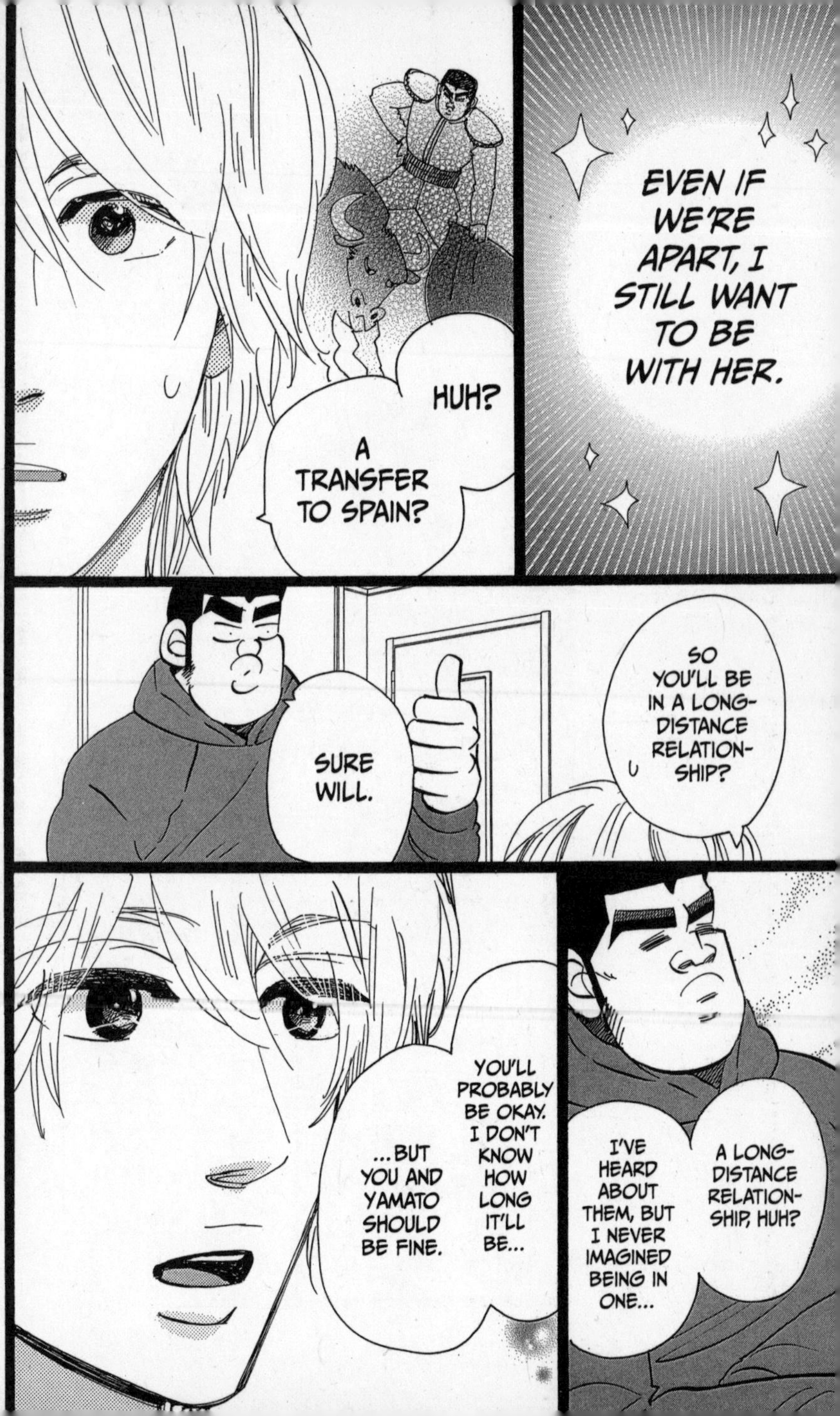
EVEN IF WE'RE APART, I STILL WANT TO BE WITH HER.
HUH?
A TRANSFER TO SPAIN?
SO YOU'LL BE IN A LONG-DISTANCE RELATIONSHIP?
SURE WILL.
A LONG-DISTANCE RELATIONSHIP, HUH?
I'VE HEARD ABOUT THEM, BUT I NEVER IMAGINED BEING IN ONE...
YOU'LL PROBABLY BE OKAY. I DON'T KNOW HOW LONG IT'LL BE...
...BUT YOU AND YAMATO SHOULD BE FINE.

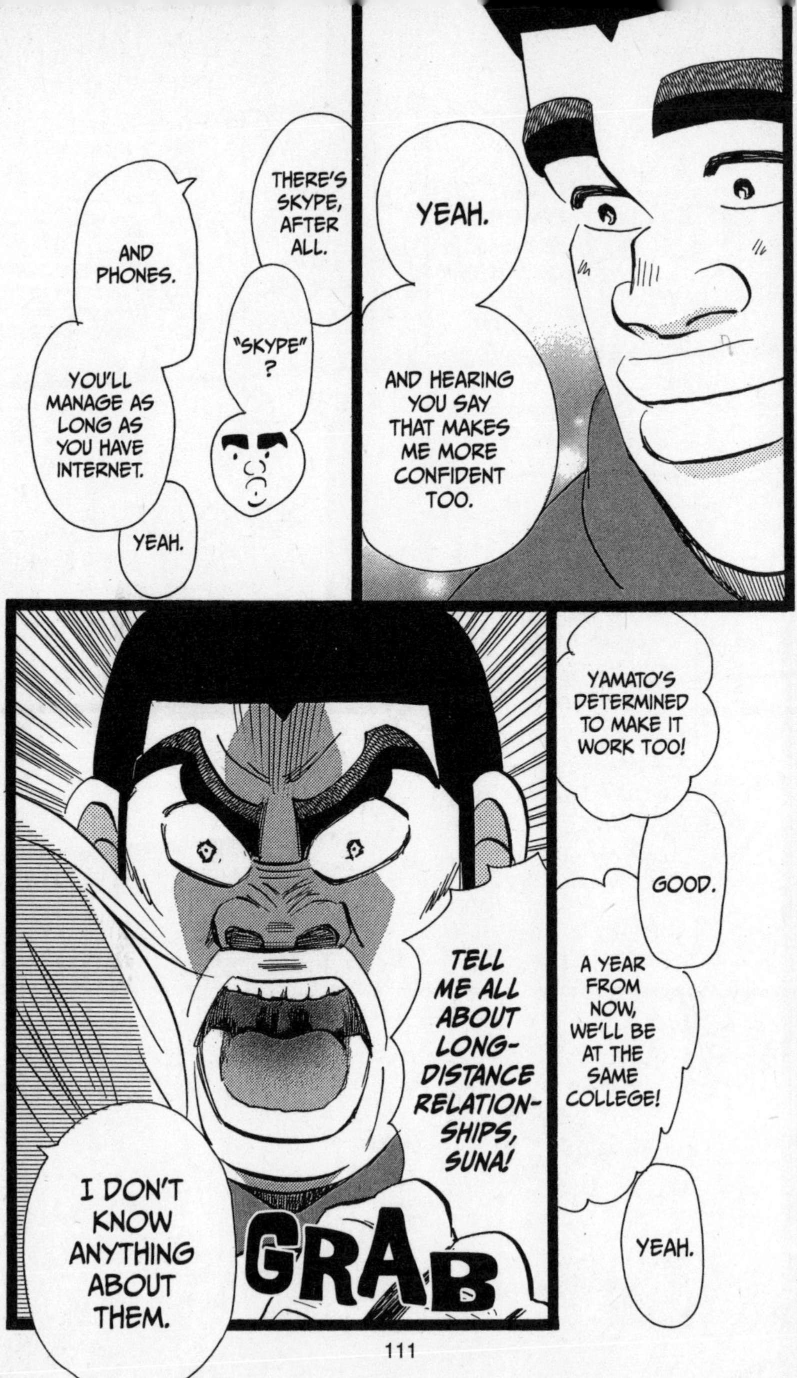
YEAH.
AND HEARING YOU SAY THAT MAKES ME MORE CONFIDENT TOO.
THERE'S SKYPE, AFTER ALL.
"SKYPE" ?
AND PHONES.
YOU'LL MANAGE AS LONG AS YOU HAVE INTERNET.
YEAH.
YAMATO'S DETERMINED TO MAKE IT WORK TOO!
GOOD.
A YEAR FROM NOW, WE'LL BE AT THE SAME COLLEGE!
YEAH.
TELL ME ALL ABOUT LONG-DISTANCE RELATIONSHIPS, SUNA!
GRAB
I DON'T KNOW ANYTHING ABOUT THEM.

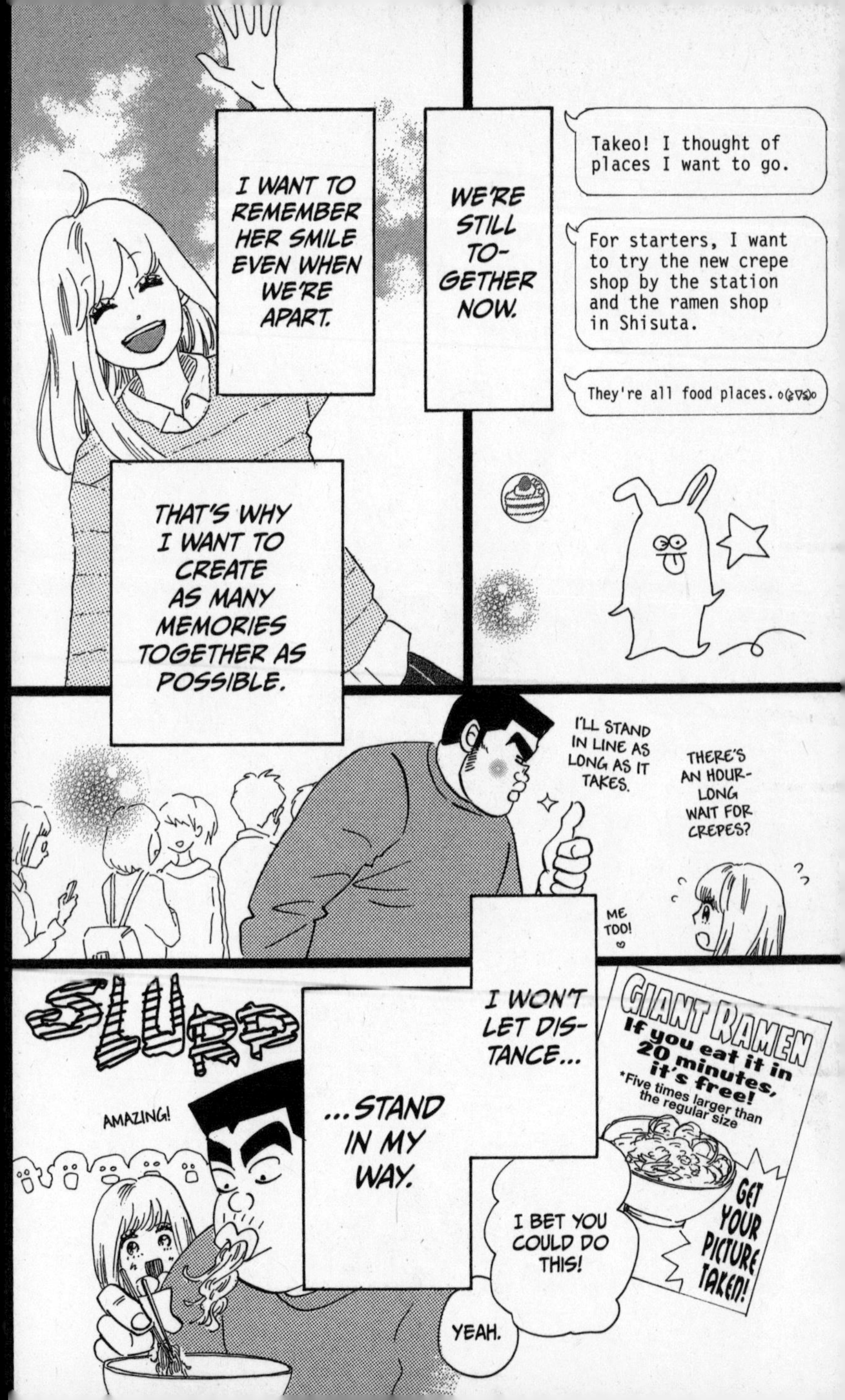
Takeo! I thought of places I want to go.
For starters, I want to try the new crepe shop by the station and the ramen shop in Shisuta.
They're all food places. o(≧▽≦)o
WE'RE STILL TO-GETHER NOW.
I WANT TO REMEMBER HER SMILE EVEN WHEN WE'RE APART.
THAT'S WHY I WANT TO CREATE AS MANY MEMORIES TOGETHER AS POSSIBLE.
THERE'S AN HOUR-LONG WAIT FOR CREPES?
I'LL STAND IN LINE AS LONG AS IT TAKES.
ME TOO!
GIANT RAMEN
If you eat it in 20 minutes, it's free!
*Five times larger than the regular size
GET YOUR PICTURE TAKEN!
I WON'T LET DIS-TANCE...
...STAND IN MY WAY.
I BET YOU COULD DO THIS!
YEAH.
SLURP
AMAZING!

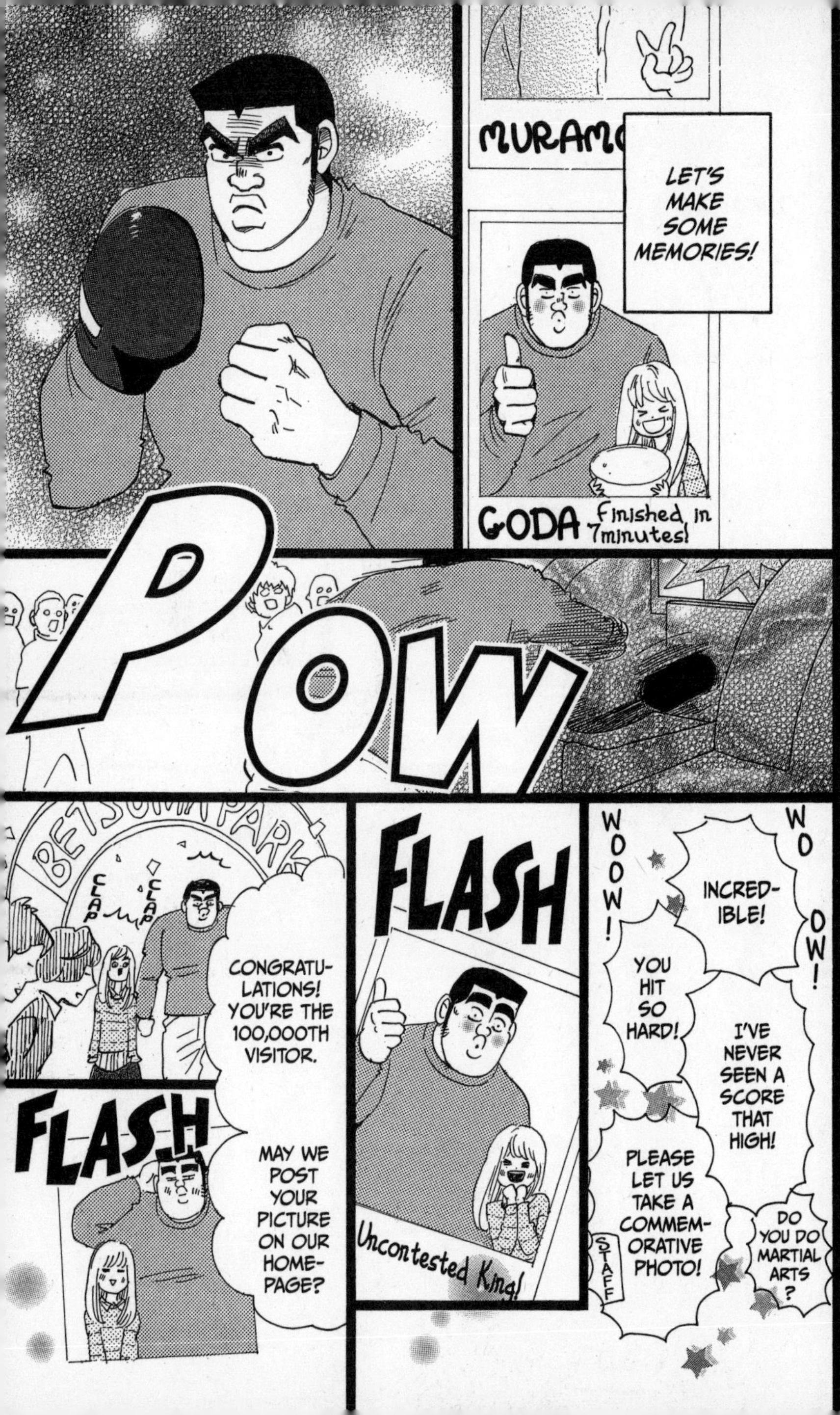
MURAMO
LET'S MAKE SOME MEMORIES!
GODA Finished in 7minutes!
POW
WO OW!
INCRED-IBLE!
WOOW!
YOU HIT SO HARD!
I'VE NEVER SEEN A SCORE THAT HIGH!
DO YOU DO MARTIAL ARTS?
STAFF
PLEASE LET US TAKE A COMMEM-ORATIVE PHOTO!
FLASH
Uncontested King!
BETSUMA PARK
CLAP CLAP
CONGRATU-LATIONS! YOU'RE THE 100,000TH VISITOR.
FLASH
MAY WE POST YOUR PICTURE ON OUR HOME-PAGE?

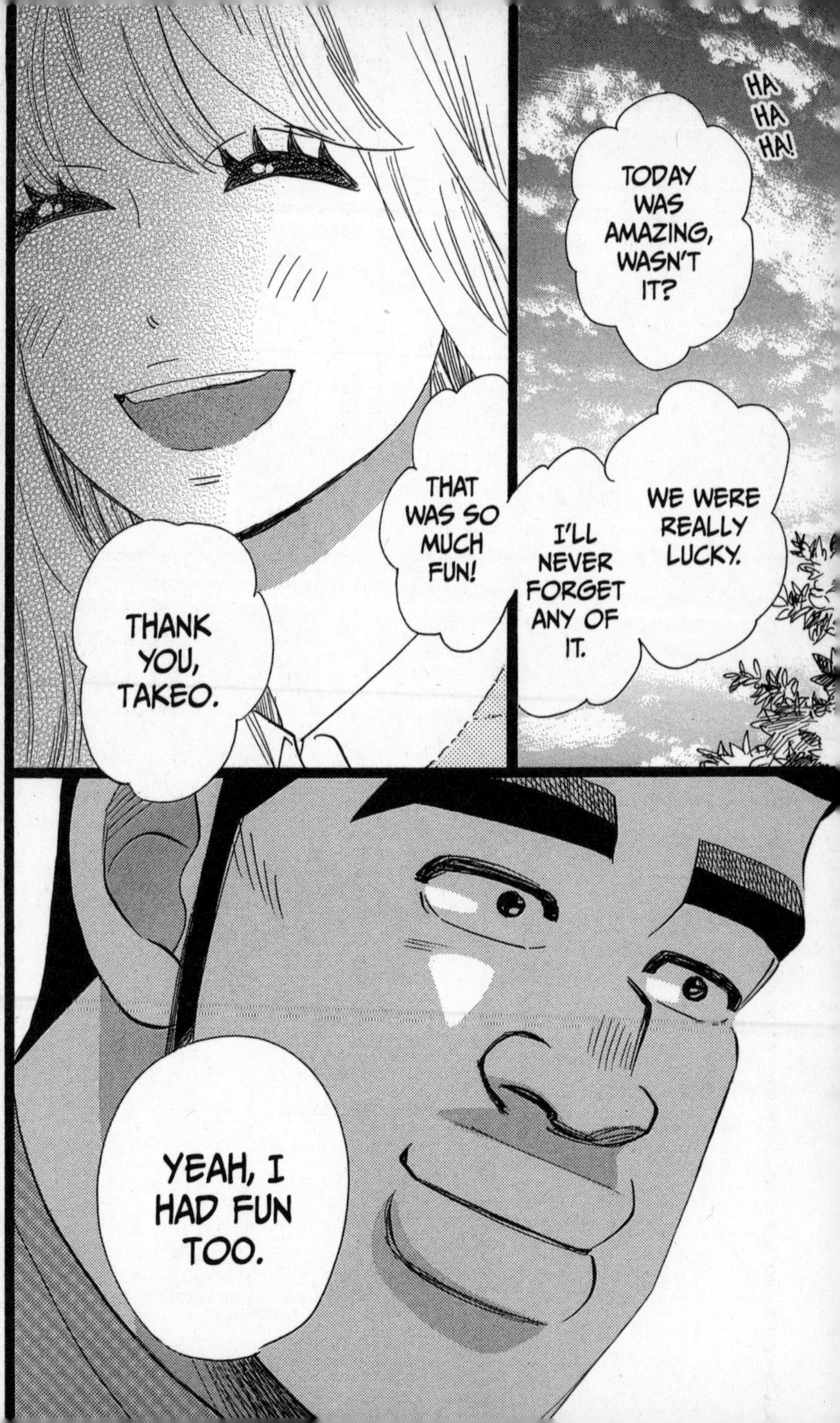
HA HA HA!
TODAY WAS AMAZING, WASN'T IT?
WE WERE REALLY LUCKY.
I'LL NEVER FORGET ANY OF IT.
THAT WAS SO MUCH FUN!
THANK YOU, TAKEO.
YEAH, I HAD FUN TOO.

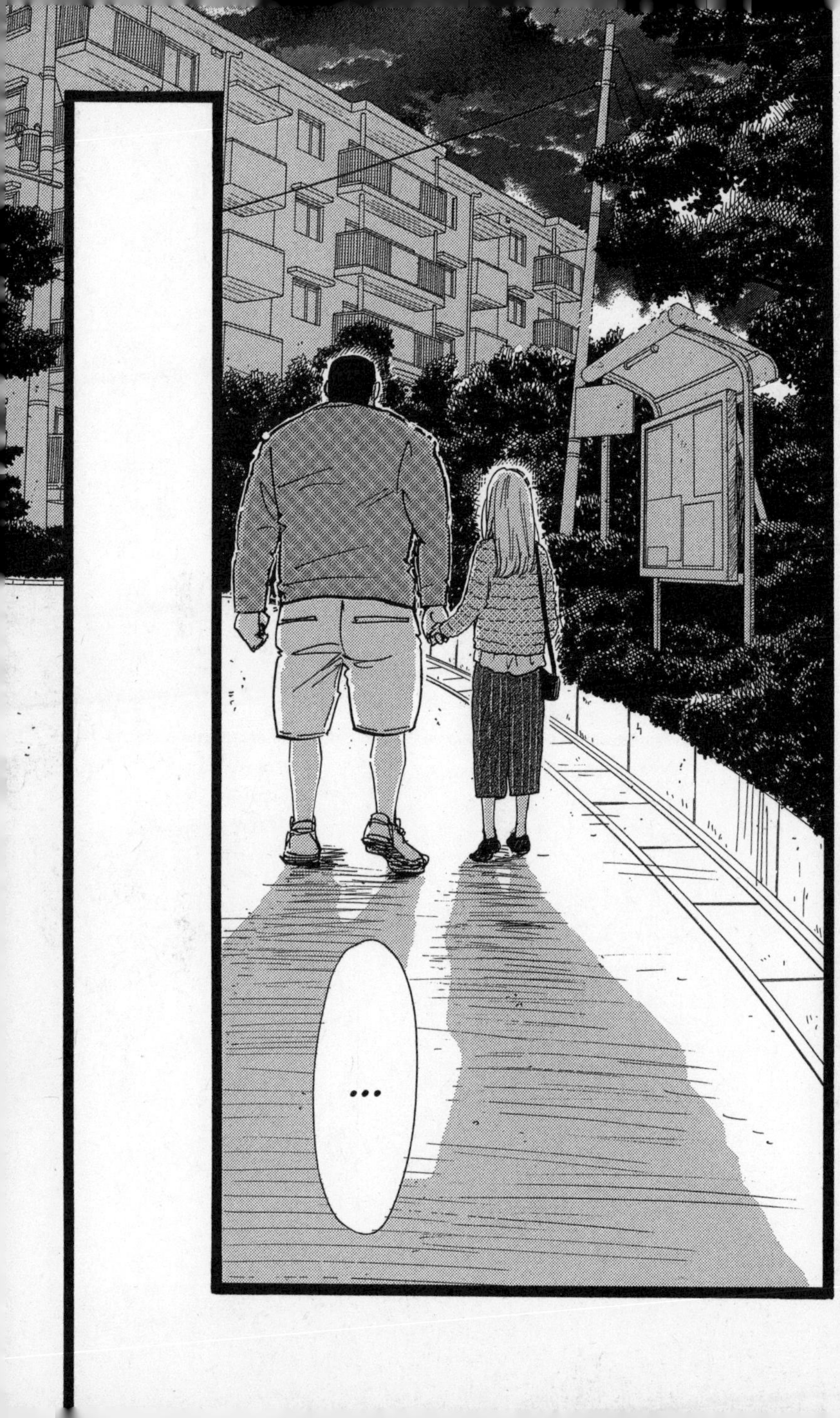
...

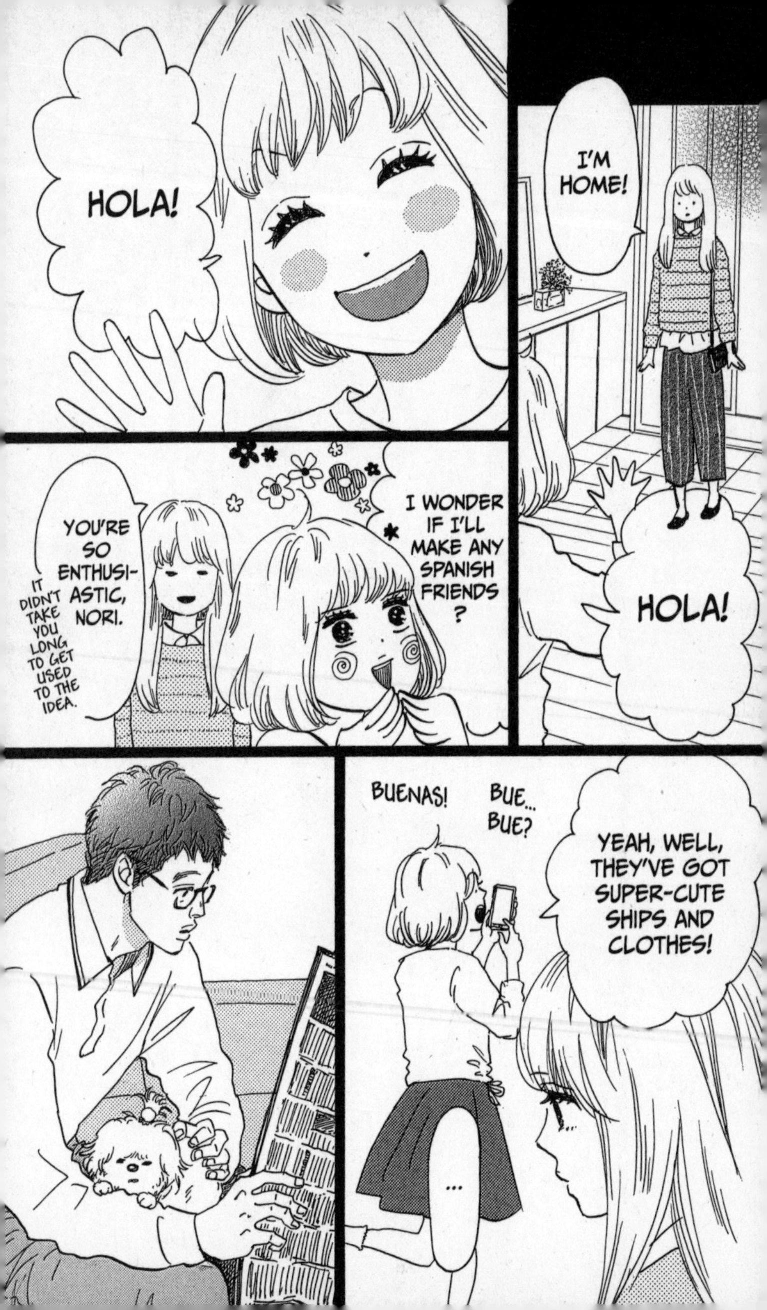
I'M HOME!
HOLA!
HOLA!
I WONDER IF I'LL MAKE ANY SPANISH FRIENDS ?
YOU'RE SO ENTHUSI-ASTIC, NORI.
IT DIDN'T TAKE YOU LONG TO GET USED TO THE IDEA.
YEAH, WELL, THEY'VE GOT SUPER-CUTE SHIPS AND CLOTHES!
BUE... BUE?
BUENAS!
...

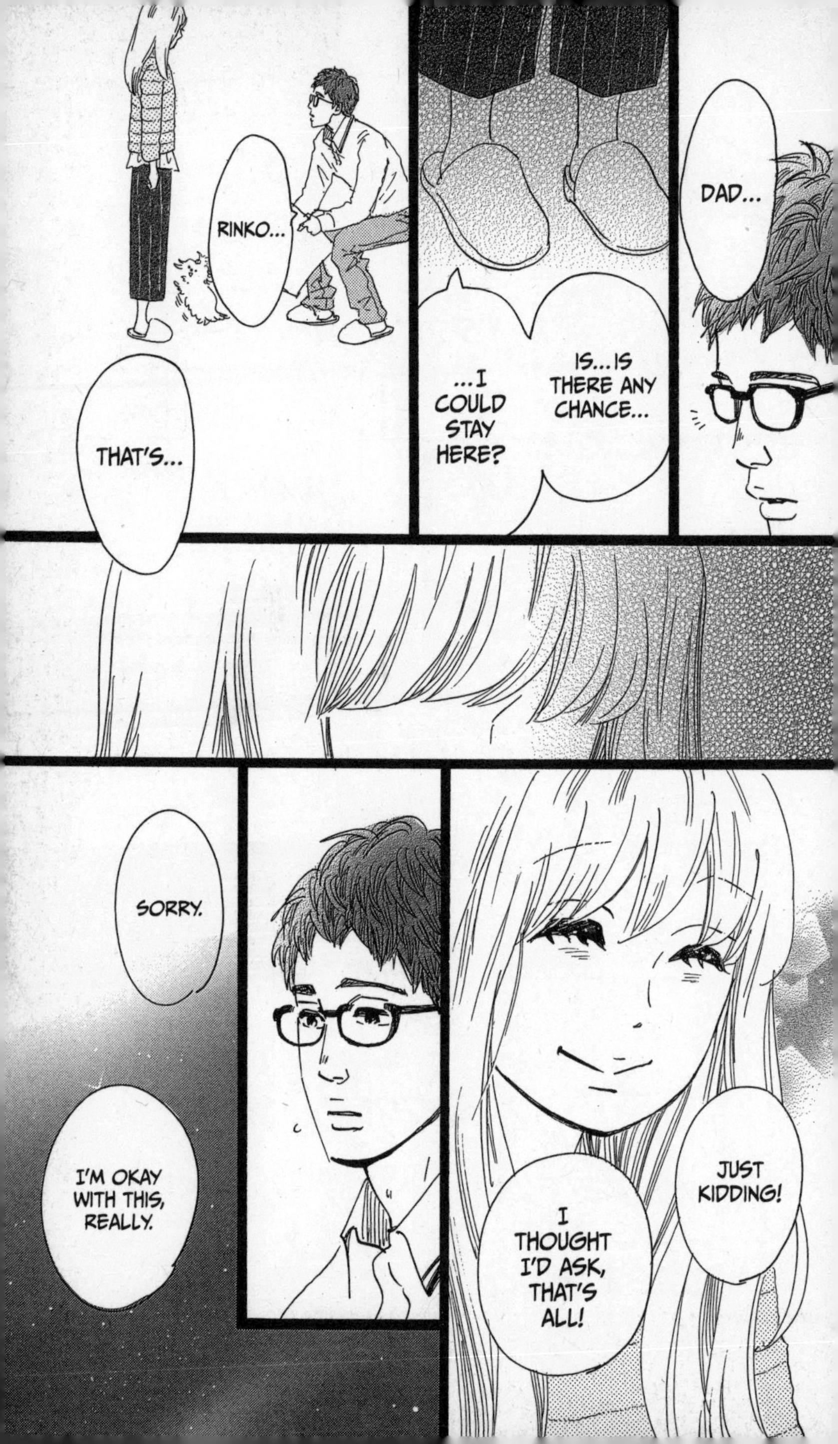
DAD...
IS... IS THERE ANY CHANCE...
...I COULD STAY HERE?
RINKO...
THAT'S...
JUST KIDDING!
I THOUGHT I'D ASK, THAT'S ALL!
SORRY.
I'M OKAY WITH THIS, REALLY.

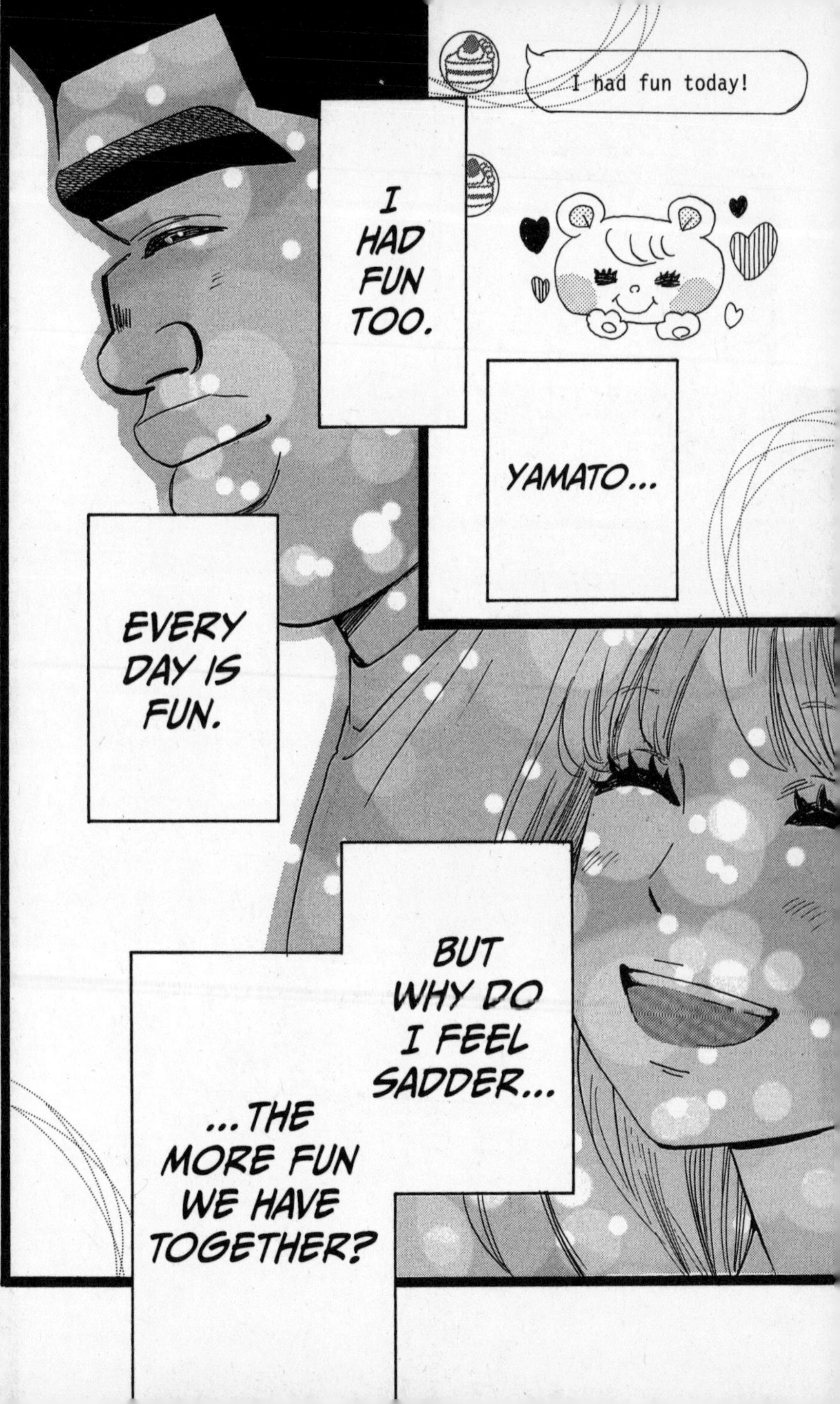
I had fun today!
YAMATO...
I HAD FUN TOO.
EVERY DAY IS FUN.
BUT WHY DO I FEEL SADDER...
...THE MORE FUN WE HAVE TOGETHER?

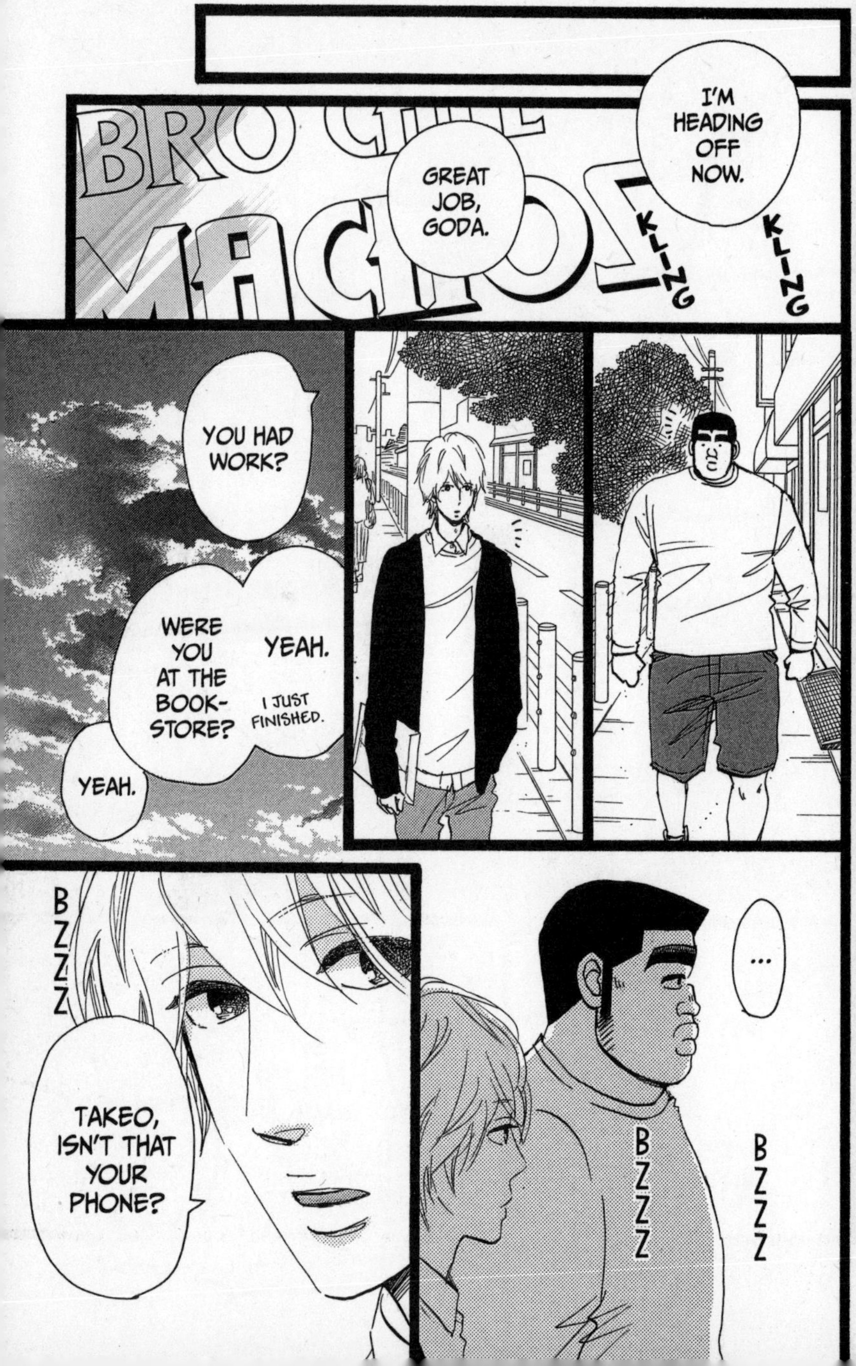

I'M HEADING OFF NOW.
KLING
GREAT JOB, GODA.
KLING
YOU HAD WORK?
YEAH.
I JUST FINISHED.
WERE YOU AT THE BOOK-STORE?
YEAH.
...
BZZZ
BZZZ
BZZZ
TAKEO, ISN'T THAT YOUR PHONE?

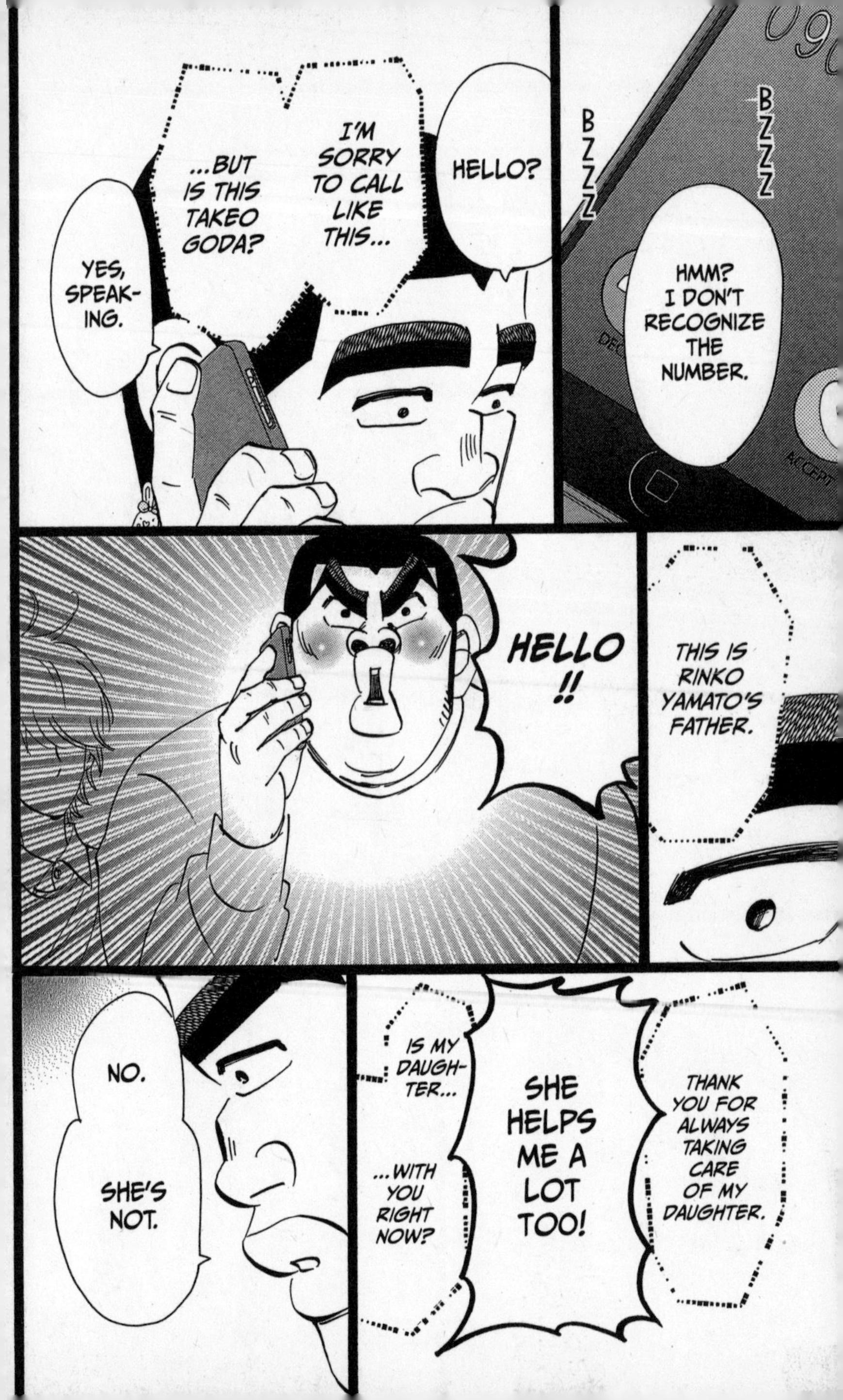
BZZZ
BZZZ
HMM? I DON'T RECOGNIZE THE NUMBER.
DECLINE
ACCEPT
HELLO?
I'M SORRY TO CALL LIKE THIS...
...BUT IS THIS TAKEO GODA?
YES, SPEAK-ING.
THIS IS RINKO YAMATO'S FATHER.
HELLO !!
THANK YOU FOR ALWAYS TAKING CARE OF MY DAUGHTER.
SHE HELPS ME A LOT TOO!
IS MY DAUGH-TER...
...WITH YOU RIGHT NOW?
NO.
SHE'S NOT.

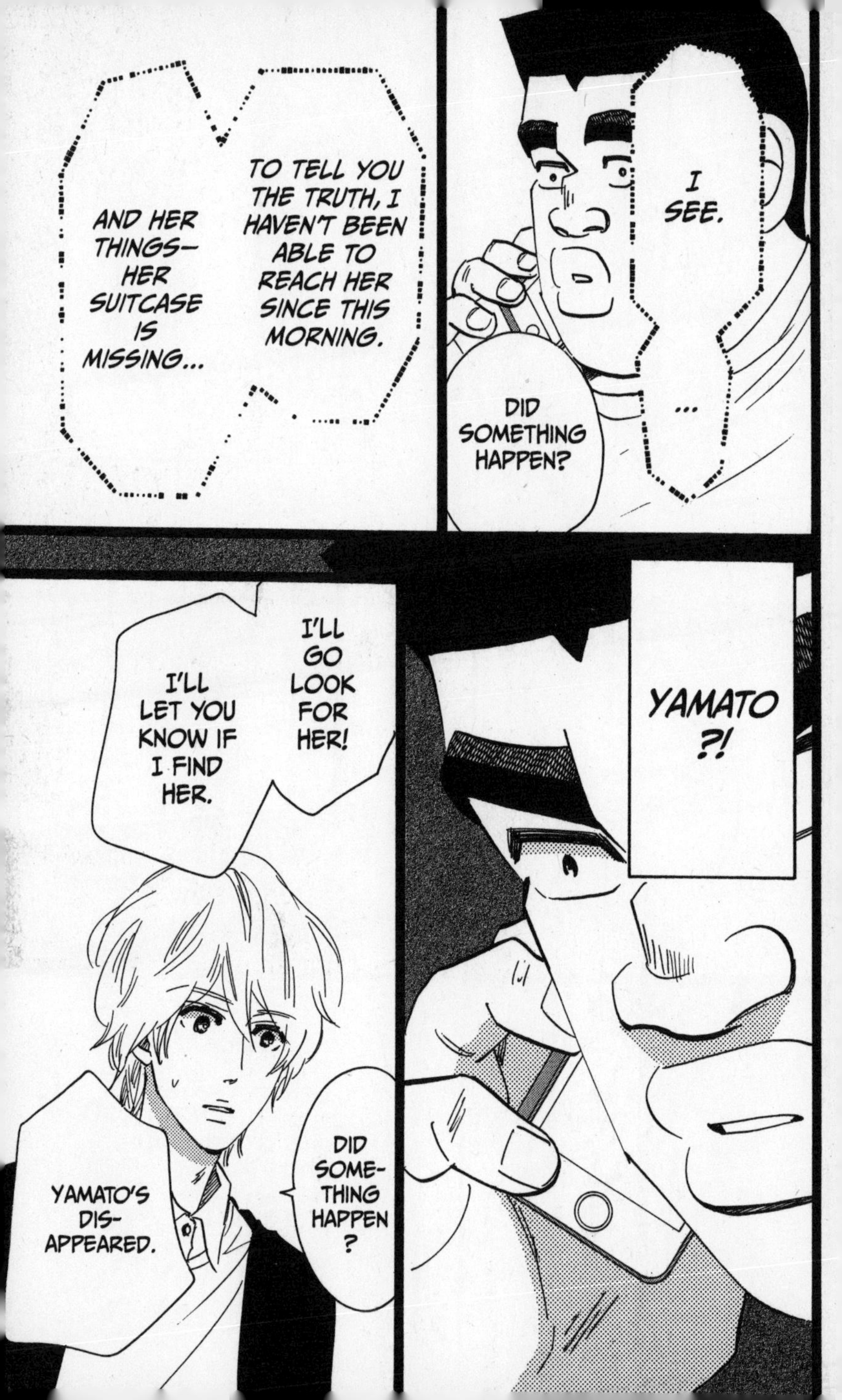
I SEE.
...
DID SOMETHING HAPPEN?
TO TELL YOU THE TRUTH, I HAVEN'T BEEN ABLE TO REACH HER SINCE THIS MORNING.
AND HER THINGS— HER SUITCASE IS MISSING...
YAMATO ?!
I'LL GO LOOK FOR HER!
I'LL LET YOU KNOW IF I FIND HER.
DID SOME-THING HAPPEN ?
YAMATO'S DIS-APPEARED.

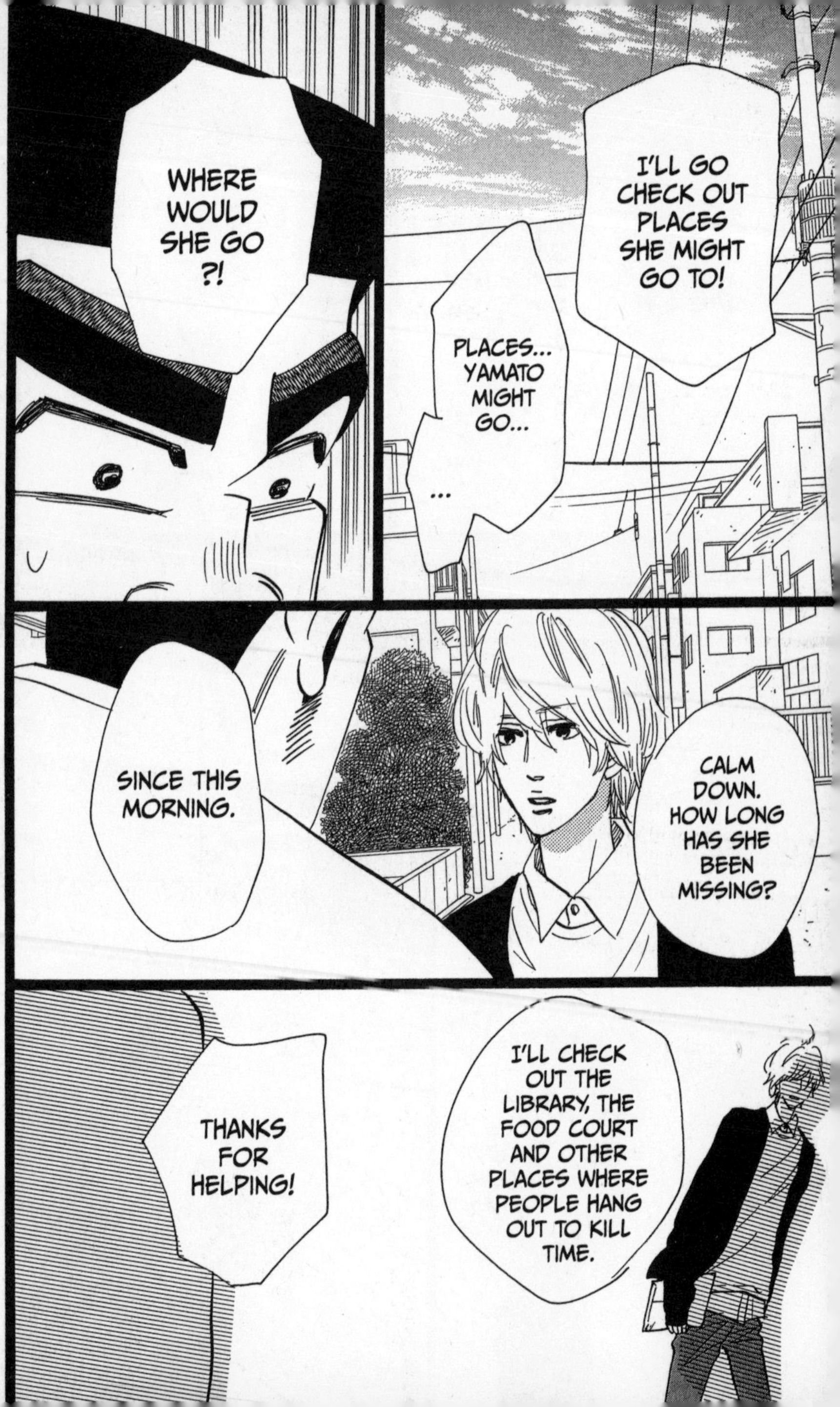
I'LL GO CHECK OUT PLACES SHE MIGHT GO TO!
PLACES... YAMATO MIGHT GO...
...
WHERE WOULD SHE GO ?!
CALM DOWN. HOW LONG HAS SHE BEEN MISSING?
SINCE THIS MORNING.
I'LL CHECK OUT THE LIBRARY, THE FOOD COURT AND OTHER PLACES WHERE PEOPLE HANG OUT TO KILL TIME.
THANKS FOR HELPING!

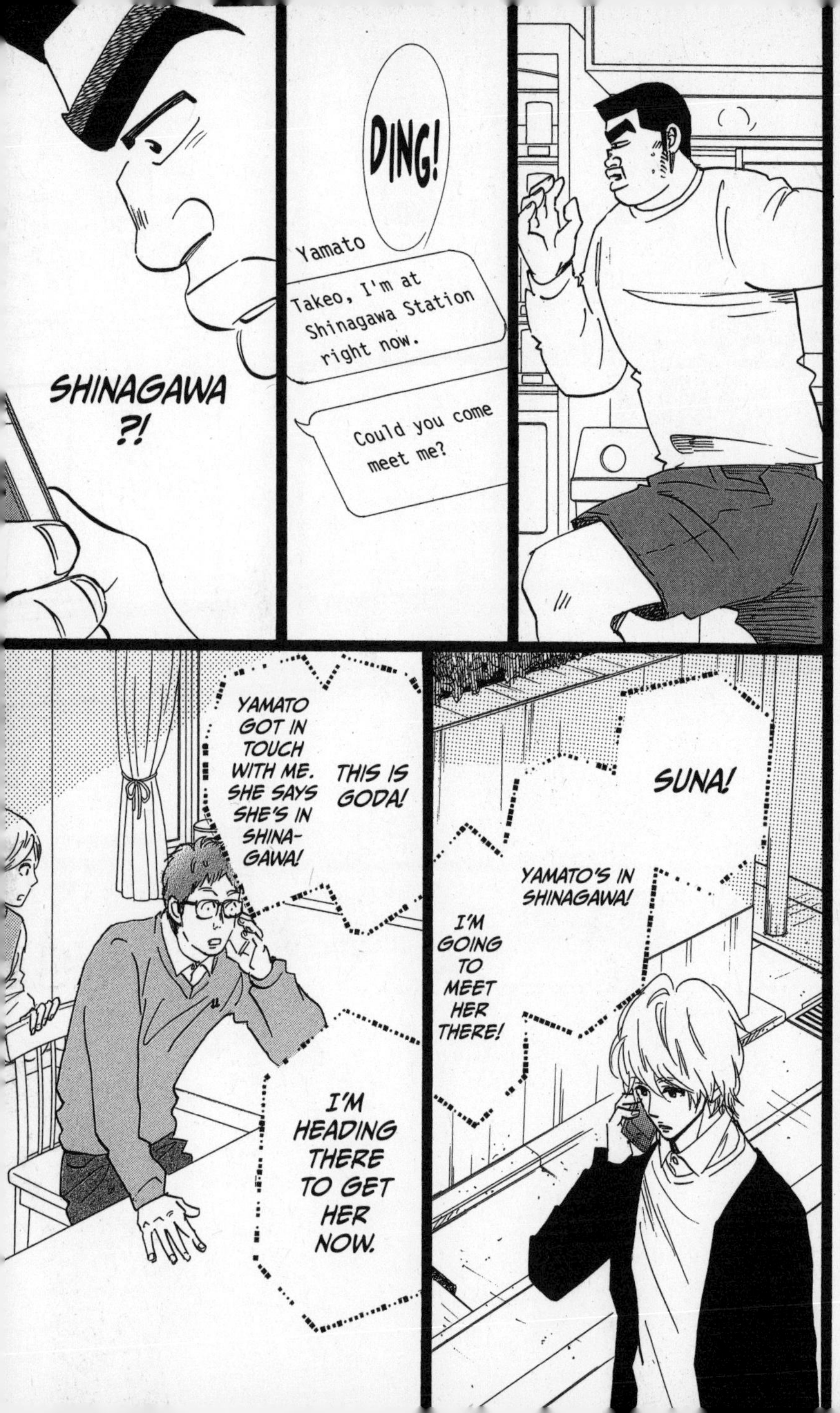
DING!
Yamato
Takeo, I'm at Shinagawa Station right now.
Could you come meet me?
SHINAGAWA ?!
SUNA!
YAMATO'S IN SHINAGAWA!
I'M GOING TO MEET HER THERE!
THIS IS GODA!
YAMATO GOT IN TOUCH WITH ME. SHE SAYS SHE'S IN SHINA-GAWA!
I'M HEADING THERE TO GET HER NOW.

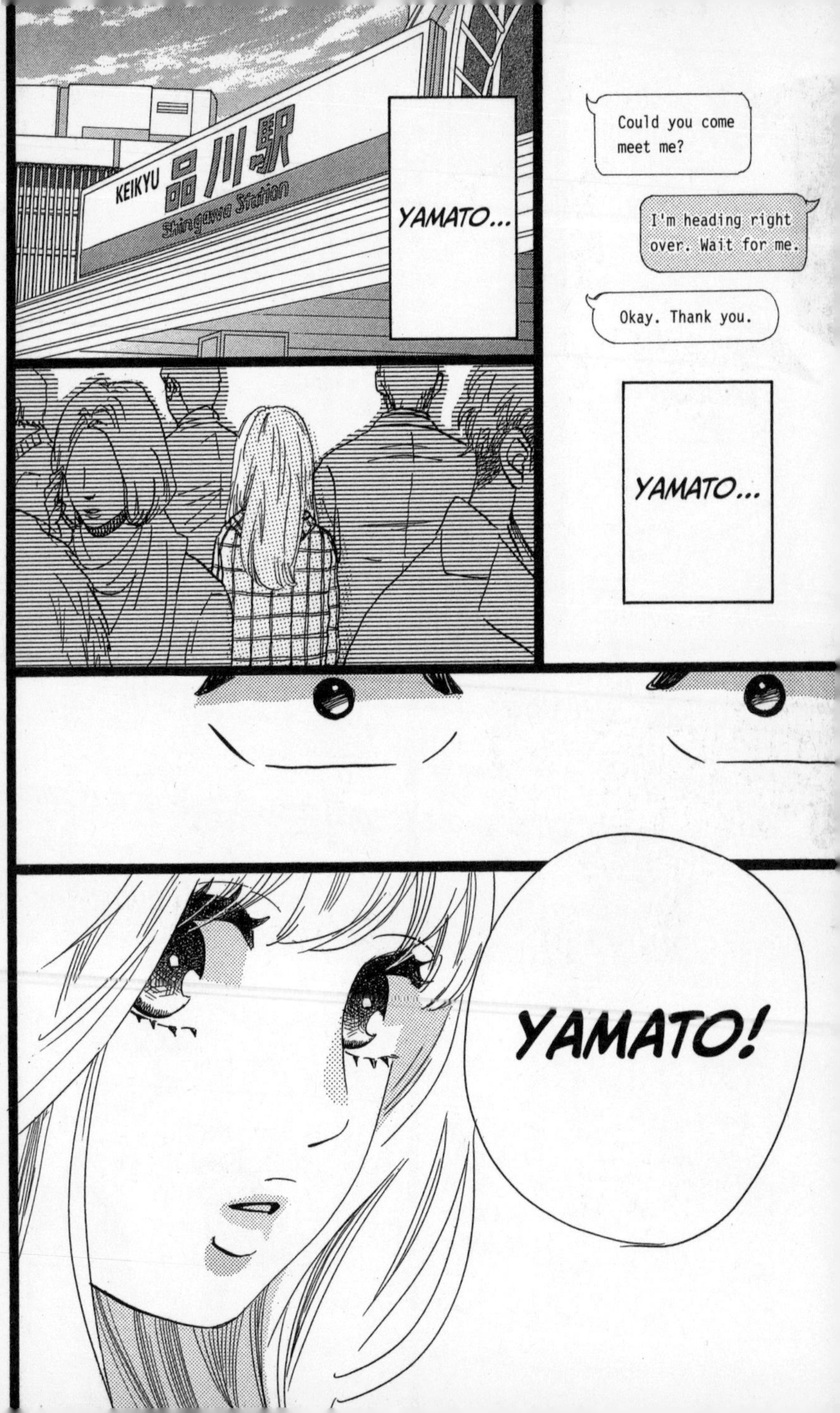
Could you come meet me?
I'm heading right over. Wait for me.
Okay. Thank you.
YAMATO...
KEIKYU 品川駅 Shingawa Station
YAMATO...
YAMATO!

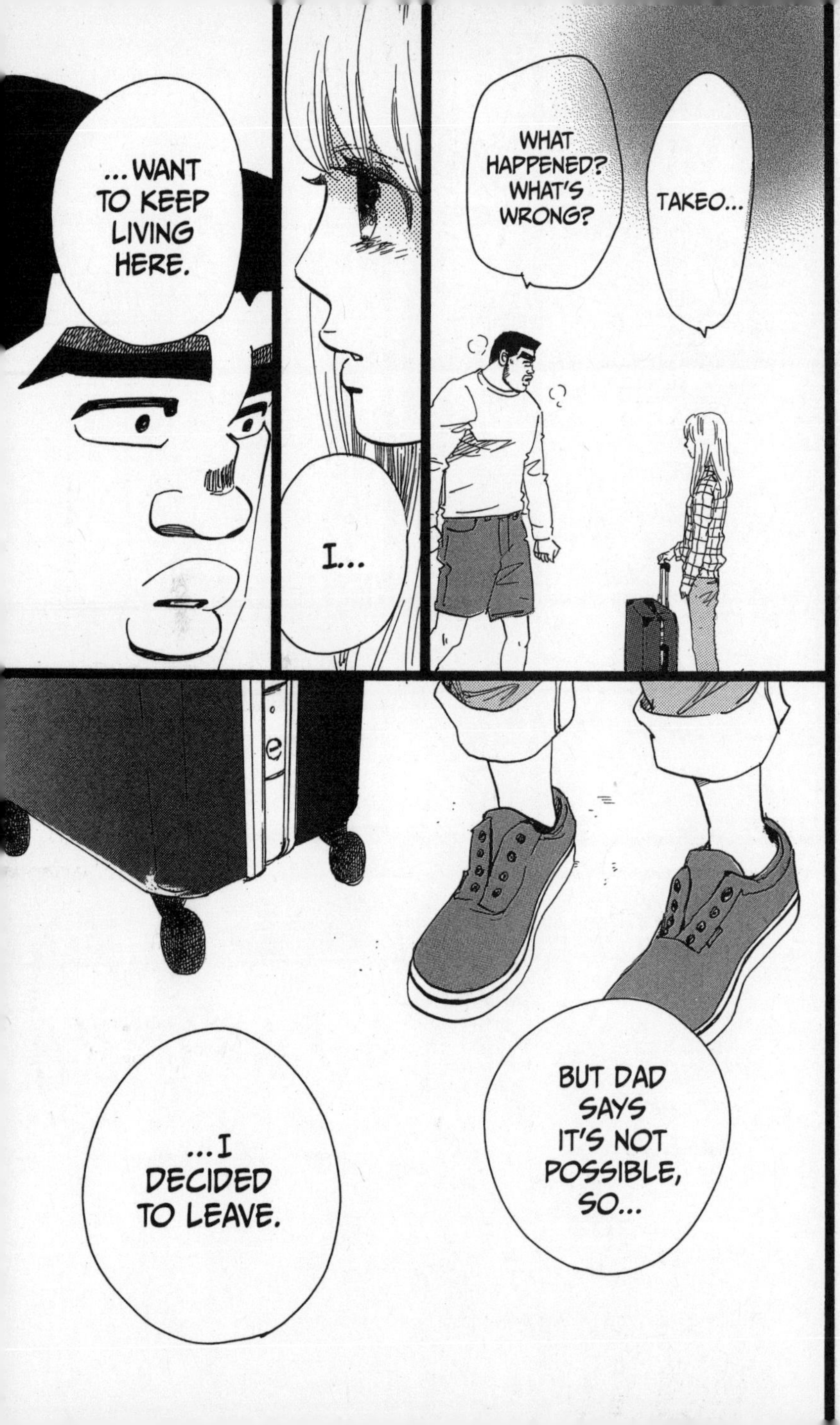
TAKEO...
WHAT HAPPENED? WHAT'S WRONG?
I...
...WANT TO KEEP LIVING HERE.
BUT DAD SAYS IT'S NOT POSSIBLE, SO...
...I DECIDED TO LEAVE.

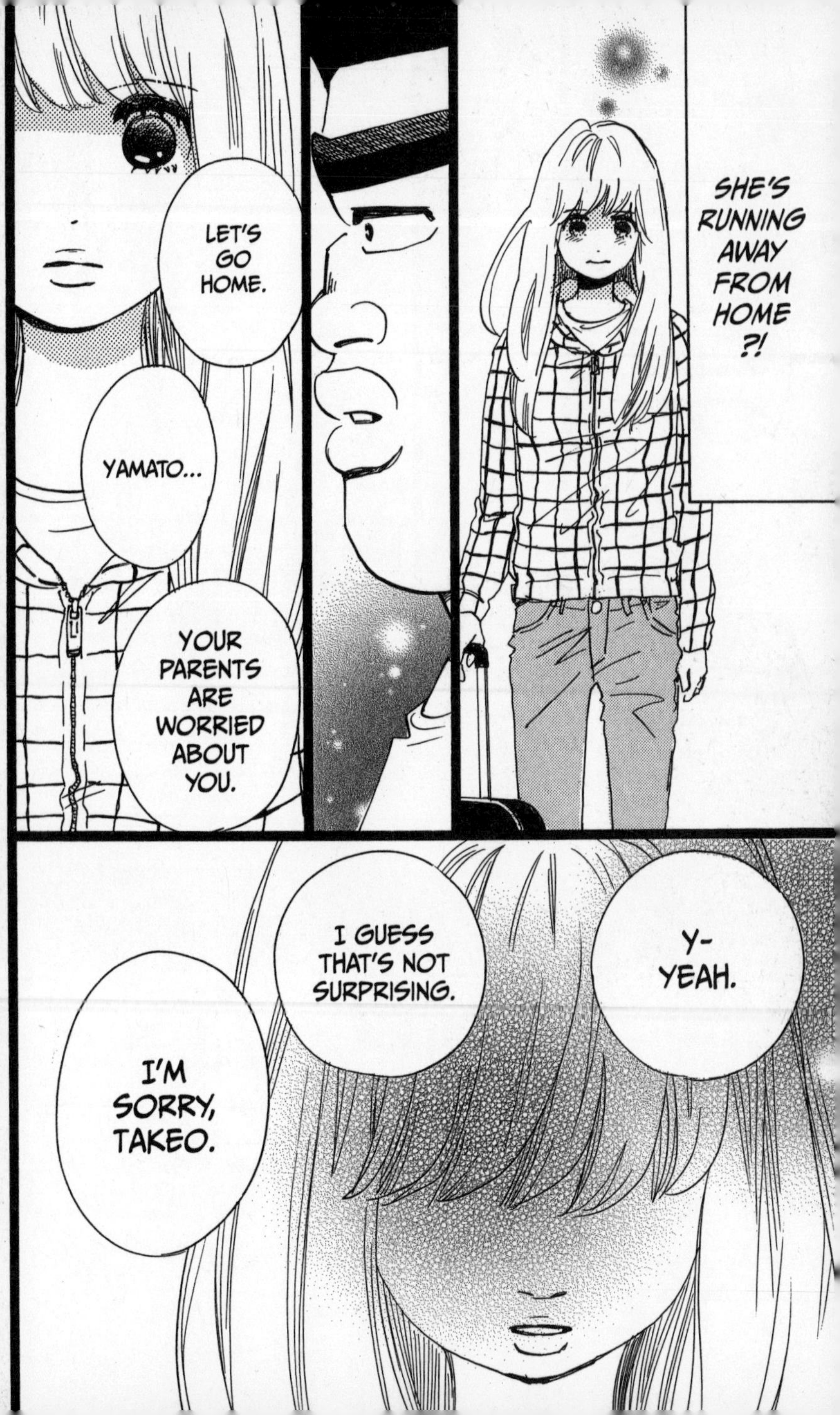
SHE'S RUNNING AWAY FROM HOME ?!
LET'S GO HOME.
YAMATO...
YOUR PARENTS ARE WORRIED ABOUT YOU.
Y-YEAH.
I GUESS THAT'S NOT SURPRISING.
I'M SORRY, TAKEO.

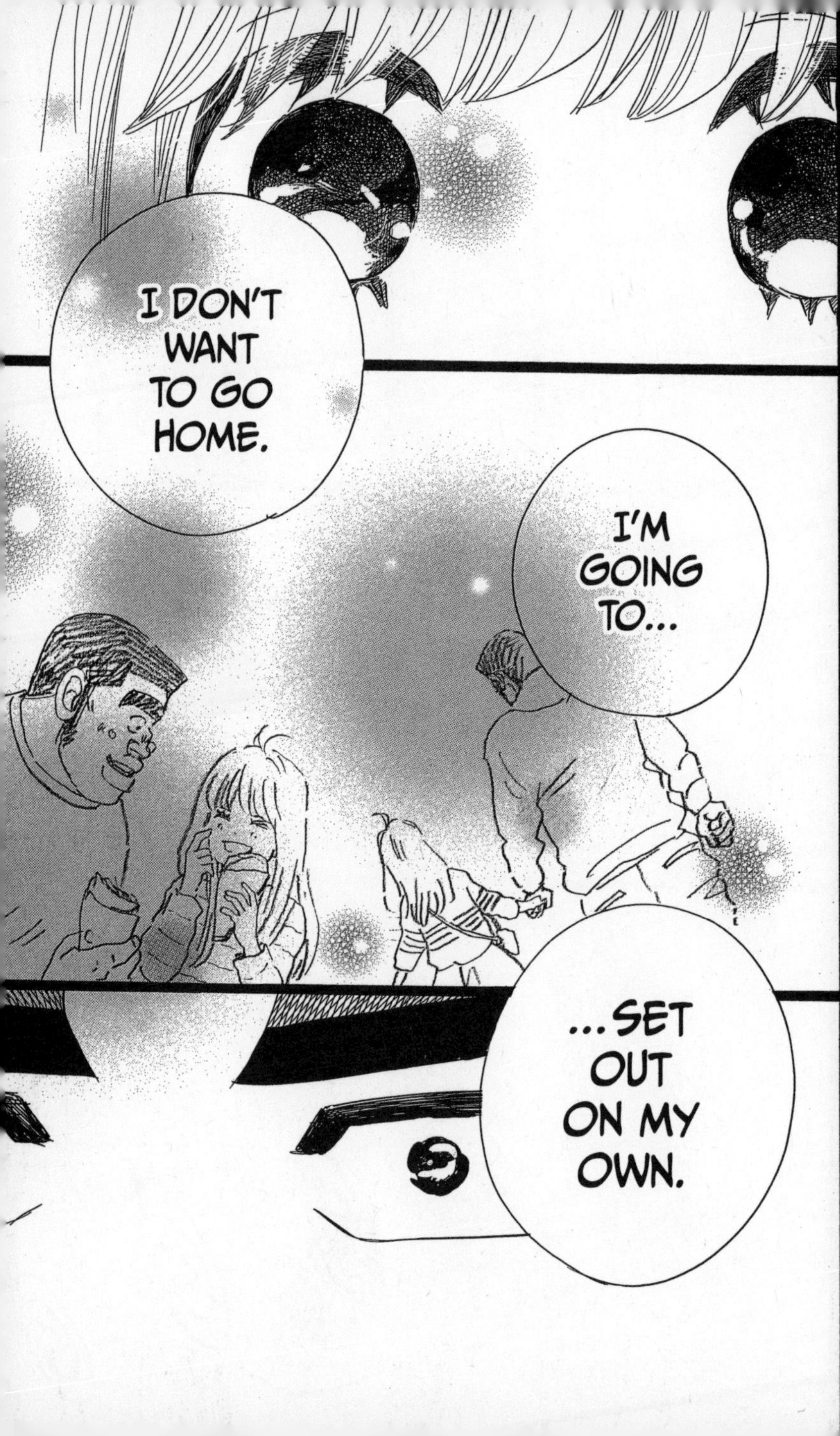
I DON'T WANT TO GO HOME.
I'M GOING TO...
...SET OUT ON MY OWN.

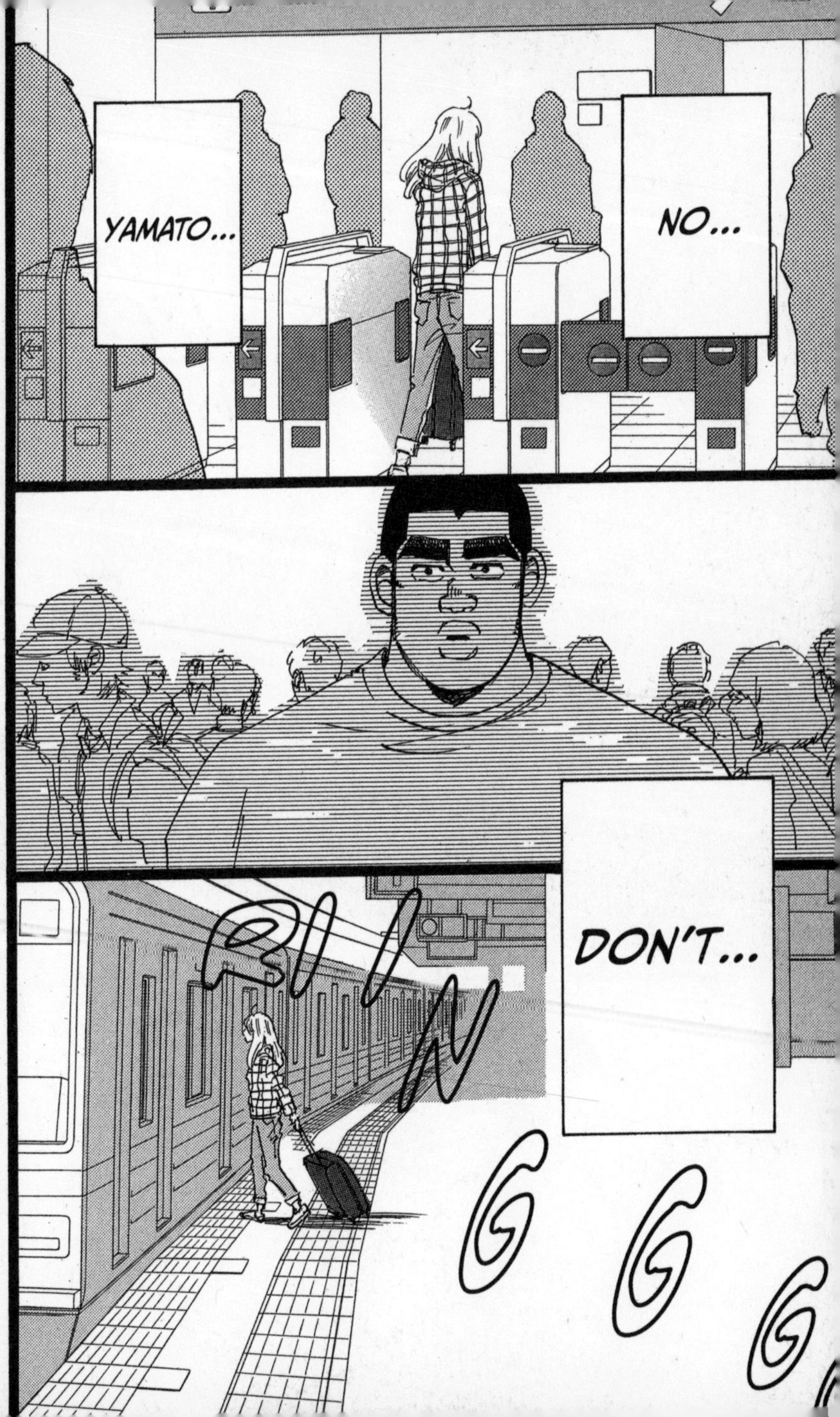
NO...
YAMATO...
DON'T...
BLIN
GGG

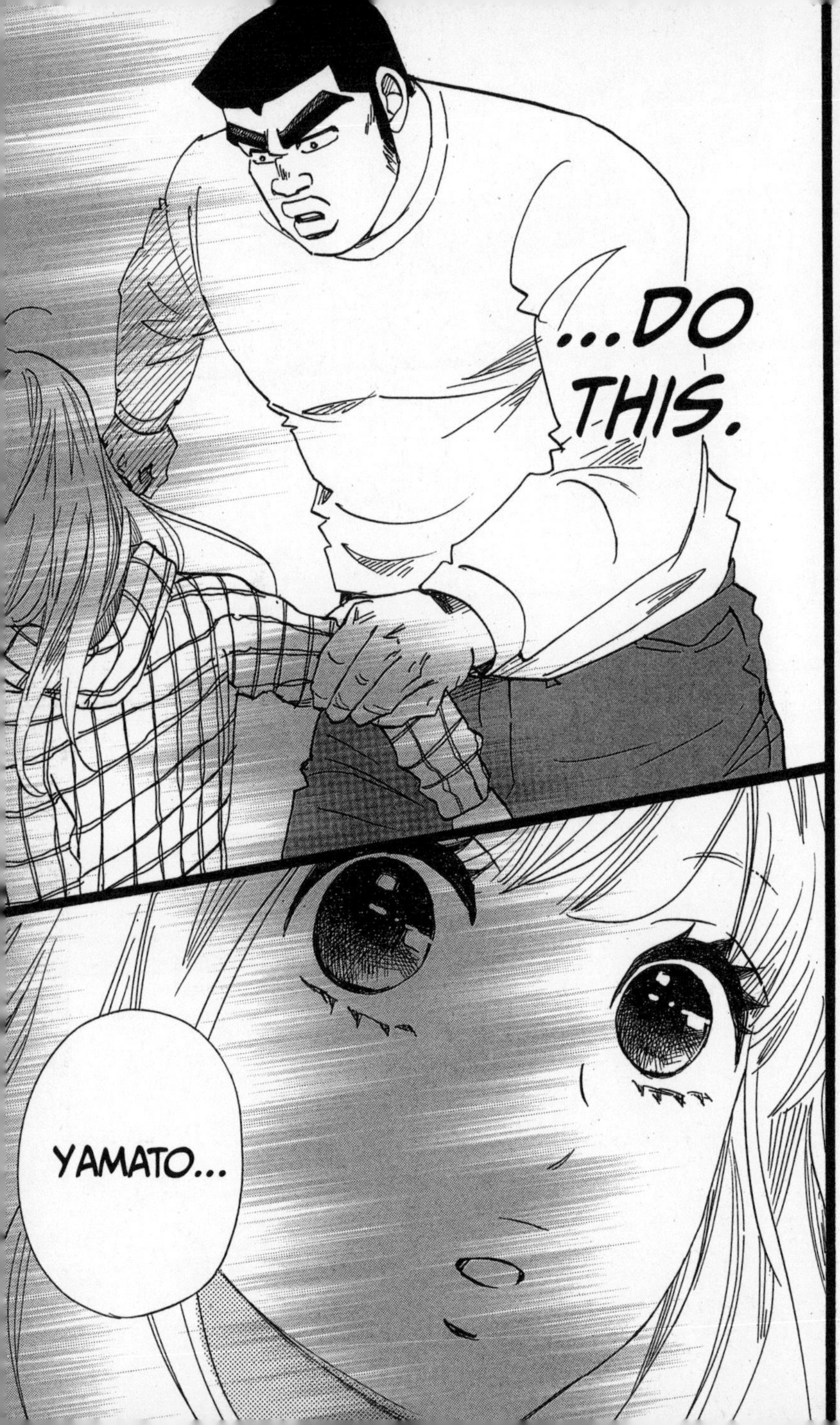
...DO THIS.
YAMATO...

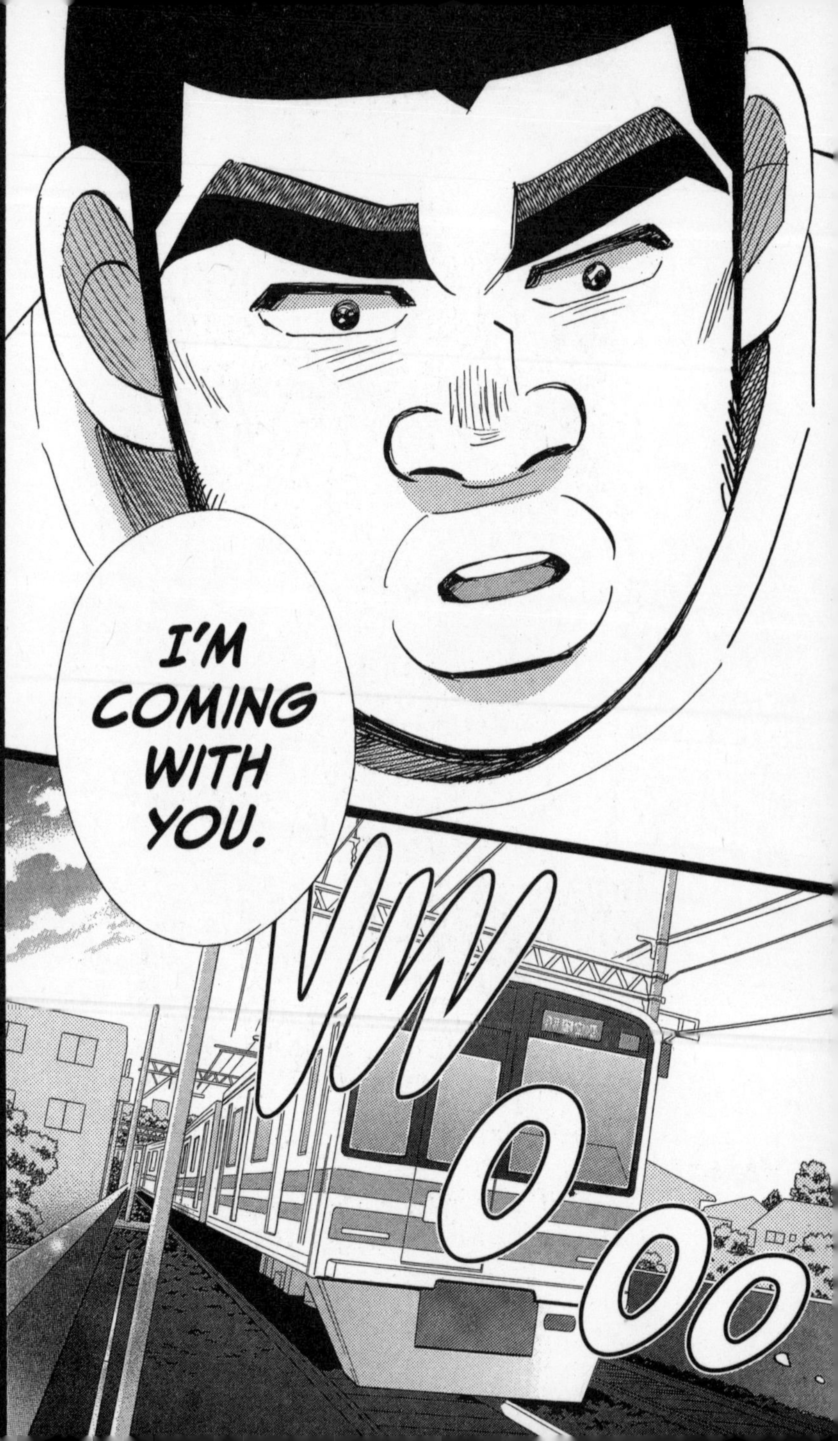
I'M COMING WITH YOU.
VWOOOO

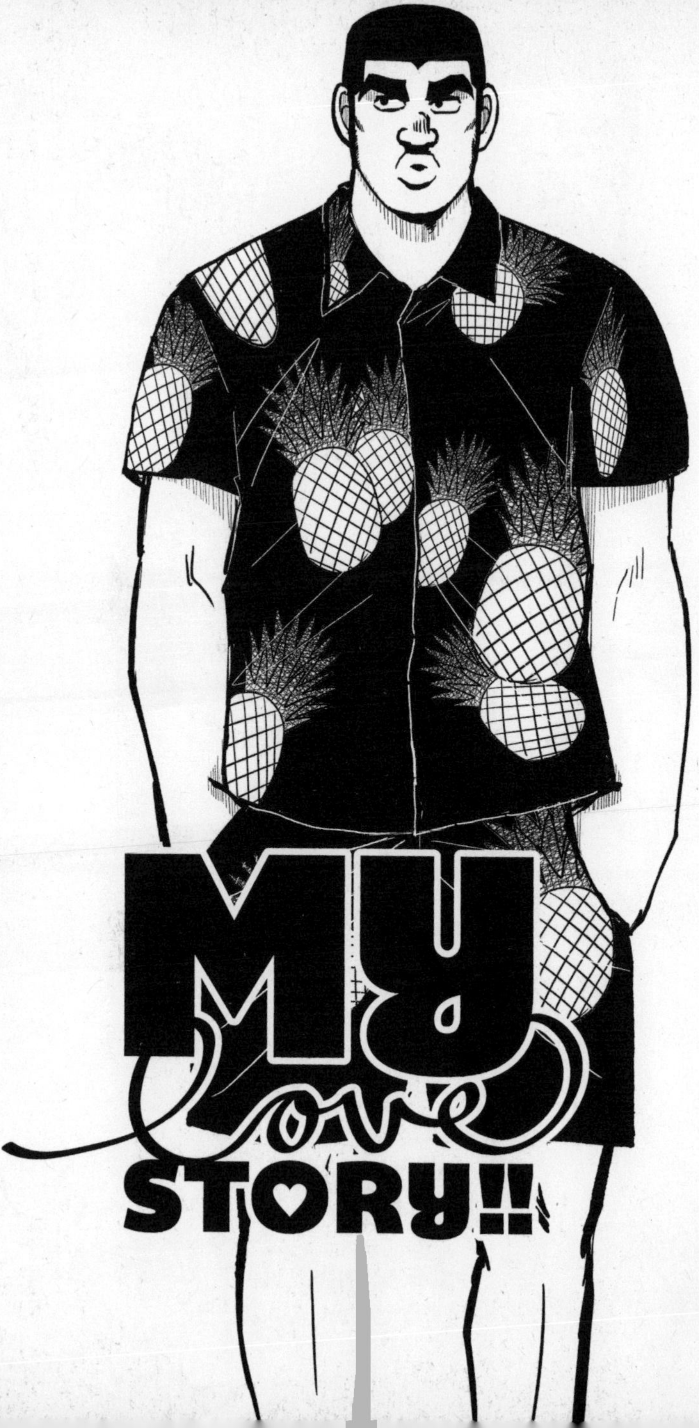
MY love STORY!!

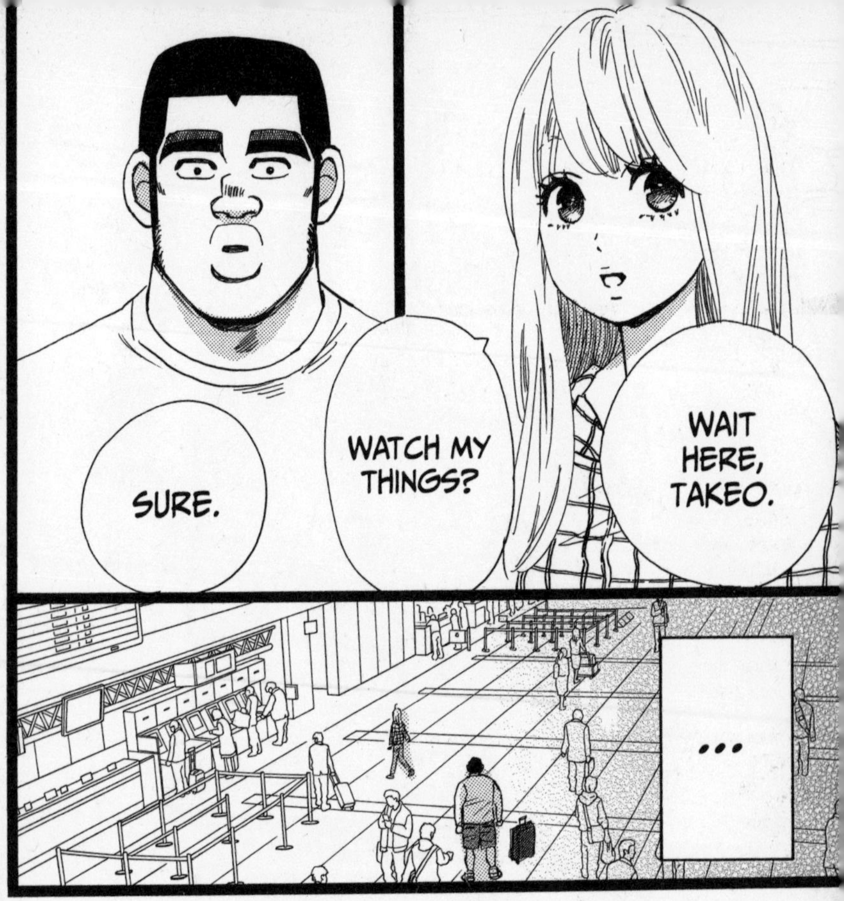
WAIT HERE, TAKEO.
WATCH MY THINGS?
SURE.
...

MY love STORY!!

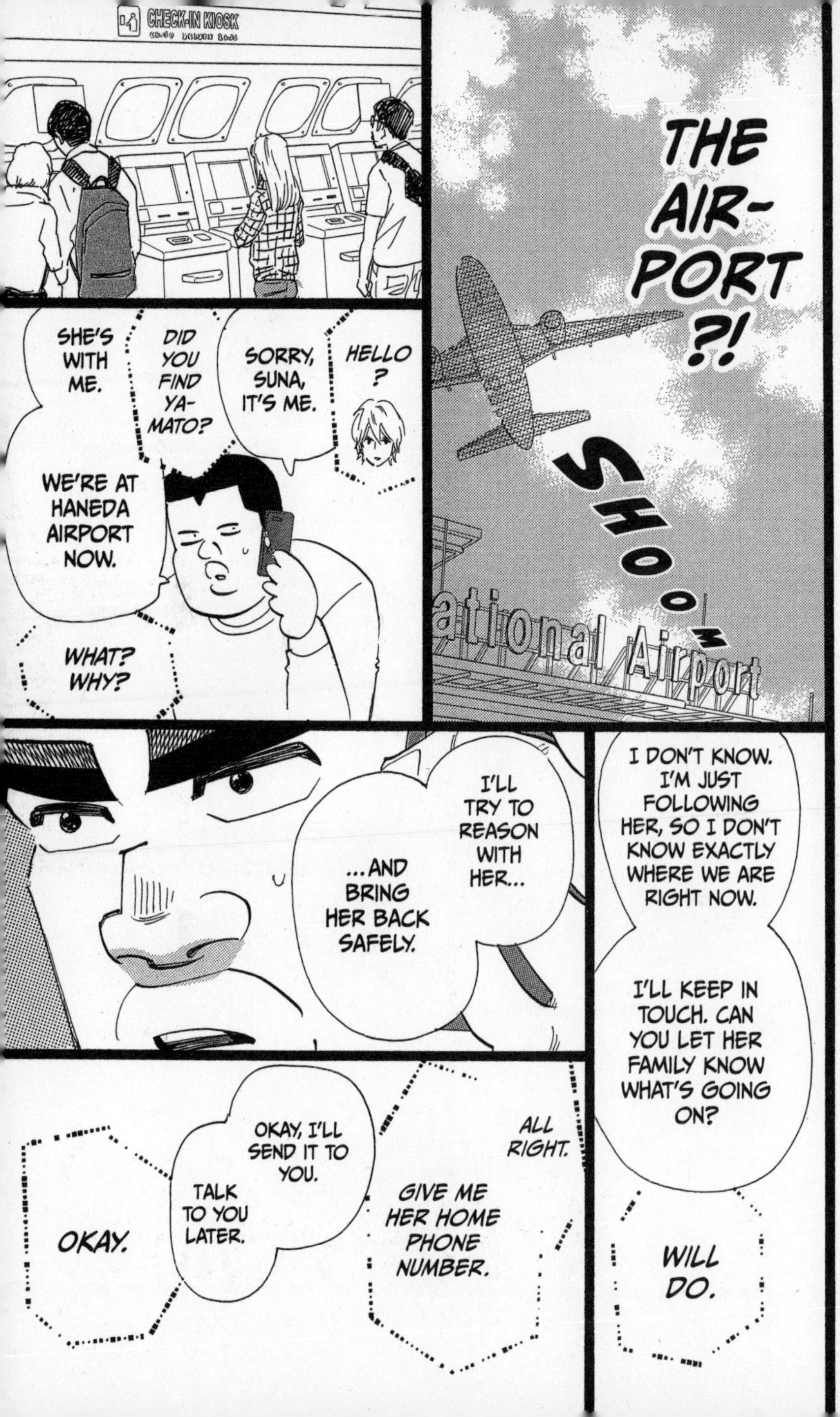
THE AIR-PORT ?!
SHOOOM
ational Airport
CHECK-IN KIOSK
HELLO ?
SORRY, SUNA, IT'S ME.
DID YOU FIND YA-MATO?
SHE'S WITH ME.
WE'RE AT HANEDA AIRPORT NOW.
WHAT? WHY?
I DON'T KNOW. I'M JUST FOLLOWING HER, SO I DON'T KNOW EXACTLY WHERE WE ARE RIGHT NOW.
I'LL KEEP IN TOUCH. CAN YOU LET HER FAMILY KNOW WHAT'S GOING ON?
I'LL TRY TO REASON WITH HER...
...AND BRING HER BACK SAFELY.
WILL DO.
ALL RIGHT.
GIVE ME HER HOME PHONE NUMBER.
OKAY, I'LL SEND IT TO YOU.
TALK TO YOU LATER.
OKAY.

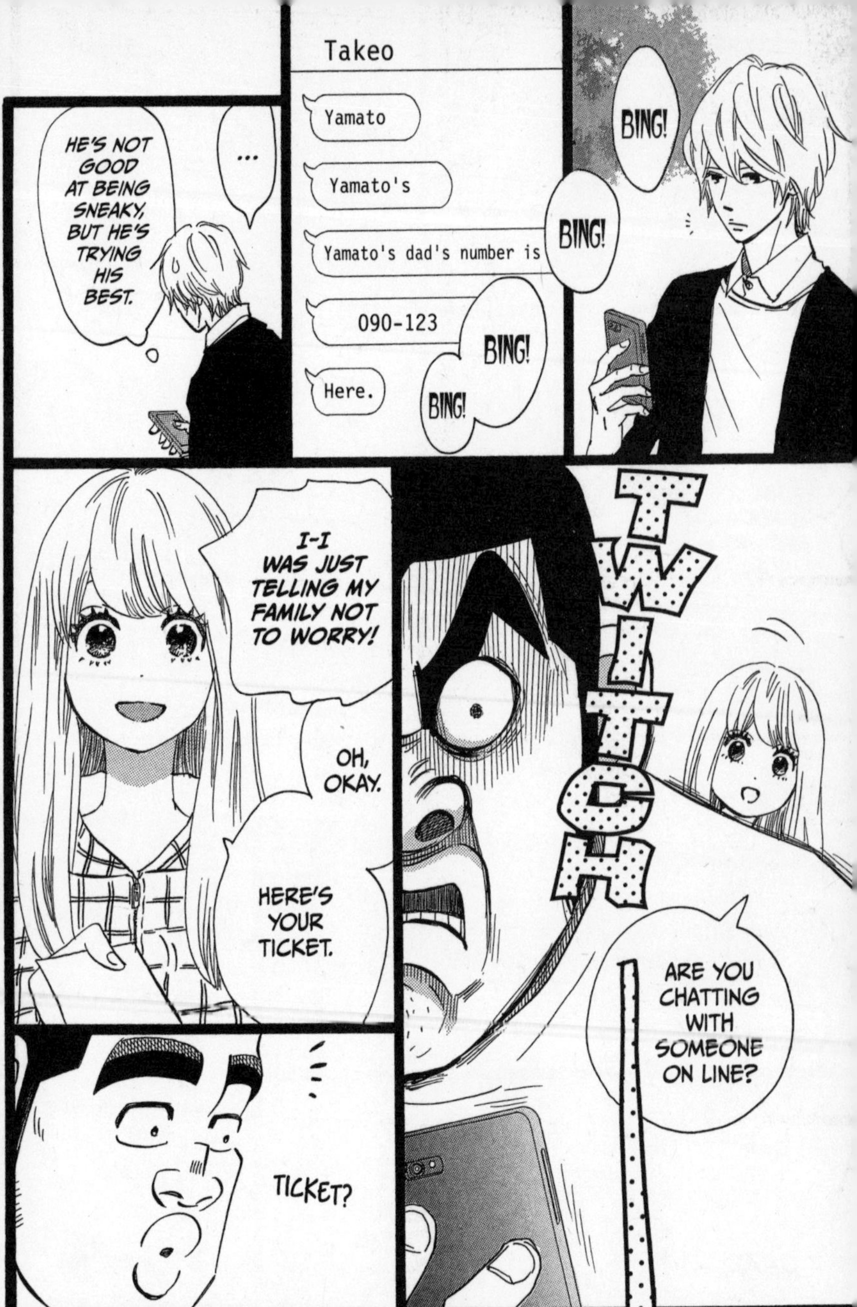
BING!
BING!
Takeo
Yamato
Yamato's
Yamato's dad's number is
090-123
Here.
BING!
BING!
...
HE'S NOT GOOD AT BEING SNEAKY, BUT HE'S TRYING HIS BEST.
TWITCH
ARE YOU CHATTING WITH SOMEONE ON LINE?
I-I WAS JUST TELLING MY FAMILY NOT TO WORRY!
OH, OKAY.
HERE'S YOUR TICKET.
TICKET?

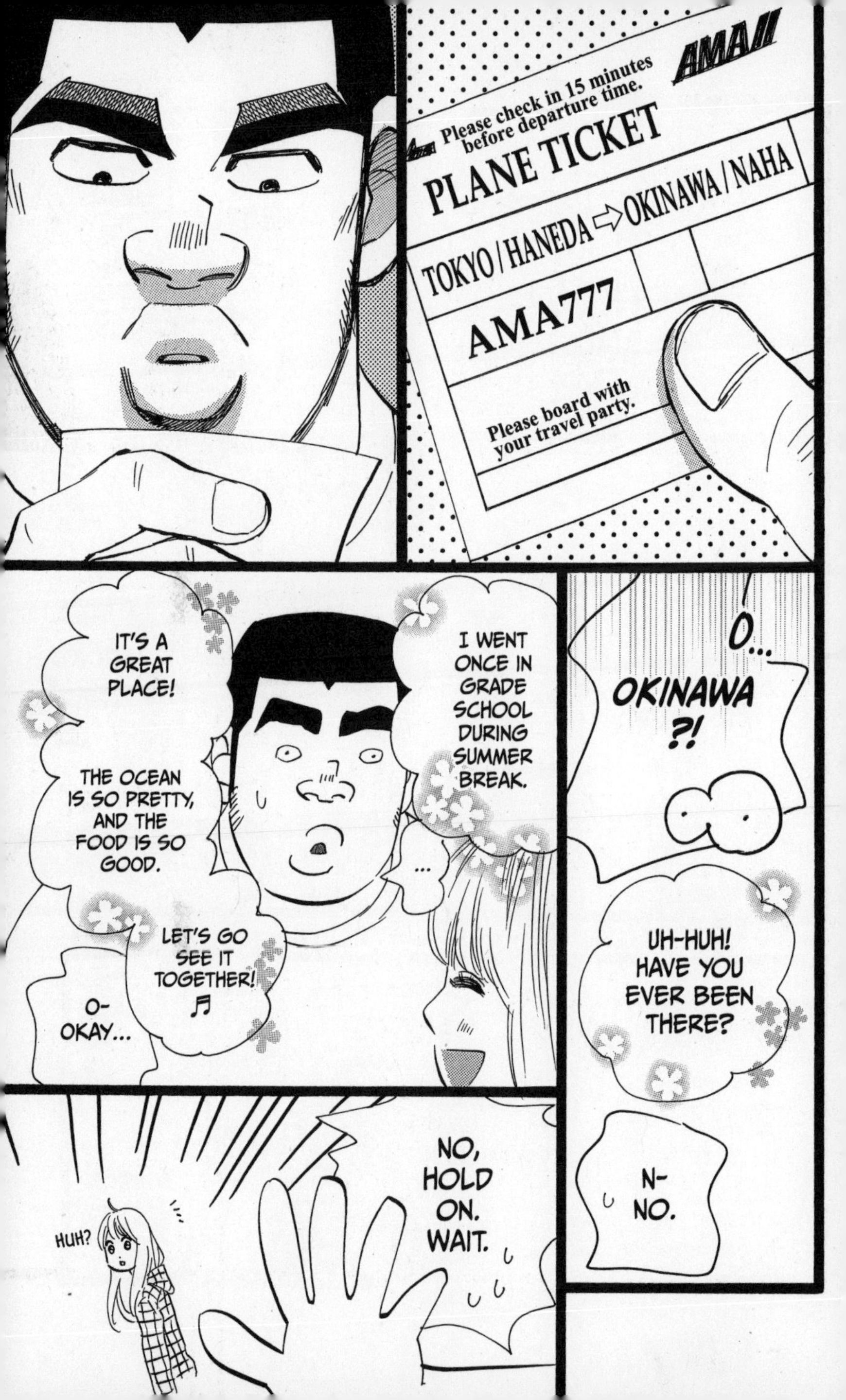
AMAII
Please check in 15 minutes before departure time.
PLANE TICKET
TOKYO / HANEDA ⇨ OKINAWA / NAHA
AMA777
Please board with your travel party.
O... OKINAWA ?!
UH-HUH! HAVE YOU EVER BEEN THERE?
N- NO.
I WENT ONCE IN GRADE SCHOOL DURING SUMMER BREAK.
IT'S A GREAT PLACE!
THE OCEAN IS SO PRETTY, AND THE FOOD IS SO GOOD.
...
LET'S GO SEE IT TOGETHER! ♬
O- OKAY...
NO, HOLD ON. WAIT.
HUH?

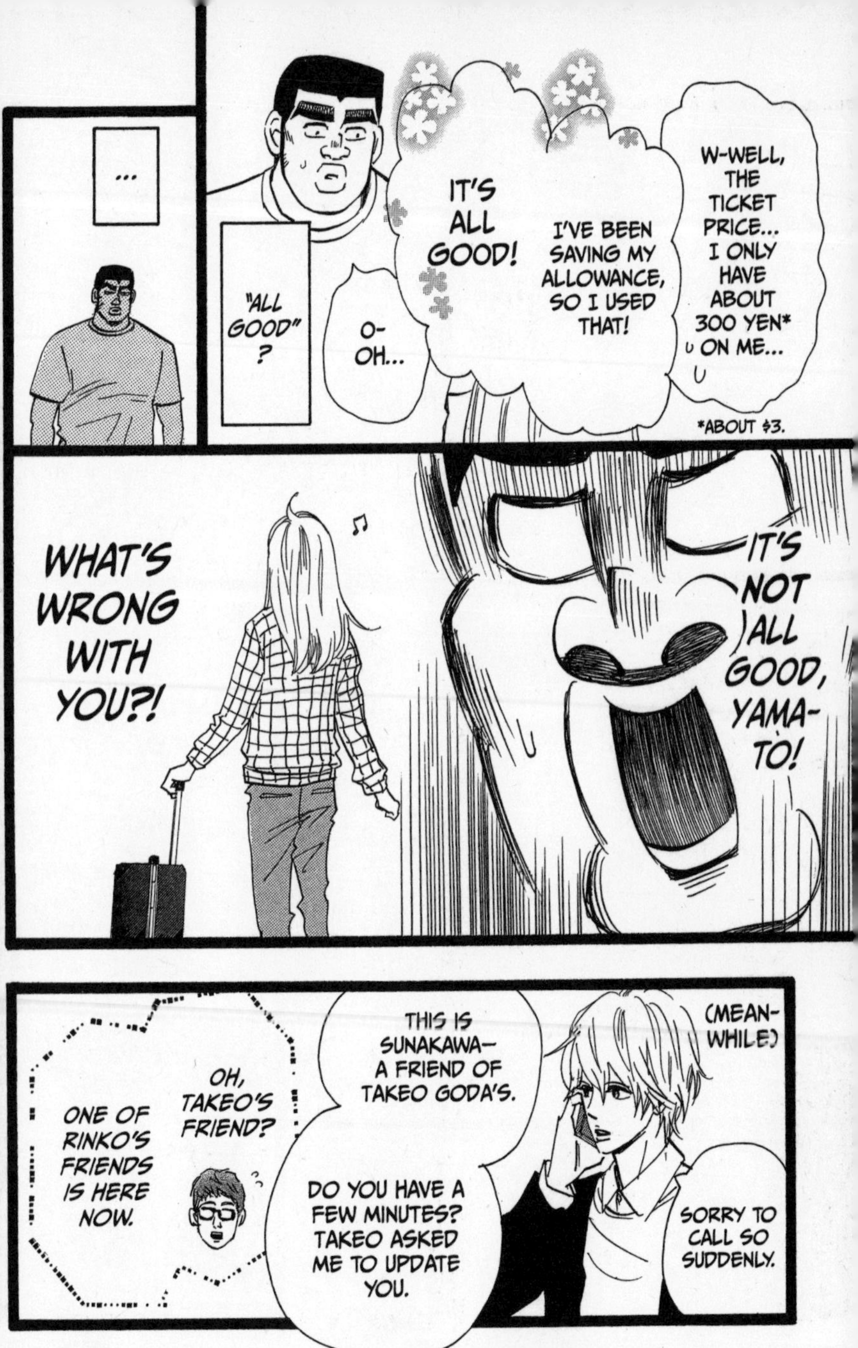
W-WELL, THE TICKET PRICE... I ONLY HAVE ABOUT 300 YEN* ON ME...
I'VE BEEN SAVING MY ALLOWANCE, SO I USED THAT!
IT'S ALL GOOD!
O-OH...
"ALL GOOD"?
...
*ABOUT $3.
IT'S NOT ALL GOOD, YAMATO!
WHAT'S WRONG WITH YOU?!
(MEANWHILE)
SORRY TO CALL SO SUDDENLY.
THIS IS SUNAKAWA—A FRIEND OF TAKEO GODA'S.
DO YOU HAVE A FEW MINUTES? TAKEO ASKED ME TO UPDATE YOU.
OH, TAKEO'S FRIEND?
ONE OF RINKO'S FRIENDS IS HERE NOW.

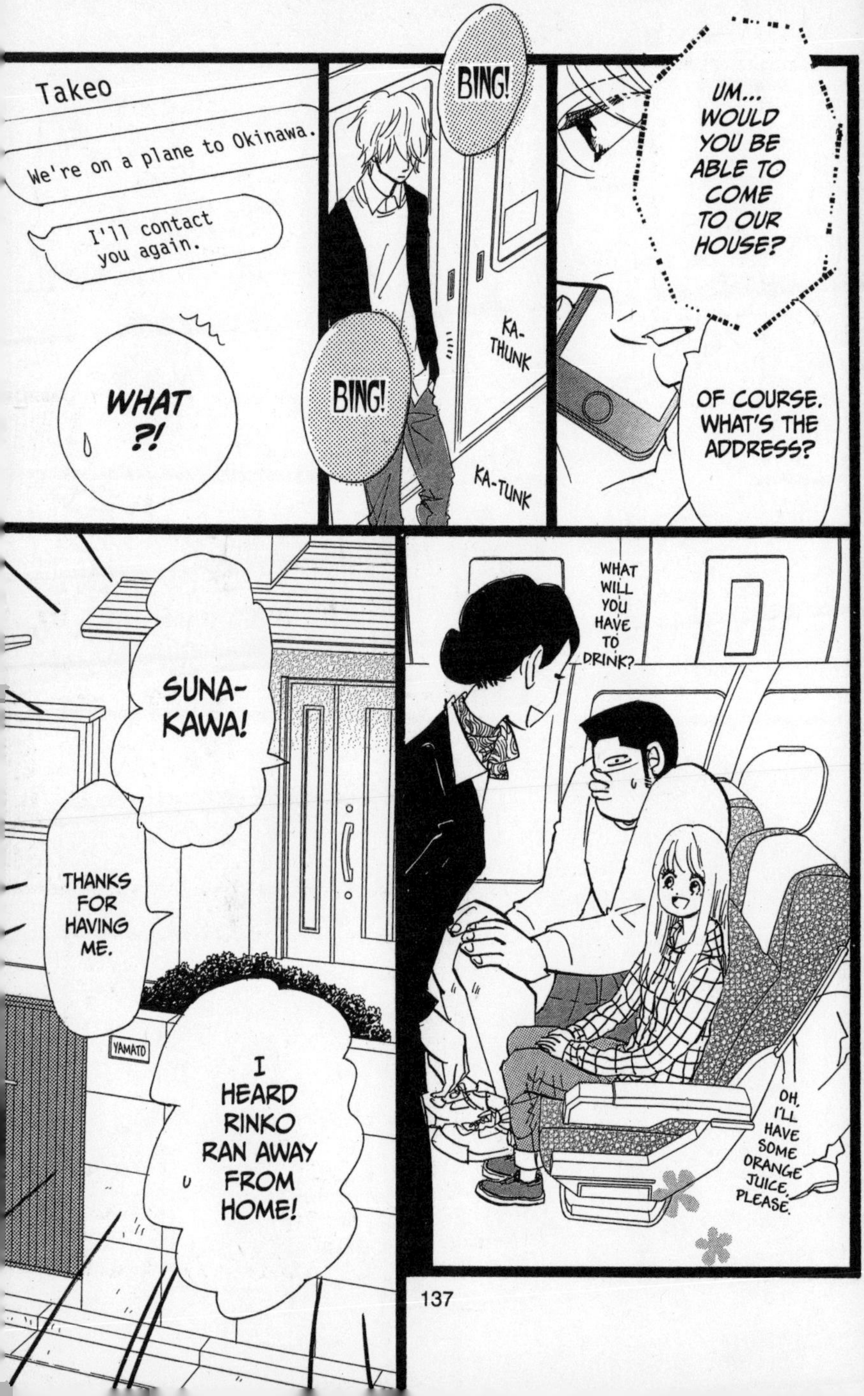
UM... WOULD YOU BE ABLE TO COME TO OUR HOUSE?
OF COURSE. WHAT'S THE ADDRESS?
BING!
KA-THUNK
BING!
KA-TUNK
Takeo
We're on a plane to Okinawa.
I'll contact you again.
WHAT ?!
WHAT WILL YOU HAVE TO DRINK?
OH, I'LL HAVE SOME ORANGE JUICE, PLEASE.
SUNA-KAWA!
THANKS FOR HAVING ME.
YAMATO
I HEARD RINKO RAN AWAY FROM HOME!

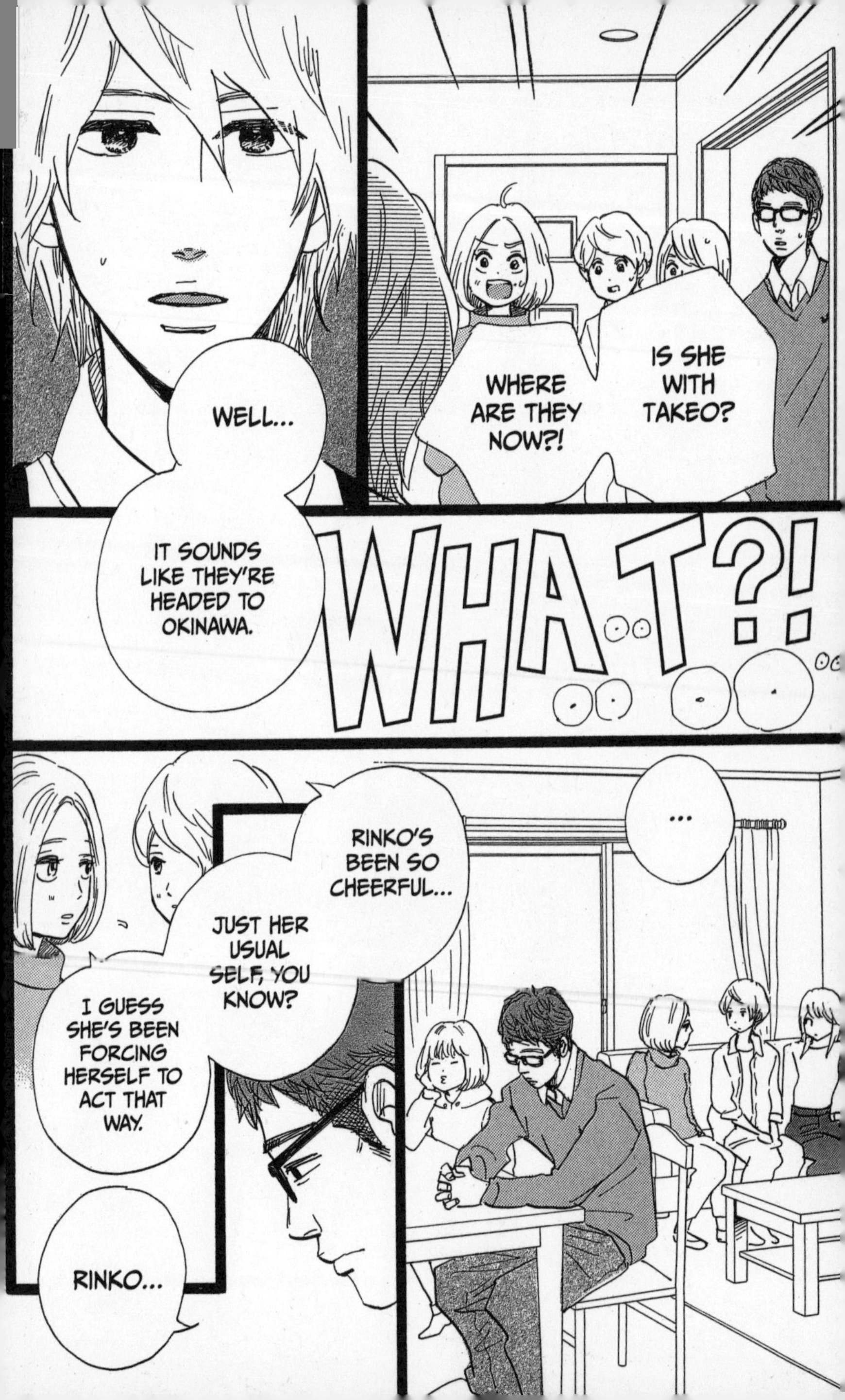
IS SHE WITH TAKEO?
WHERE ARE THEY NOW?!
WELL...
IT SOUNDS LIKE THEY'RE HEADED TO OKINAWA.
WHAT?!
...
RINKO'S BEEN SO CHEERFUL...
JUST HER USUAL SELF, YOU KNOW?
I GUESS SHE'S BEEN FORCING HERSELF TO ACT THAT WAY.
RINKO...

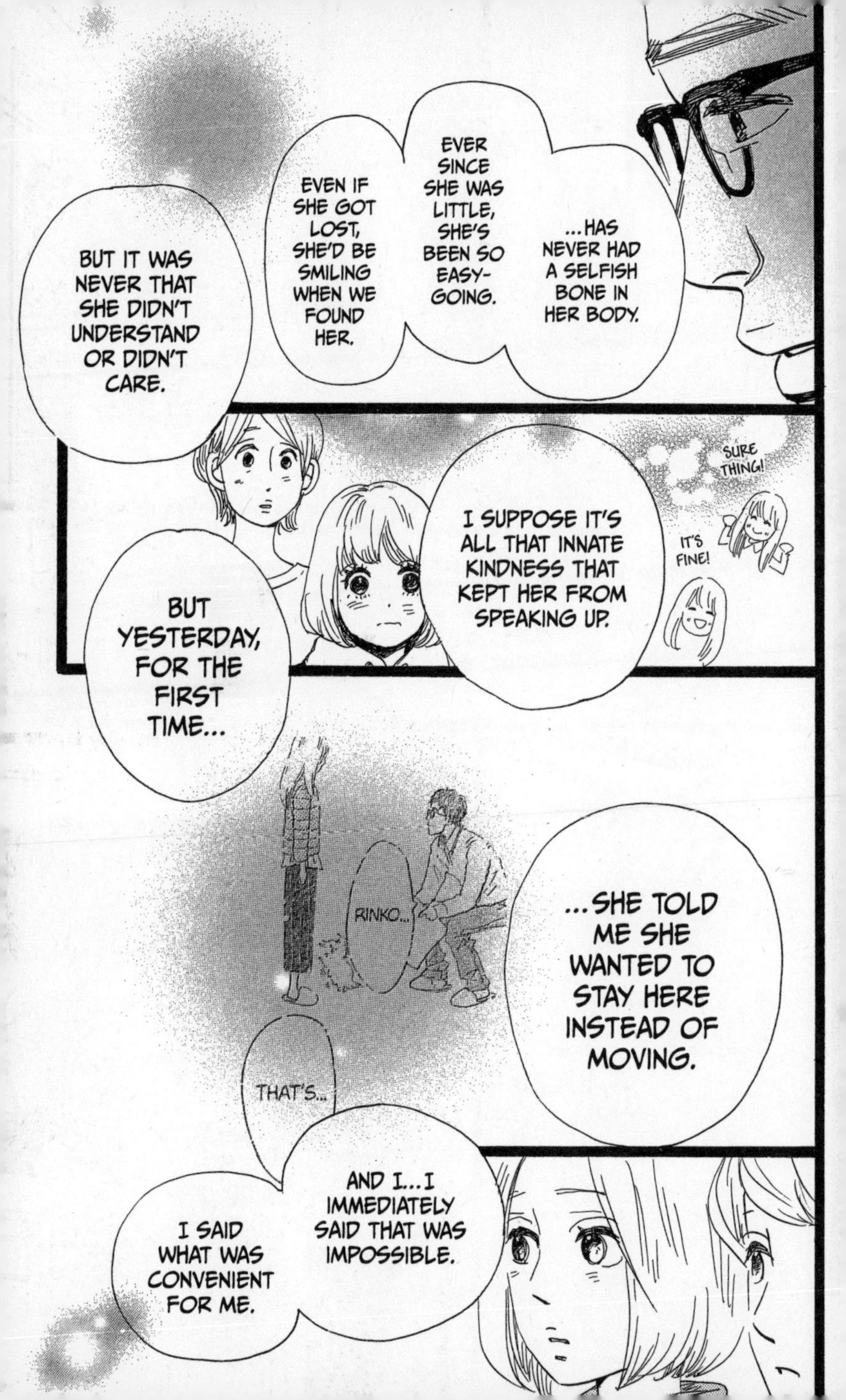
...HAS NEVER HAD A SELFISH BONE IN HER BODY.
EVER SINCE SHE WAS LITTLE, SHE'S BEEN SO EASY-GOING.
EVEN IF SHE GOT LOST, SHE'D BE SMILING WHEN WE FOUND HER.
BUT IT WAS NEVER THAT SHE DIDN'T UNDERSTAND OR DIDN'T CARE.
SURE THING!
IT'S FINE!
I SUPPOSE IT'S ALL THAT INNATE KINDNESS THAT KEPT HER FROM SPEAKING UP.
BUT YESTERDAY, FOR THE FIRST TIME...
...SHE TOLD ME SHE WANTED TO STAY HERE INSTEAD OF MOVING.
RINKO...
THAT'S...
AND I...I IMMEDIATELY SAID THAT WAS IMPOSSIBLE.
I SAID WHAT WAS CONVENIENT FOR ME.

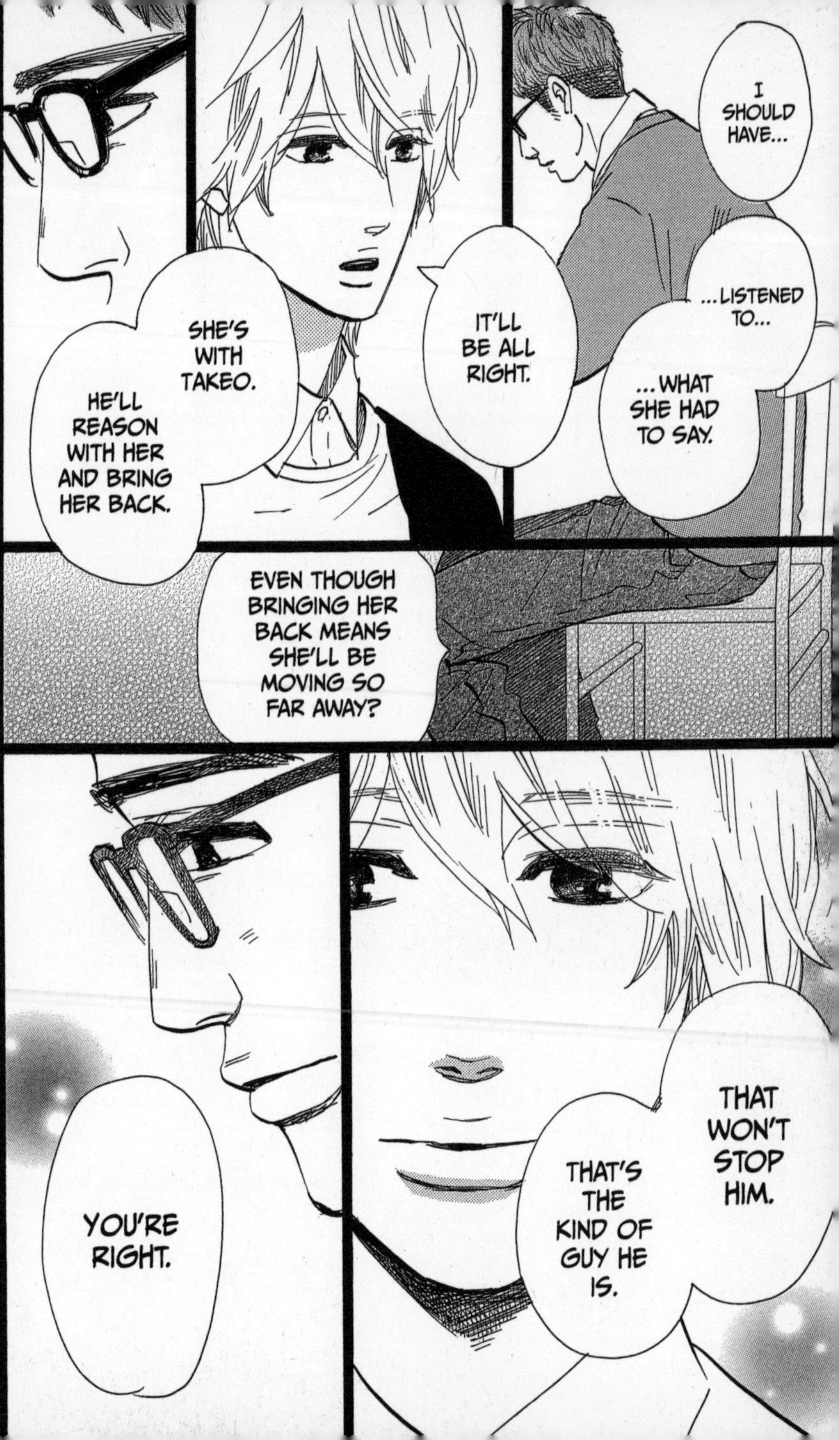
I SHOULD HAVE...
...LISTENED TO...
...WHAT SHE HAD TO SAY.
IT'LL BE ALL RIGHT.
SHE'S WITH TAKEO.
HE'LL REASON WITH HER AND BRING HER BACK.
EVEN THOUGH BRINGING HER BACK MEANS SHE'LL BE MOVING SO FAR AWAY?
THAT WON'T STOP HIM.
THAT'S THE KIND OF GUY HE IS.
YOU'RE RIGHT.

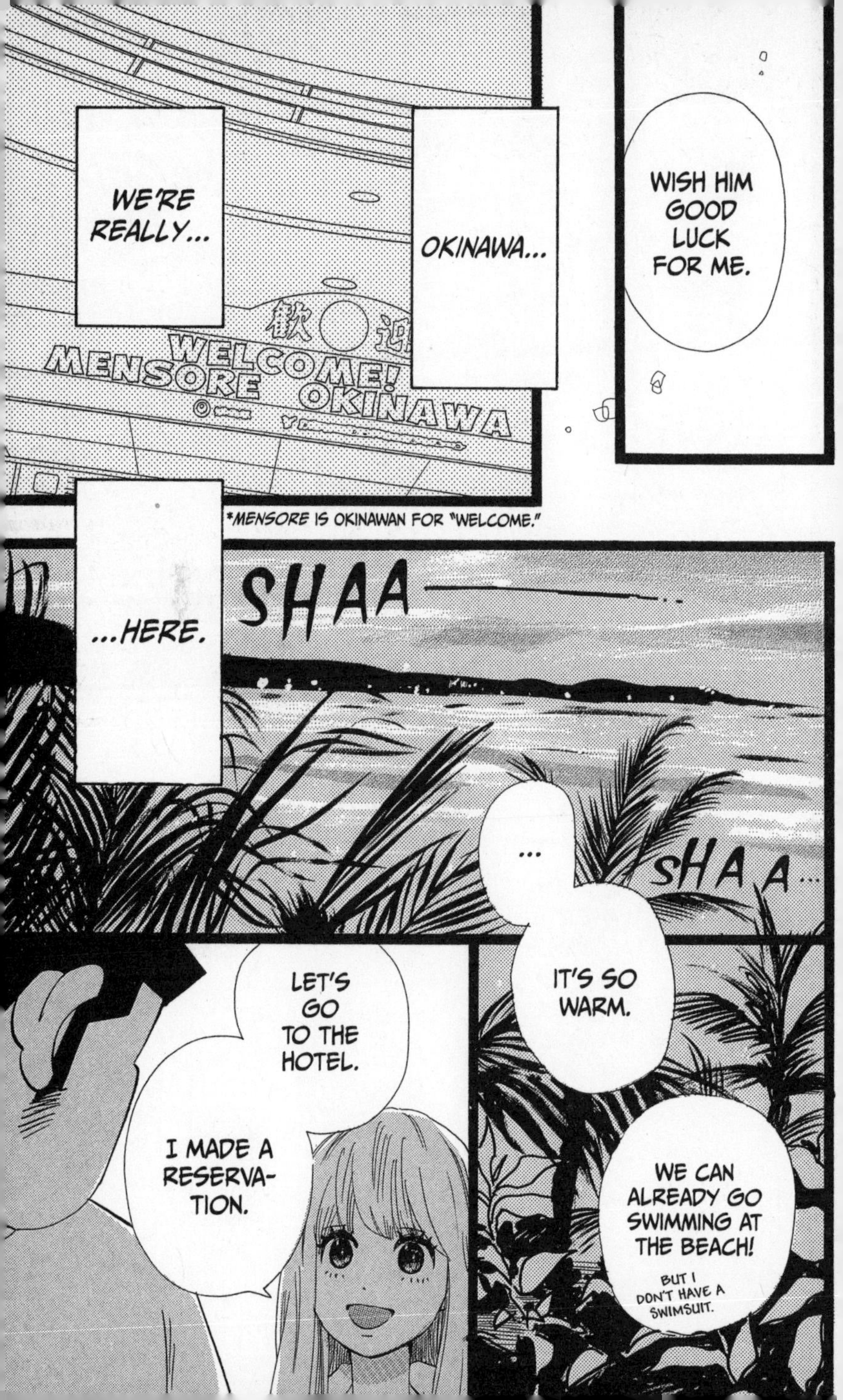
WISH HIM GOOD LUCK FOR ME.
OKINAWA...
WE'RE REALLY...
歓迎
WELCOME! MENSORE OKINAWA
...HERE.
*MENSORE IS OKINAWAN FOR "WELCOME."
SHAA
...
SHAA...
IT'S SO WARM.
WE CAN ALREADY GO SWIMMING AT THE BEACH!
BUT I DON'T HAVE A SWIMSUIT.
LET'S GO TO THE HOTEL.
I MADE A RESERVA-TION.

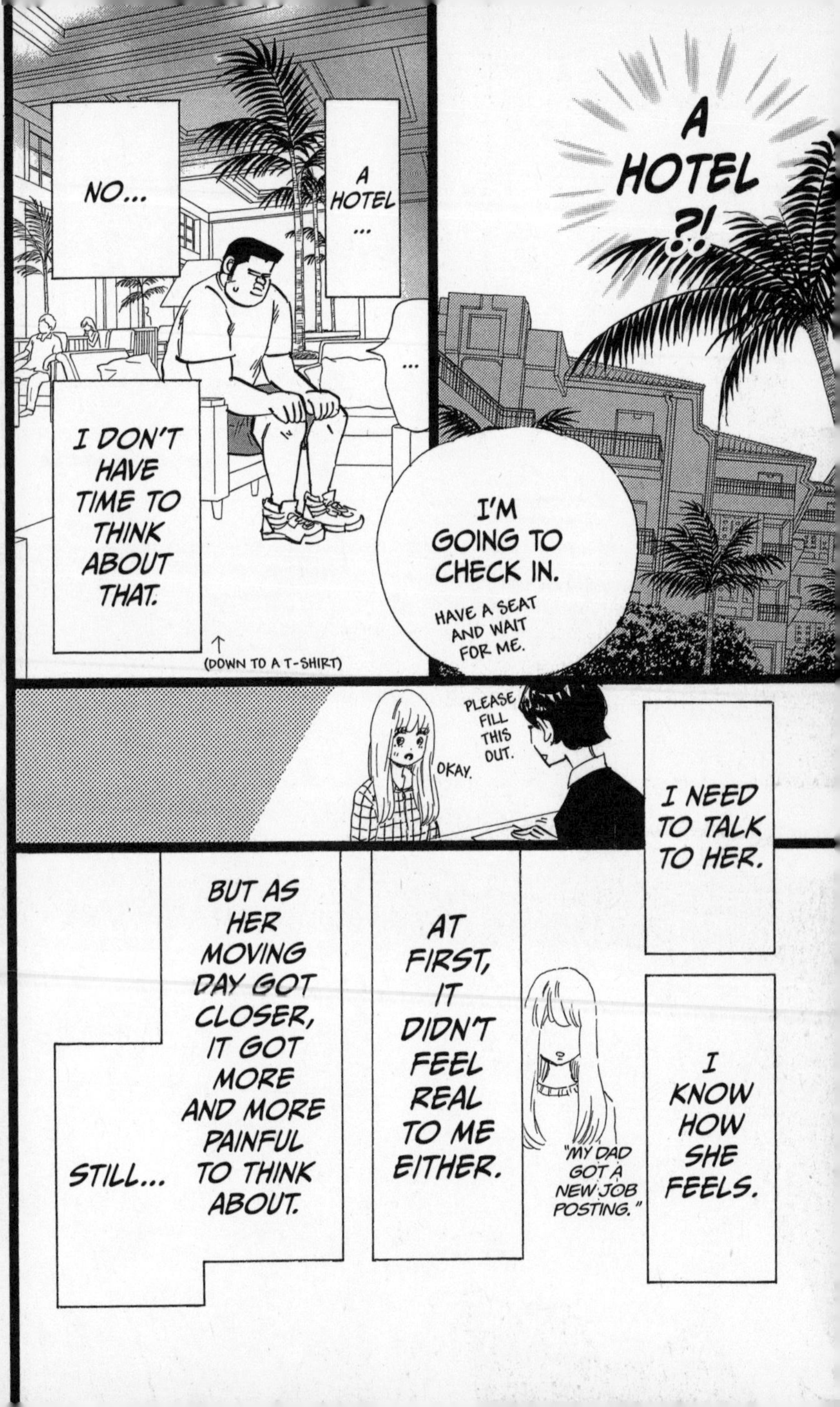
A HOTEL ?!
I'M GOING TO CHECK IN.
HAVE A SEAT AND WAIT FOR ME.
A HOTEL...
NO...
...
I DON'T HAVE TIME TO THINK ABOUT THAT.
(DOWN TO A T-SHIRT)
I NEED TO TALK TO HER.
PLEASE FILL THIS OUT.
OKAY.
I KNOW HOW SHE FEELS.
"MY DAD GOT A NEW JOB POSTING."
AT FIRST, IT DIDN'T FEEL REAL TO ME EITHER.
BUT AS HER MOVING DAY GOT CLOSER, IT GOT MORE AND MORE PAINFUL TO THINK ABOUT.
STILL...

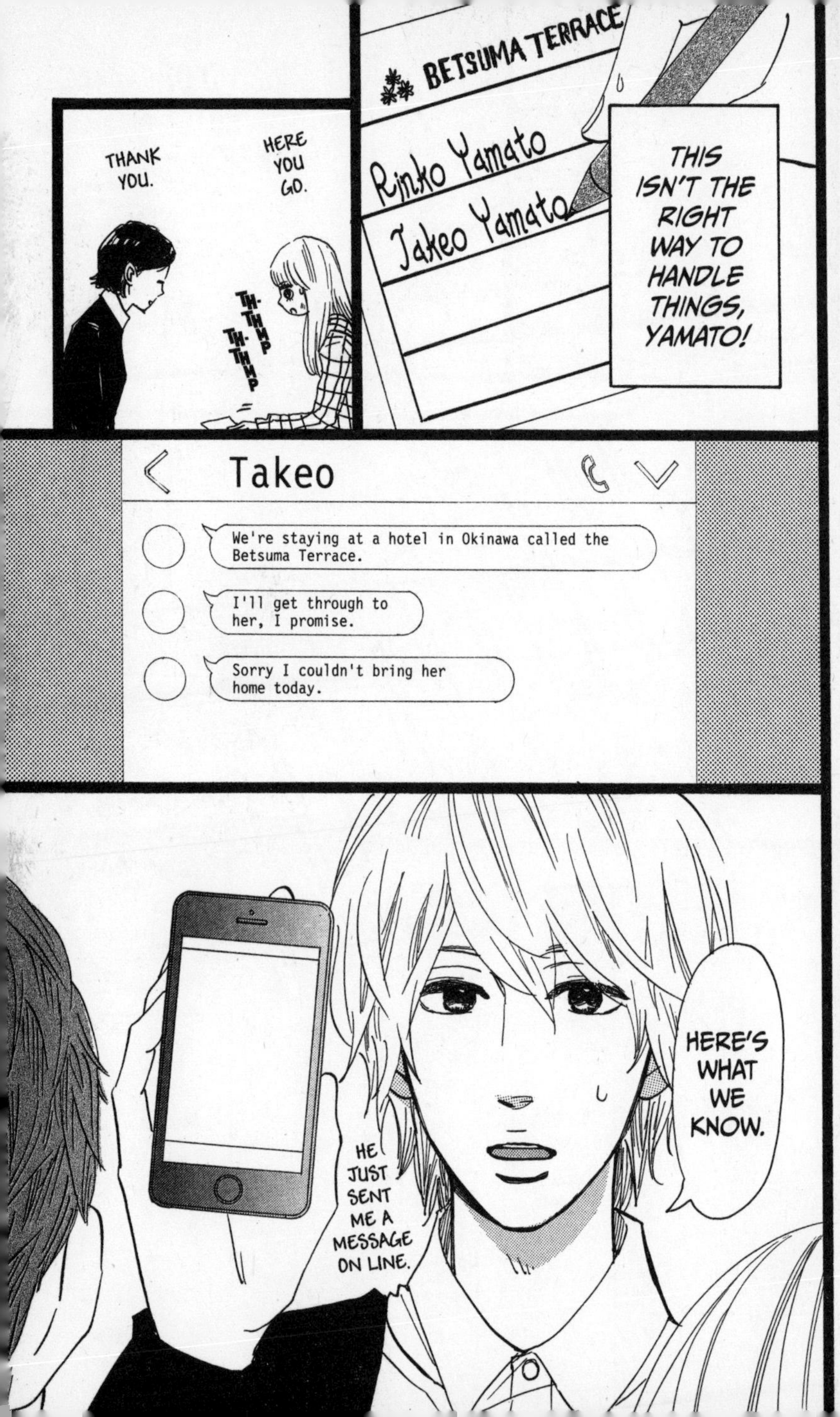
BETSUMA TERRACE
Rinko Yamato
Takeo Yamato
THIS ISN'T THE RIGHT WAY TO HANDLE THINGS, YAMATO!
HERE YOU GO.
THANK YOU.
TH-THMP TH-THMP
Takeo
We're staying at a hotel in Okinawa called the Betsuma Terrace.
I'll get through to her, I promise.
Sorry I couldn't bring her home today.
HERE'S WHAT WE KNOW.
HE JUST SENT ME A MESSAGE ON LINE.

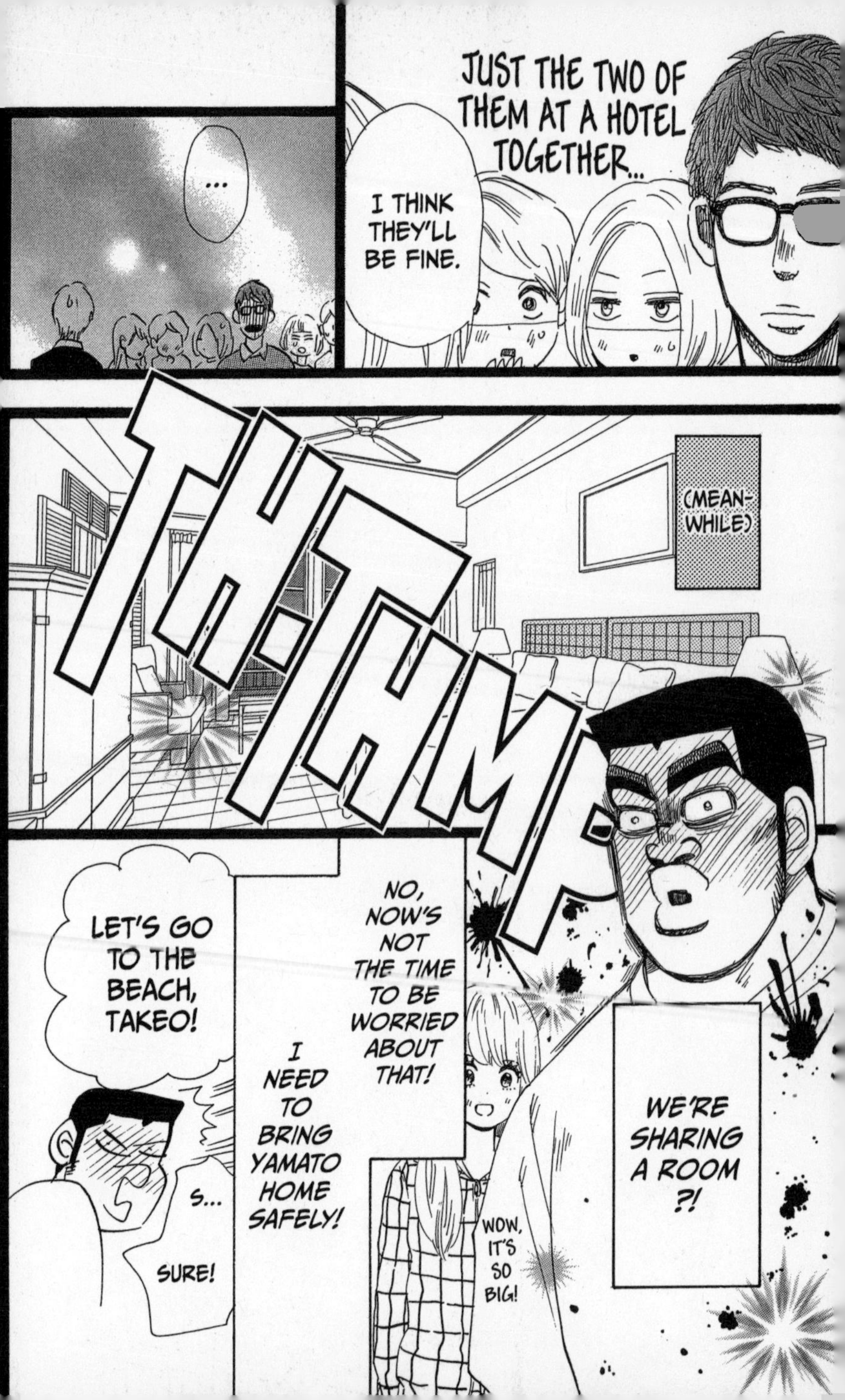
JUST THE TWO OF THEM AT A HOTEL TOGETHER...
I THINK THEY'LL BE FINE.
...
(MEAN-WHILE)
THUMP
WE'RE SHARING A ROOM ?!
WOW, IT'S SO BIG!
NO, NOW'S NOT THE TIME TO BE WORRIED ABOUT THAT!
I NEED TO BRING YAMATO HOME SAFELY!
LET'S GO TO THE BEACH, TAKEO!
S...
SURE!

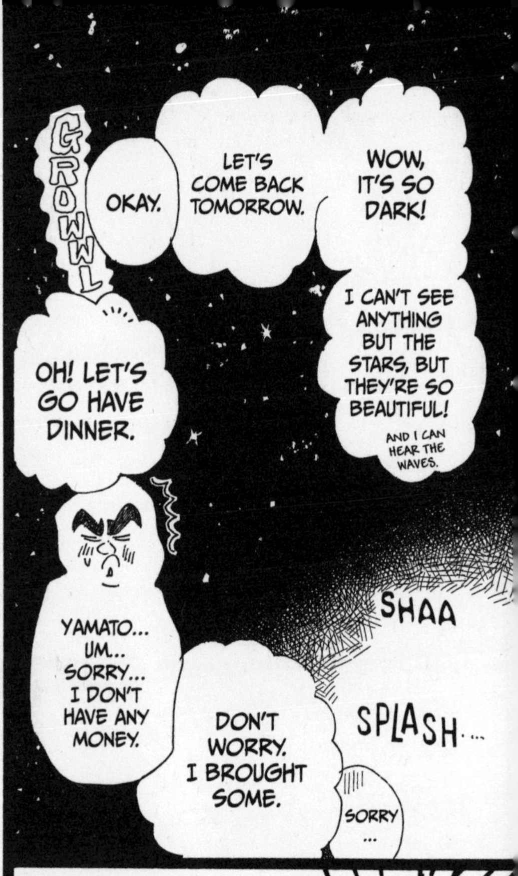
WOW, IT'S SO DARK!
I CAN'T SEE ANYTHING BUT THE STARS, BUT THEY'RE SO BEAUTIFUL!
AND I CAN HEAR THE WAVES.
LET'S COME BACK TOMORROW.
OKAY.
GROWWL
OH! LET'S GO HAVE DINNER.
SHAA
YAMATO... UM... SORRY... I DON'T HAVE ANY MONEY.
SPLASH...
DON'T WORRY. I BROUGHT SOME.
SORRY...
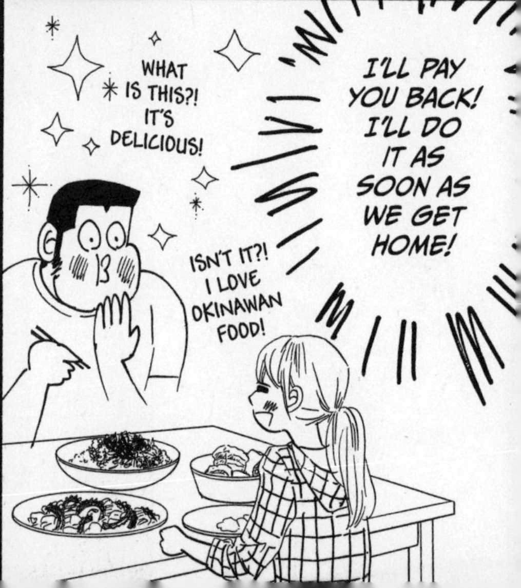
I'LL PAY YOU BACK! I'LL DO IT AS SOON AS WE GET HOME!
WHAT IS THIS?! IT'S DELICIOUS!
ISN'T IT?! I LOVE OKINAWAN FOOD!
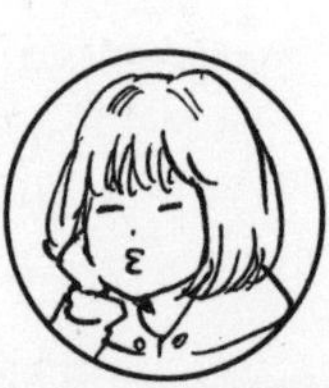

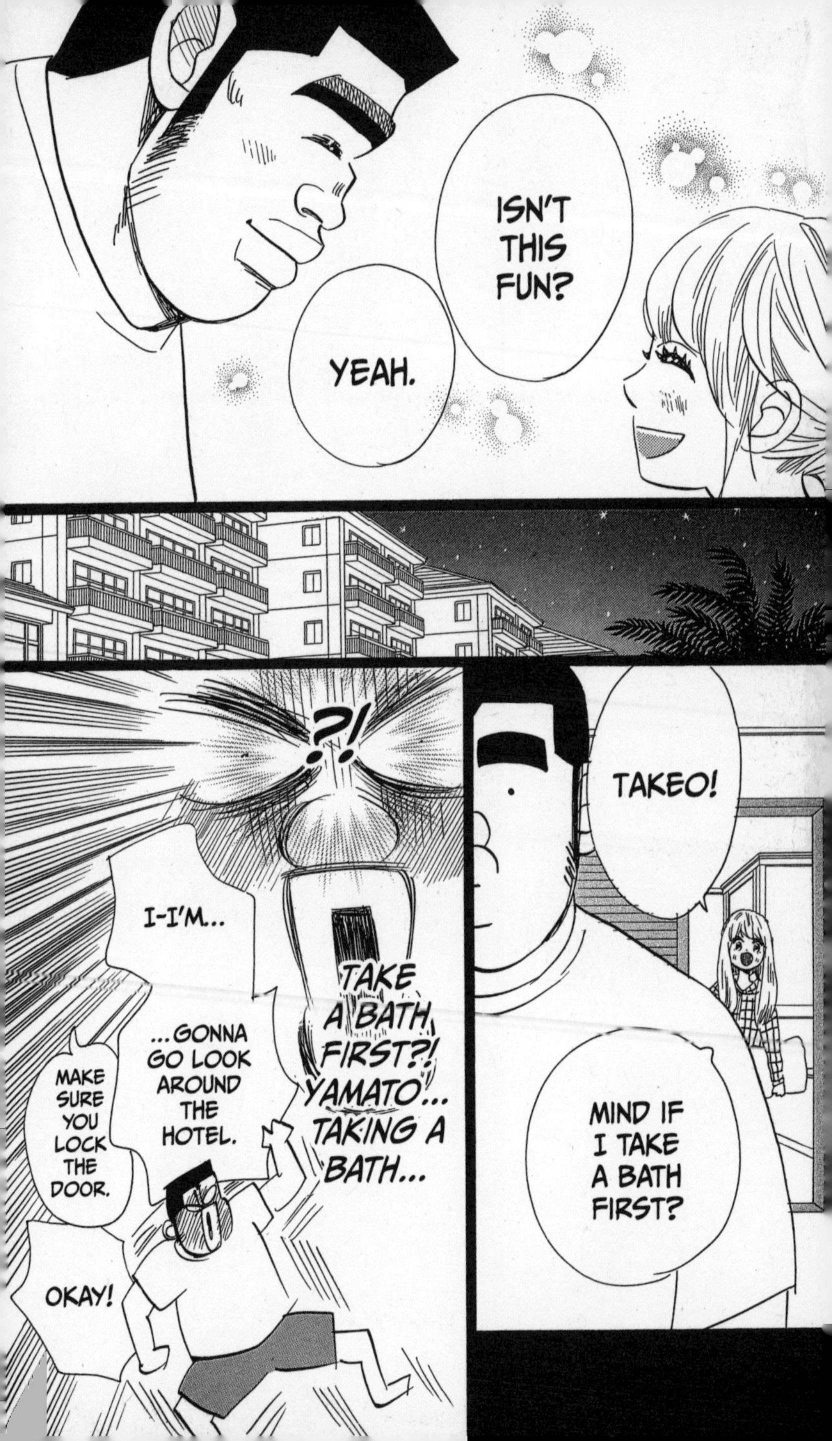
ISN'T THIS FUN?
YEAH.
TAKEO!
MIND IF I TAKE A BATH FIRST?
?!
TAKE A BATH FIRST?! YAMATO... TAKING A BATH...
I-I'M...
...GONNA GO LOOK AROUND THE HOTEL.
MAKE SURE YOU LOCK THE DOOR.
OKAY!

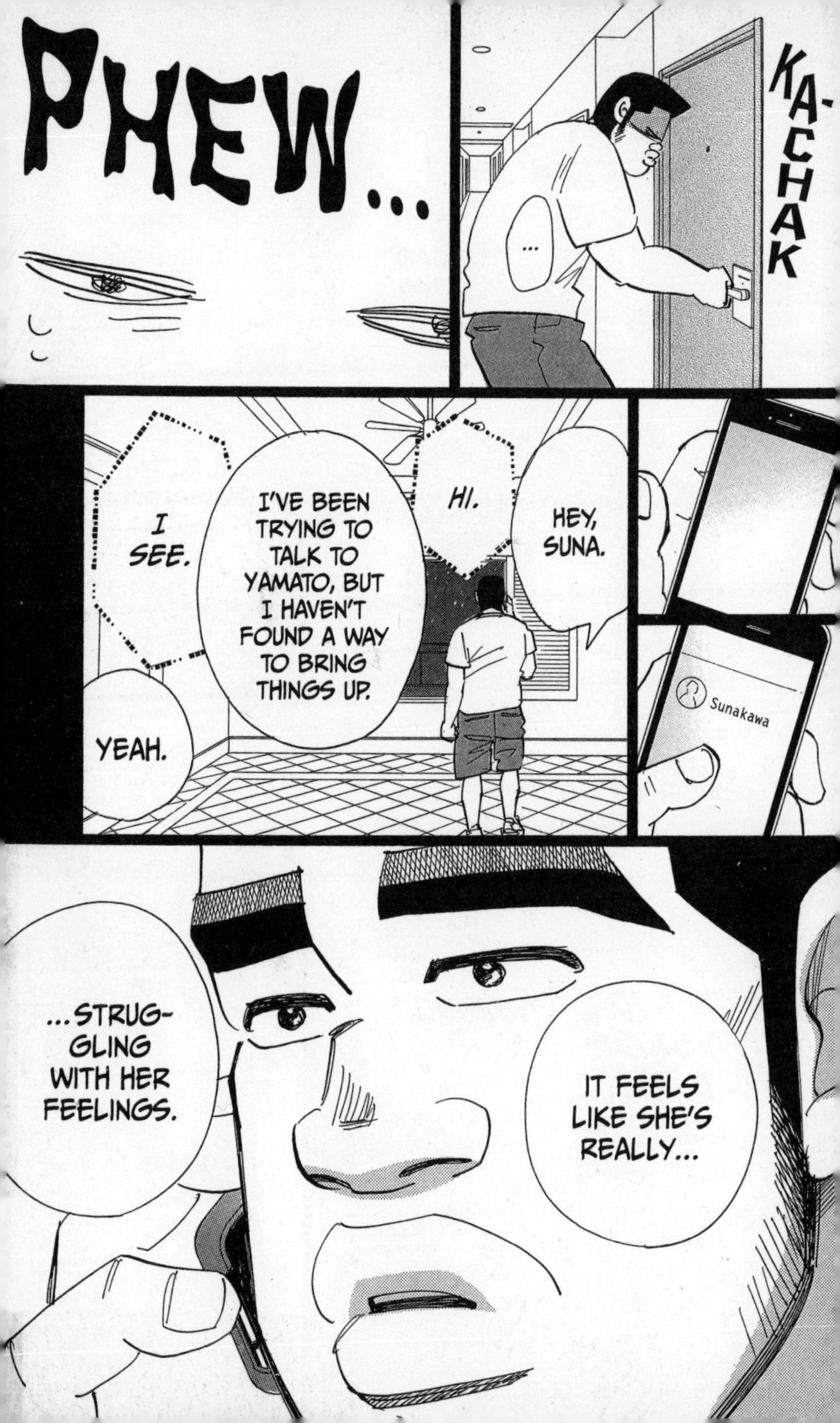
KA-CHAK
...
PHEW...
Sunakawa
HEY, SUNA.
HI.
I'VE BEEN TRYING TO TALK TO YAMATO, BUT I HAVEN'T FOUND A WAY TO BRING THINGS UP.
I SEE.
YEAH.
IT FEELS LIKE SHE'S REALLY...
...STRUG-GLING WITH HER FEELINGS.

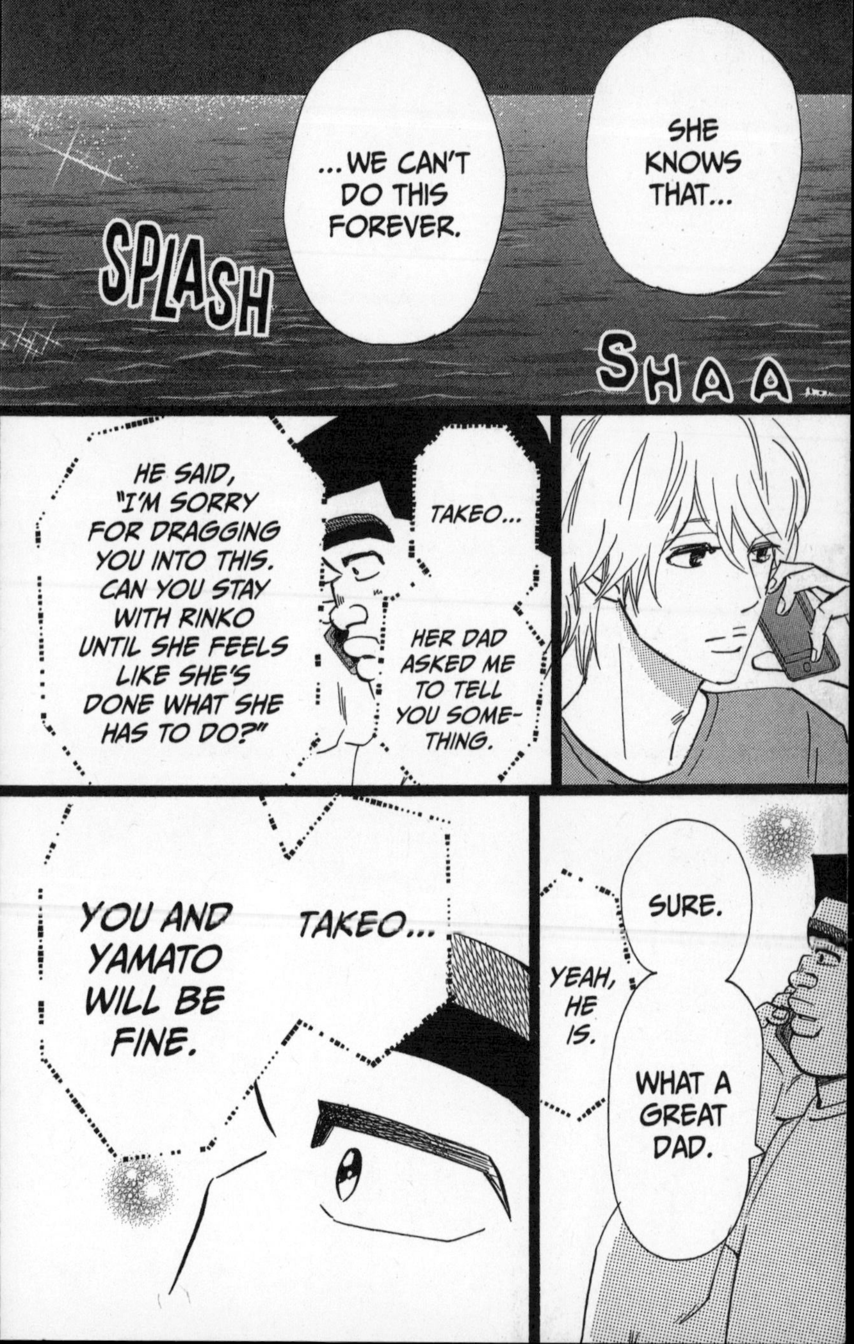
SHE KNOWS THAT...
SHAA...
...WE CAN'T DO THIS FOREVER.
SPLASH
TAKEO...
HER DAD ASKED ME TO TELL YOU SOME-THING.
HE SAID, "I'M SORRY FOR DRAGGING YOU INTO THIS. CAN YOU STAY WITH RINKO UNTIL SHE FEELS LIKE SHE'S DONE WHAT SHE HAS TO DO?"
SURE.
WHAT A GREAT DAD.
YEAH, HE IS.
TAKEO...
YOU AND YAMATO WILL BE FINE.

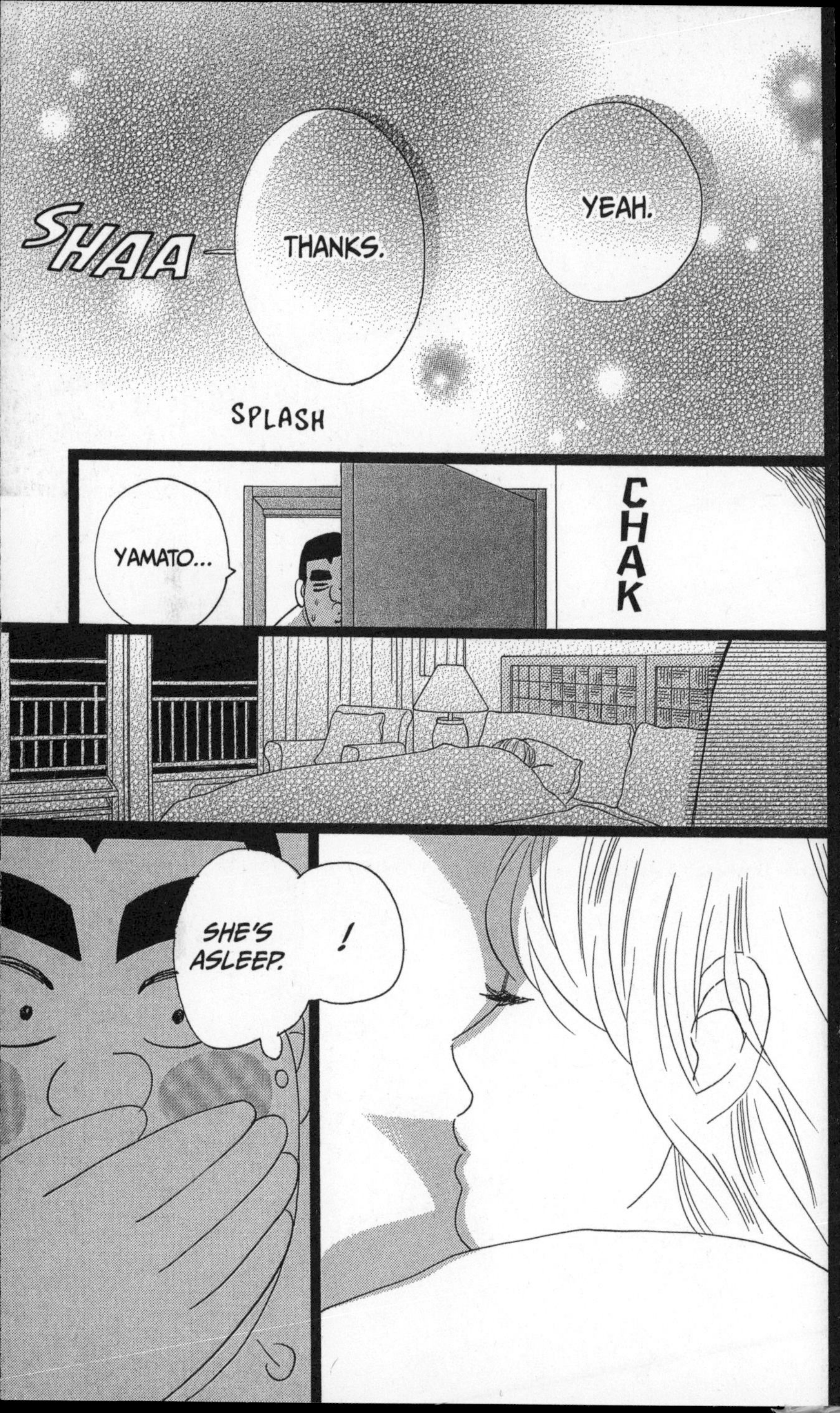
YEAH.
THANKS.
SHAA
SPLASH
CHAK
YAMATO...
!
SHE'S ASLEEP.

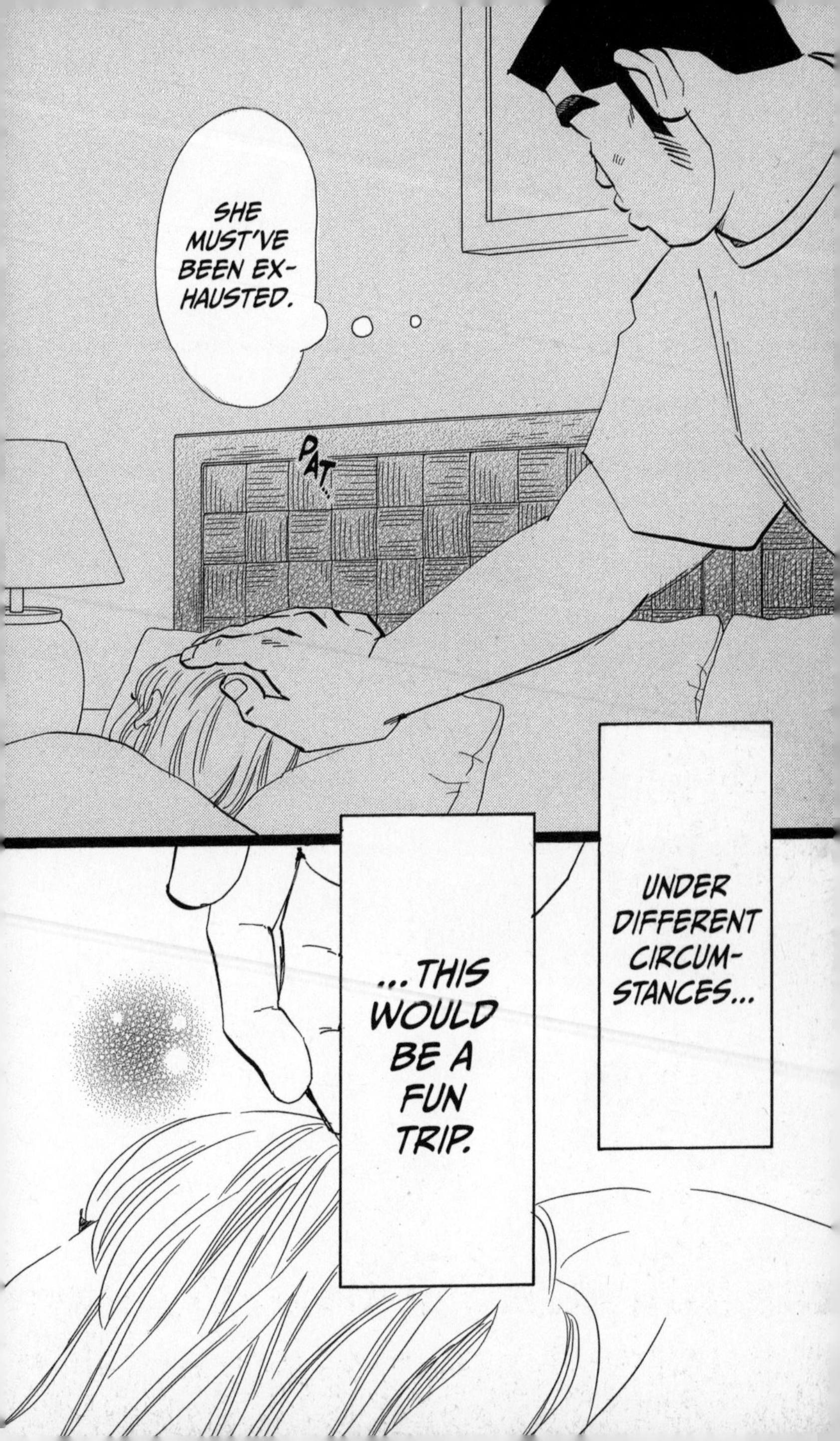
SHE MUST'VE BEEN EX-HAUSTED.
PAT...
UNDER DIFFERENT CIRCUM-STANCES...
...THIS WOULD BE A FUN TRIP.

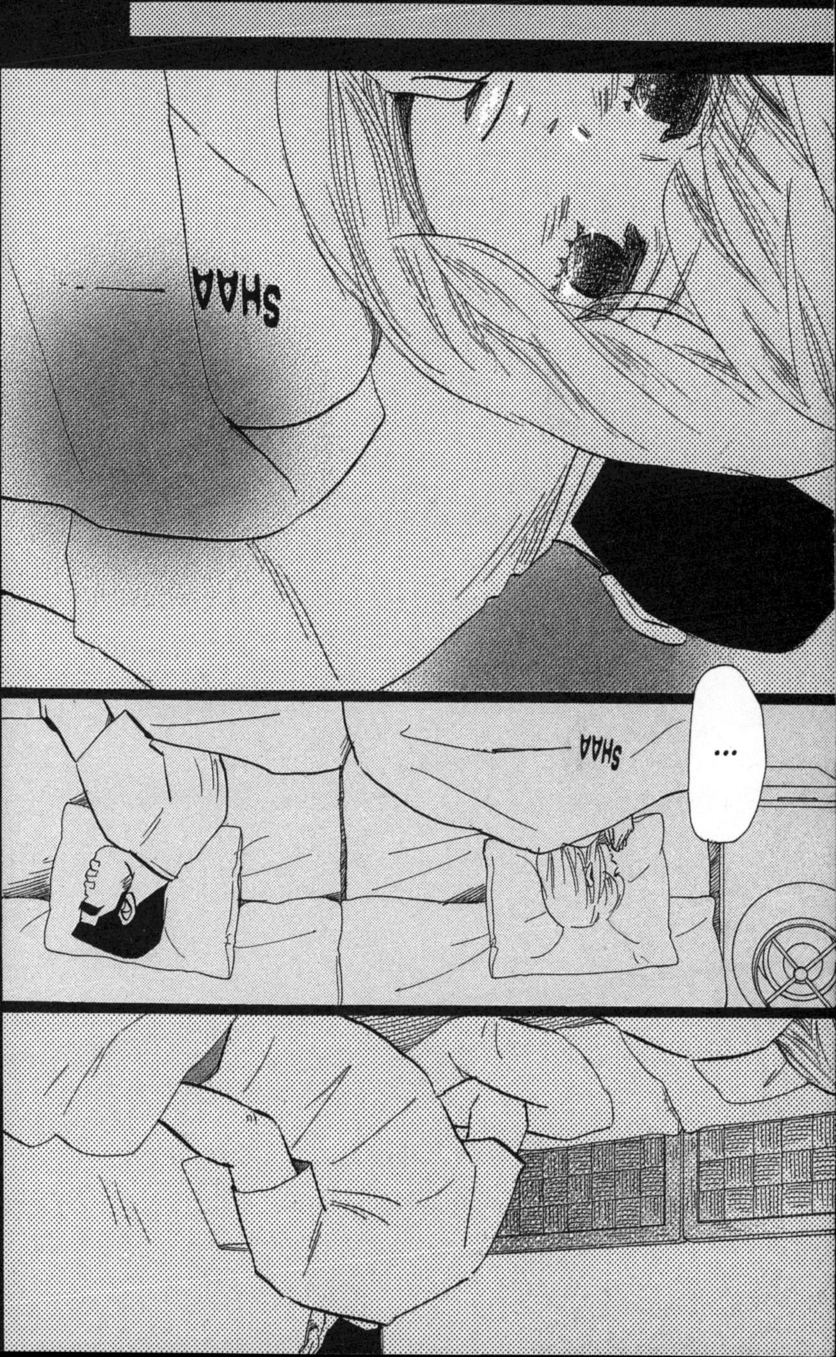
SHAA
...
SHAA

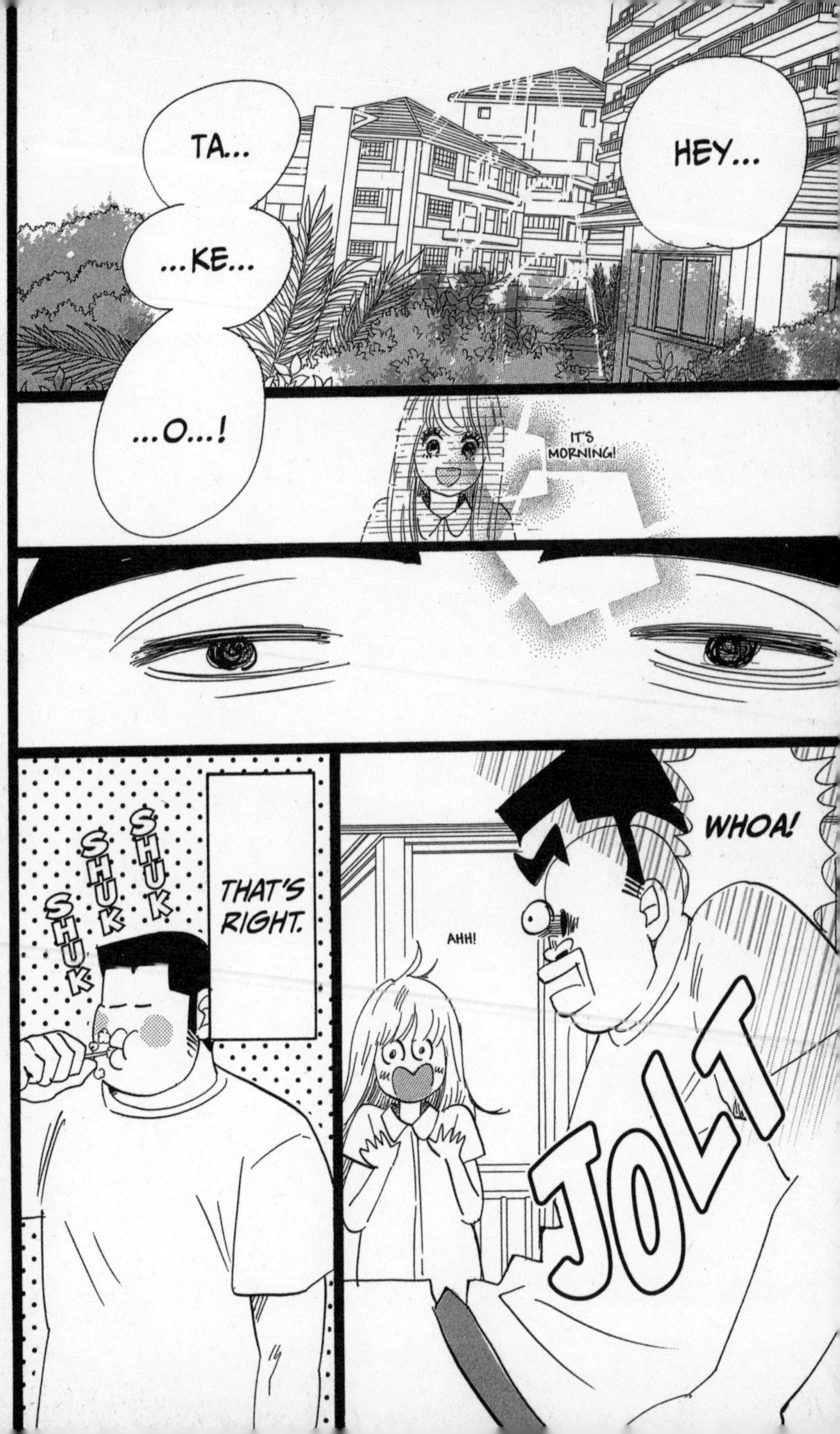
HEY...
TA...
...KE...
...O...!
IT'S MORNING!
WHOA!
JOLT
AHH!
THAT'S RIGHT.
SHUK SHUK SHUK

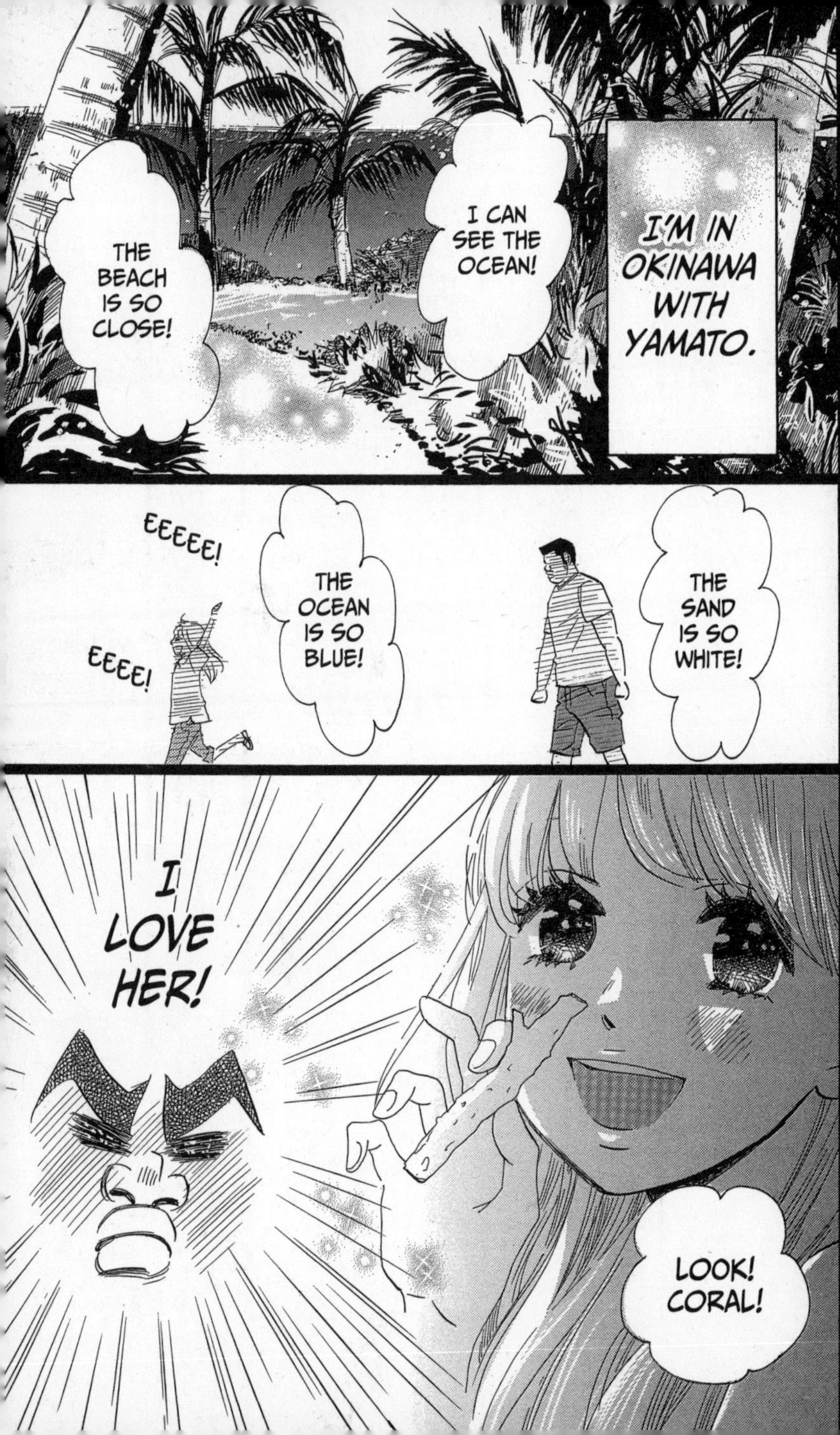
I'M IN OKINAWA WITH YAMATO.
I CAN SEE THE OCEAN!
THE BEACH IS SO CLOSE!
THE SAND IS SO WHITE!
THE OCEAN IS SO BLUE!
EEEEEE!
EEEE!
LOOK! CORAL!
I LOVE HER!

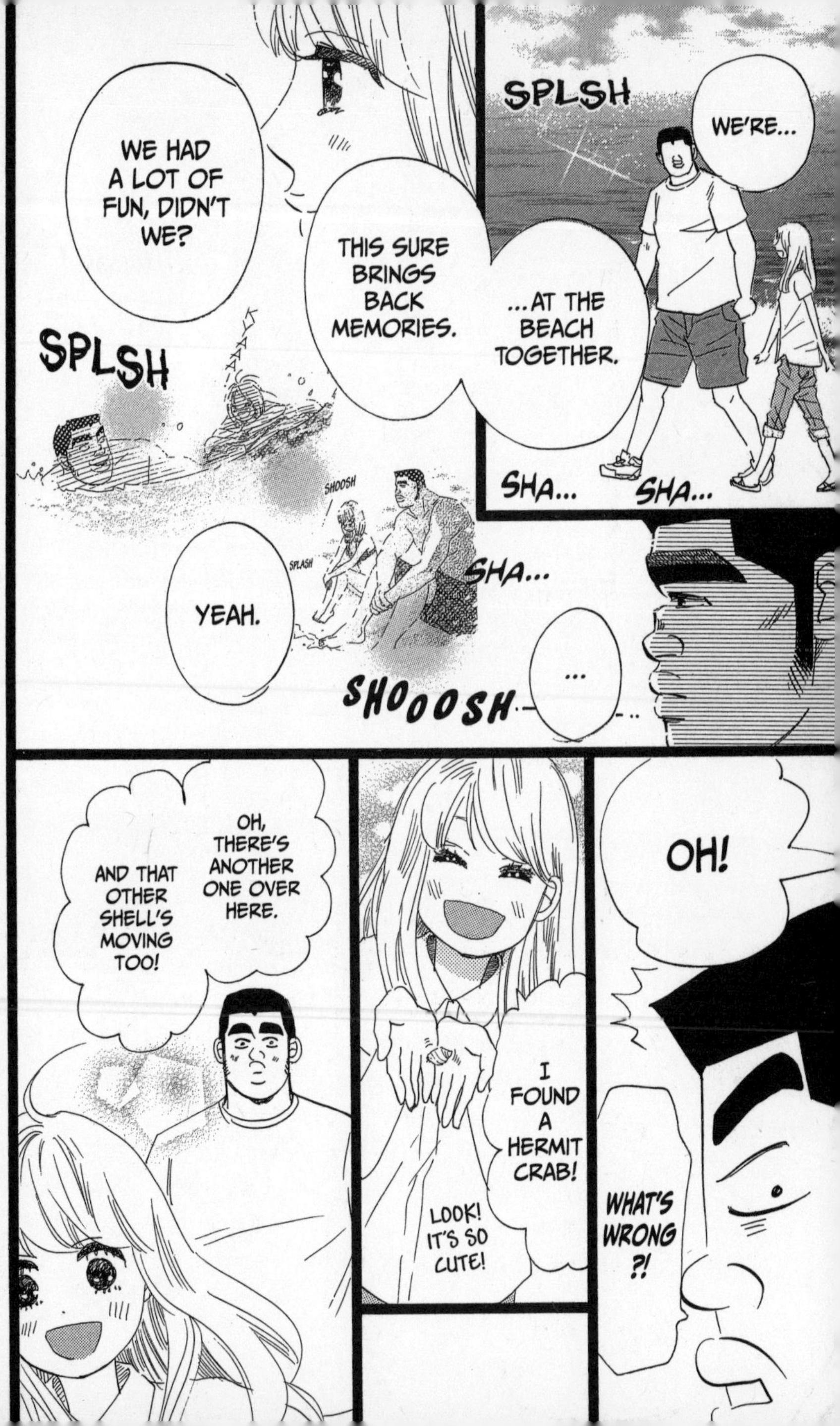
SPLSH
WE'RE...
...AT THE BEACH TOGETHER.
THIS SURE BRINGS BACK MEMORIES.
SHA... SHA...
...
SHA...
SHOOOSH
WE HAD A LOT OF FUN, DIDN'T WE?
SPLSH
SHOOSH
SPLASH
YEAH.
OH!
WHAT'S WRONG ?!
I FOUND A HERMIT CRAB!
LOOK! IT'S SO CUTE!
OH, THERE'S ANOTHER ONE OVER HERE.
AND THAT OTHER SHELL'S MOVING TOO!

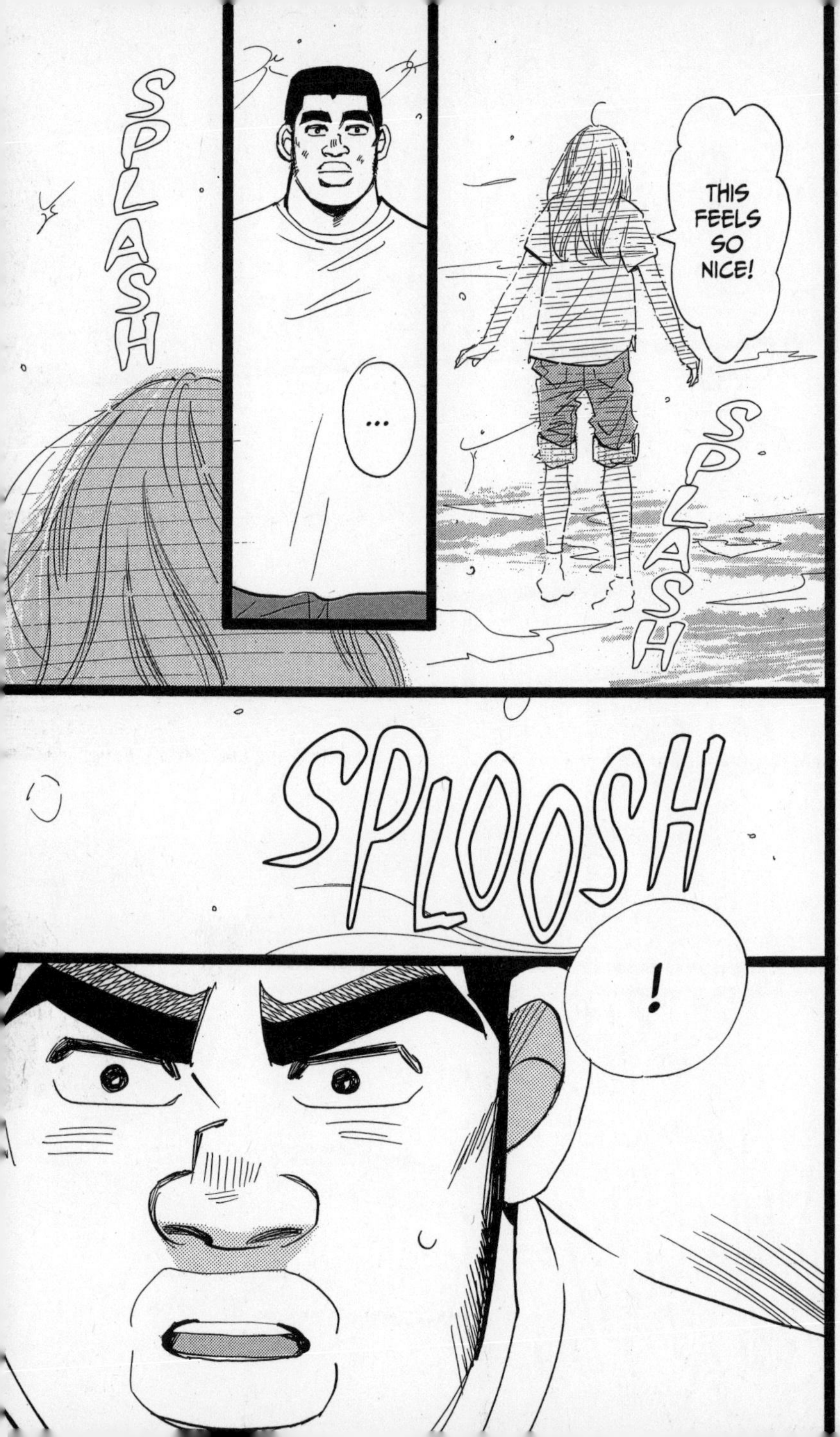
THIS FEELS SO NICE!
SPLASH
SPLASH
...
SPLOOSH
!

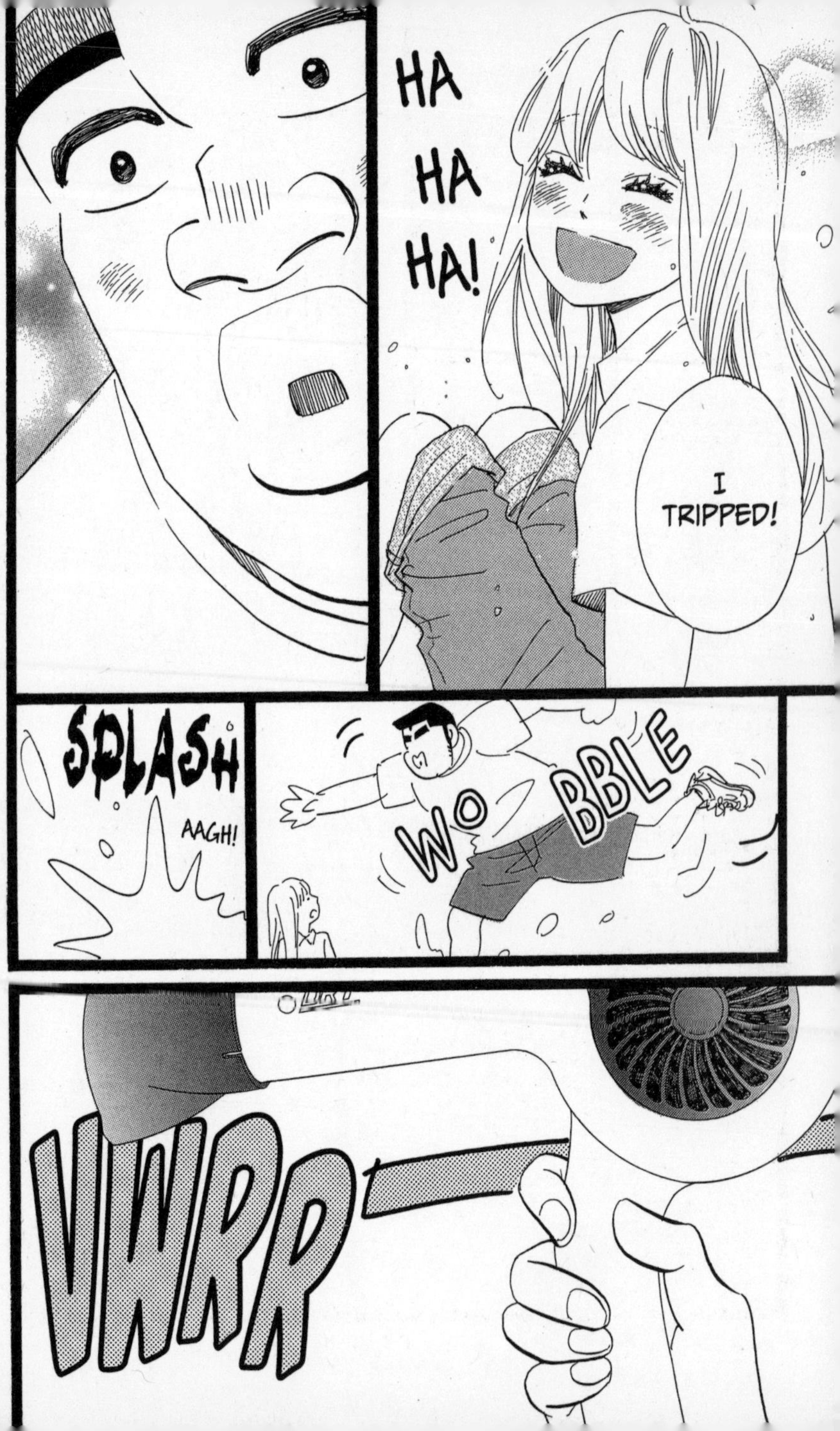
I TRIPPED!
HA HA HA!
WOBBLE
SPLASH
AAGH!
VWRR

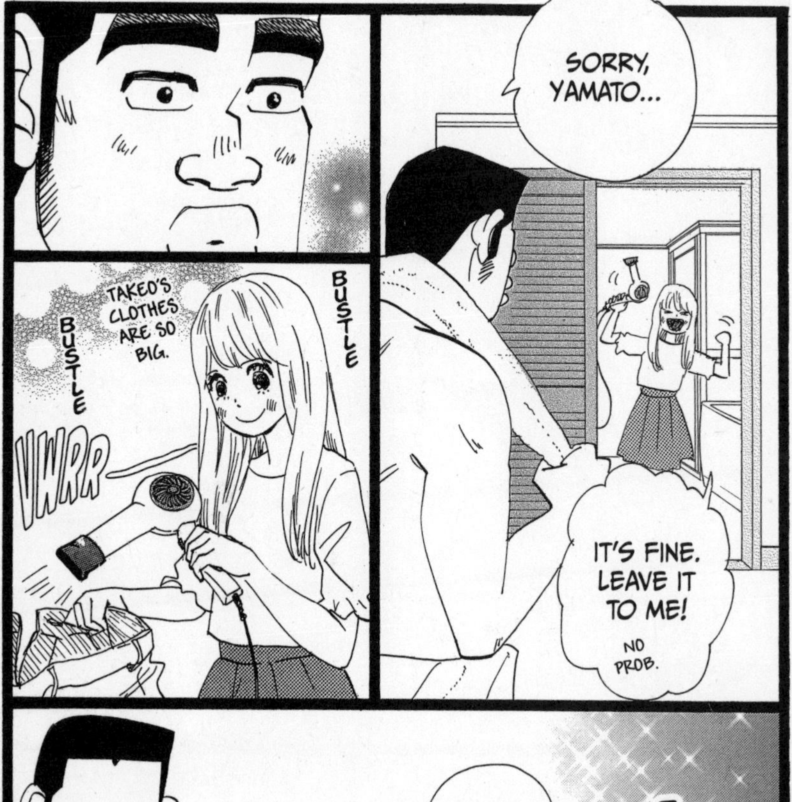
SORRY, YAMATO...
IT'S FINE. LEAVE IT TO ME!
NO PROB.
BUSTLE
TAKEO'S CLOTHES ARE SO BIG.
BUSTLE
VWRR
I LOVE HER!!
I CAN DO THAT.
YOUR ARMS MUST BE TIRED.
NOPE! IT'S A COMFORTABLE POSITION, SO I'M FINE.
MAKE SURE YOU TOWEL OFF, TAKEO.
SORRY I GOT CHANGED WHEN YOU CAN'T...
THANKS.
I DIDN'T HAVE MONEY FOR NEW CLOTHES.

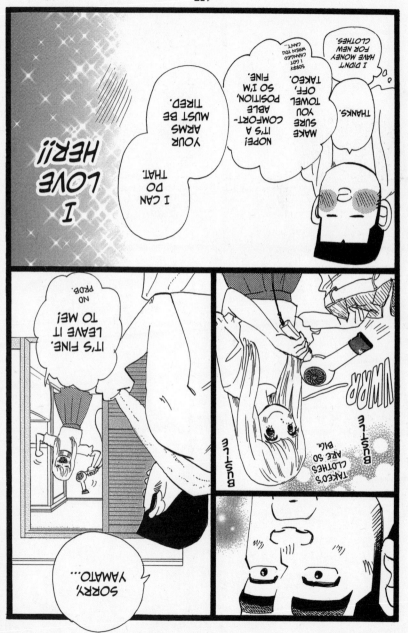

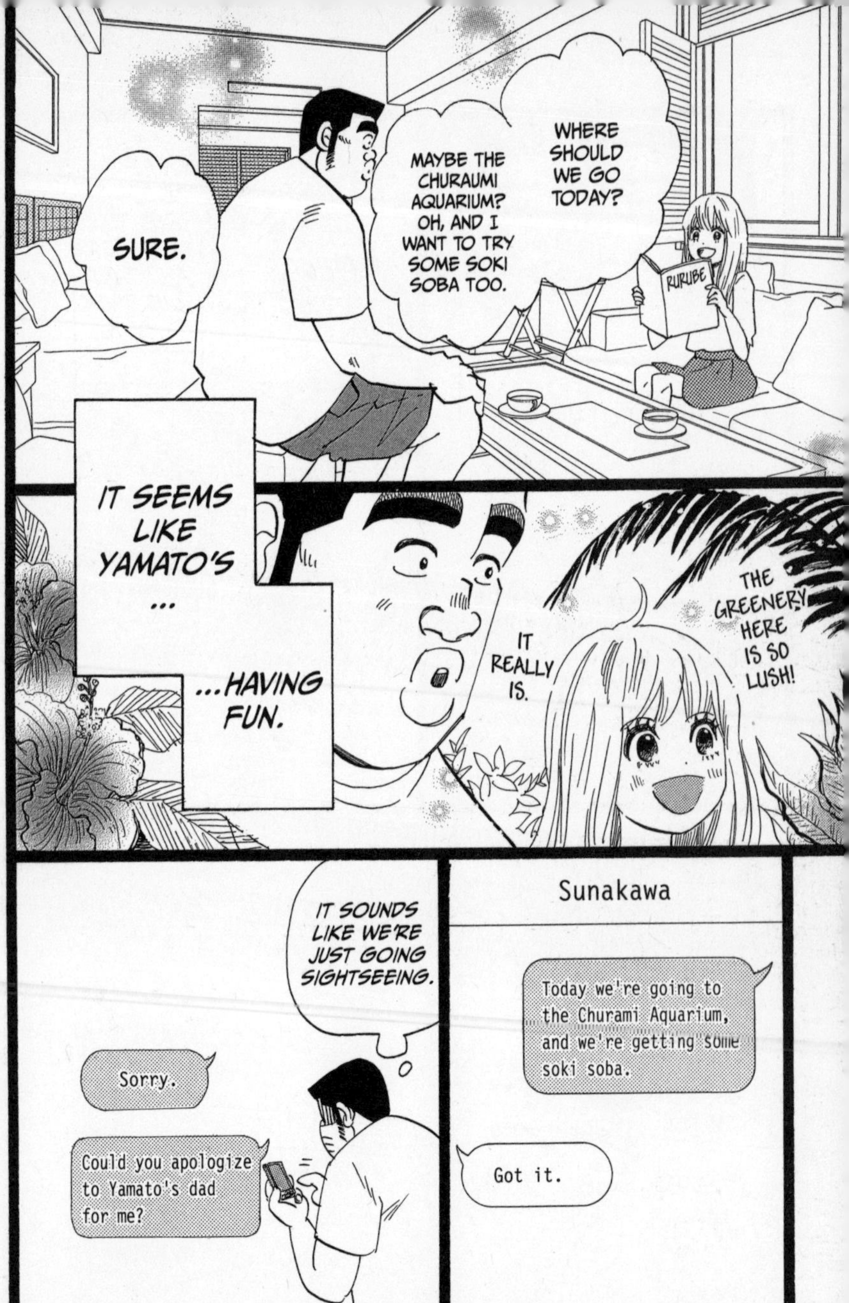
RURUBE
WHERE SHOULD WE GO TODAY?
MAYBE THE CHURAUMI AQUARIUM? OH, AND I WANT TO TRY SOME SOKI SOBA TOO.
SURE.
THE GREENERY HERE IS SO LUSH!
IT REALLY IS.
IT SEEMS LIKE YAMATO'S ...
...HAVING FUN.
Sunakawa
Today we're going to the Churami Aquarium, and we're getting some soki soba.
Got it.
IT SOUNDS LIKE WE'RE JUST GOING SIGHTSEEING.
Sorry.
Could you apologize to Yamato's dad for me?

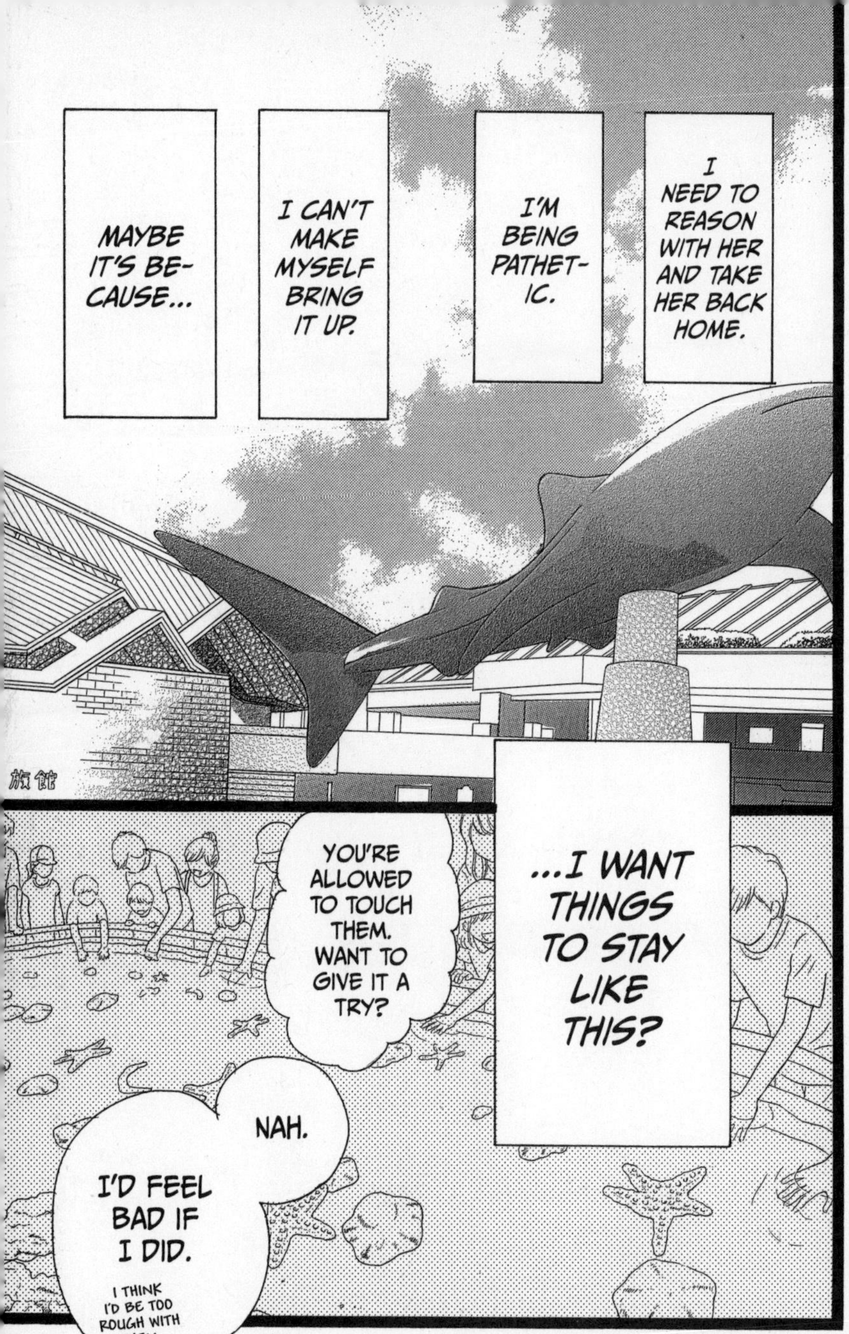
I NEED TO REASON WITH HER AND TAKE HER BACK HOME.
I'M BEING PATHET-IC.
I CAN'T MAKE MYSELF BRING IT UP.
MAYBE IT'S BE-CAUSE...
...I WANT THINGS TO STAY LIKE THIS?
YOU'RE ALLOWED TO TOUCH THEM. WANT TO GIVE IT A TRY?
NAH.
I'D FEEL BAD IF I DID.
I THINK I'D BE TOO ROUGH WITH THEM.

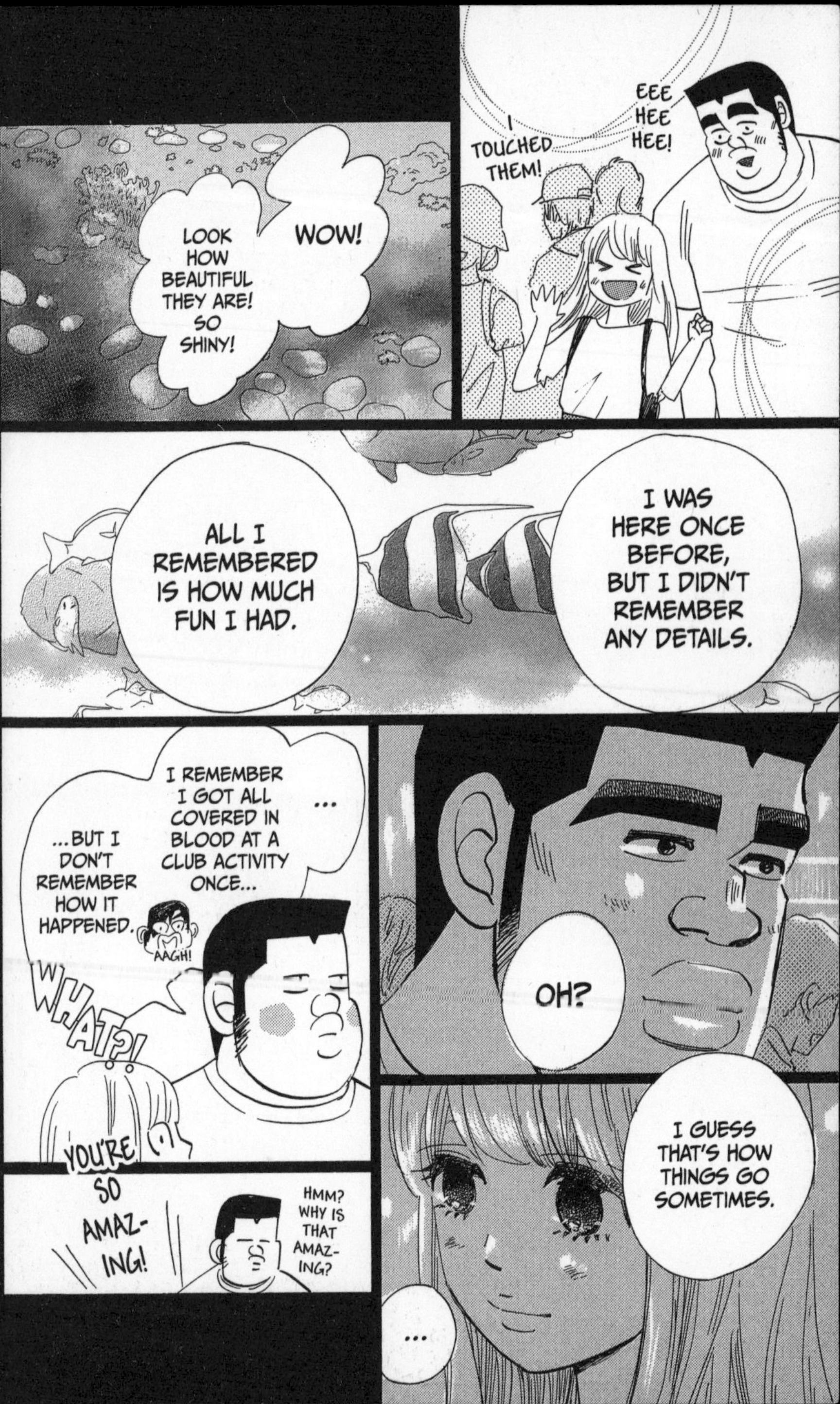
EEE HEE HEE!
I TOUCHED THEM!
WOW!
LOOK HOW BEAUTIFUL THEY ARE! SO SHINY!
I WAS HERE ONCE BEFORE, BUT I DIDN'T REMEMBER ANY DETAILS.
ALL I REMEMBERED IS HOW MUCH FUN I HAD.
OH?
I REMEMBER I GOT ALL COVERED IN BLOOD AT A CLUB ACTIVITY ONCE...
...
...BUT I DON'T REMEMBER HOW IT HAPPENED.
AAGH!
WHAT?!
I GUESS THAT'S HOW THINGS GO SOMETIMES.
...
YOU'RE SO AMAZING!
HMM? WHY IS THAT AMAZING?

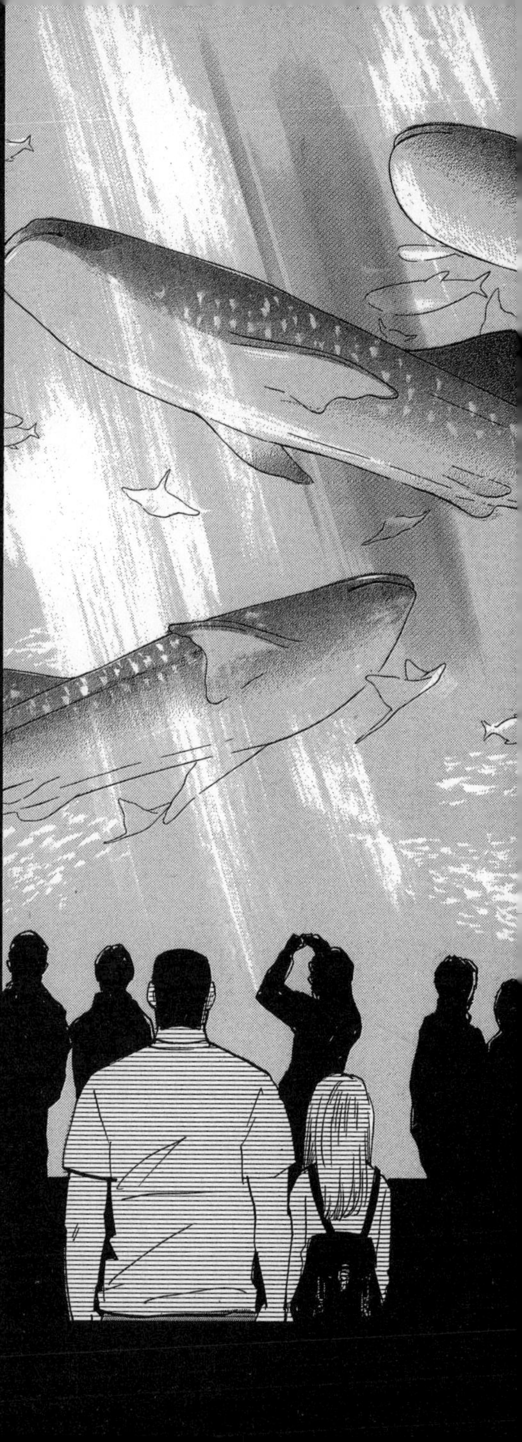
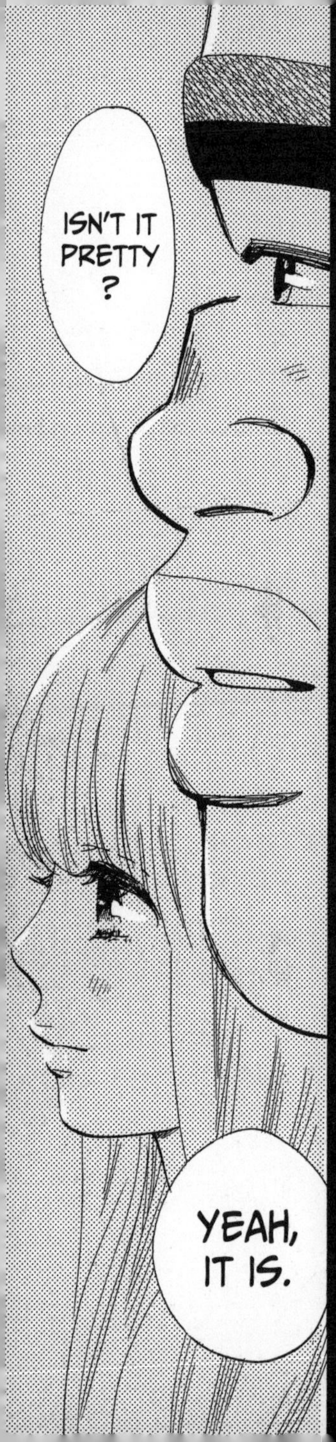
ISN'T IT PRETTY ?
YEAH, IT IS.

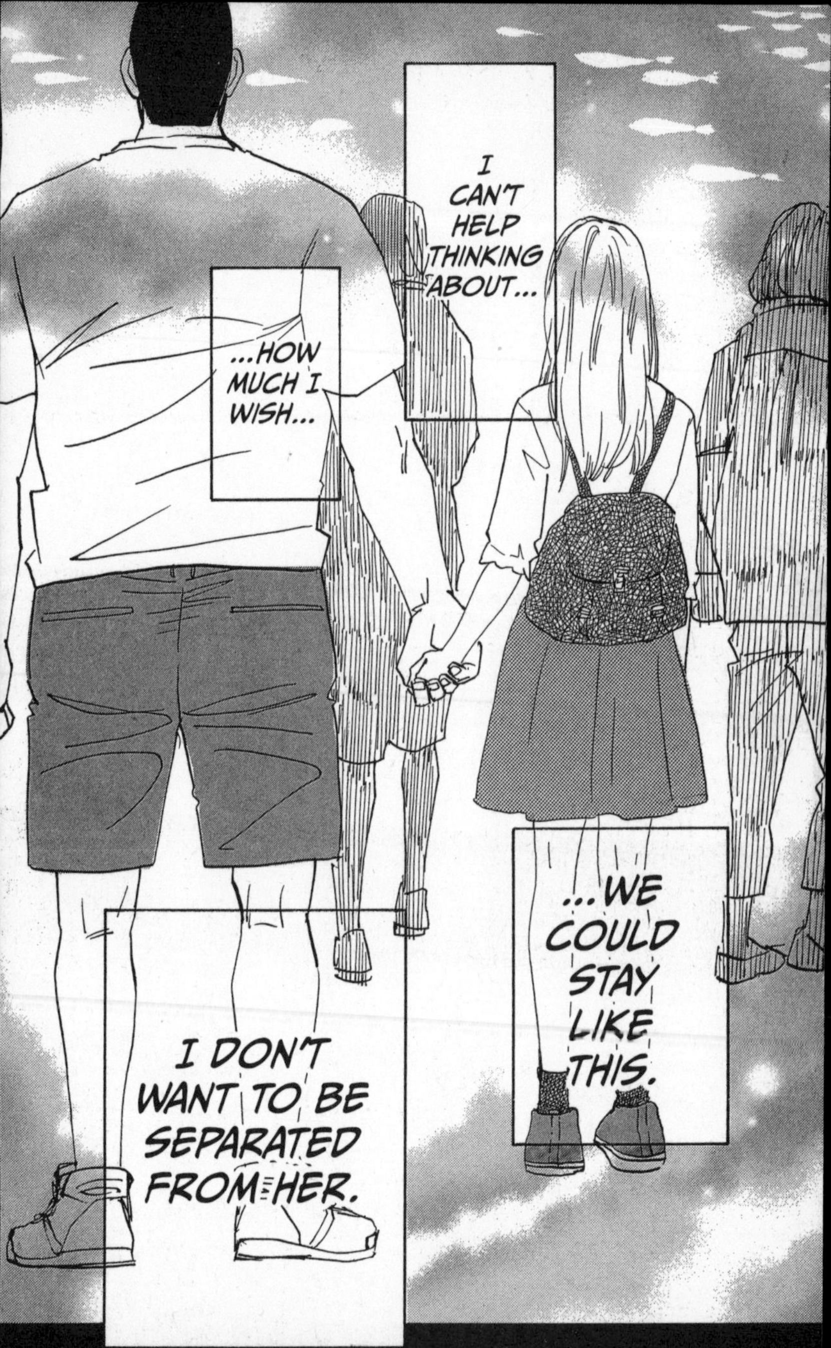
I CAN'T HELP THINKING ABOUT...
...HOW MUCH I WISH...
...WE COULD STAY LIKE THIS.
I DON'T WANT TO BE SEPARATED FROM HER.

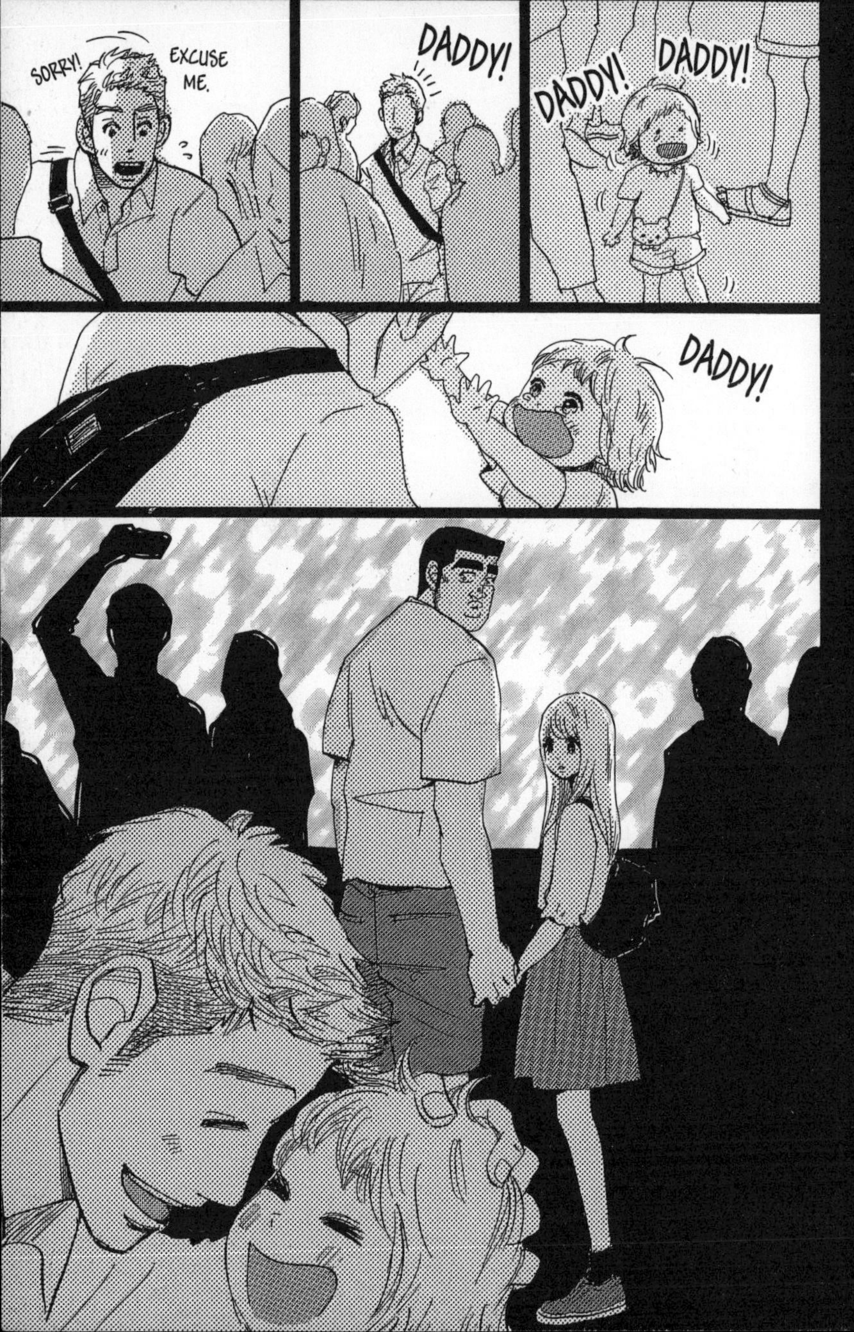
DADDY!
DADDY!
DADDY!
SORRY!
EXCUSE ME.
DADDY!

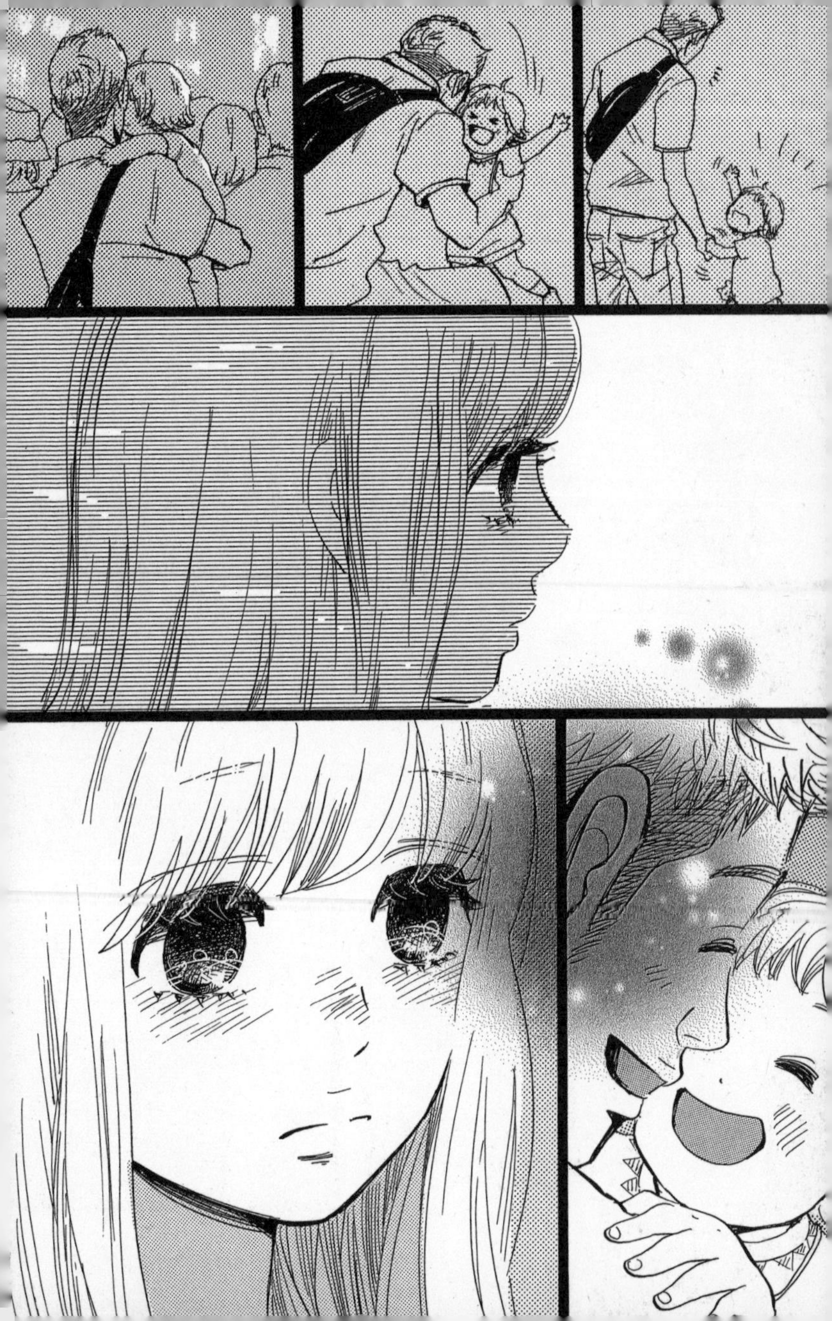

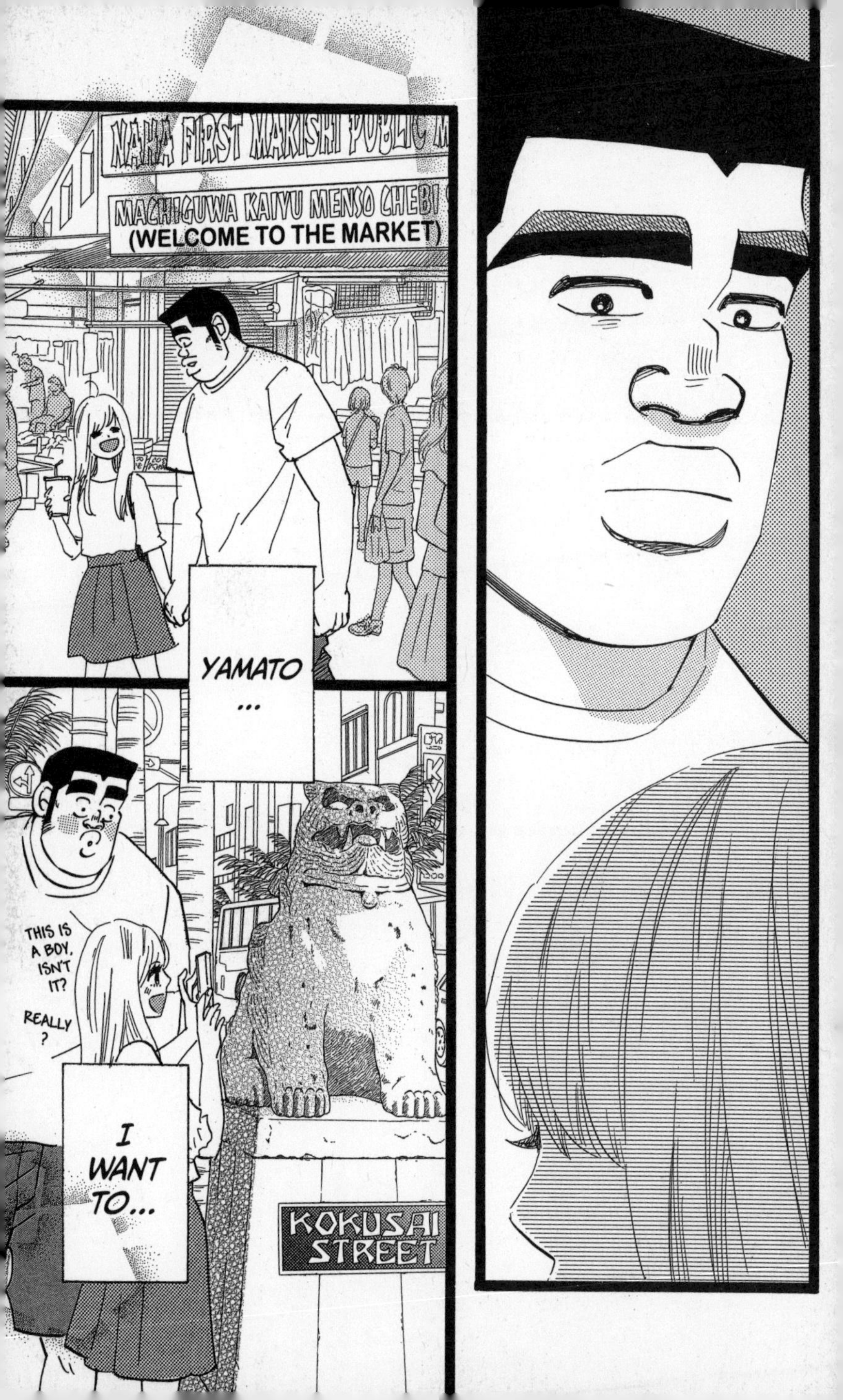
NAHA FIRST MAKISHI PUBLIC M
MACHIGUWA KAIYU MENSO CHEBI
(WELCOME TO THE MARKET)
YAMATO ...
THIS IS A BOY, ISN'T IT?
REALLY ?
I WANT TO...
KOKUSAI STREET

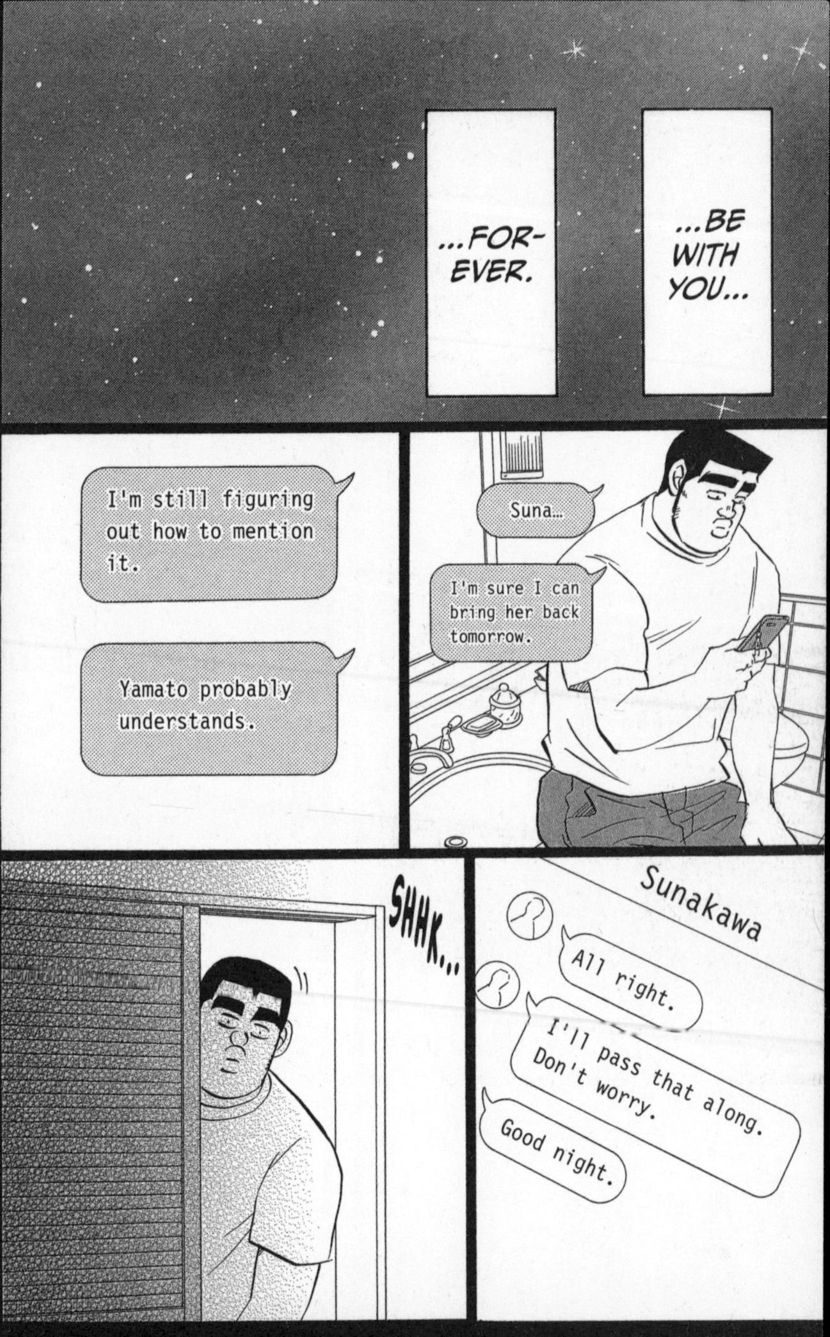
...BE WITH YOU...
...FOR-EVER.
Suna...
I'm sure I can bring her back tomorrow.
I'm still figuring out how to mention it.
Yamato probably understands.
Sunakawa
All right.
I'll pass that along. Don't worry.
Good night.
SHHK...

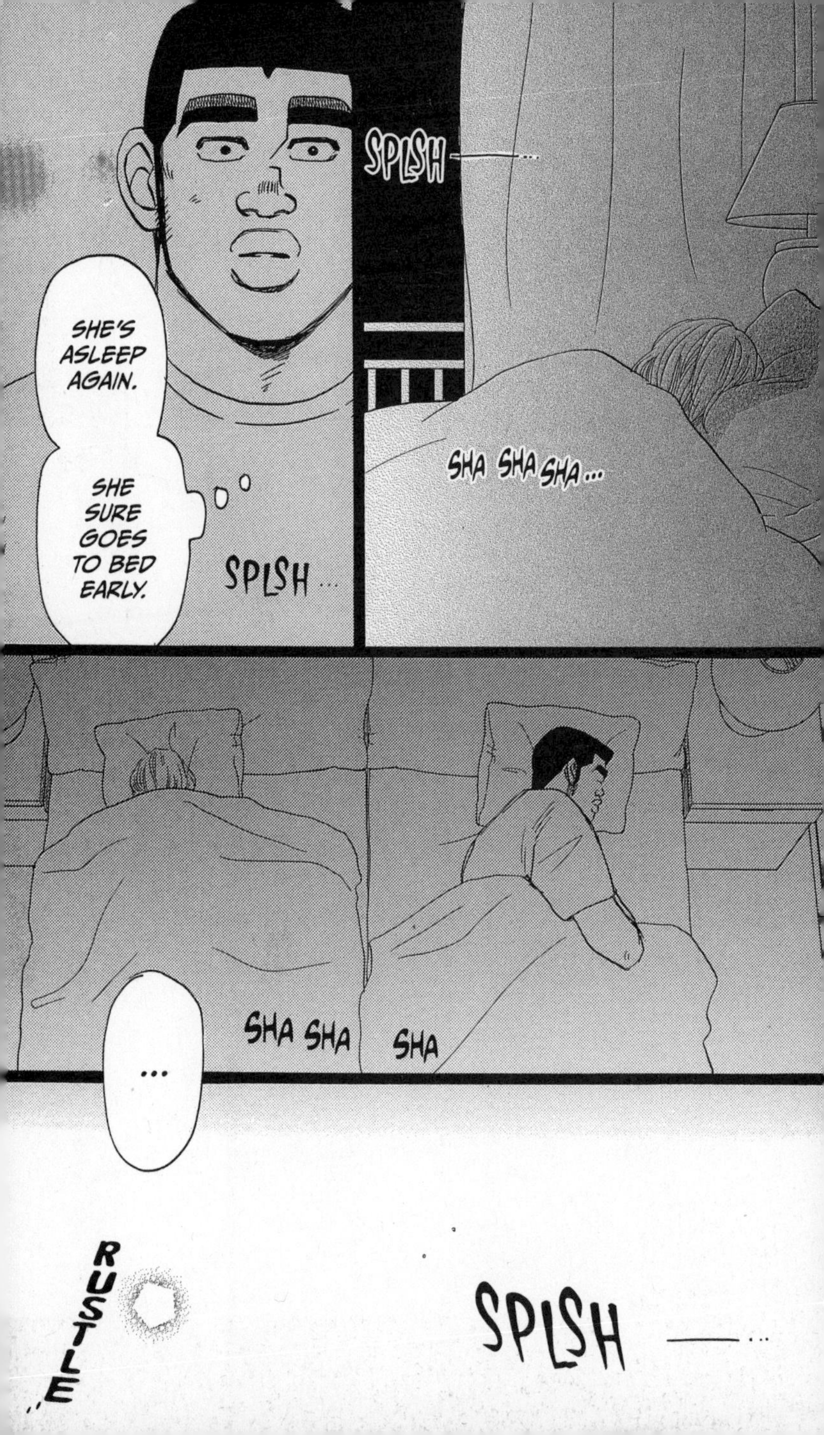
SPLSH —...
SHA SHA SHA...
SHE'S ASLEEP AGAIN.
SHE SURE GOES TO BED EARLY.
SPLSH...
SHA SHA SHA
...
SPLSH —...
RUSTLE

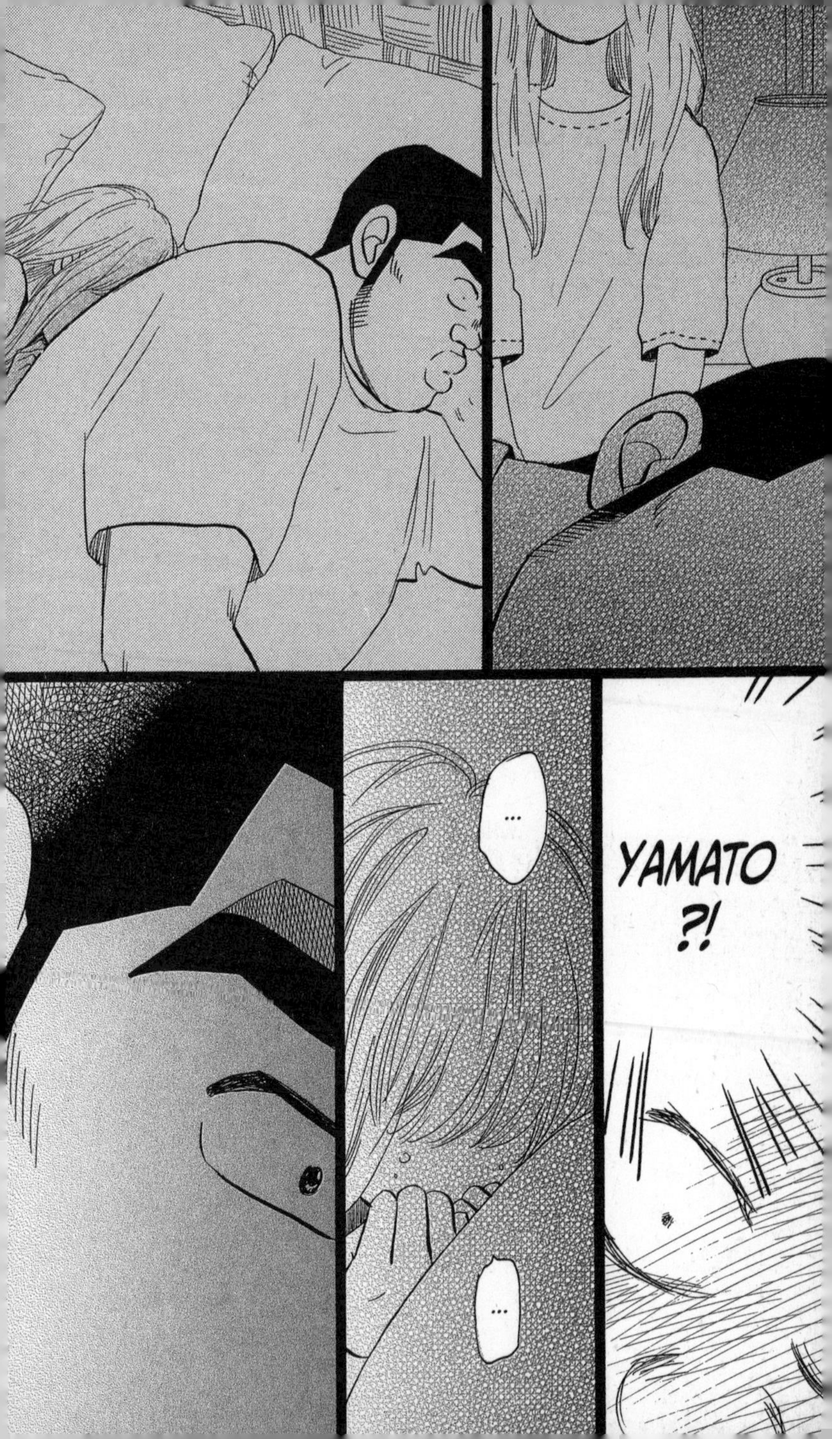
YAMATO ?!
...
...

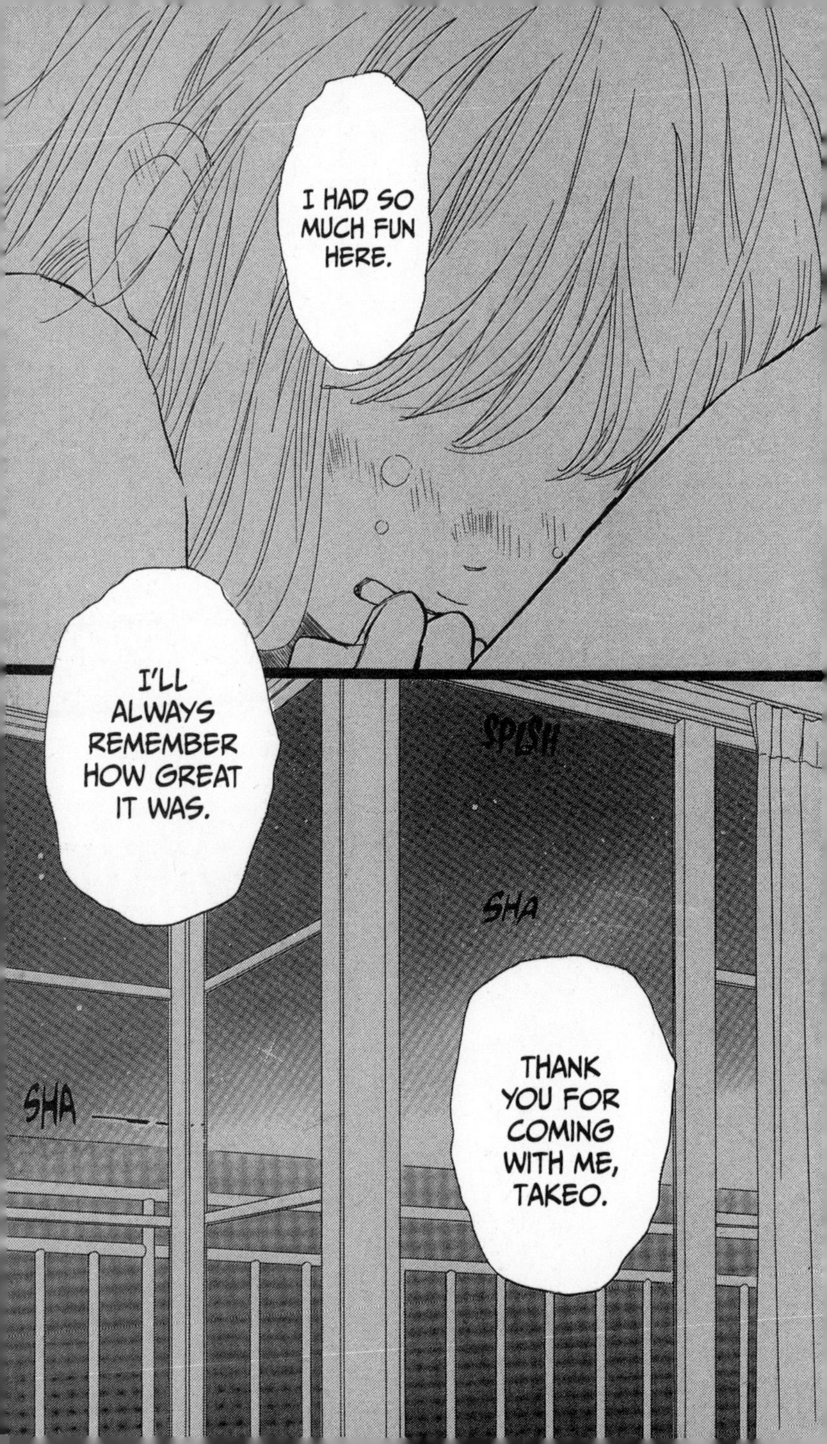
I HAD SO MUCH FUN HERE.
I'LL ALWAYS REMEMBER HOW GREAT IT WAS.
SPLSH
SHA
THANK YOU FOR COMING WITH ME, TAKEO.
SHA

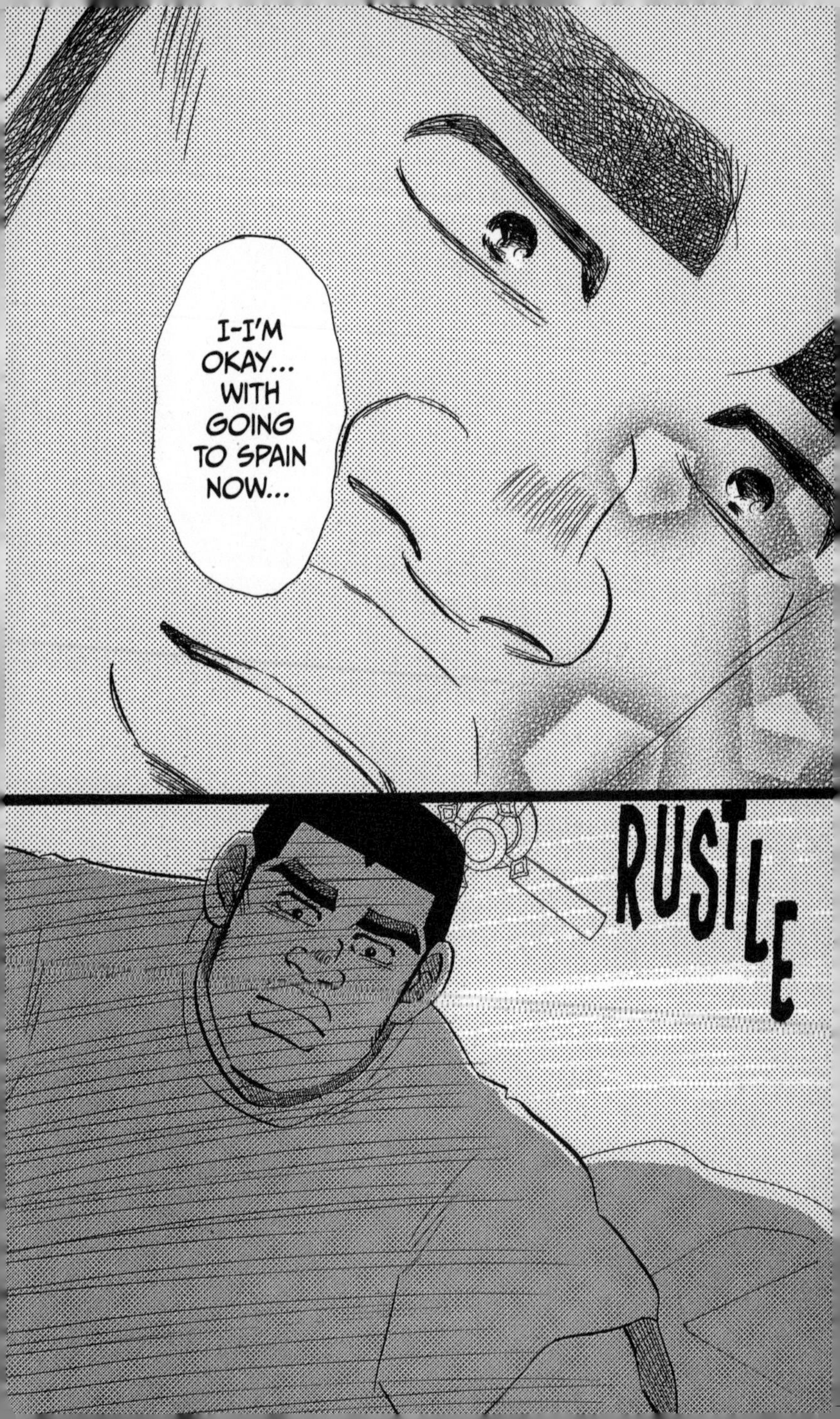
I-I'M OKAY... WITH GOING TO SPAIN NOW...
RUSTLE

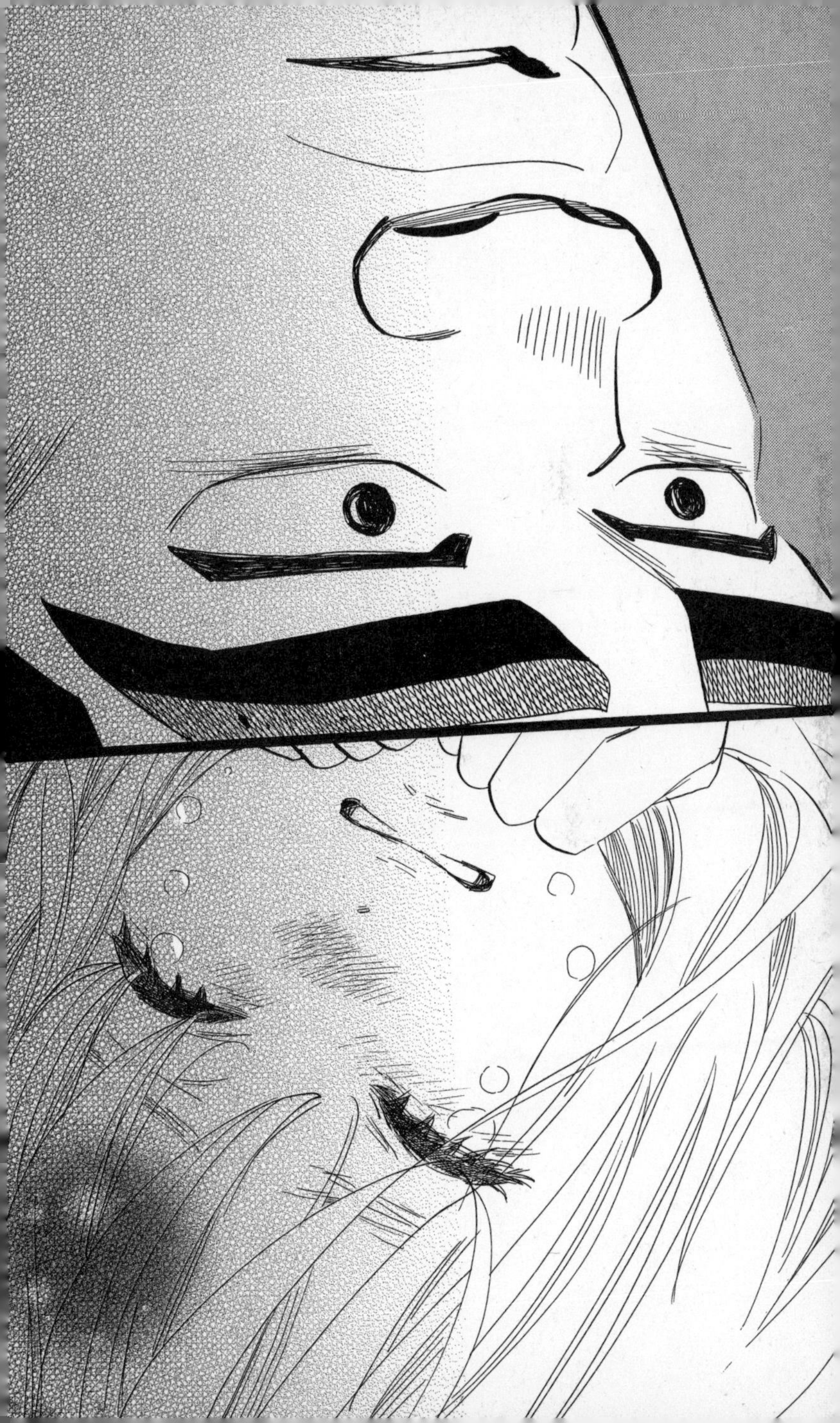

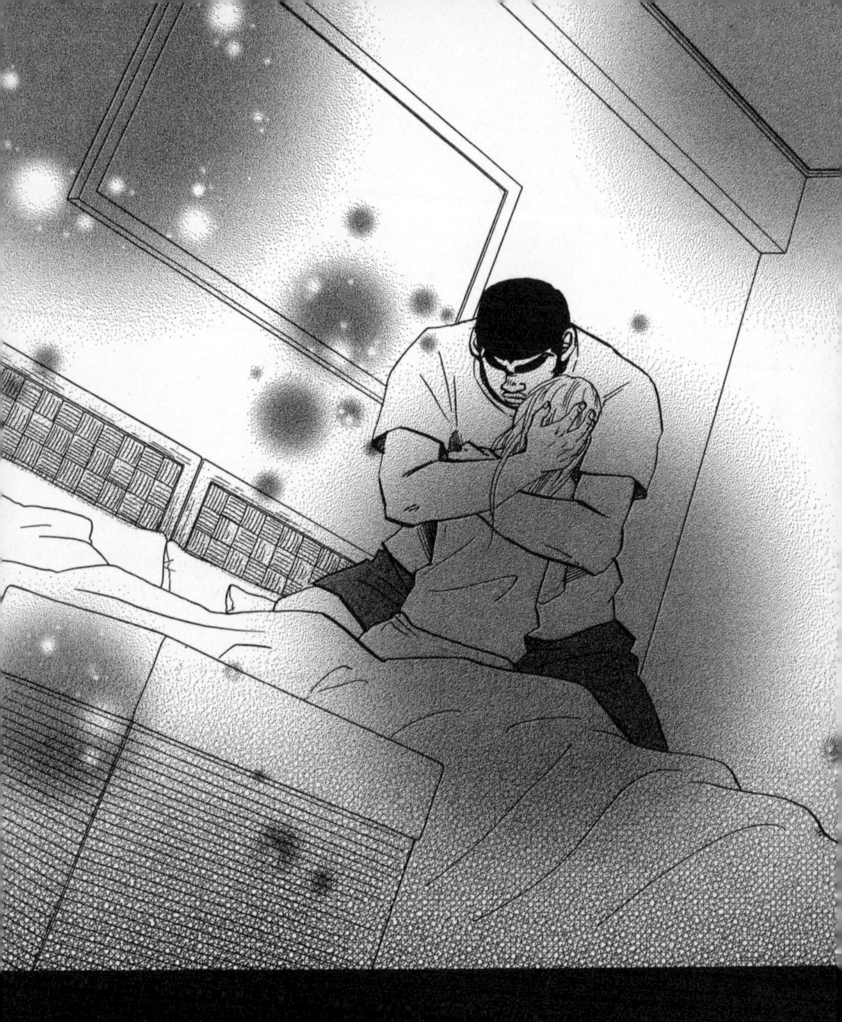

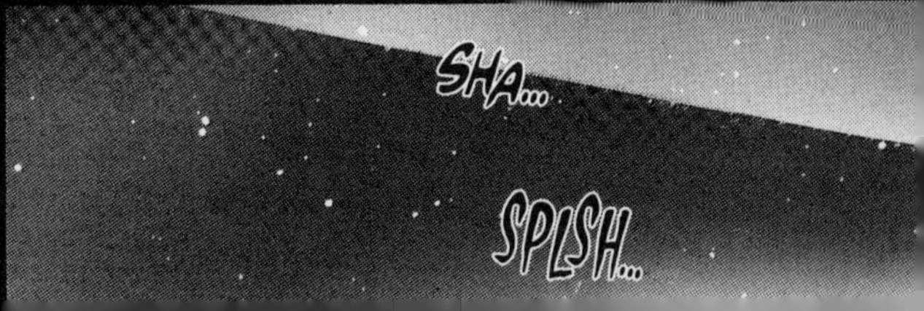
SHA...
SPLSH...

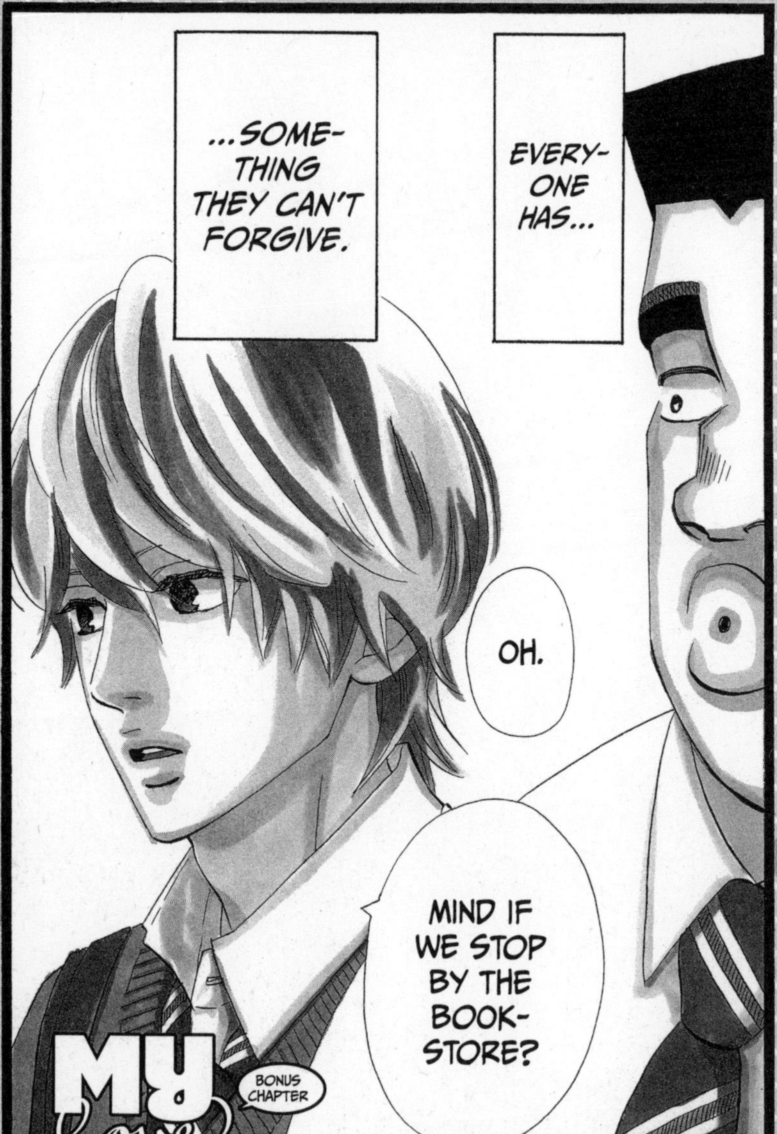
EVERY-ONE HAS...
...SOME-THING THEY CAN'T FORGIVE.
OH.
MIND IF WE STOP BY THE BOOK-STORE?
MY love STORY!!
BONUS CHAPTER

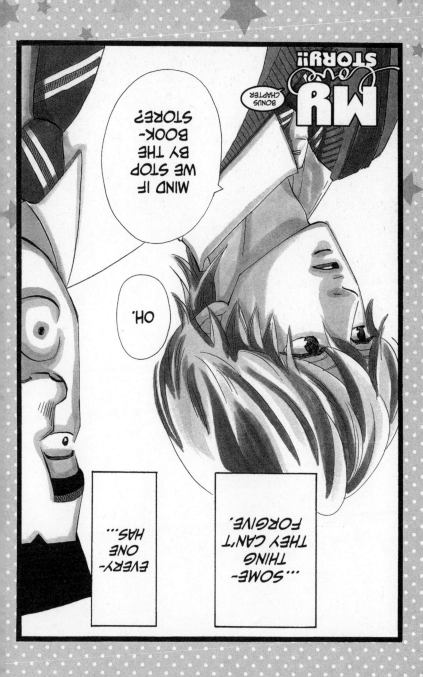

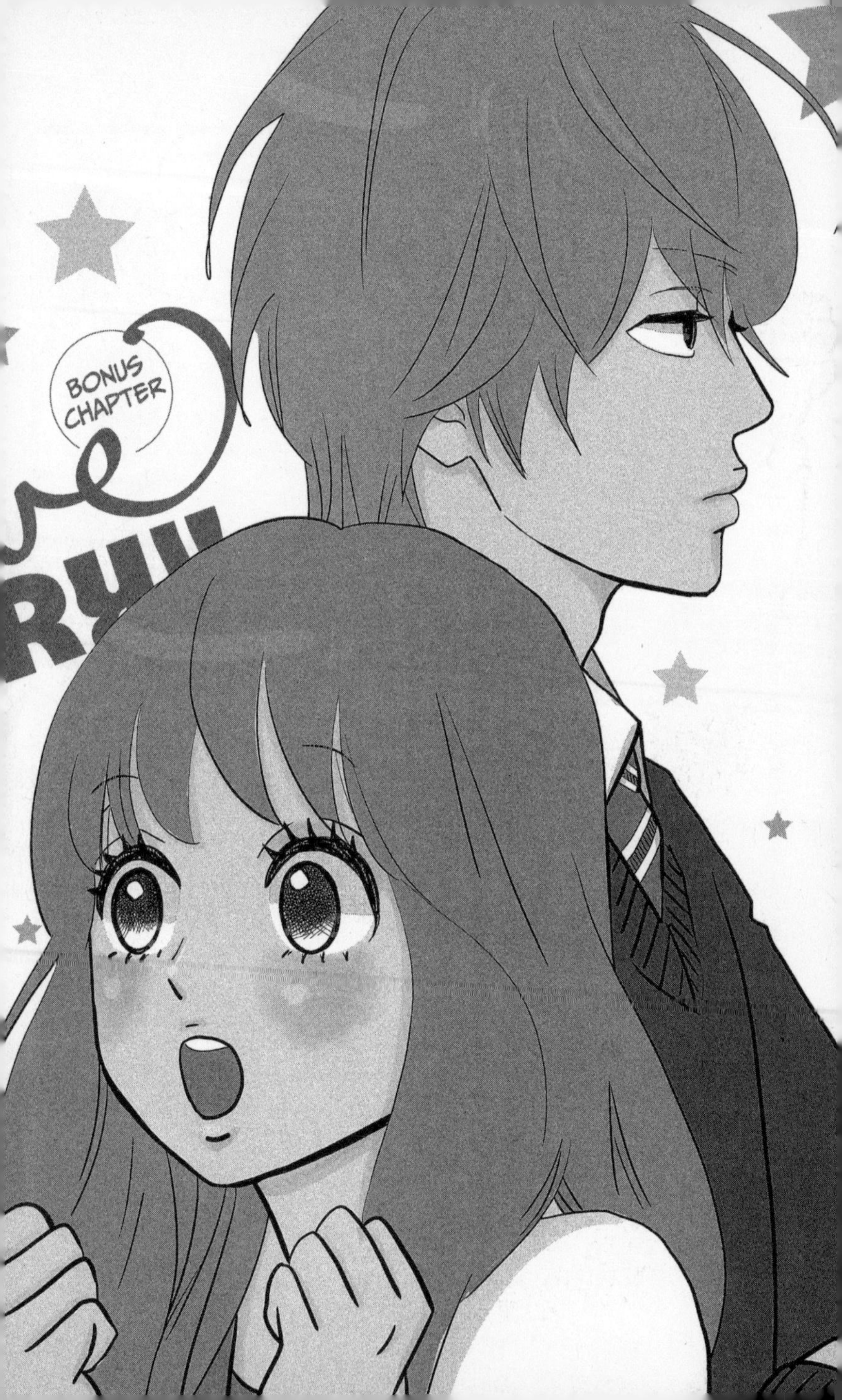
BONUS CHAPTER

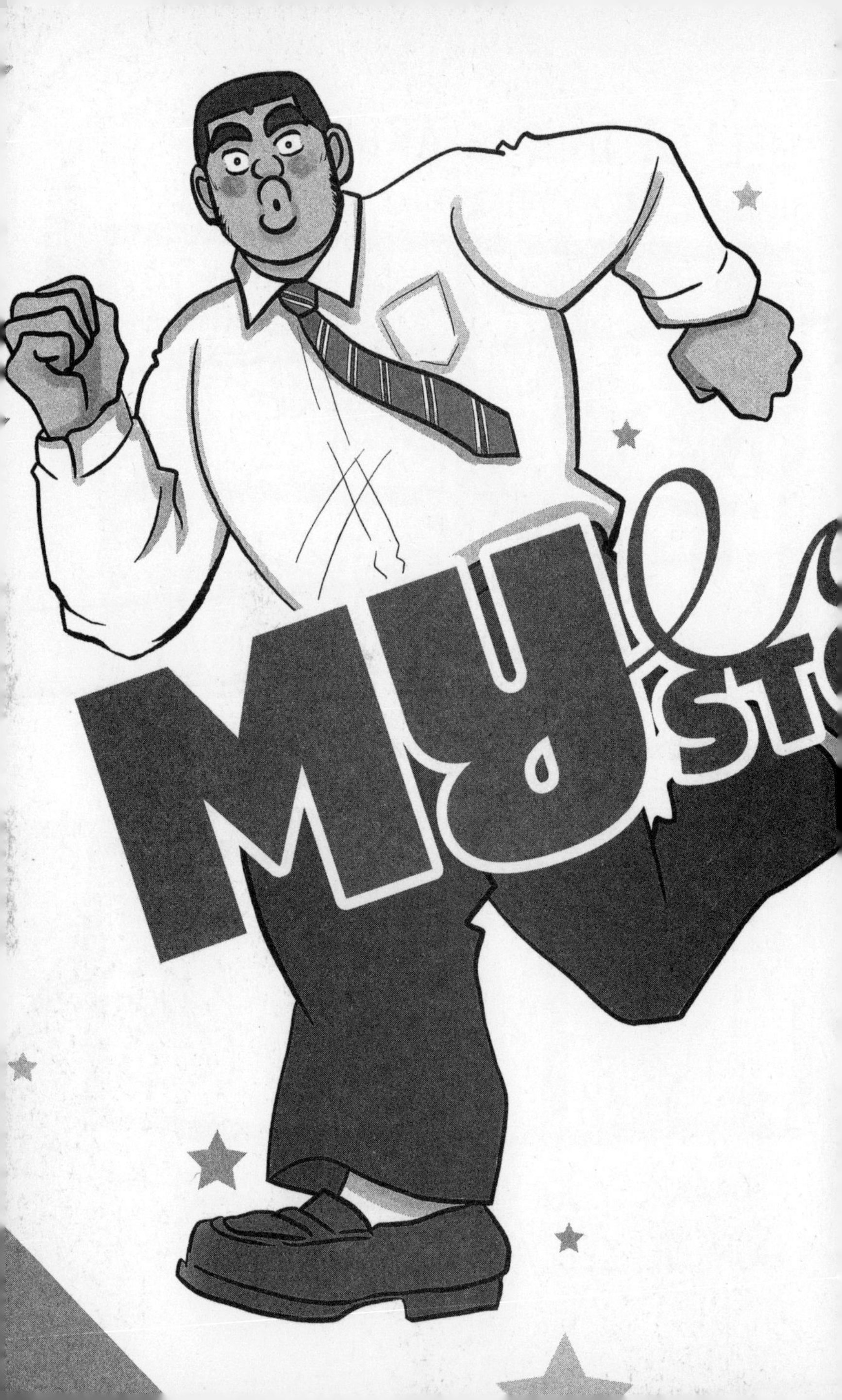
MY

HELLO! THIS IS ARUKO!

THANK YOU FOR PICKING UP VOLUME 12!

I'M GOING TO SKETCH A FEW LITTLE THINGS THAT HAPPENED.

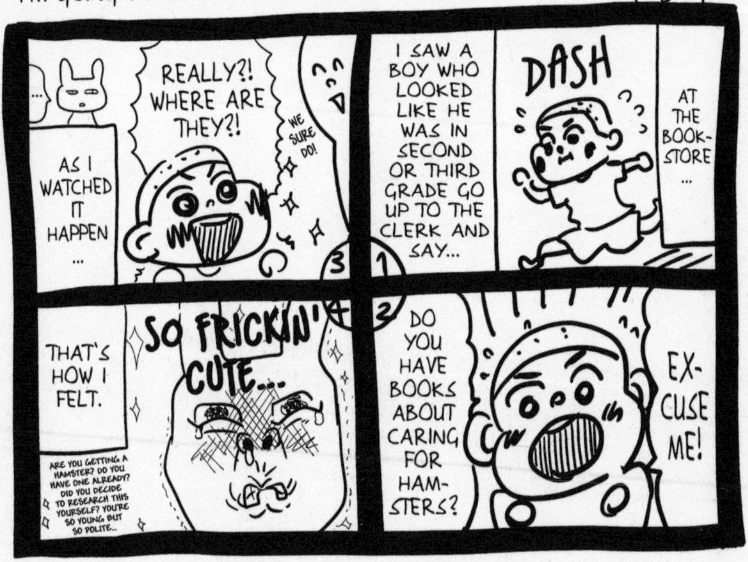
AT THE BOOKSTORE...
DASH
I SAW A BOY WHO LOOKED LIKE HE WAS IN SECOND OR THIRD GRADE GO UP TO THE CLERK AND SAY...
EXCUSE ME!
DO YOU HAVE BOOKS ABOUT CARING FOR HAMSTERS?
AS I WATCHED IT HAPPEN...
...
REALLY?! WHERE ARE THEY?!
WE SURE DO!
THAT'S HOW I FELT.
SO FRICKIN' CUTE...
ARE YOU GETTING A HAMSTER? DO YOU HAVE ONE ALREADY? DID YOU DECIDE TO RESEARCH THIS YOURSELF? YOU'RE SO YOUNG BUT SO POLITE...

IT WAS SO HEARTWARMING THAT I TEARED UP.

THE OTHER DAY, WHILE MY DAUGHTER WAS TAKING A BATH...

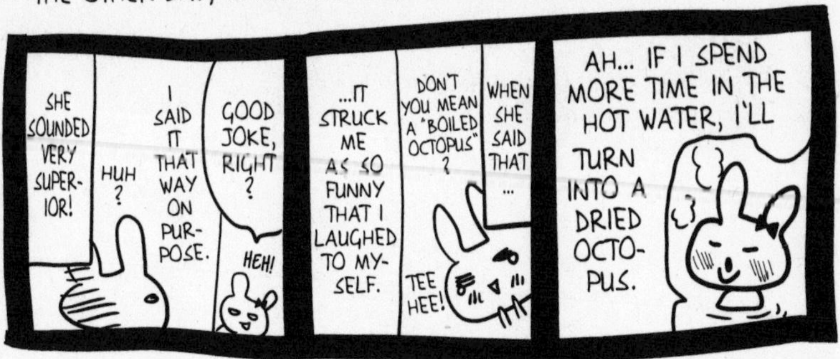
AH... IF I SPEND MORE TIME IN THE HOT WATER, I'LL
TURN INTO A DRIED OCTOPUS.
WHEN SHE SAID THAT...
DON'T YOU MEAN A "BOILED OCTOPUS"?
TEE HEE!
...IT STRUCK ME AS SO FUNNY THAT I LAUGHED TO MYSELF.
GOOD JOKE, RIGHT?
HEH!
I SAID IT THAT WAY ON PURPOSE.
HUH?
SHE SOUNDED VERY SUPERIOR!

THANK YOU VERY MUCH!

I HOPE TO SEE YOU IN VOLUME 13!

SPRING 2016

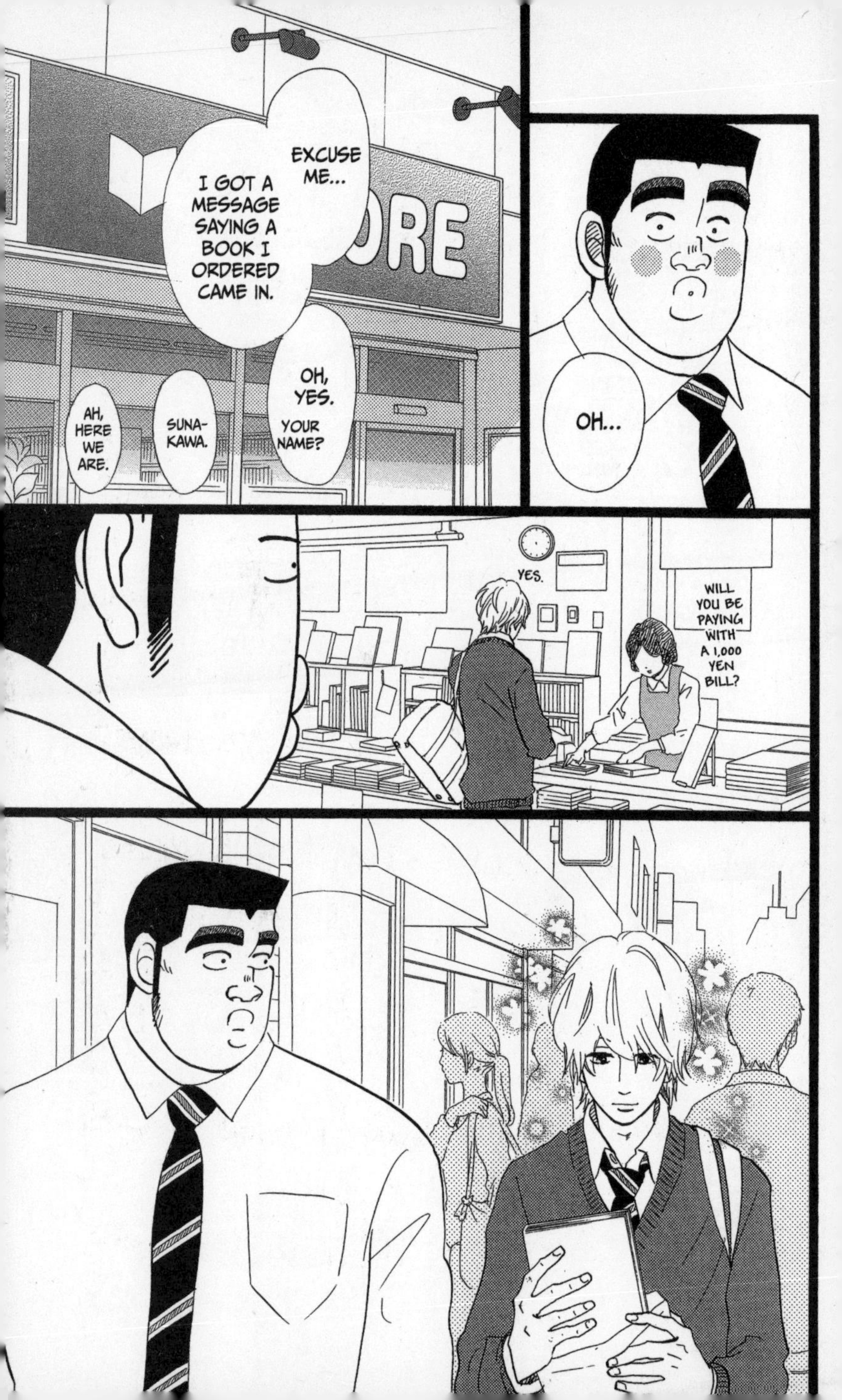
OH...
EXCUSE ME...
I GOT A MESSAGE SAYING A BOOK I ORDERED CAME IN.
OH, YES.
YOUR NAME?
SUNA-KAWA.
AH, HERE WE ARE.
WILL YOU BE PAYING WITH A 1,000 YEN BILL?
YES.

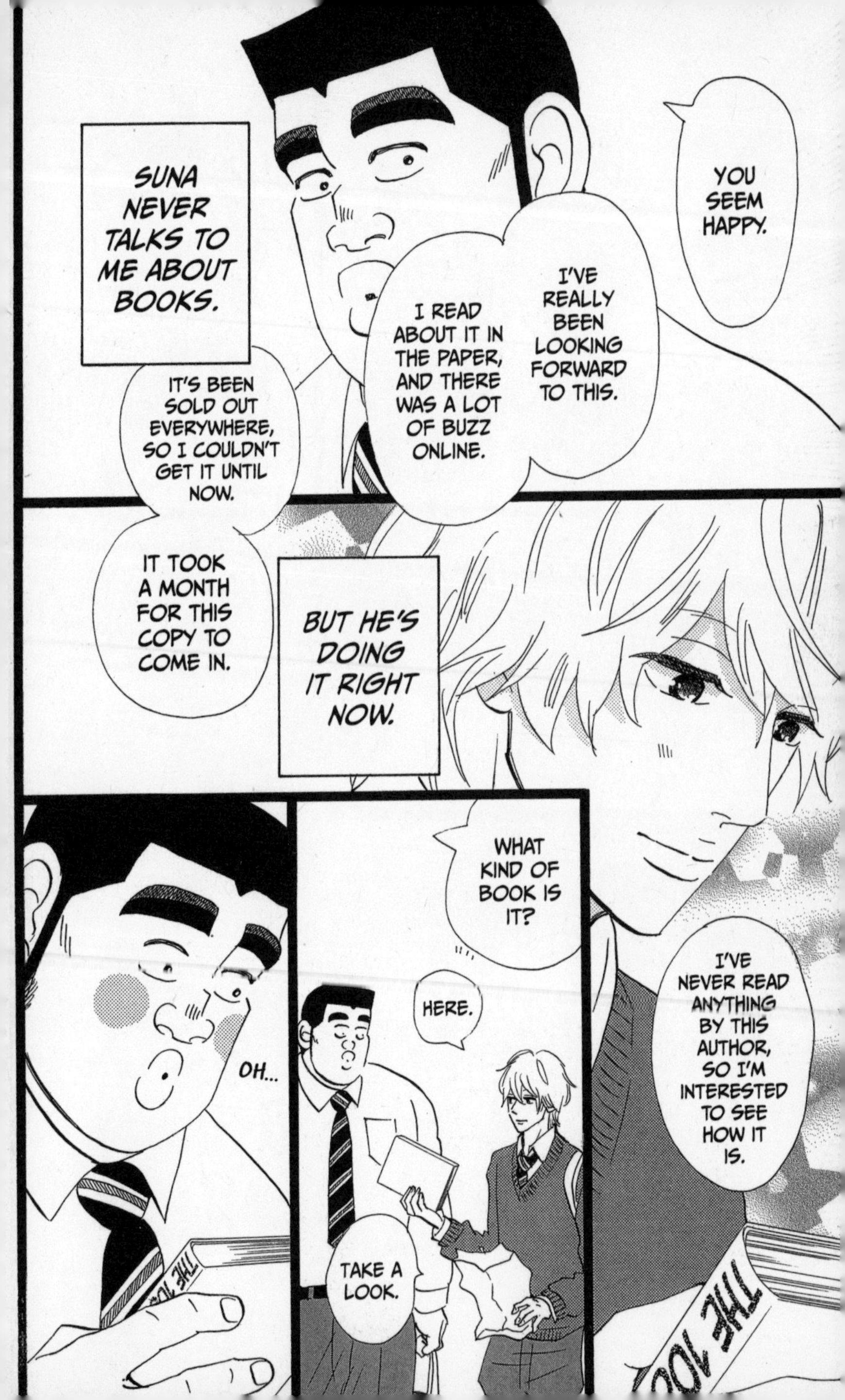
YOU SEEM HAPPY.
I'VE REALLY BEEN LOOKING FORWARD TO THIS.
I READ ABOUT IT IN THE PAPER, AND THERE WAS A LOT OF BUZZ ONLINE.
SUNA NEVER TALKS TO ME ABOUT BOOKS.
IT'S BEEN SOLD OUT EVERYWHERE, SO I COULDN'T GET IT UNTIL NOW.
IT TOOK A MONTH FOR THIS COPY TO COME IN.
BUT HE'S DOING IT RIGHT NOW.
I'VE NEVER READ ANYTHING BY THIS AUTHOR, SO I'M INTERESTED TO SEE HOW IT IS.
WHAT KIND OF BOOK IS IT?
HERE.
TAKE A LOOK.
OH...

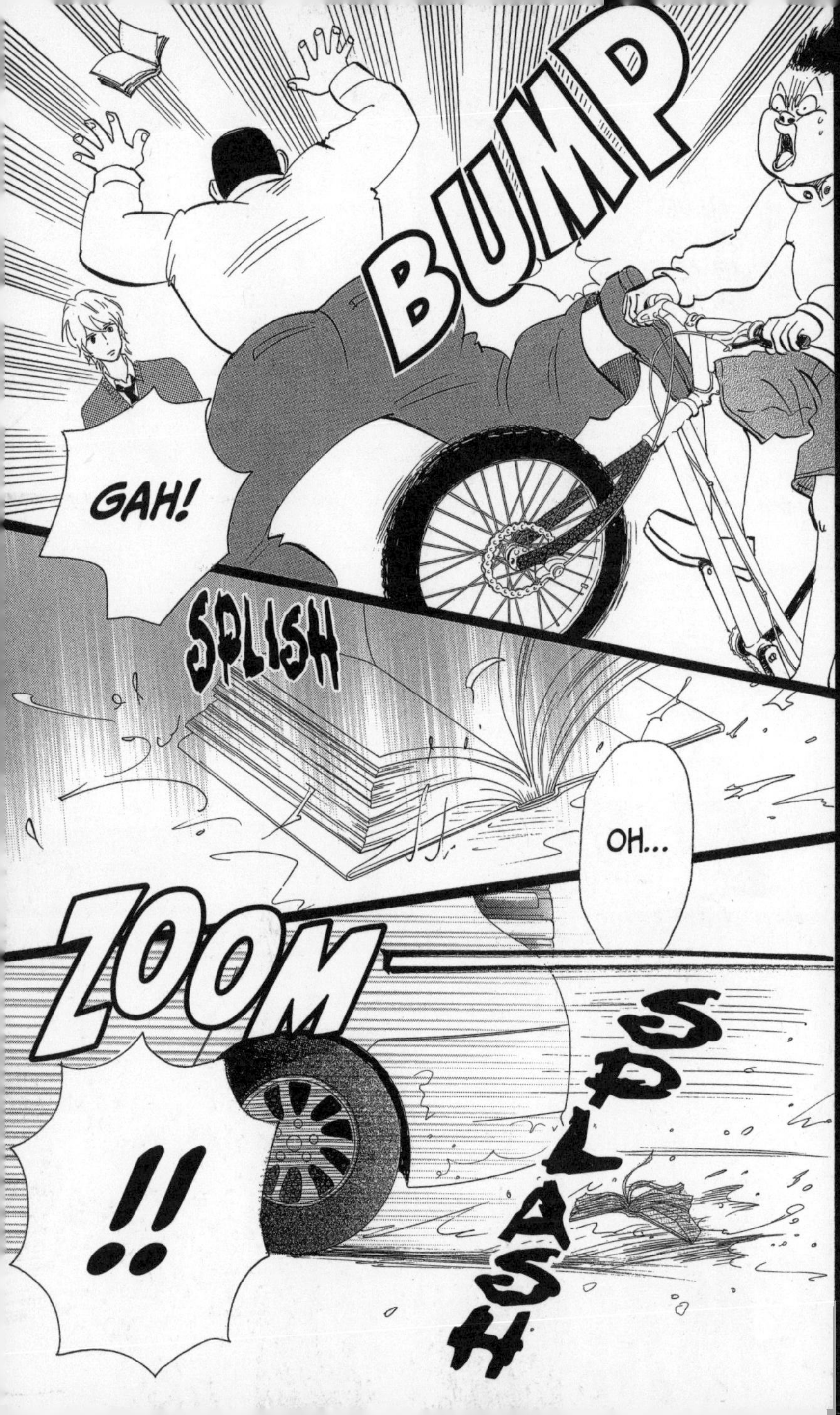
BUMP
GAH!
SPLISH
OH...
ZOOM
SPLASH
!!

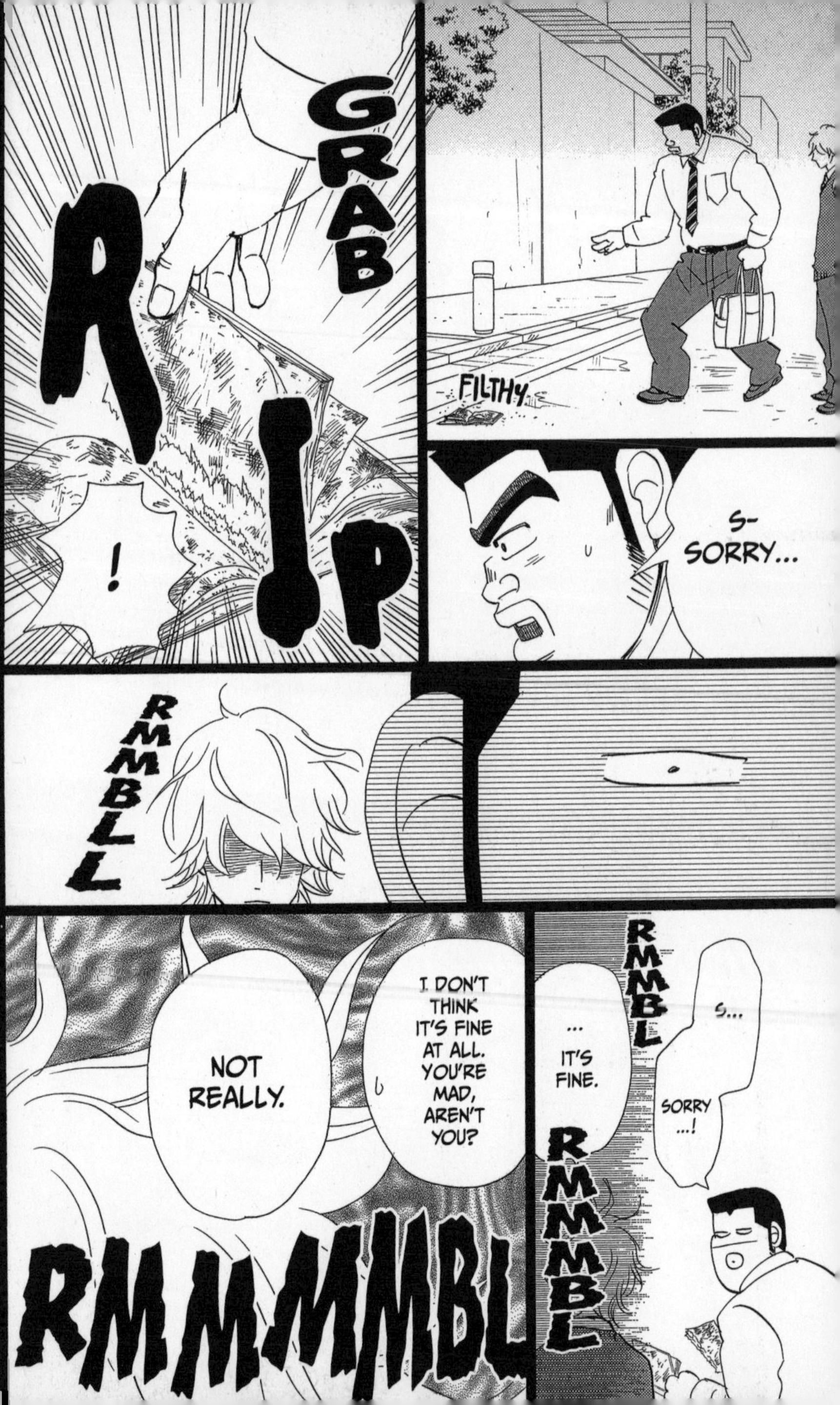
FILTHY
GRAB
RIP
!
S-
SORRY...
RMMBLL
S...
SORRY
...!
RMMBL
...
IT'S
FINE.
RMMMBL
I DON'T THINK IT'S FINE AT ALL. YOU'RE MAD, AREN'T YOU?
NOT REALLY.
RMMMMBL

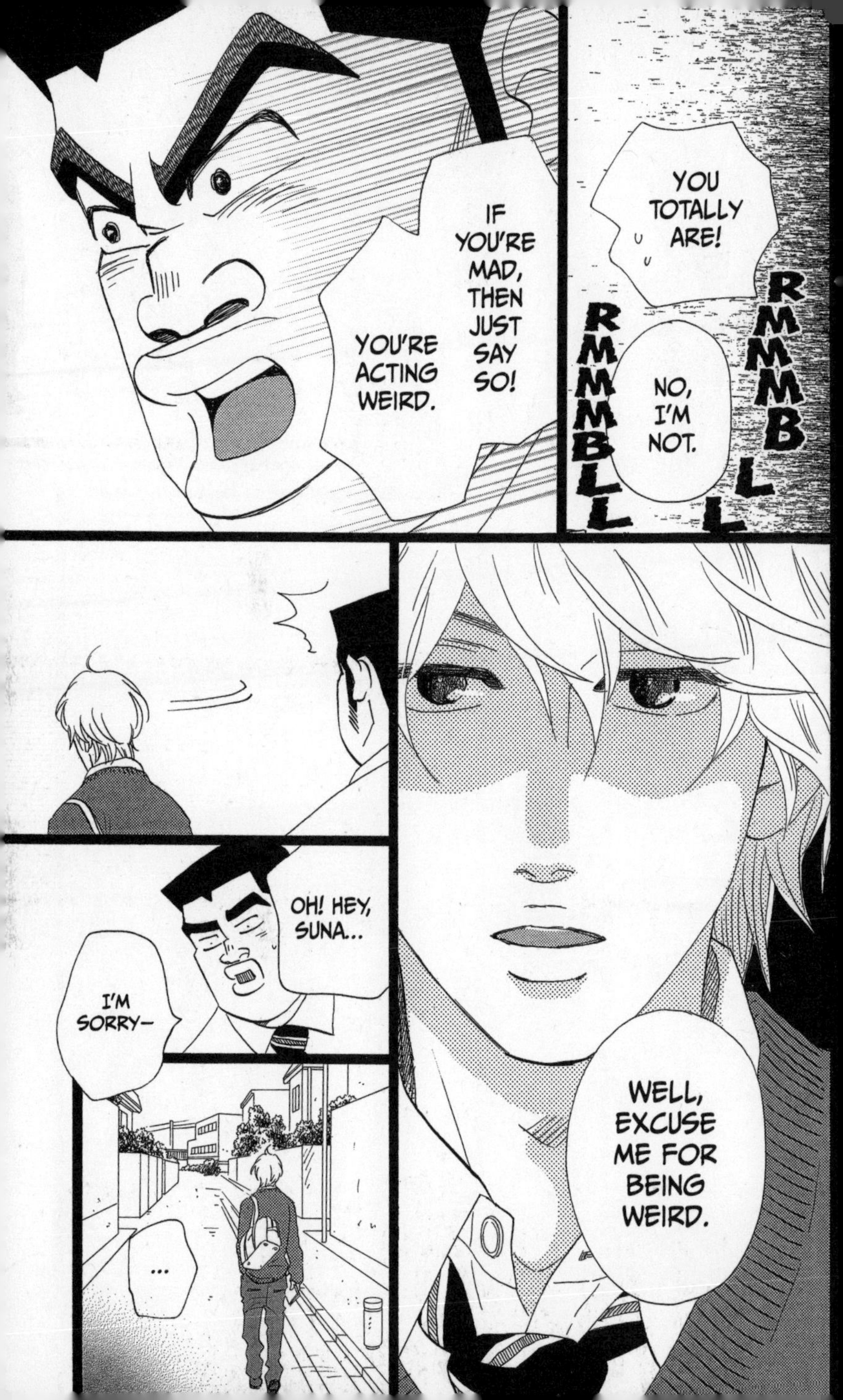
YOU TOTALLY ARE!
RMMMBLL
NO, I'M NOT.
RMMMBLL
IF YOU'RE MAD, THEN JUST SAY SO!
YOU'RE ACTING WEIRD.
WELL, EXCUSE ME FOR BEING WEIRD.
OH! HEY, SUNA...
I'M SORRY—
...

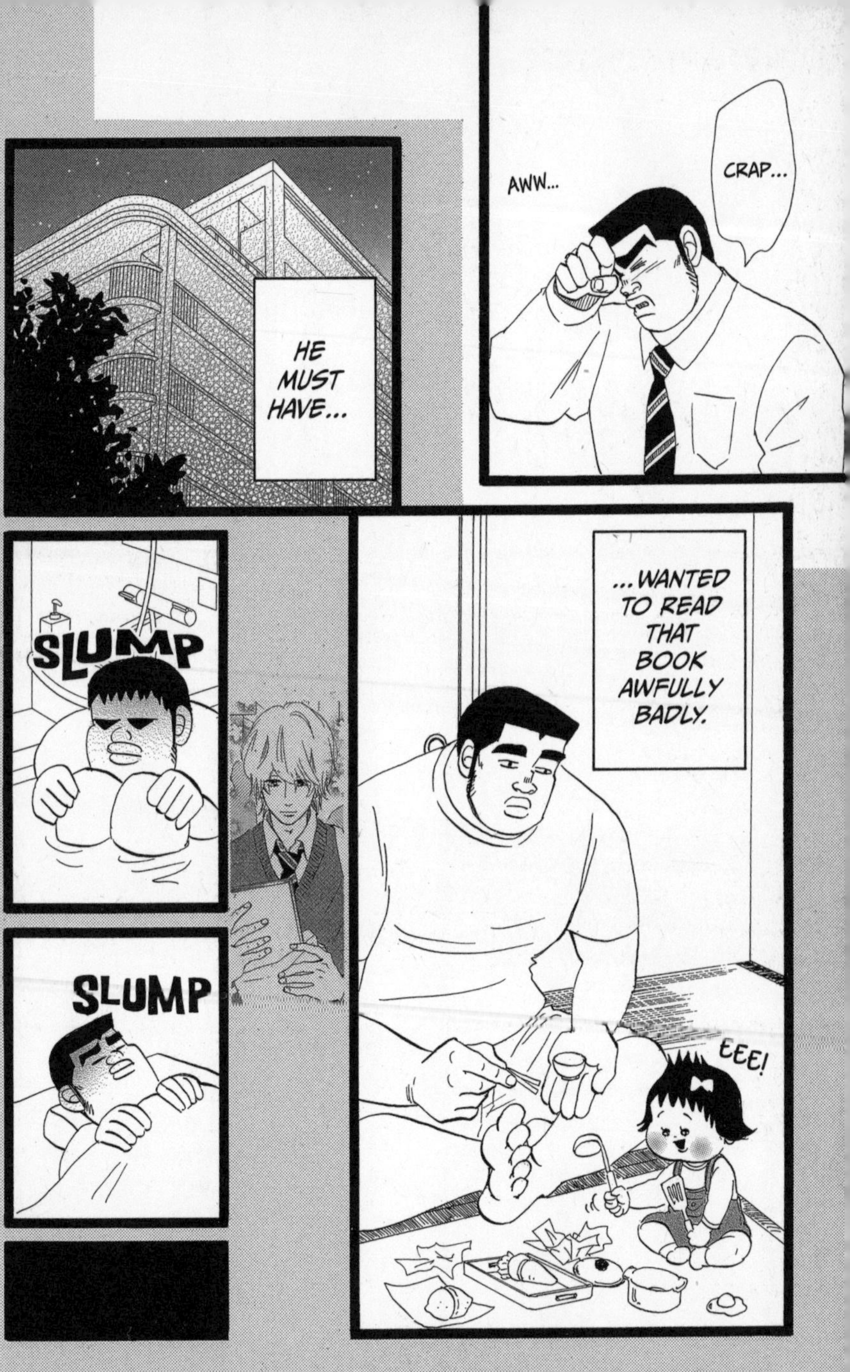
AWW...
CRAP...
HE MUST HAVE...
...WANTED TO READ THAT BOOK AWFULLY BADLY.
EEE!
SLUMP
SLUMP

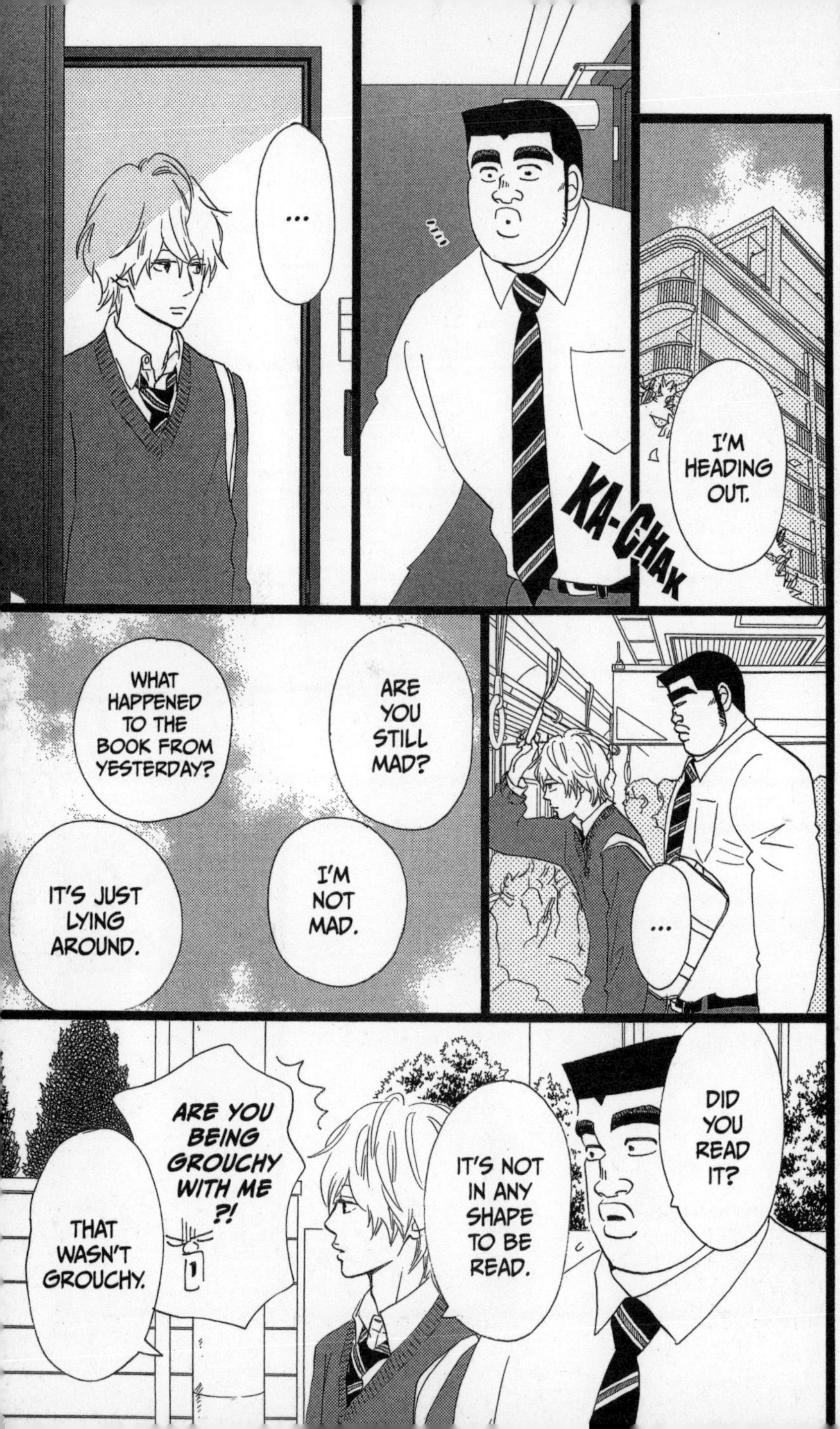
I'M HEADING OUT.
KA-CHAX
...
...
...
ARE YOU STILL MAD?
WHAT HAPPENED TO THE BOOK FROM YESTERDAY?
I'M NOT MAD.
IT'S JUST LYING AROUND.
DID YOU READ IT?
IT'S NOT IN ANY SHAPE TO BE READ.
ARE YOU BEING GROUCHY WITH ME ?!
THAT WASN'T GROUCHY.

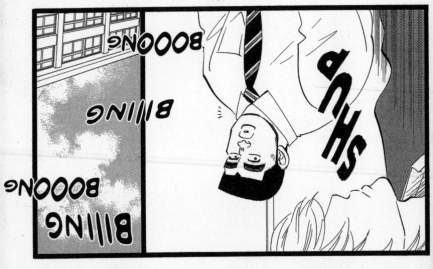

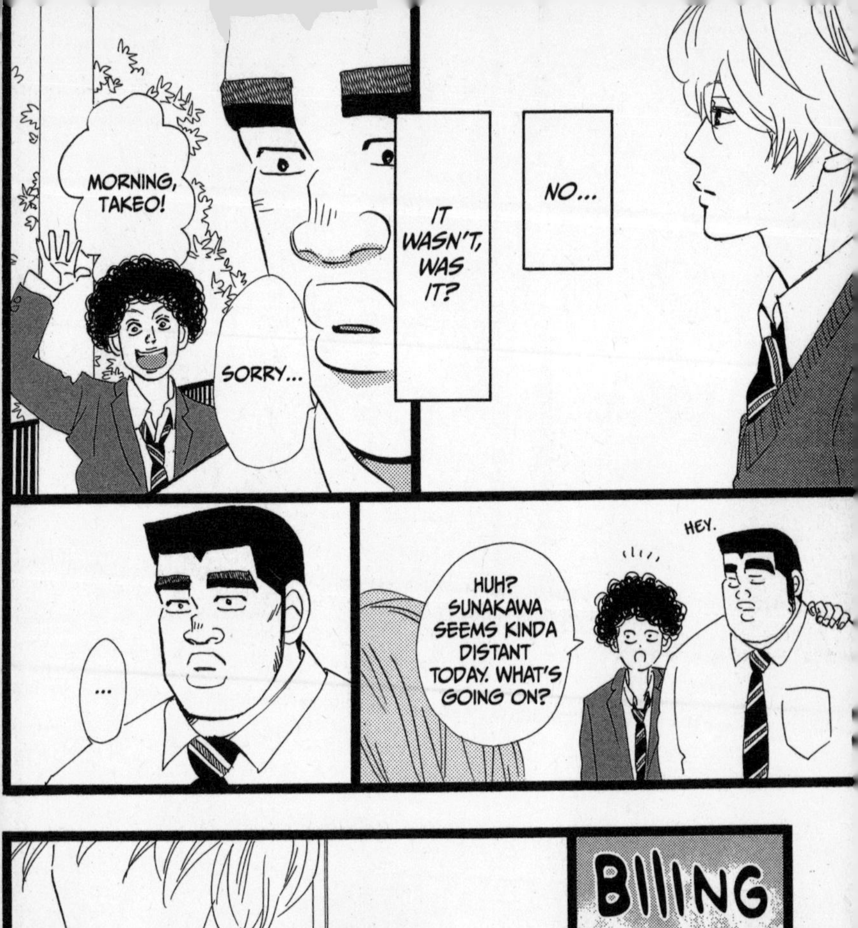
NO...
IT WASN'T, WAS IT?
MORNING, TAKEO!
SORRY...
HEY.
HUH? SUNAKAWA SEEMS KINDA DISTANT TODAY. WHAT'S GOING ON?
...
BIIING
BOOONG
BIIING
BOOONG
SHUP

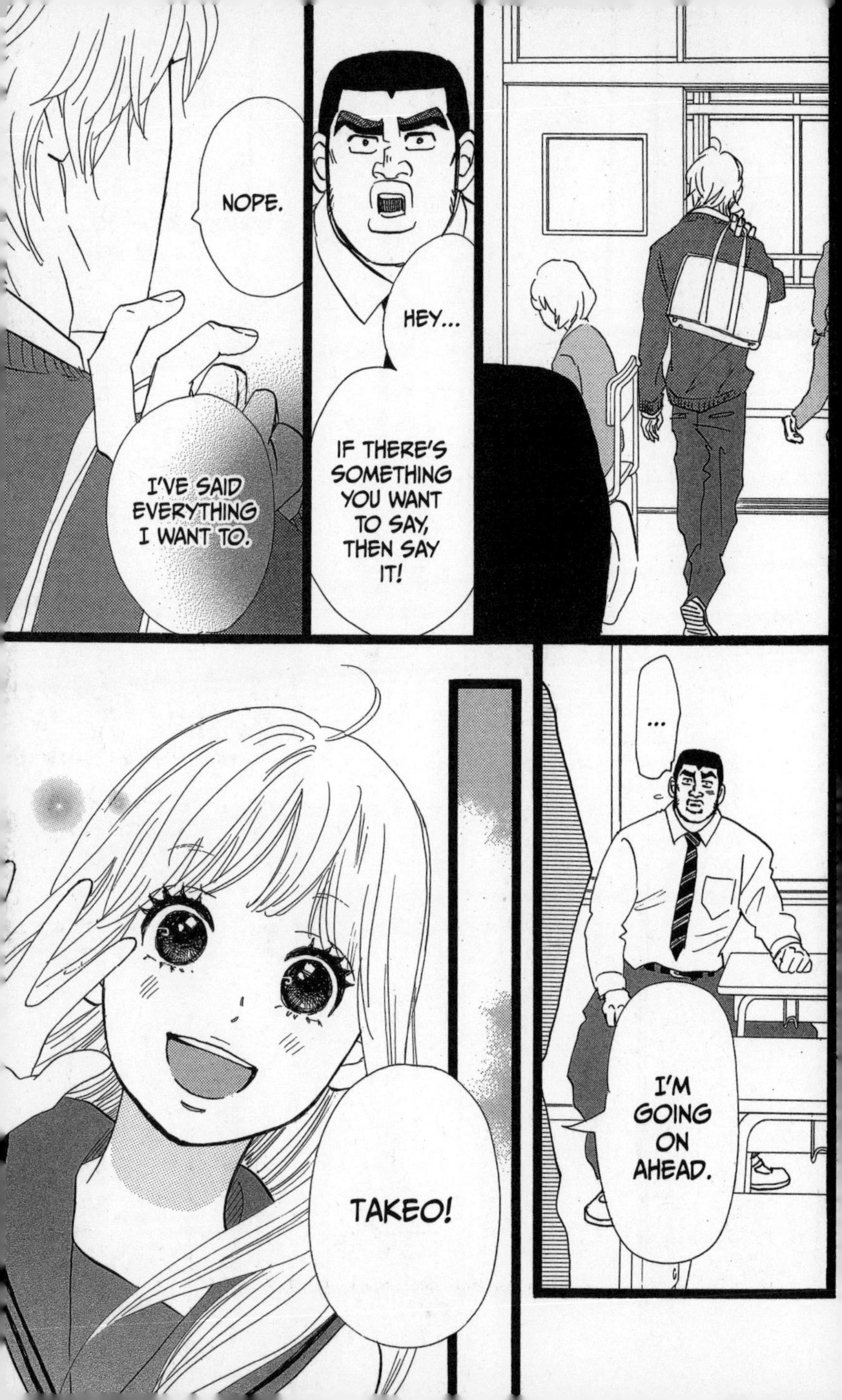
HEY...
IF THERE'S SOMETHING YOU WANT TO SAY, THEN SAY IT!
NOPE.
I'VE SAID EVERYTHING I WANT TO.
...
I'M GOING ON AHEAD.
TAKEO!

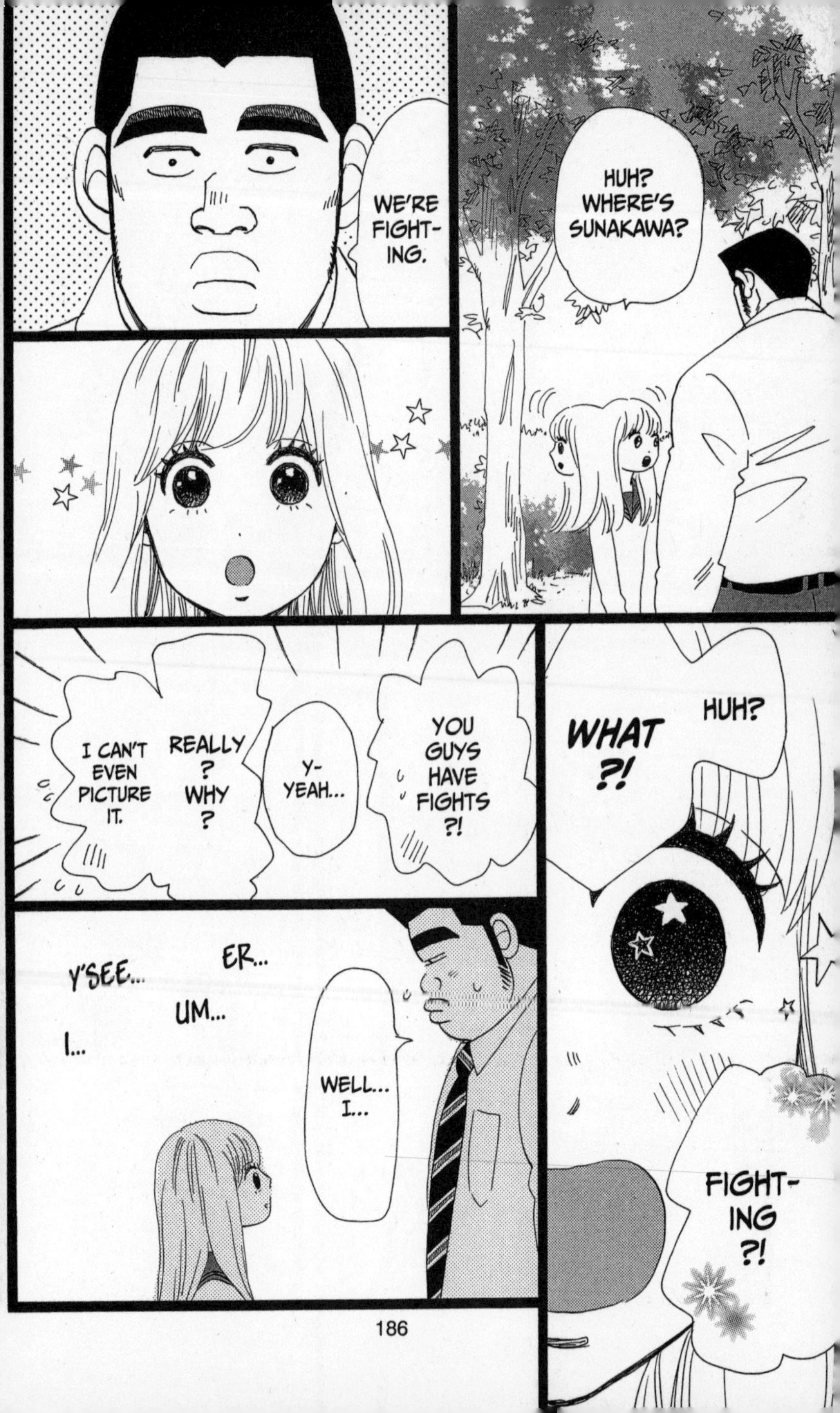
HUH? WHERE'S SUNAKAWA?
WE'RE FIGHT-ING.
HUH?
WHAT ?!
FIGHT-ING ?!
YOU GUYS HAVE FIGHTS ?!
Y-YEAH...
REALLY ? WHY ?
I CAN'T EVEN PICTURE IT.
WELL... I...
ER...
UM...
Y'SEE...
I...

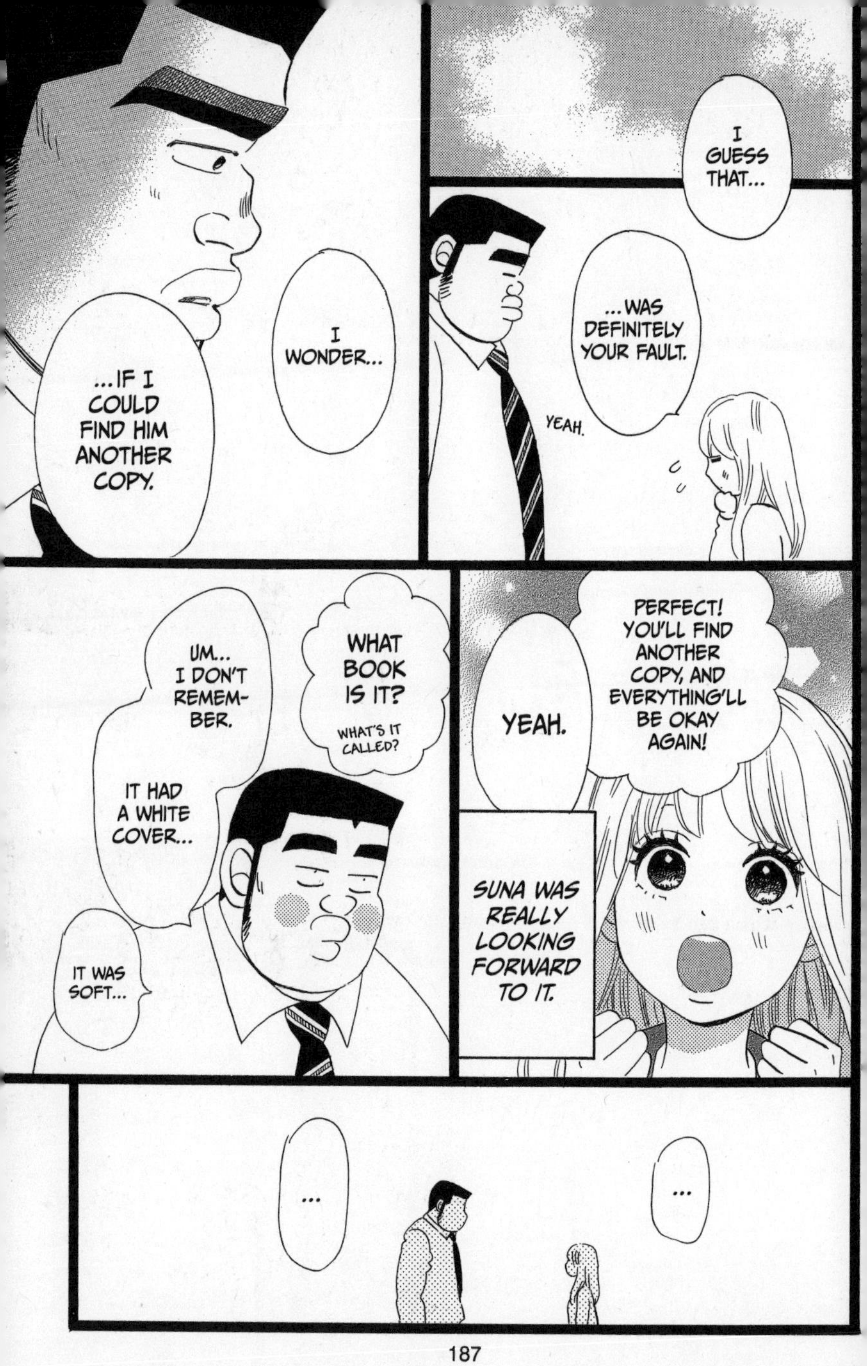
I GUESS THAT...
...WAS DEFINITELY YOUR FAULT.
YEAH.
I WONDER...
...IF I COULD FIND HIM ANOTHER COPY.
PERFECT! YOU'LL FIND ANOTHER COPY, AND EVERYTHING'LL BE OKAY AGAIN!
YEAH.
SUNA WAS REALLY LOOKING FORWARD TO IT.
WHAT BOOK IS IT?
WHAT'S IT CALLED?
UM... I DON'T REMEMBER.
IT HAD A WHITE COVER...
IT WAS SOFT...
...
...

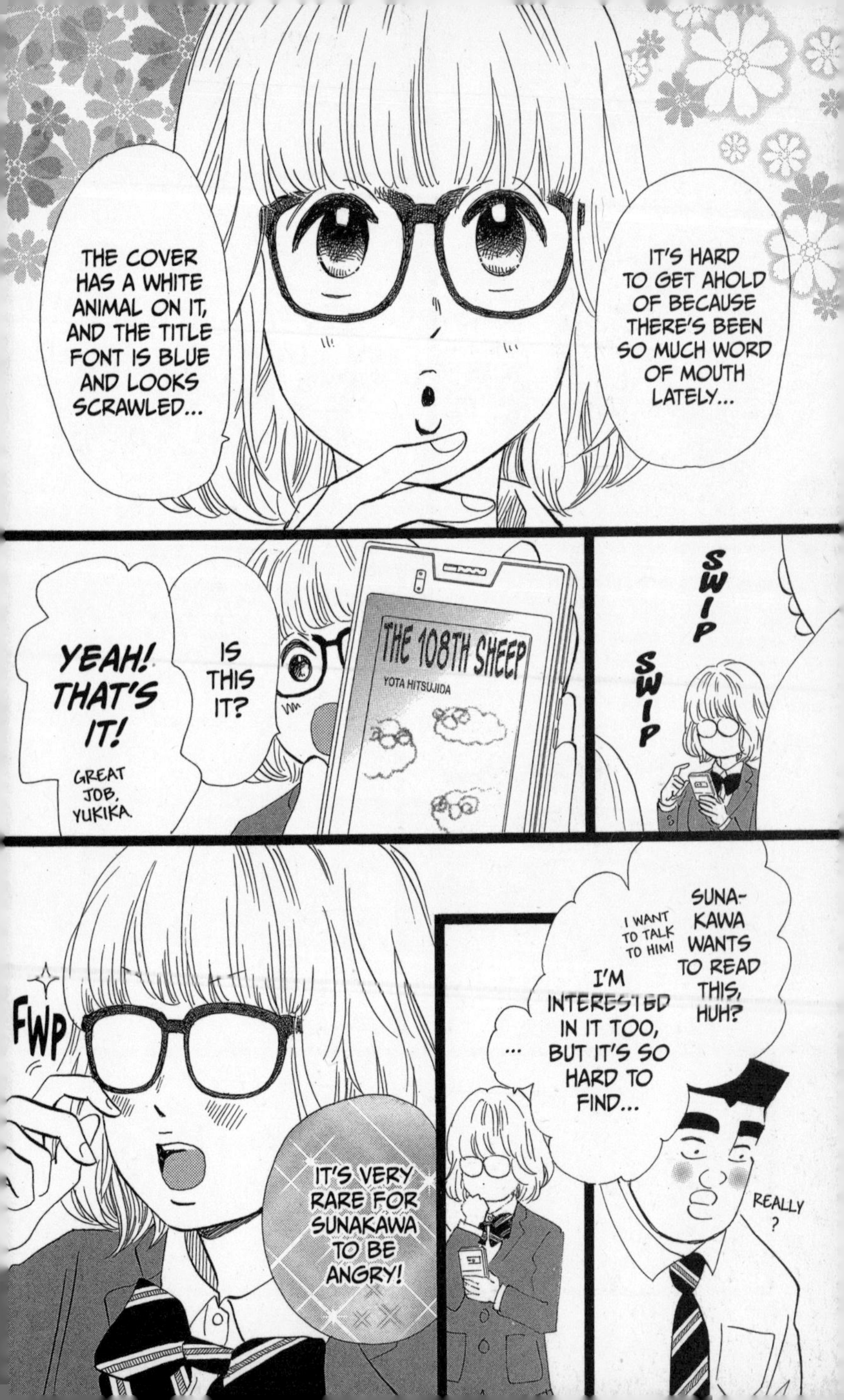
IT'S HARD TO GET AHOLD OF BECAUSE THERE'S BEEN SO MUCH WORD OF MOUTH LATELY...
THE COVER HAS A WHITE ANIMAL ON IT, AND THE TITLE FONT IS BLUE AND LOOKS SCRAWLED...
SWIP SWIP
THE 108TH SHEEP
YOTA HITSUJIDA
IS THIS IT?
YEAH! THAT'S IT!
GREAT JOB, YUKIKA.
SUNAKAWA WANTS TO READ THIS, HUH?
I WANT TO TALK TO HIM!
I'M INTERESTED IN IT TOO, BUT IT'S SO HARD TO FIND...
...
REALLY?
IT'S VERY RARE FOR SUNAKAWA TO BE ANGRY!
FWP

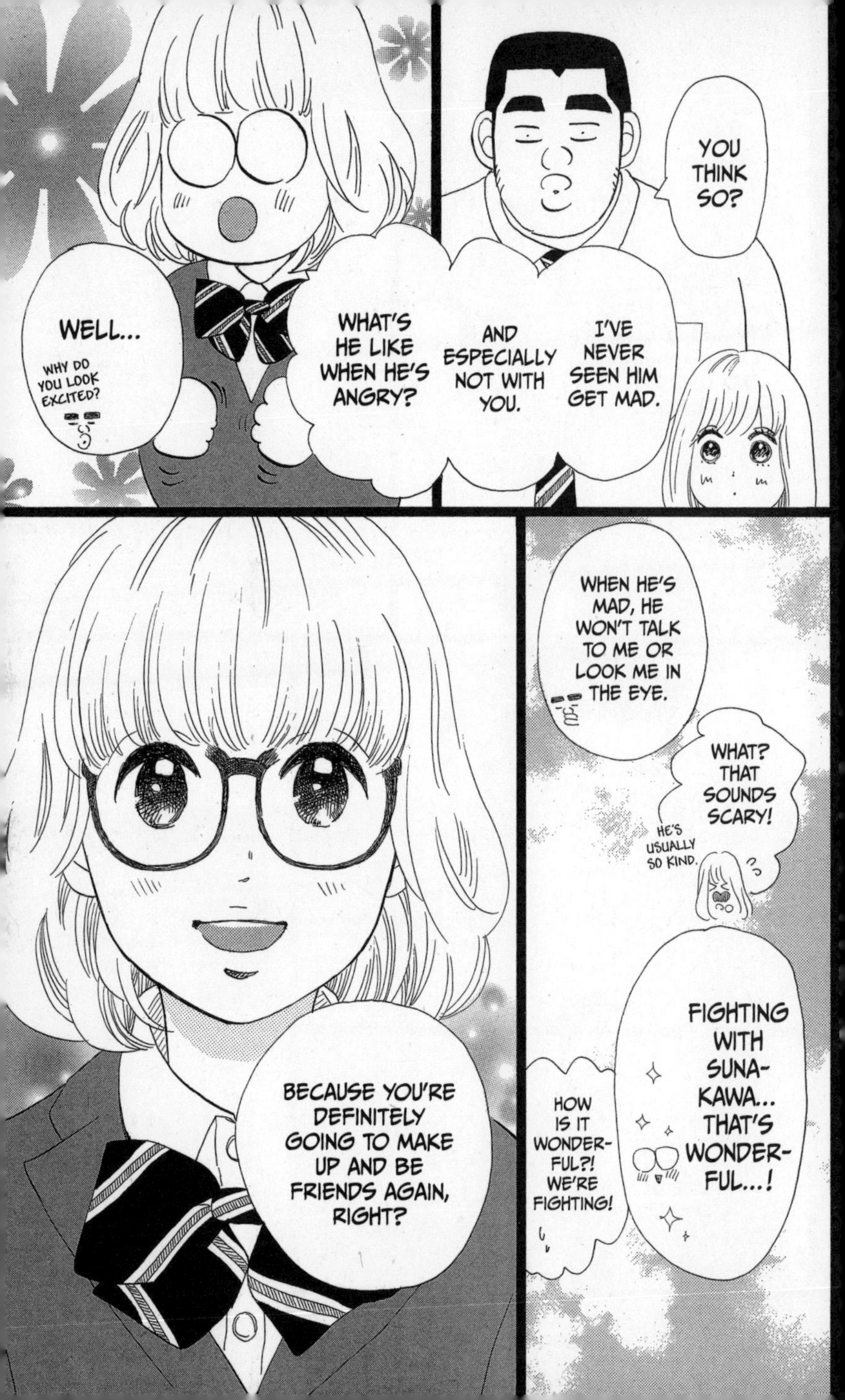
YOU THINK SO?
I'VE NEVER SEEN HIM GET MAD.
AND ESPECIALLY NOT WITH YOU.
WHAT'S HE LIKE WHEN HE'S ANGRY?
WELL...
WHY DO YOU LOOK EXCITED?
WHEN HE'S MAD, HE WON'T TALK TO ME OR LOOK ME IN THE EYE.
WHAT? THAT SOUNDS SCARY!
HE'S USUALLY SO KIND.
FIGHTING WITH SUNA-KAWA... THAT'S WONDER-FUL...!
HOW IS IT WONDER-FUL?! WE'RE FIGHTING!
BECAUSE YOU'RE DEFINITELY GOING TO MAKE UP AND BE FRIENDS AGAIN, RIGHT?

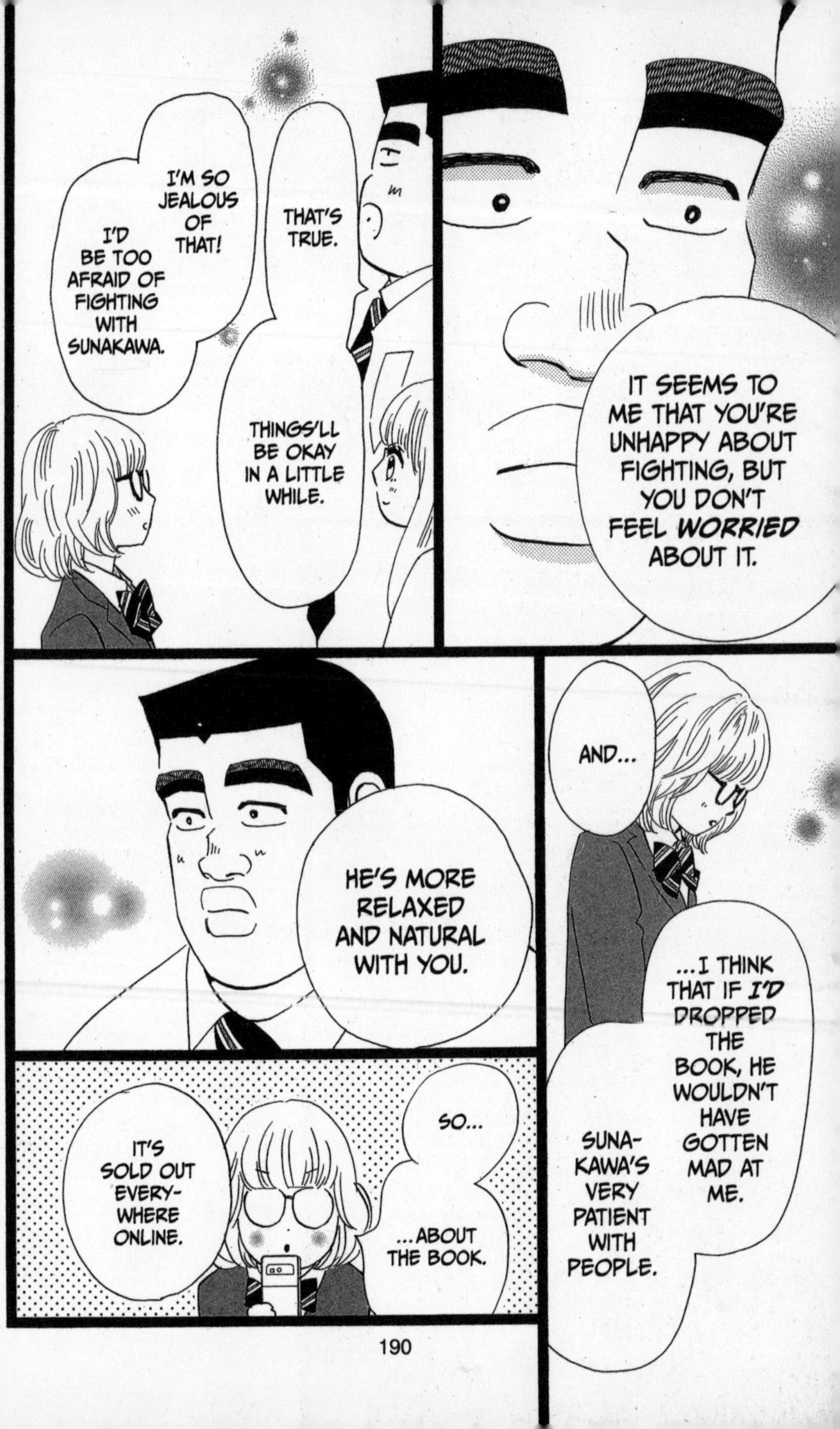
IT SEEMS TO ME THAT YOU'RE UNHAPPY ABOUT FIGHTING, BUT YOU DON'T FEEL *WORRIED* ABOUT IT.
THAT'S TRUE.
I'M SO JEALOUS OF THAT!
I'D BE TOO AFRAID OF FIGHTING WITH SUNAKAWA.
THINGS'LL BE OKAY IN A LITTLE WHILE.
AND...
...I THINK THAT IF *I'D* DROPPED THE BOOK, HE WOULDN'T HAVE GOTTEN MAD AT ME.
SUNA-KAWA'S VERY PATIENT WITH PEOPLE.
HE'S MORE RELAXED AND NATURAL WITH YOU.
SO...
...ABOUT THE BOOK.
IT'S SOLD OUT EVERY-WHERE ONLINE.

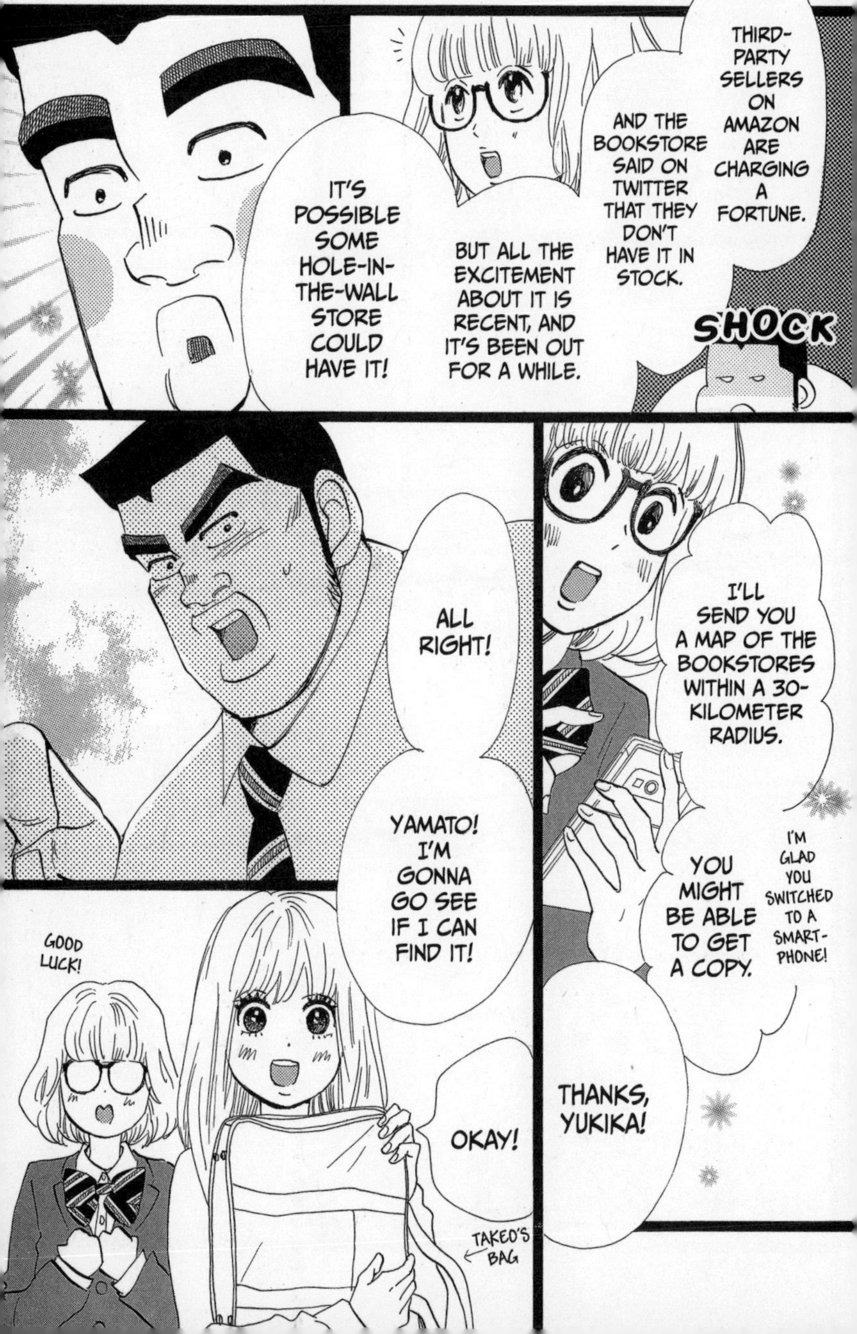
THIRD-PARTY SELLERS ON AMAZON ARE CHARGING A FORTUNE.
AND THE BOOKSTORE SAID ON TWITTER THAT THEY DON'T HAVE IT IN STOCK.
SHOCK
BUT ALL THE EXCITEMENT ABOUT IT IS RECENT, AND IT'S BEEN OUT FOR A WHILE.
IT'S POSSIBLE SOME HOLE-IN-THE-WALL STORE COULD HAVE IT!
I'LL SEND YOU A MAP OF THE BOOKSTORES WITHIN A 30-KILOMETER RADIUS.
I'M GLAD YOU SWITCHED TO A SMART-PHONE!
YOU MIGHT BE ABLE TO GET A COPY.
THANKS, YUKIKA!
ALL RIGHT!
YAMATO! I'M GONNA GO SEE IF I CAN FIND IT!
OKAY!
TAKEO'S BAG
GOOD LUCK!

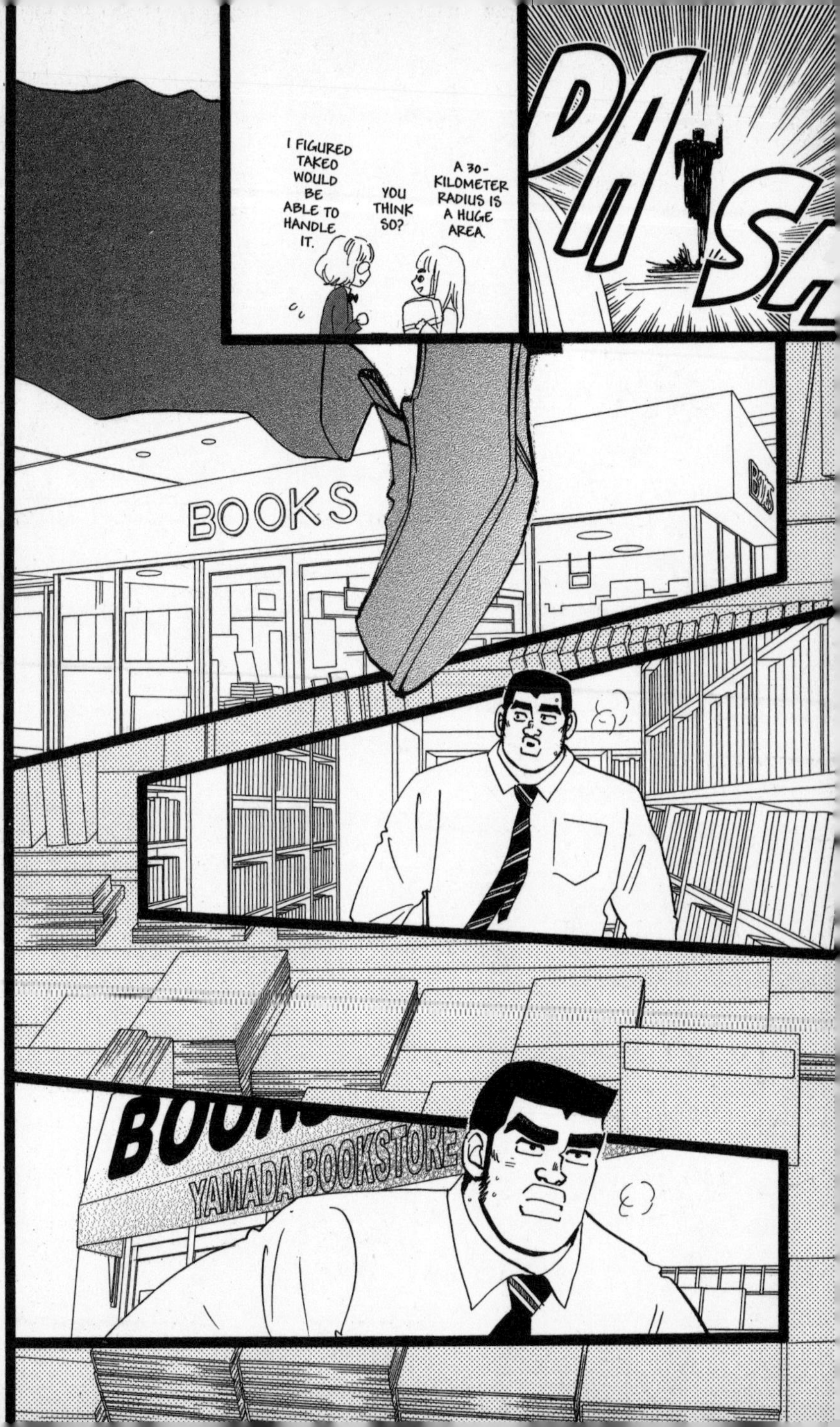
DASH
A 30-KILOMETER RADIUS IS A HUGE AREA.
YOU THINK SO?
I FIGURED TAKEO WOULD BE ABLE TO HANDLE IT.
BOOKS
YAMADA BOOKSTORE

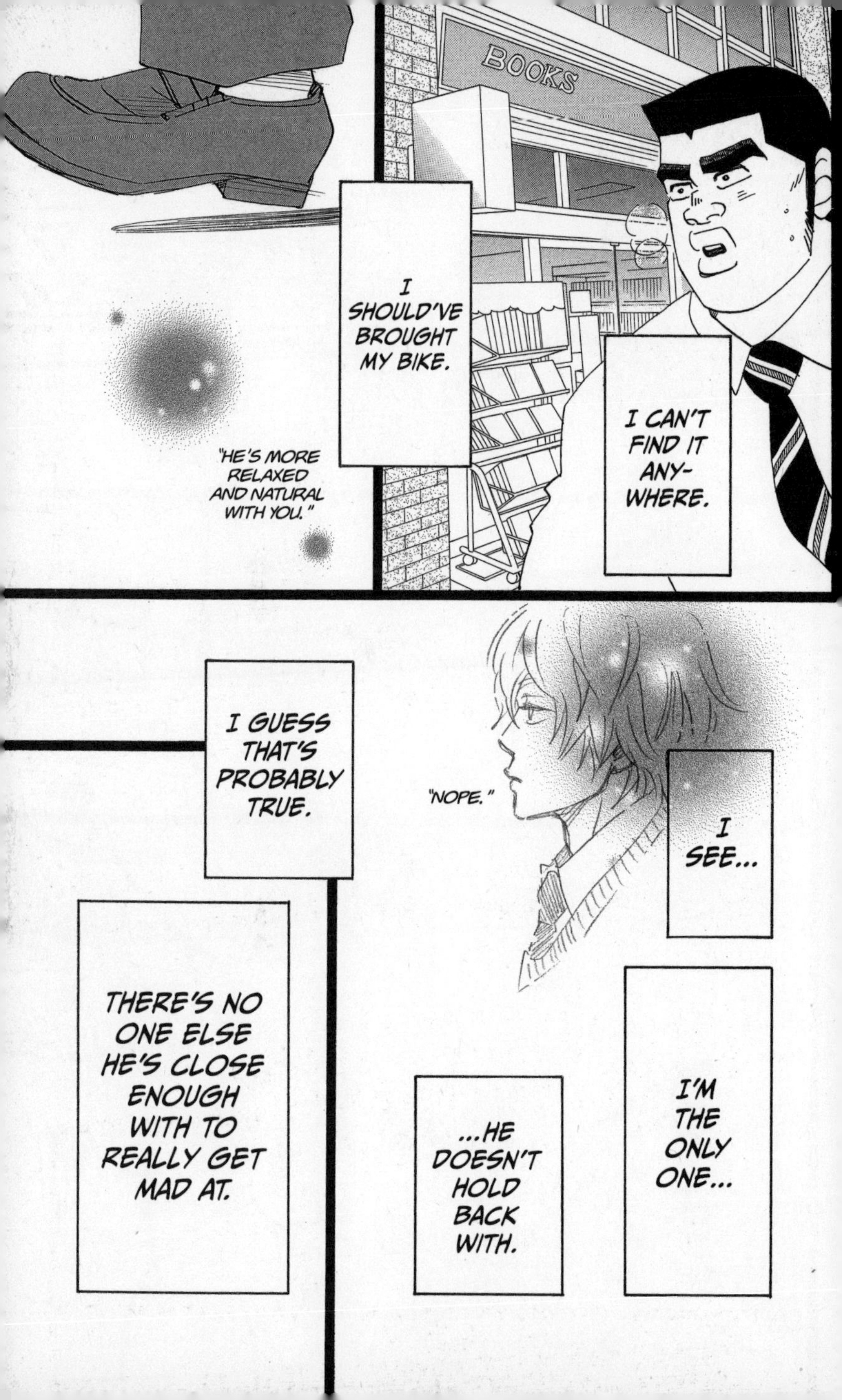
BOOKS
I CAN'T FIND IT ANY-WHERE.
I SHOULD'VE BROUGHT MY BIKE.
"HE'S MORE RELAXED AND NATURAL WITH YOU."
I SEE...
"NOPE."
I GUESS THAT'S PROBABLY TRUE.
I'M THE ONLY ONE...
...HE DOESN'T HOLD BACK WITH.
THERE'S NO ONE ELSE HE'S CLOSE ENOUGH WITH TO REALLY GET MAD AT.

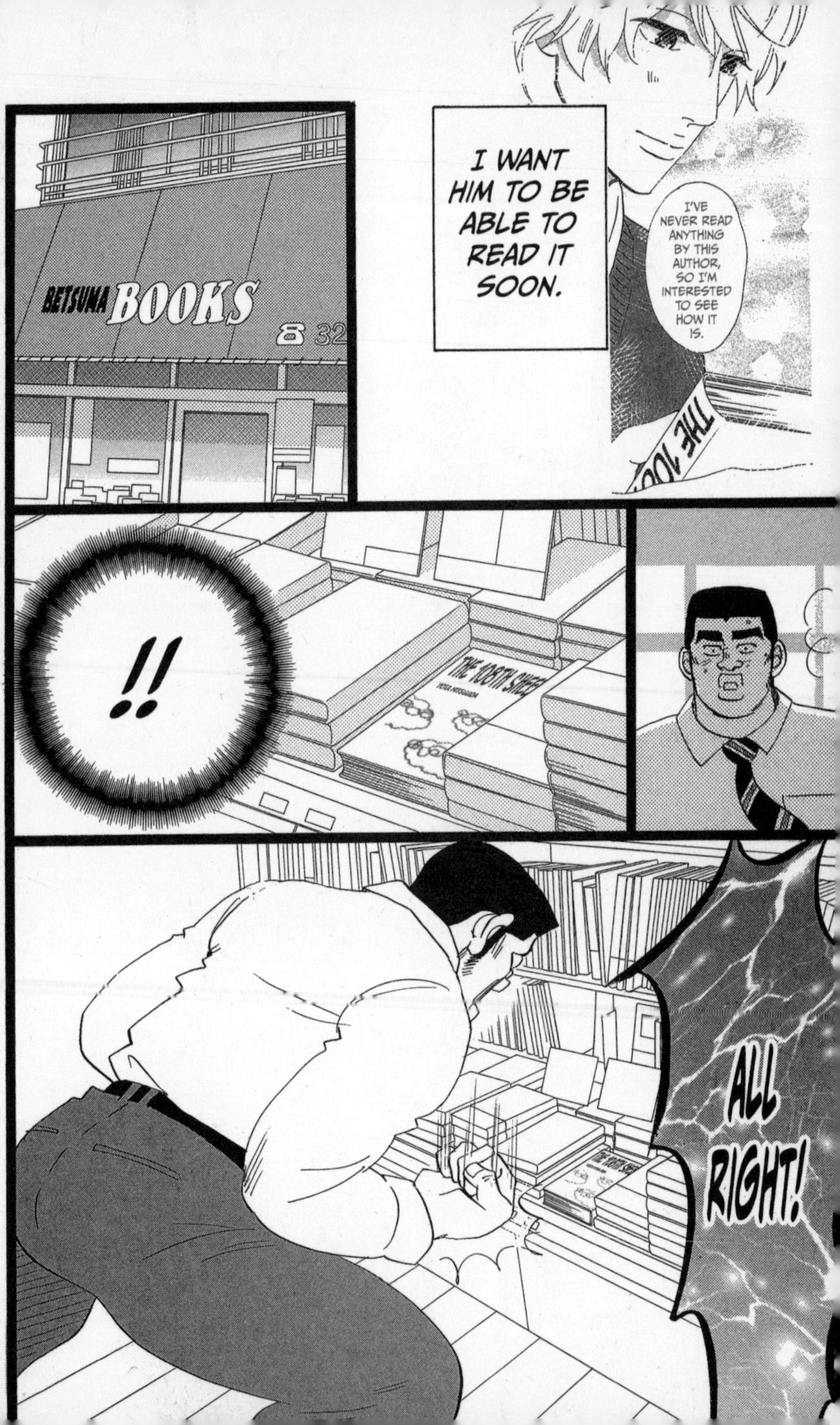
I'VE NEVER READ ANYTHING BY THIS AUTHOR, SO I'M INTERESTED TO SEE HOW IT IS.
THE 10
I WANT HIM TO BE ABLE TO READ IT SOON.
BETSUMA BOOKS
32
THE 108TH SHEE
!!
ALL RIGHT!
THE 108TH SHEE

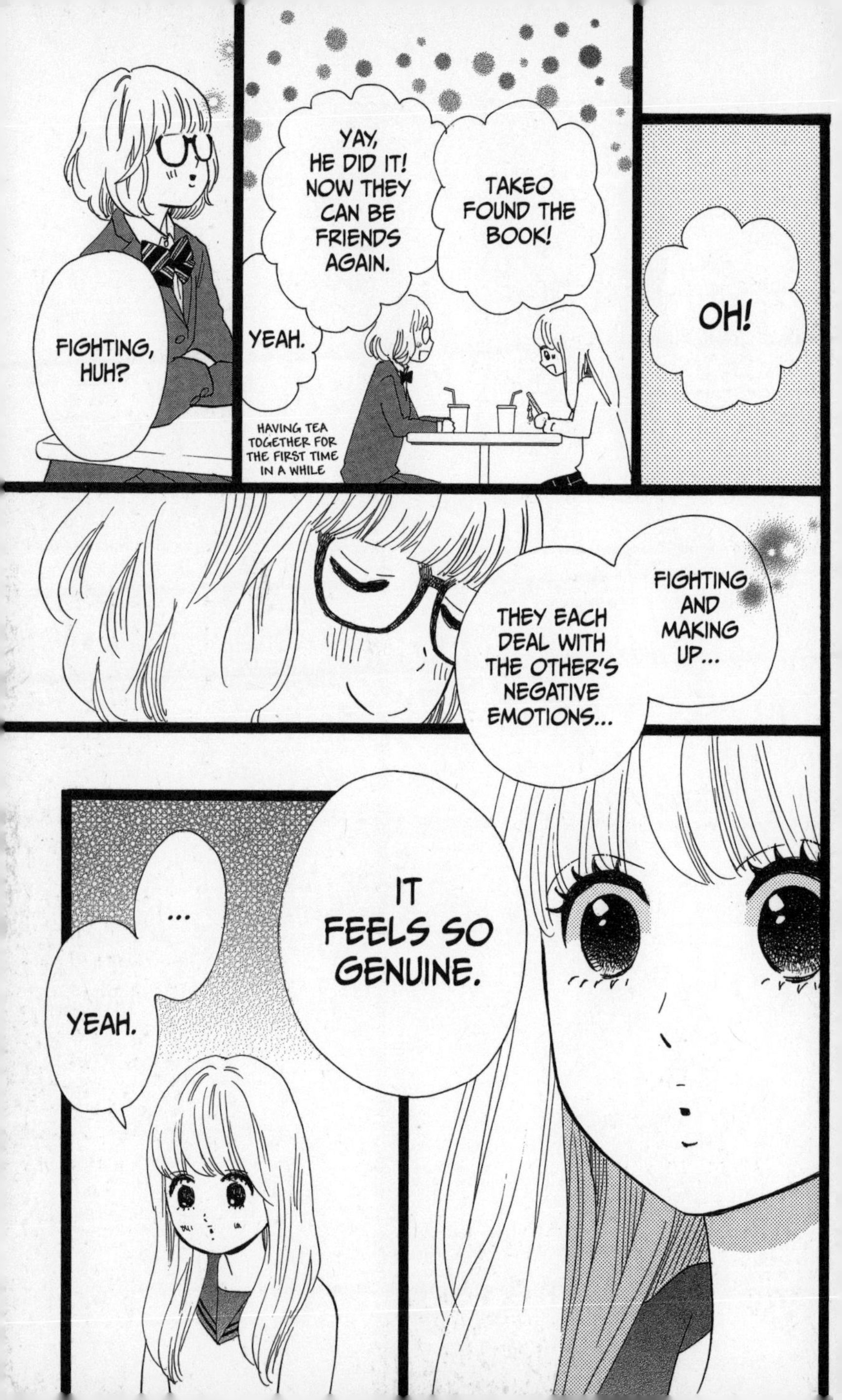
OH!
TAKEO FOUND THE BOOK!
YAY, HE DID IT! NOW THEY CAN BE FRIENDS AGAIN.
YEAH.
HAVING TEA TOGETHER FOR THE FIRST TIME IN A WHILE
FIGHTING, HUH?
FIGHTING AND MAKING UP...
THEY EACH DEAL WITH THE OTHER'S NEGATIVE EMOTIONS...
IT FEELS SO GENUINE.
...
YEAH.

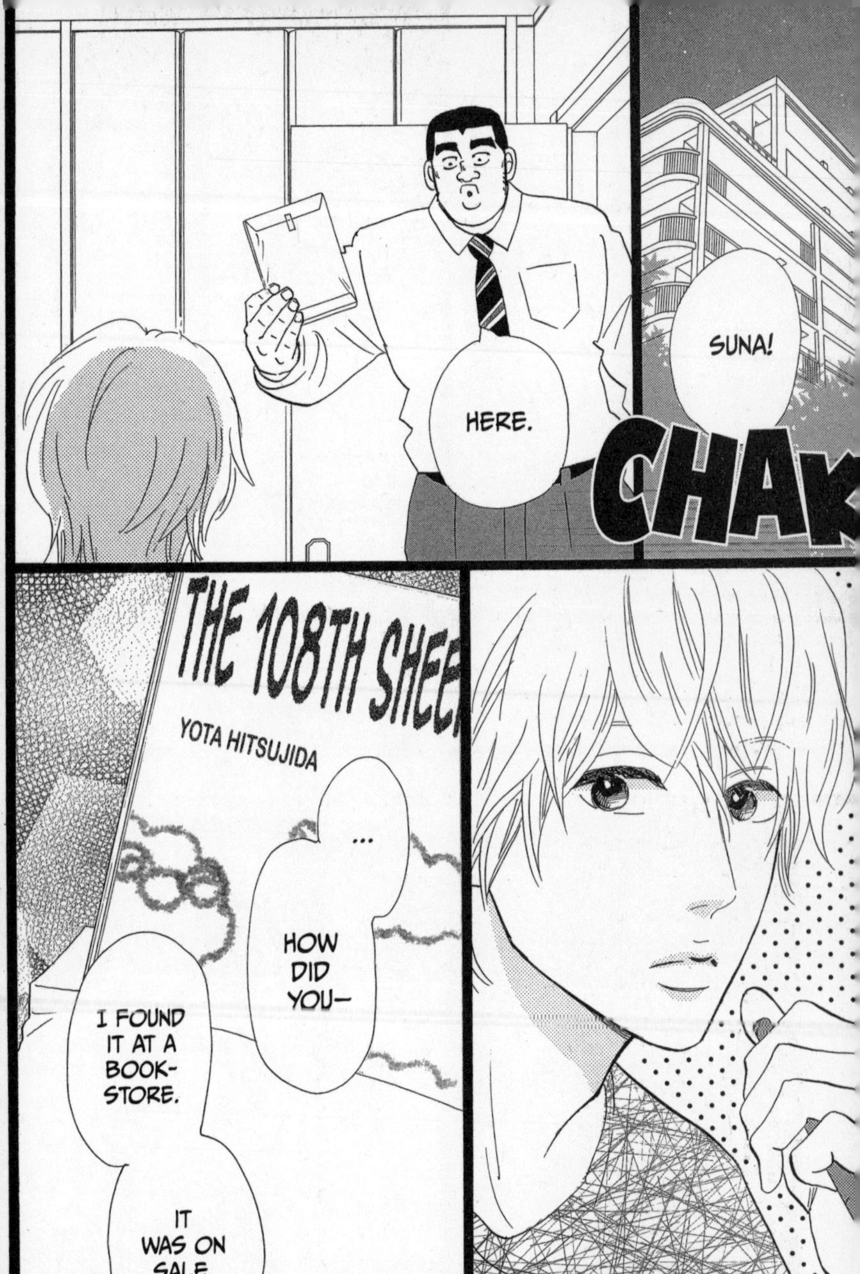
SUNA!
CHAK
HERE.
...
HOW DID YOU—
THE 108TH SHEE
YOTA HITSUJIDA
I FOUND IT AT A BOOK-STORE.
IT WAS ON SALE.

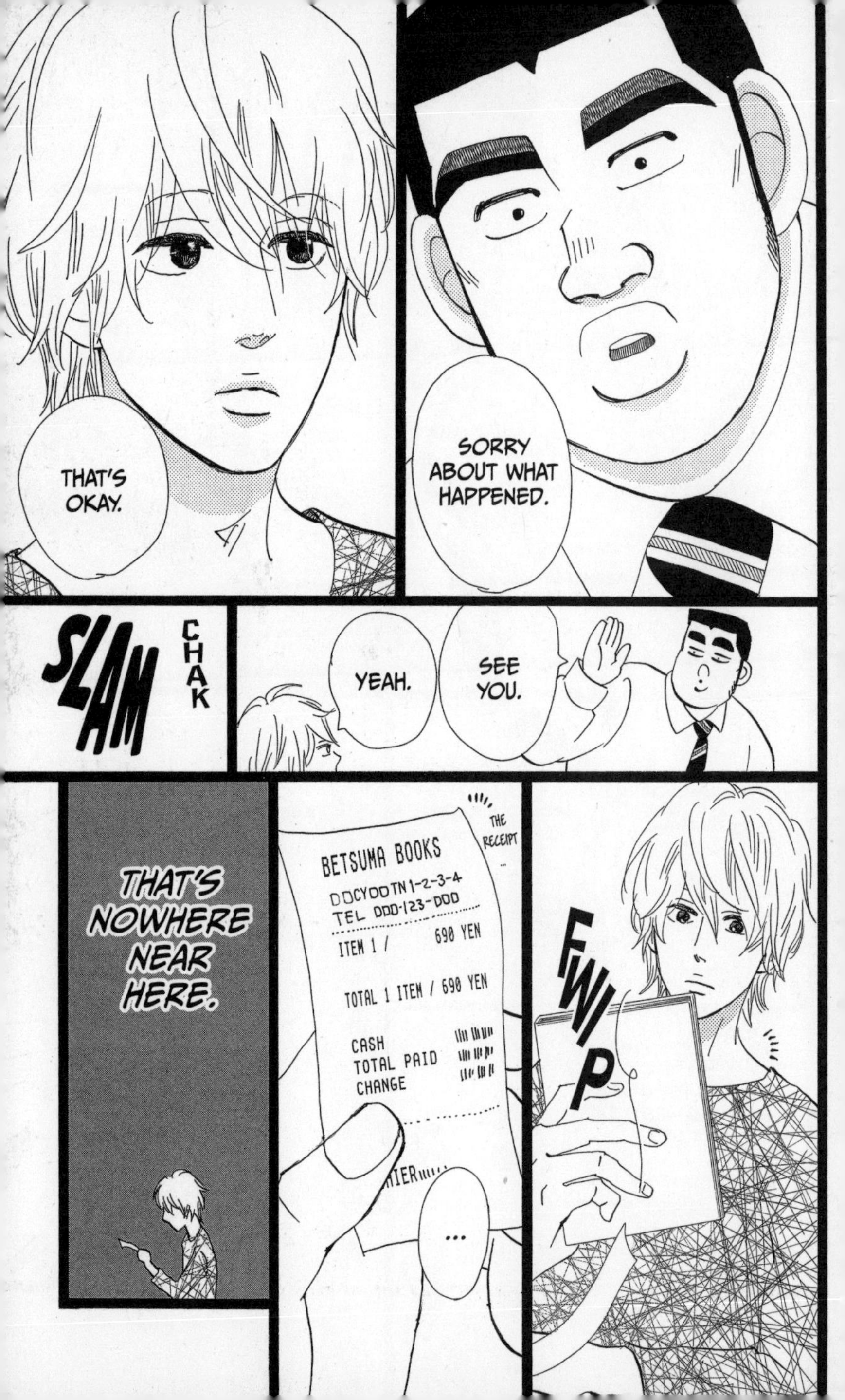
SORRY ABOUT WHAT HAPPENED.
THAT'S OKAY.
SEE YOU.
YEAH.
CHAK
SLAM
FWIP
THE RECEIPT...
BETSUMA BOOKS
DDCYDDTN 1-2-3-4
TEL DDD-123-DDD
ITEM 1 / 690 YEN
TOTAL 1 ITEM / 690 YEN
CASH
TOTAL PAID
CHANGE
...
THAT'S NOWHERE NEAR HERE.

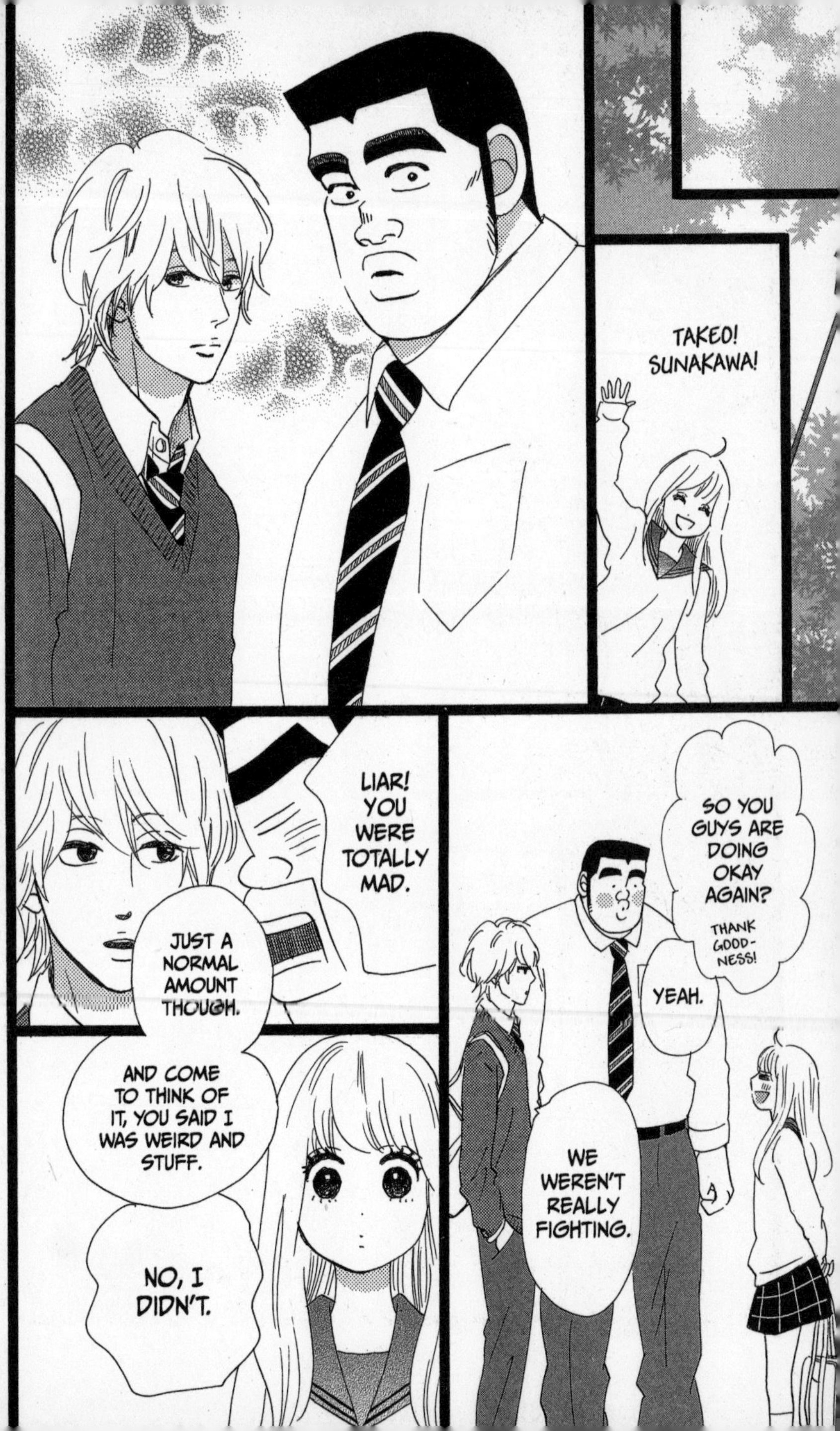
TAKEO! SUNAKAWA!
SO YOU GUYS ARE DOING OKAY AGAIN?
THANK GOOD-NESS!
YEAH.
WE WEREN'T REALLY FIGHTING.
LIAR! YOU WERE TOTALLY MAD.
JUST A NORMAL AMOUNT THOUGH.
AND COME TO THINK OF IT, YOU SAID I WAS WEIRD AND STUFF.
NO, I DIDN'T.

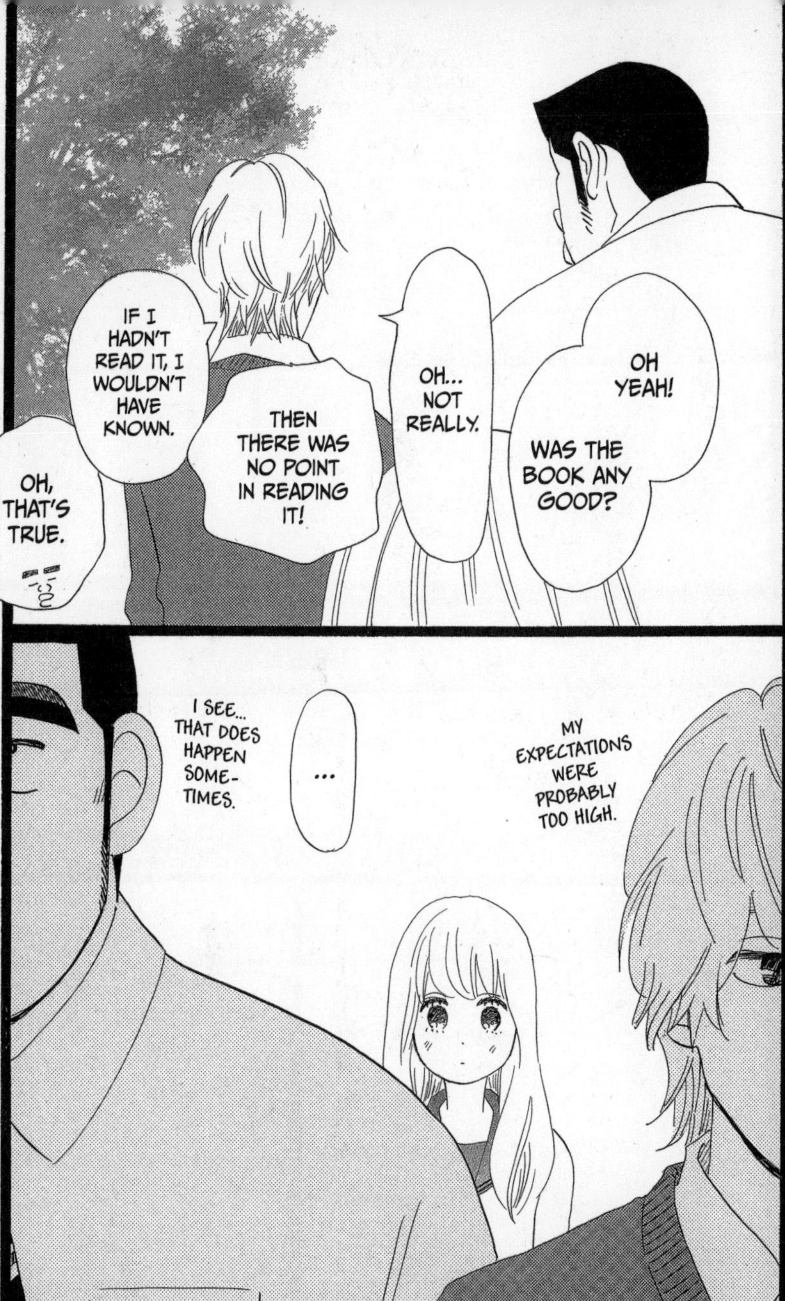
OH YEAH!
WAS THE BOOK ANY GOOD?
OH... NOT REALLY.
THEN THERE WAS NO POINT IN READING IT!
IF I HADN'T READ IT, I WOULDN'T HAVE KNOWN.
OH, THAT'S TRUE.
MY EXPECTATIONS WERE PROBABLY TOO HIGH.
...
I SEE... THAT DOES HAPPEN SOME-TIMES.

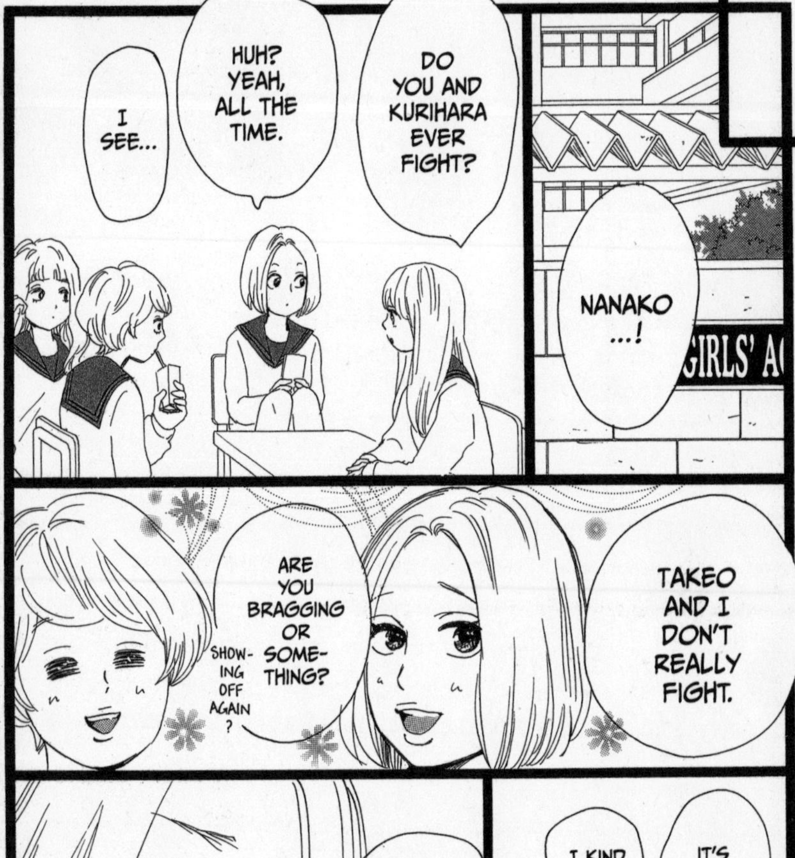

NANAKO ...!
GIRLS' A
DO YOU AND KURIHARA EVER FIGHT?
HUH? YEAH, ALL THE TIME.
I SEE...
TAKEO AND I DON'T REALLY FIGHT.
ARE YOU BRAGGING OR SOME-THING?
SHOW-ING OFF AGAIN?
IT'S NOT LIKE THAT...
I KIND OF WANT TO FIGHT.
IT MAKES THINGS FEEL MORE GENUINE, RIGHT?
LISTEN, WE FIGHT BECAUSE WE'RE ANNOYED AT ONE ANOTHER. IT'S GOT NOTHING TO DO WITH BEING GENUINE.

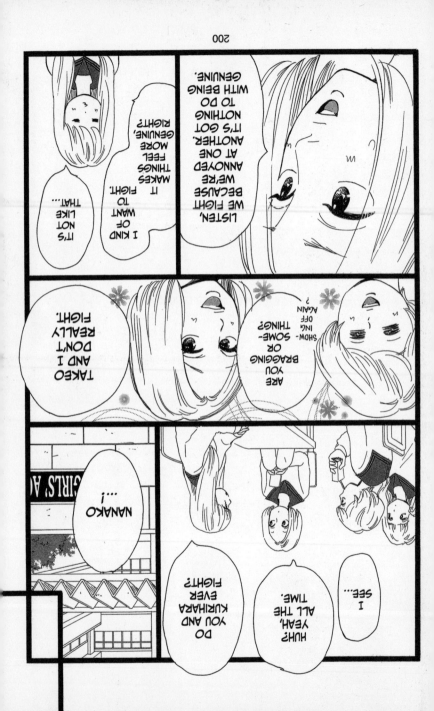

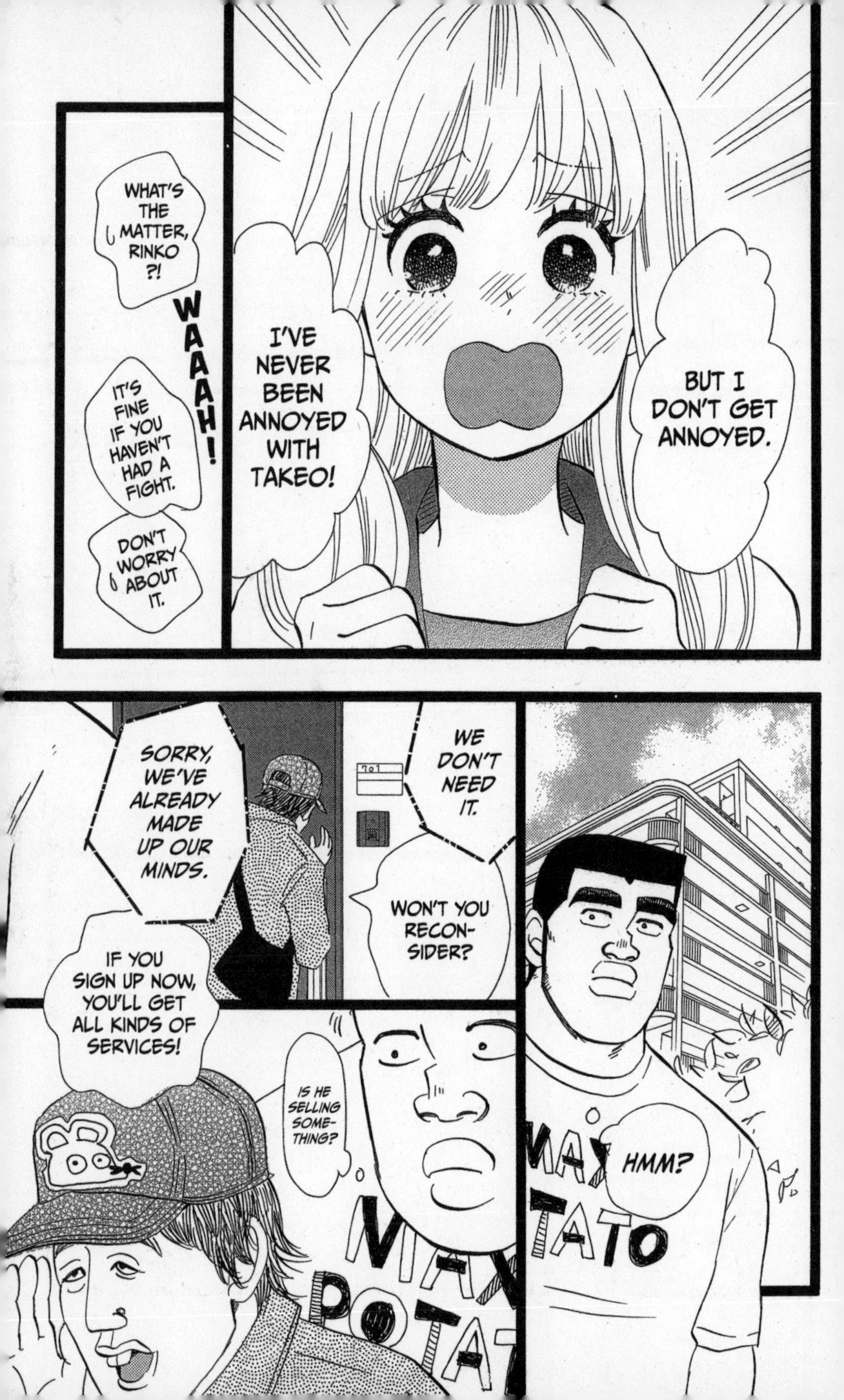
BUT I DON'T GET ANNOYED.
I'VE NEVER BEEN ANNOYED WITH TAKEO!
WHAT'S THE MATTER, RINKO ?!
WAAAAH!
IT'S FINE IF YOU HAVEN'T HAD A FIGHT.
DON'T WORRY ABOUT IT.
HMM?
MAX POTATO
WE DON'T NEED IT.
WON'T YOU RECONSIDER?
SORRY, WE'VE ALREADY MADE UP OUR MINDS.
IF YOU SIGN UP NOW, YOU'LL GET ALL KINDS OF SERVICES!
IS HE SELLING SOME-THING?
MAX POTAT

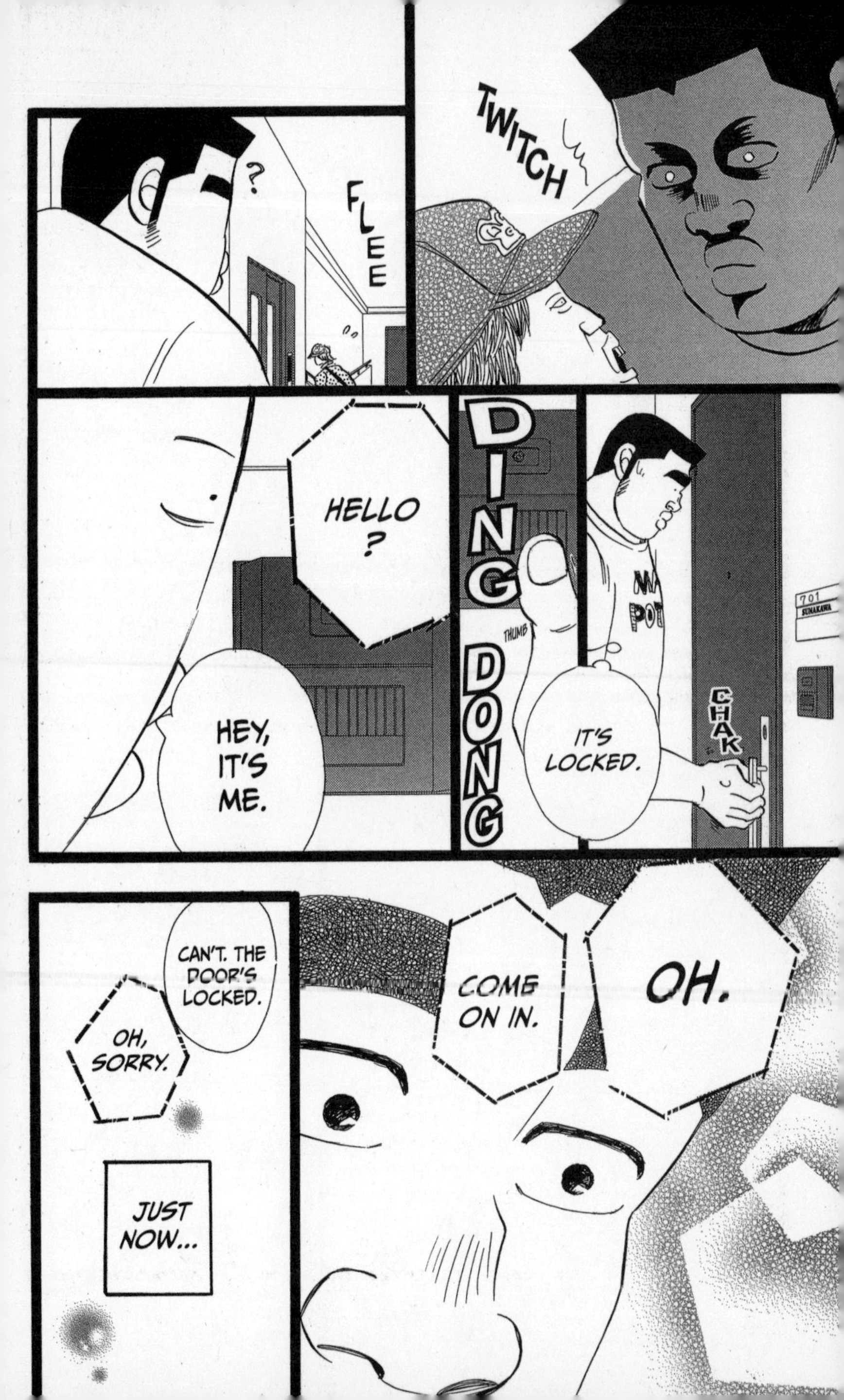
TWITCH
FLEE
?
701 SUNAKAWA
CHAK
IT'S LOCKED.
THUMB
DING DONG
HELLO ?
HEY, IT'S ME.
OH.
COME ON IN.
CAN'T. THE DOOR'S LOCKED.
OH, SORRY.
JUST NOW...

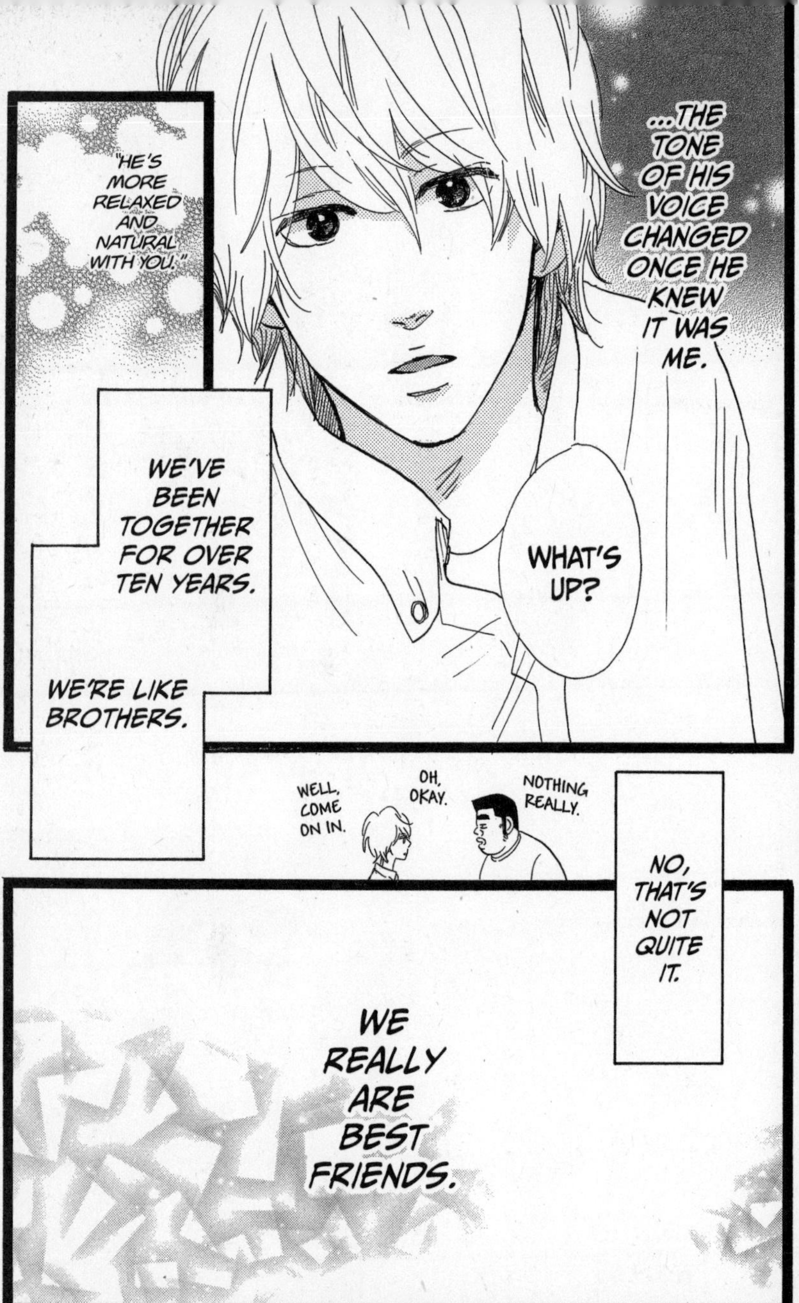
...THE TONE OF HIS VOICE CHANGED ONCE HE KNEW IT WAS ME.
WHAT'S UP?
"HE'S MORE RELAXED AND NATURAL WITH YOU."
WE'VE BEEN TOGETHER FOR OVER TEN YEARS.
WE'RE LIKE BROTHERS.
NOTHING REALLY.
OH, OKAY.
WELL, COME ON IN.
NO, THAT'S NOT QUITE IT.
WE REALLY ARE BEST FRIENDS.

THE END

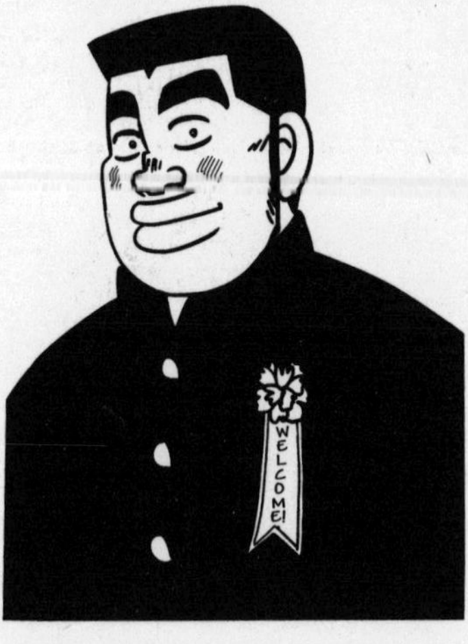
WELCOME!

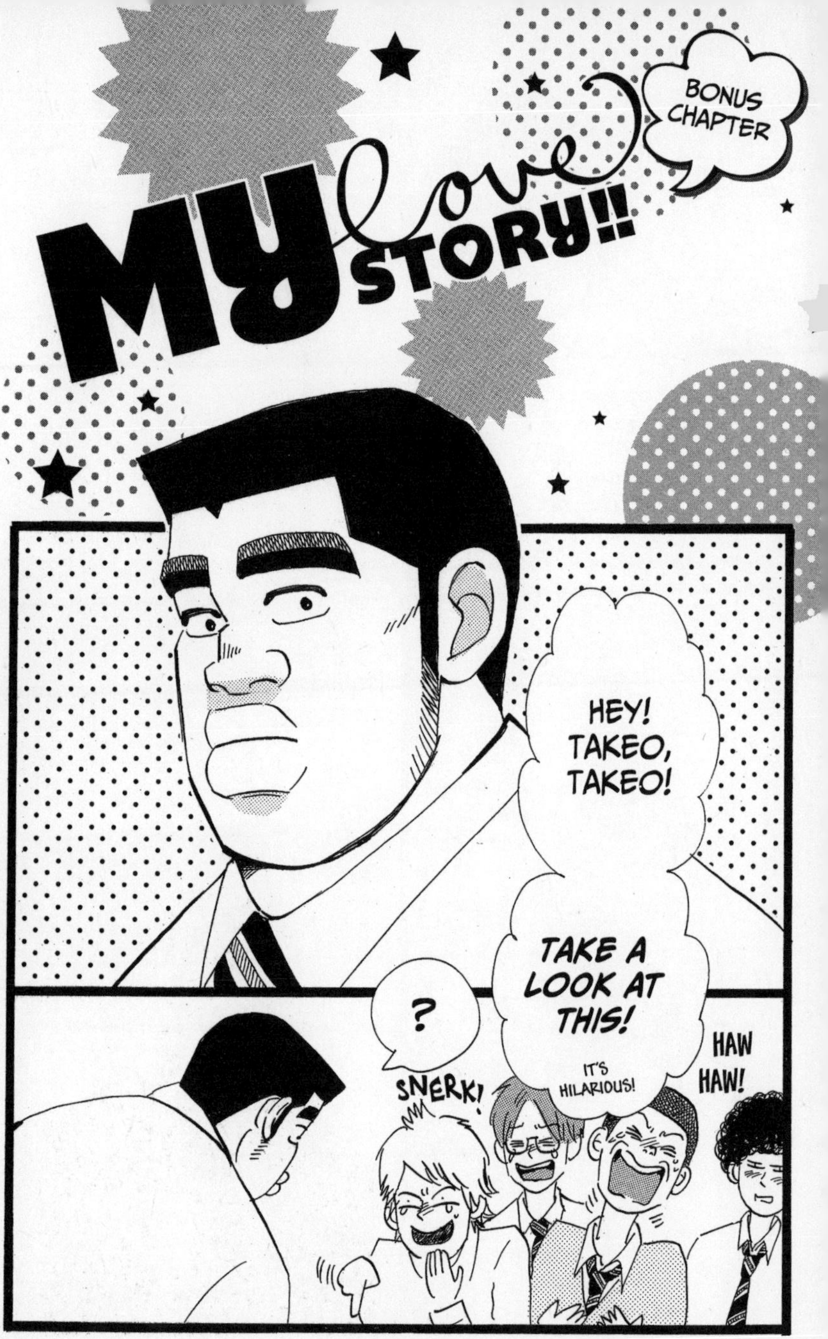
MY love STORY!!
BONUS CHAPTER
HEY! TAKEO, TAKEO!
TAKE A LOOK AT THIS!
IT'S HILARIOUS!
HAW HAW!
?
SNERK!

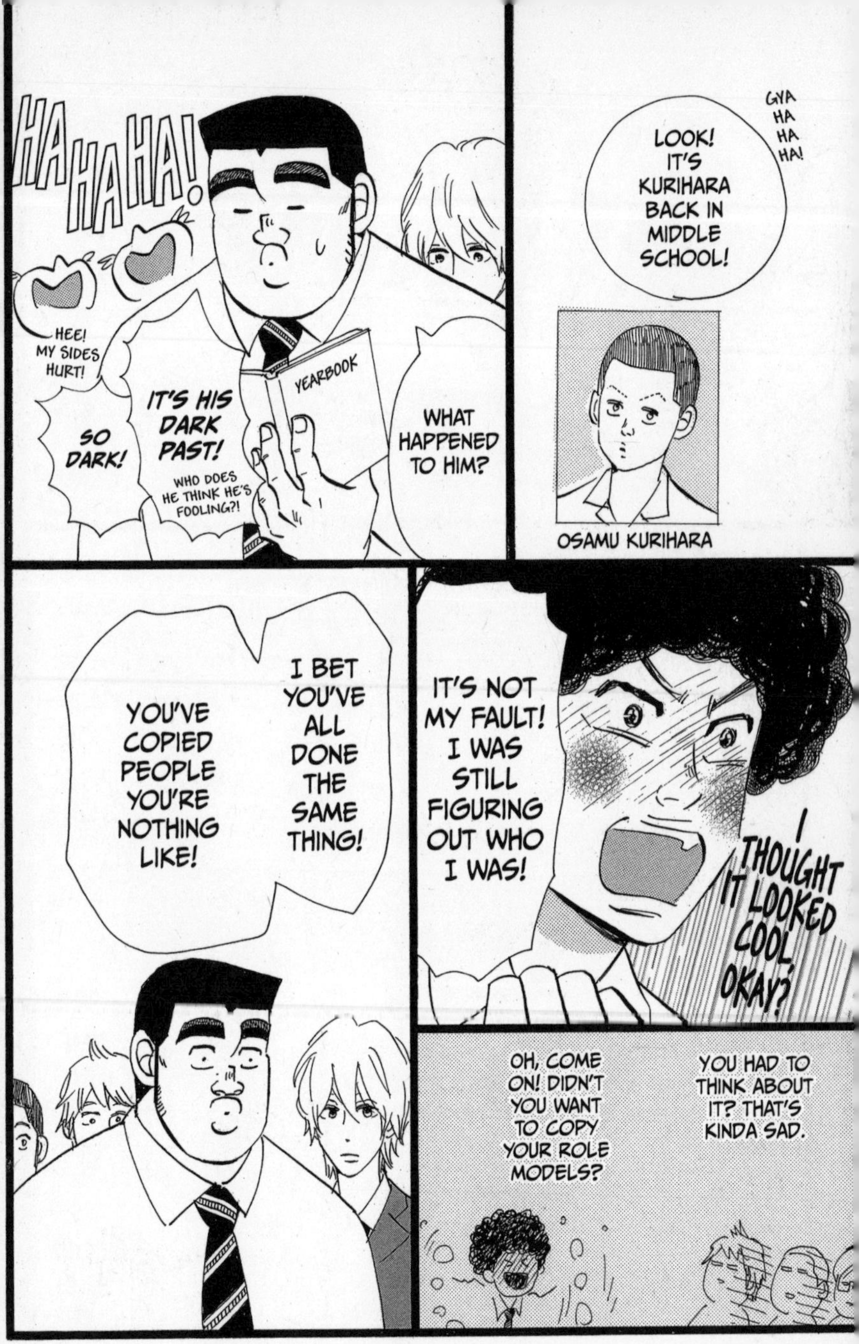
LOOK! IT'S KURIHARA BACK IN MIDDLE SCHOOL!
GYA HA HA HA!
OSAMU KURIHARA
HAHAHA!
WHAT HAPPENED TO HIM?
YEARBOOK
IT'S HIS DARK PAST!
WHO DOES HE THINK HE'S FOOLING?!
HEE! MY SIDES HURT!
SO DARK!
IT'S NOT MY FAULT! I WAS STILL FIGURING OUT WHO I WAS!
I THOUGHT IT LOOKED COOL, OKAY?
I BET YOU'VE ALL DONE THE SAME THING!
YOU'VE COPIED PEOPLE YOU'RE NOTHING LIKE!
YOU HAD TO THINK ABOUT IT? THAT'S KINDA SAD.
OH, COME ON! DIDN'T YOU WANT TO COPY YOUR ROLE MODELS?

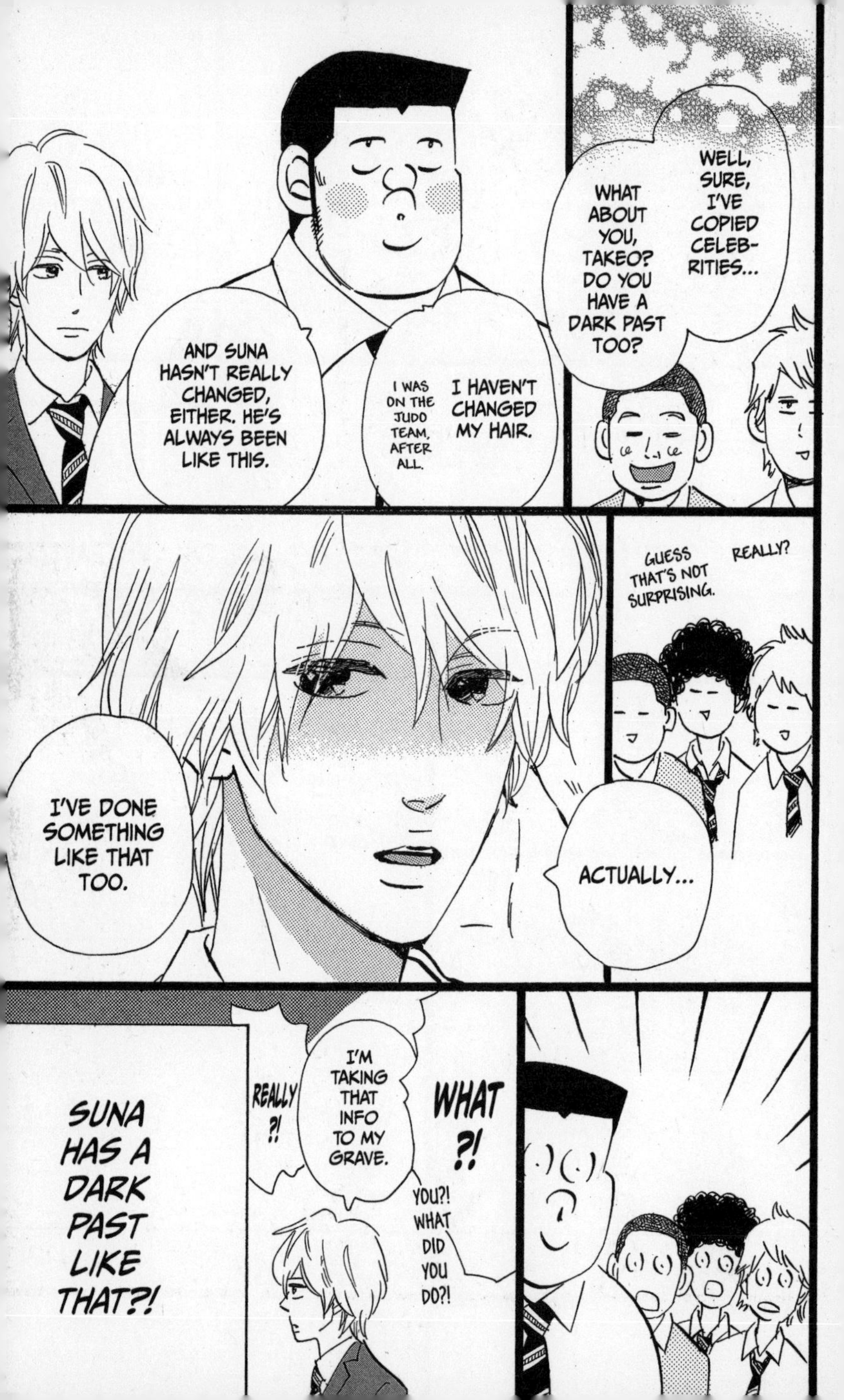
WELL, SURE, I'VE COPIED CELEB-RITIES...
WHAT ABOUT YOU, TAKEO? DO YOU HAVE A DARK PAST TOO?
I HAVEN'T CHANGED MY HAIR.
I WAS ON THE JUDO TEAM, AFTER ALL.
AND SUNA HASN'T REALLY CHANGED, EITHER. HE'S ALWAYS BEEN LIKE THIS.
REALLY?
GUESS THAT'S NOT SURPRISING.
ACTUALLY...
I'VE DONE SOMETHING LIKE THAT TOO.
WHAT ?!
YOU?! WHAT DID YOU DO?!
I'M TAKING THAT INFO TO MY GRAVE.
REALLY ?!
SUNA HAS A DARK PAST LIKE THAT?!

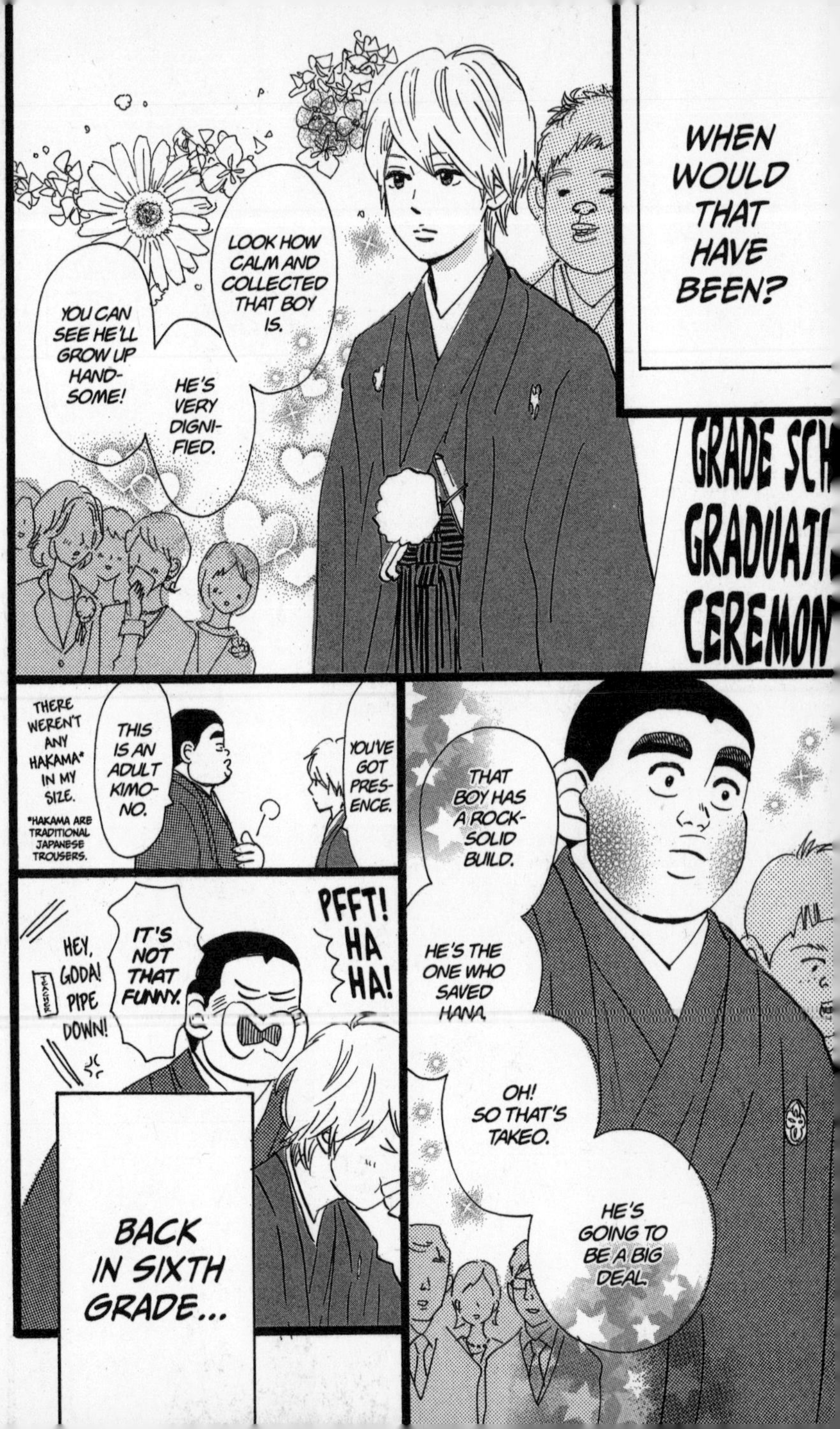
WHEN WOULD THAT HAVE BEEN?
GRADE SCH
GRADUATI
CEREMON
LOOK HOW CALM AND COLLECTED THAT BOY IS.
YOU CAN SEE HE'LL GROW UP HAND-SOME!
HE'S VERY DIGNI-FIED.
THAT BOY HAS A ROCK-SOLID BUILD.
HE'S THE ONE WHO SAVED HANA.
OH! SO THAT'S TAKEO.
HE'S GOING TO BE A BIG DEAL.
YOU'VE GOT PRES-ENCE.
THIS IS AN ADULT KIMO-NO.
THERE WEREN'T ANY HAKAMA* IN MY SIZE.
*HAKAMA ARE TRADITIONAL JAPANESE TROUSERS.
PFFT! HA HA!
IT'S NOT THAT FUNNY.
TEACHER
HEY, GODA! PIPE DOWN!
BACK IN SIXTH GRADE...

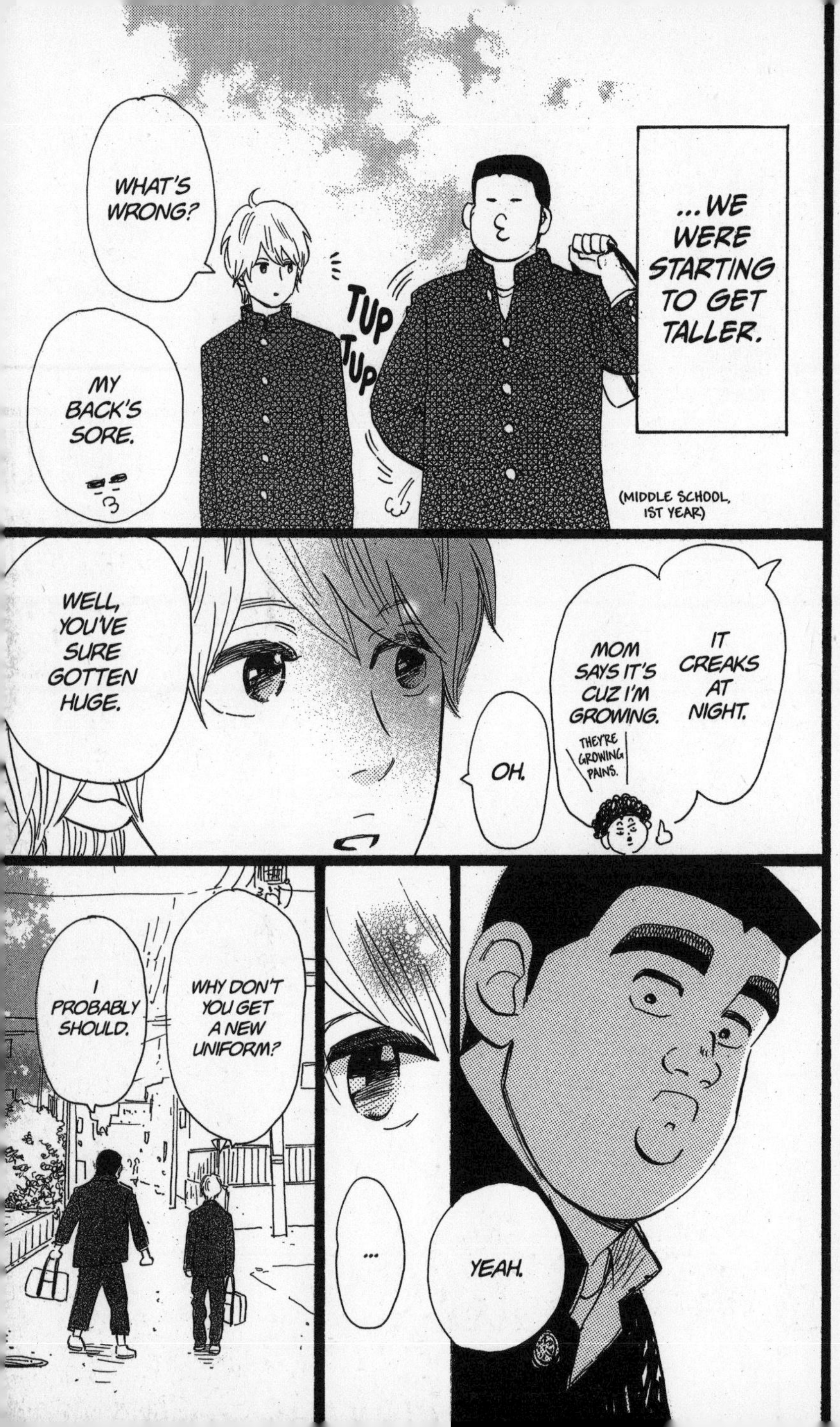
...WE WERE STARTING TO GET TALLER.
(MIDDLE SCHOOL, 1ST YEAR)
TUP TUP
WHAT'S WRONG?
MY BACK'S SORE.
IT CREAKS AT NIGHT.
MOM SAYS IT'S CUZ I'M GROWING.
THEY'RE GROWING PAINS.
OH.
WELL, YOU'VE SURE GOTTEN HUGE.
YEAH.
...
WHY DON'T YOU GET A NEW UNIFORM?
I PROBABLY SHOULD.

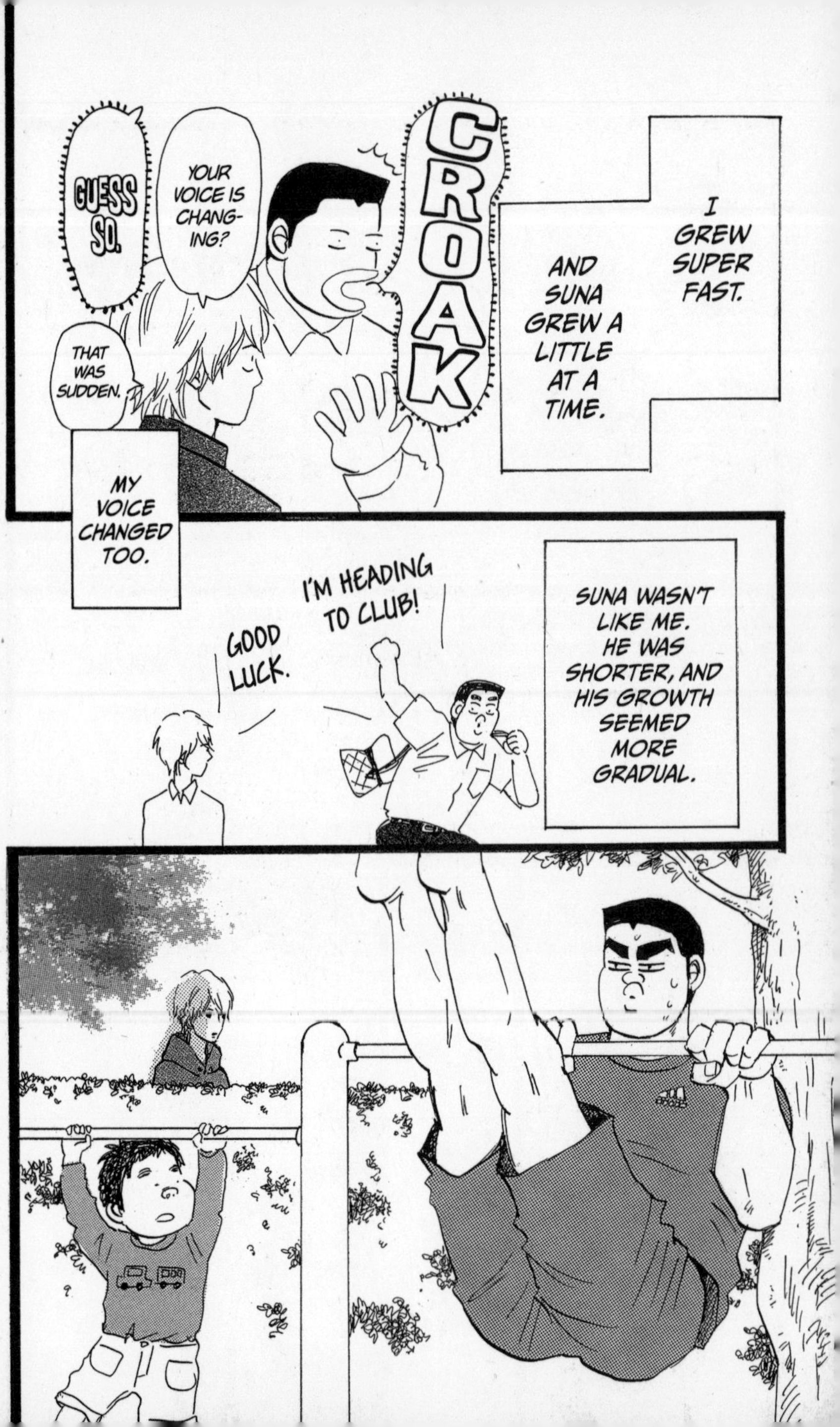
I GREW SUPER FAST.
AND SUNA GREW A LITTLE AT A TIME.
CROAK
YOUR VOICE IS CHANGING?
GUESS SO.
THAT WAS SUDDEN.
MY VOICE CHANGED TOO.
SUNA WASN'T LIKE ME. HE WAS SHORTER, AND HIS GROWTH SEEMED MORE GRADUAL.
I'M HEADING TO CLUB!
GOOD LUCK.

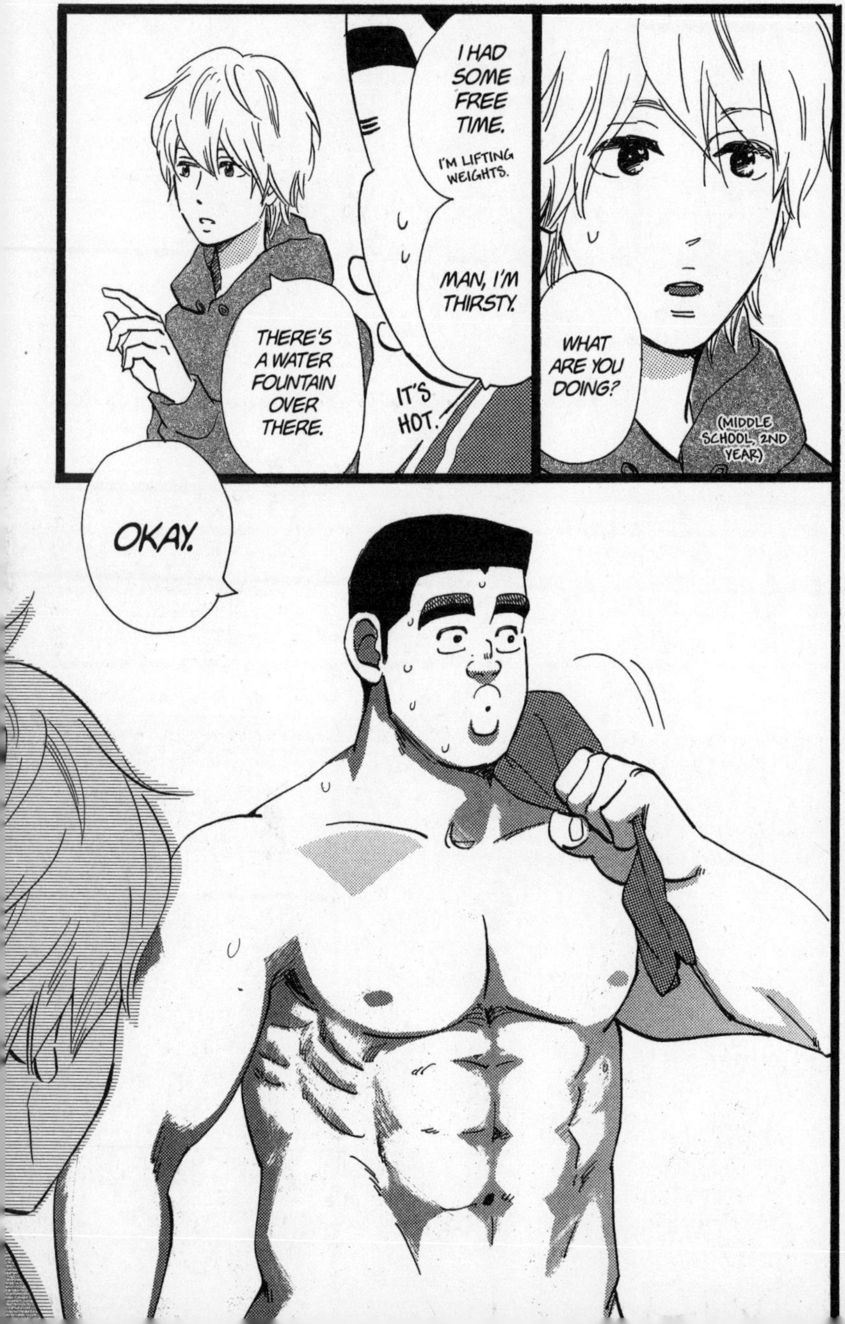
WHAT ARE YOU DOING?
(MIDDLE SCHOOL, 2ND YEAR)
I HAD SOME FREE TIME.
I'M LIFTING WEIGHTS.
MAN, I'M THIRSTY.
IT'S HOT.
THERE'S A WATER FOUNTAIN OVER THERE.
OKAY.

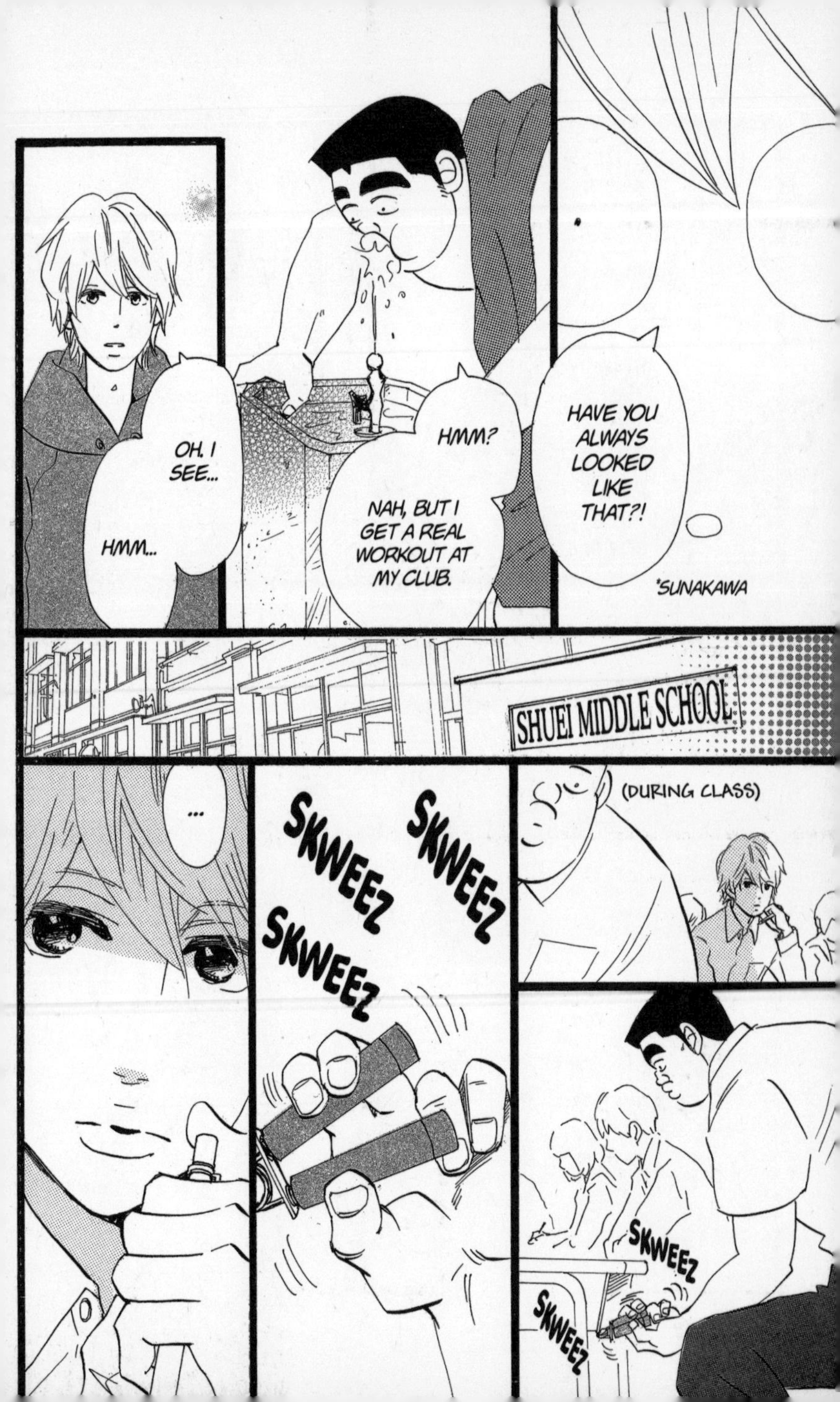
HAVE YOU ALWAYS LOOKED LIKE THAT?!
*SUNAKAWA
HMM?
NAH, BUT I GET A REAL WORKOUT AT MY CLUB.
OH. I SEE...
HMM...
SHUEI MIDDLE SCHOOL
(DURING CLASS)
SKWEEZ
SKWEEZ
SKWEEZ
SKWEEZ
SKWEEZ
...

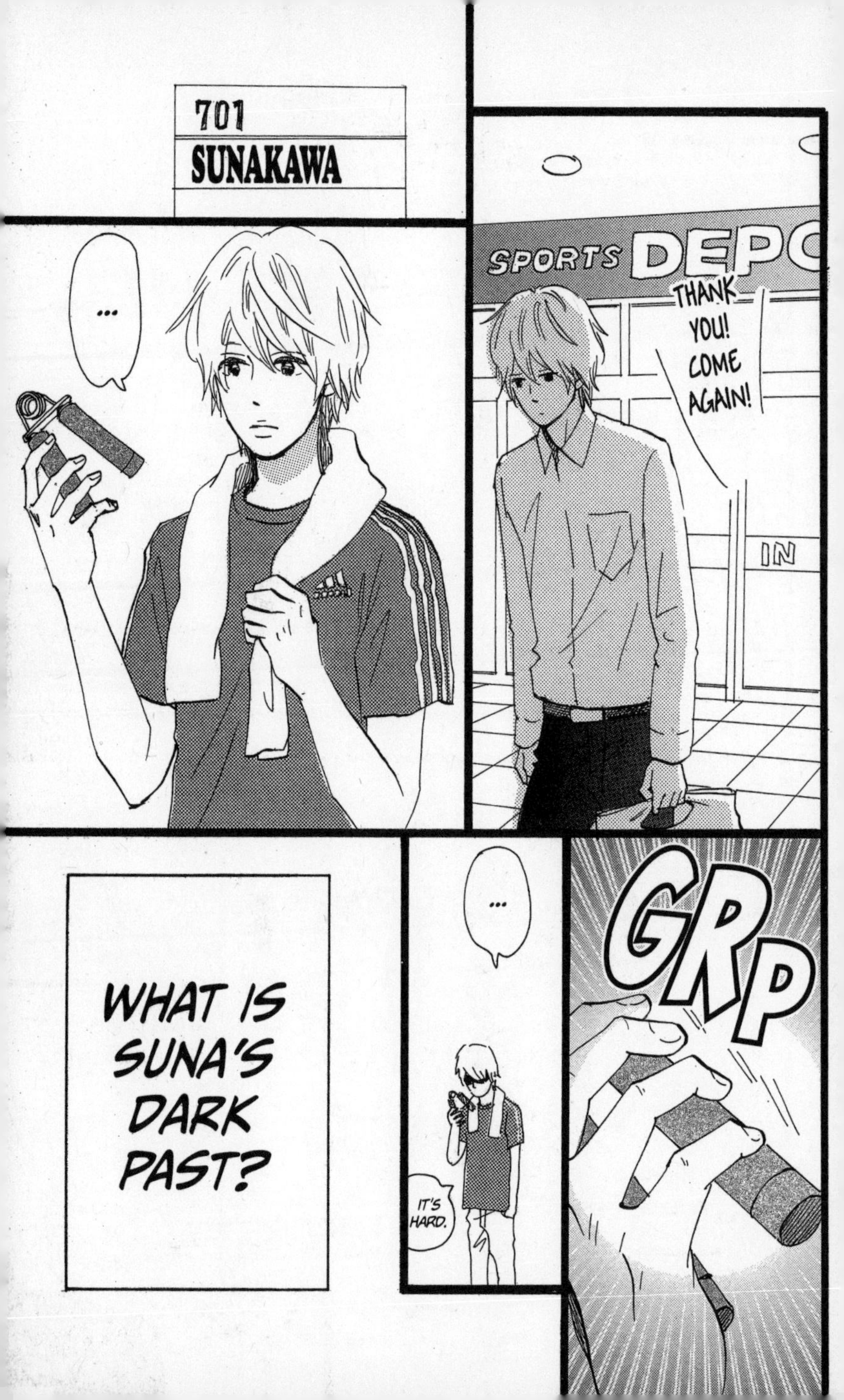
SPORTS DEPO
THANK YOU! COME AGAIN!
IN
701
SUNAKAWA
...
GRP
...
IT'S HARD.
WHAT IS SUNA'S DARK PAST?

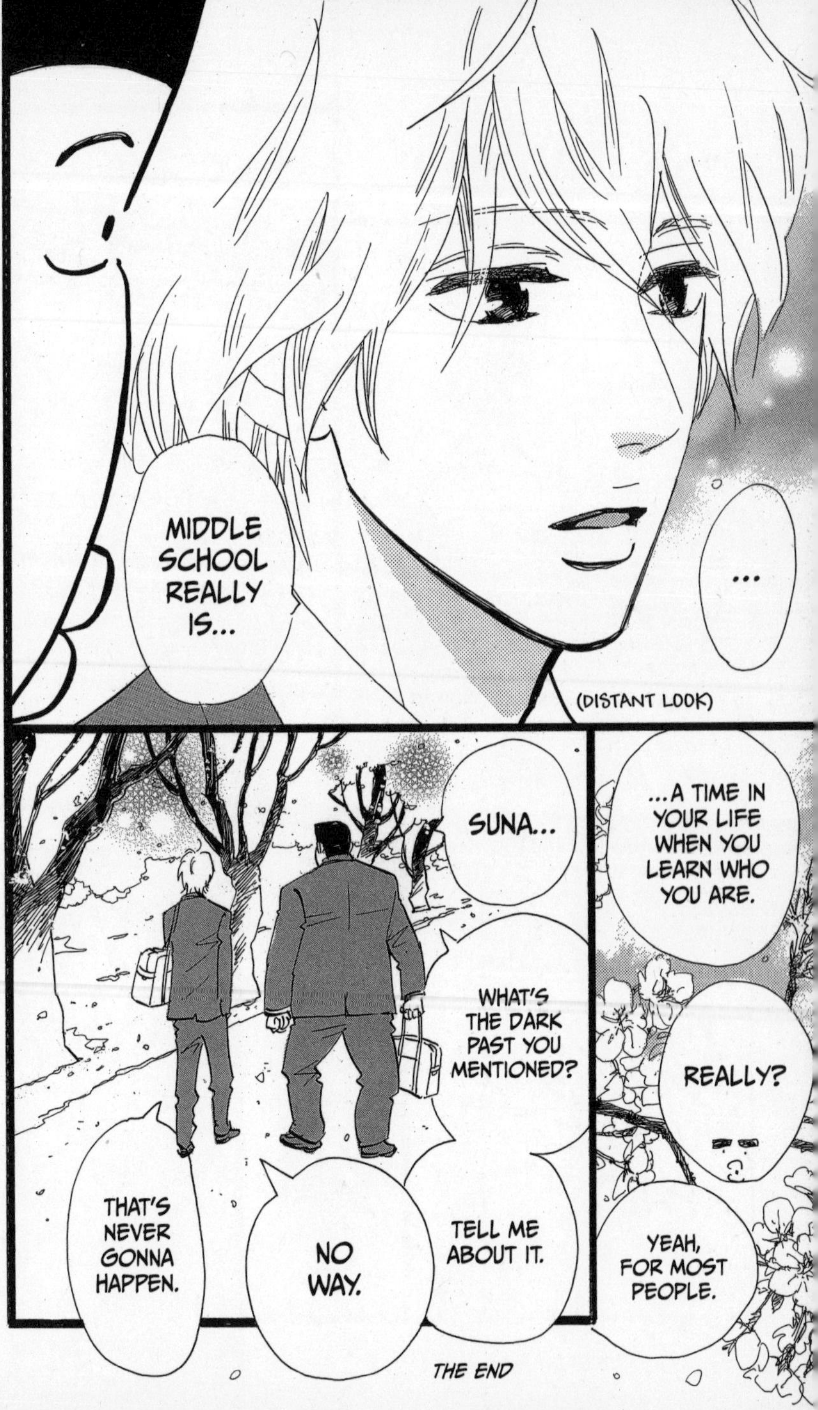
...
MIDDLE SCHOOL REALLY IS...
(DISTANT LOOK)
...A TIME IN YOUR LIFE WHEN YOU LEARN WHO YOU ARE.
REALLY?
YEAH, FOR MOST PEOPLE.
SUNA...
WHAT'S THE DARK PAST YOU MENTIONED?
TELL ME ABOUT IT.
NO WAY.
THAT'S NEVER GONNA HAPPEN.

THE END

I don't have any confidence in my tastes, so whenever I have to give a present or a gift, I never know what to choose. But when I think about how happy I feel when I receive something, no matter what it may be, I remember that it's the thought that counts so I should just pick something out. It feels good to make people happy!
– Kazune Kawahara

ARUKO is from Ishikawa Prefecture in Japan and was born on July 26 (a Leo!). She made her manga debut with *Ame Nochi Hare* (Clear After the Rain). Her other works include *Yasuko to Kenji*, and her hobbies include laughing and getting lost.

KAZUNE KAWAHARA is from Hokkaido Prefecture in Japan and was born on March 11 (a Pisces!). She made her manga debut at age 18 with *Kare no Ichiban Sukina Hito* (His Most Favorite Person). Her best-selling shojo manga series *High School Debut* is available in North America from VIZ Media. Her hobby is interior redecorating.

Spring is getting warm and making me sleepy. The hot summer sun makes me sleepy. Long autumn nights make me sleepy. And winter makes me so sleepy I want to hibernate. Sunny days pleasantly warm me and make me sleepy. And the low atmospheric pressure of rainy days makes me sleepy. I wish I could be a baby! All I'd do is sleep and be pampered.
– Aruko

MY LOVE STORY!!

Volume 12
Shojo Beat Edition

Story by **KAZUNE KAWAHARA**
Art by **ARUKO**

———————————//———————————

English Adaptation ♡ **Ysabet Reinhardt MacFarlane**
Translation ♡ **JN Productions**
Touch-up Art & Lettering ♡ **Mark McMurray**
Design ♡ **Fawn Lau**
Editor ♡ **Amy Yu**

———————————//———————————

ORE MONOGATARI!!
© 2011 by Kazune Kawahara, Aruko
All rights reserved.
First published in Japan in 2011 by SHUEISHA Inc., Tokyo
English translation rights arranged by SHUEISHA Inc.

Printed in the U.S.A.

Published by VIZ Media, LLC
P.O. Box 77010
San Francisco, CA 94107

10 9 8 7 6 5 4 3 2 1
First printing, May 2017

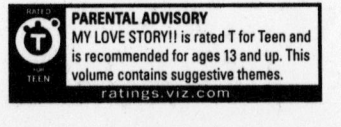